THE AMERI⬛⬛⬛ ⬛⬛ ⬛⬛⬛ ⬛N

LEGAL GUIDE
FOR
SMALL
BUSINESS

SECOND EDITION

THE AMERICAN BAR ASSOCIATION

LEGAL GUIDE
FOR
SMALL
BUSINESS

SECOND EDITION

Everything You Need to Know About
Small Business, from **Start-Up** to
Employment Laws to **Financing** and **Selling**

RANDOM HOUSE REFERENCE
NEW YORK   TORONTO   LONDON   SYDNEY   AUCKLAND

Library of Congress Cataloging-in-Publication Data

The American Bar Association legal guide for small business : everything you need to know
about small business, from start-up to employment to financing and selling.—2nd ed.
p. cm.
Includes index.
ISBN: 978-0-375-72303-2
1. Small business—Law and legislation—United States—Popular works.
I. American Bar Association.   II. Title: Legal guide for small business.
KF1659.A96 2010
346.73'0652—dc22   2009049394

Printed in the United States of America

10 9 8 7 6 5 4 3 2 1

Second Edition

AMERICAN BAR ASSOCIATION

Carolyn B. Lamm
President

Mabel C. McKinney-Browning
Director, Division for Public Education

Charles Williams
Catherine Hawke
Series Editors

PRINCIPAL AUTHOR OF SECOND EDITION

Robert D. Sprague
Assistant Professor
University of Wyoming College of Business

REVIEWERS, SECOND EDITION

Rupert M. Barkoff Atlanta, Georgia	William Dixon Haught Little Rock, Arkansas
Lena S. Barnett Silver Spring, Maryland	Barbara Jones Richfield, Minnesota
Matthew H. Bindford Scottsdale, Arizona	Jim Morgan Chico, California
Michael Greenfield St. Louis, Missouri	Joshua Perlman Pittsburgh, Pennsylvania and Phoenix, Arizona
Jay Grenig Milwaukee, Wisconsin	Andrew Selden Minneapolis, Minnesota

PREVIOUS EDITION AUTHORS AND REVIEWERS

Harry Haynsworth	Michael Flowers
Jane Easter Bahls	Patricia A. Frishkoff
Ron Coleman	Sidney S. Goldstein
Christopher Drew	Joe M. Goodman
John Drew	David L. Haron
Barbara Fick	Nancy Hauserman

TABLE OF CONTENTS

FOREWORD

Carolyn B. Lamm, *President*
American Bar Association

The American Bar Association is the nation's premier source of legal information. With more than 400,000 members, representing every specialty and every type of legal practice, the ABA is in a unique position to deliver accurate, up-to-date, unbiased legal information to its members, and to the general public. This book allows you to benefit from the ABA's network of legal professionals.

This edition of the *American Bar Association Legal Guide for Small Business* was revised, updated, and tailored for the modern, technological business environment by Robert D. Sprague, a professor of business and law at the University of Wyoming. The reviewing committee once again comes from the wide-ranging breadth of ABA membership, guaranteeing that the concerns of small-business owners are addressed in language that is straightforward and easily understood.

Thanks to all the lawyers who volunteered to write, review, and update this book, you can be sure that the information you are about to read is: useful, helpful, unbiased, current, written in a reader-friendly style, and, most importantly, reflective of the national picture, because ABA members practice in all jurisdictions.

Public education and public service are two of the most important goals of the American Bar Association. The members and staff of the ABA Standing Committee on Public Education provided excellent leadership for this project and are dedicated to helping experts communicate the law to the public. Indeed, this book is a fine example of how the ABA takes an active role in providing the public with critical information it can use.

The American Bar Association is the largest voluntary association in the world. Besides its commitment to public education, the ABA provides programs to assist lawyers and judges in their work and leads initiatives to improve the legal system for the public, including promoting fast, affordable alternatives to lawsuits, such as mediation, arbitration, conciliation, and small claims courts. Through ABA support for lawyer referral programs and pro bono services (where lawyers donate their time), many more people have been able to find the best lawyer for their particular case and obtain quality legal help within their budgets.

Carolyn B. Lamm is president of the American Bar Association and is a partner with White and Case in Washington, D.C. Her practice focuses on international arbitration, international trade, and litigation.

INTRODUCTION

Eduardo Roberto Rodriguez
Chair, ABA Standing Committee on Public Education

Owning your own business has always been part of the American dream, even during difficult financial times. For many, it is a way to reach for a brighter tomorrow and establish financial security.

This book is designed to help you make that dream come true. Understanding your legal rights and responsibilities as a business owner and being aware of your options are some of the keys to success.

Whether you have been in business for years or are just now contemplating going out on your own, you are going to have plenty of legal questions. That is where this book can help—by sorting out issues, providing background information, and suggesting the pros and cons of various courses of action.

This book aims to help you:

• Spot problems while they are manageable and least costly to fix.

• Avoid false starts by doing it right the first time.

• Minimize the time and expenses that do not make you money.

• Minimize your tax bill.

• Learn how to protect your business—and much more.

In addition, you will find practical, down-to-earth information about locating your business (at home or rented office space), evaluating a franchise opportunity, buying an existing business, dealing with customers, and managing finances.

These topics and more are covered in plain, direct language. No legal jargon or obscure technical language here—just concise, straightforward discussions of how the law affects businesses every day.

HOW TO USE THIS BOOK

We have made a special effort to make this book practical by using situations and problems you are likely to encounter. Each chapter is clearly laid out, and begins with a real-life situation that shows the practical ramifications of the subject. You will want to keep this book handy and refer to it often at the various stages of business ownership. It is clearly organized so you can easily find the specific help you need as a new issue or opportunity arises.

Part One—First Steps will get your business off to a successful start including tackling issues of naming your business, protecting your concepts, and helping you find the necessary legal help.

Part Two—Setting Up Shop will alert you to the legal pitfalls to watch for as you determine where to locate your business (kitchen table or new office?) and will help you identify the risks to your business once you have things up and running.

Part Three—Types of Business Organizations will explore the organizational options, from being a sole proprietor to being a part of a partnership, or a corporation, or organizing your business as a limited liability company, and the tax consequences and legal liability of each choice.

Part Four—A Section About People will give you the legal lowdown on the people who work for you as employees, as well as the customers you serve.

Part Five—Running the Business will offer tips regarding the contracts necessary for running your business and how to handle some pitfalls that many business owners experience: disputes, small business scams, and conflicts over intellectual property.

Part Six—The Taxman Cometh will alert you that the law has a number of provisions that can help you save on taxes.

Part Seven—Various Endings will give you the tools to see that you close your business experience in the best possible way by addressing how to handle a faltering business, selling a business, retirement, and, in the worst-case scenario, death.

Within chapters, sidebars will highlight important points. Some provide you with easy-to-understand definitions of key legal terms, while others give you practical tips, warn about pitfalls, or list important steps to avoid them. We conclude the book with a resource guide that points you to the best places on the Web to find more help with running your small business.

In this changing economy, competition is fierce, and there are no guarantees of success. We recognize that you need every edge you can get. Sometimes a problem will be so complex or have so much at stake, that you will want to seek immediate legal advice from an attorney who knows the facts of your particular case and can give you advice tailored to your situation. With this book, you will be able to make informed decisions about a wide range of problems and opportunities. Armed with knowledge and insights, you can be confident that the decisions you make will be in your best interests.

Eduardo Roberto Rodriguez is a Senior Partner with Rodriguez, Colvin, Chaney & Saenz, L.L.P., in Brownsville, Texas.

PART I

First Steps

So you've decided to take the plunge. You're starting your own business. You'll be your own boss.

Of course, you want to get started on becoming the national standard in your industry immediately. But first, take some time to look at how the law affects your start-up business—a little planning now might save plenty of time, money, and heartache down the line.

This section takes a look at some of the very first issues any new business owner must consider:

- Will your idea work?
- Do you need a lawyer and how will you find one who is right for you and your business?
- Should you buy an existing business rather than start a new one?
- What about franchising? What is it and is it right for you?

CHAPTER 1

Getting Started

Business Ideas—and Funding Them

Cory knows that to make it in a start-up business she'll need plenty of head and heart. She's got an idea for a business that she knows will work, and she's willing to take certain risks and work hard to make it happen. But it's all so confusing. How does she start? Where does she start? What about getting the money to start? How is the law involved?

This chapter deals with some of the very first issues you'll face before starting your small business.

THE VERY FIRST STEP— THE BUSINESS PLAN

Of course you're excited about your idea for a business, and you can't wait to get it going and watch the money roll in. Even so, don't commit yourself until you've prepared a business plan.

Many new business owners believe a business plan is needed only for raising money (capital) for the business. But preparing a business plan forces you to consider critical issues that can determine the success, or failure, of your enterprise. The basic elements of a business plan include: a description of your business and its mission statement; an analysis of the business environment; a thorough discussion of the business's product(s) and/or service(s); an analysis of the competition; a discussion of your competitive advantage; pricing strategies; sales and credit policies; your marketing and promotional strategy; a discussion of your management, organizational structure, and key personnel; start-up costs and financing, including financial forecasts; a discussion of legal issues, including any intellectual property your business may own or use; a discussion of risks and insurance coverage; and a description of your critical suppliers. Part of your discussion of your competition and competitive advantage will include a SWOT analysis: your strengths (attributes of your business and personnel that will contribute to its success), weaknesses (any shortcomings within your business that may be an impediment to your success), opportunities (external conditions that can help lead your business to success), and threats (external challenges that may be an impediment to your success). A business plan will help you analyze the market and develop your overall business strategy. One of the first elements of a business plan is an analysis of the business environment:

- Are there global, national, local, or industry trends that can impact your business?
- Are there global, national, or local demographic trends that can impact your business?
- Have there been recent changes in the law that can have a significant impact on your business?
- Have there been technological developments that can help or hurt your business?
- How will near-term trends in the local, national, and global economy impact your business?

Of course, you'll want to make sure your idea is lawful, does not require special licenses or permits, and has no restrictions that might create problems. For example, a great idea for a bar might not be feasible if you can't qualify for a liquor license.

For the most part, your business plan will have relatively minor legal considerations, but we include a very brief discussion of the basic components of the business plan because they're so fundamental. There are plenty of sources for more information about business plans, and we refer you to some of them in this chapter.

How Sound Is Your Business Idea?

A sound business idea is one that makes economic sense based on *your* experience and background. You'll usually want to choose a type of business that you're familiar with and have some experience in. If you have no experience in food service operations, it's probably not a good idea to open up or buy a restaurant. (But if you really want to run a restaurant, maybe you should consider taking a job in one for a year or two before trying one on your own.)

Operating a successful business requires hard work and expertise. Hard-earned experience will save you the time and expense of scrambling under the gun to develop the know-how a particular business requires to be successful. If you're considering a business in an area you're not personally familiar with, be sure to hire or consult others with expertise and exposure. People who have been there are usually willing to provide advice, and there are many retired business executives just waiting to help.

 GETTING STARTED

Besides numerous popular books and magazines that deal with small business start-ups, there are many terrific Web sites with information. Take a look at:

- www.score.org, a nonprofit resource partner with the U.S. Small Business Administration that provides entrepreneurial education and links entrepreneurs with experienced business mentors;

- www.sba.gov/smallbusinessplanner, a guide for managing your business from start to finish, provided by the U.S. Small Business Administration (SBA);

- www.bsorchecklist.org, which contains a comprehensive small business start-up checklist; and

- www.smartbiz.com, to see how you fit the profile of an entrepreneur.

Market Research

The failure rate for new businesses is high. Data indicate that 20 percent of new businesses do not last more than one year, and that over half of new businesses do not last five years. Before you commit yourself and your hard-earned money, determine whether a market exists for your service or product. Have similar businesses in this area failed? Can you determine why? If a market does exist for what you're thinking of offering, what's the best way to exploit it? One major goal of your business plan is to determine how your business will compete in the marketplace, which will usually include these steps:

• create a detailed description of the products and/or services you will provide;

• analyze your competition;

• identify any competitive advantage that you may have;

• examine your pricing structure and establish a customer credit policy;

• profile your target market; and

• determine how you will promote your product and/or services.

Use the resources of your library and the Internet (we suggest some helpful sites at the end of this book) to find out as much as you can about the industry or service you're interested in. Be especially concerned with actual and potential competitors—who are they, what are their strengths and weaknesses, and do you feel you have an edge on them?

One important issue is the location of the business. Obviously, you don't want to open up a greeting-card shop across the street from another greeting-card shop in a small town. But two greeting-card stores located in different parts of a major shopping center might both be successful. You will also want to take into consideration whether there are any legal restrictions (for example, zoning) that might limit your location.

Your market research will help you understand what your buyers want and how to communicate that your new business

MARKET RESEARCH

To help you get started with market research, take a look at:

- www.bsorchecklist.org/marketresearch.htm, which has tips for conducting market research and analysis;

- www.managementhelp.org (type "market research" into the search field), providing sources for market research information; and

- www.ohioline.osu.edu (click on "Business," then "Small Business Series" and select the article on Conducting Market Research).

can meet that need. You may wish to consider local colleges as a source of help and information for conducting market analysis. For example, marketing students at a local business college may be interested in performing a marketing analysis for you as a class project.

Developing a Financial Plan

Lots of new businesses fail for one very simple reason: They don't establish a sound financial forecast, leading to inadequate or unwise financing. The financial requirements of businesses vary greatly. However, it is critical that you adequately estimate your start-up and operating costs. Fortunately, you can probably find resources to help you figure out your particular business's needs and, in particular, its cash flow situation.

- Trade associations are often a good source of information about the capital needs of a particular business.
- The local office of the federal Small Business Administration (SBA) and the equivalent state business development office can also assist with financial planning for a new business.
- An accountant, financial planner, or business lawyer who has experience with start-up businesses can be invaluable.

• A business banker will have useful information and may provide professionals to help in developing a business plan.

• If you're purchasing a business, look at prior financial statements and information on taxes paid, including sales taxes and payroll returns as well as the overall return. These should give you a basis for forecasting costs. The process of buying a business is discussed in chapter 5.

• If the business is going to be run as a franchise operation, the franchisor is required to provide information about many aspects of the business, which will help you determine the financial resources you will need. Franchise operations will be discussed in greater detail in chapters 6 and 7.

• Finally, software can be really helpful—there are good budgeting programs and overall business planning programs that can take you through some key steps.

Once you have gathered this information, you are in position to develop a financial plan. One very important element of your financial plan is calculating your break-even point (the point at which revenues begin to exceed expenses). A break-even analysis will force you to calculate your costs of doing business and help you realize just how much revenue your business will need to generate in order to become profitable.

 FINANCIAL PLANS

• www.sba.gov/smallbusinessplanner (click on "Finance Start-Up") provides links to important financial considerations, including break-even analysis, for start-up businesses; and

• www.bplans.com, a for-profit service, provides information on business plans, including sample plans, a section on start-up business planning, and a guide to finding your local small business development center.

SECURING CAPITAL

Capital is another word for *money.* By any name, it's the lifeblood of any new business. There are usually several potential sources of capital for a new business:
- contributions made by you;
- loans from family and friends;
- loans from banks and other financial institutions;
- loans underwritten by a government agency;
- investments made by others who will be actively involved in the management of the business; and
- investments from other individuals and institutions who won't be actively involved in the business and are just looking at the profit potential.

There are two basic forms of capital: equity and debt. Equity capital represents ownership in the business. You don't have to pay back equity capital, but you give up some ownership, and possibly some control, of the business to raise equity capital. Debt capital is a loan to the business—it must be repaid, with interest.

How and where the funds come from have many significant legal considerations.

Contributions Made by You

Let's begin with the first alternative. Getting capital from yourself can be the simplest possibility but may not meet the needs of your business.

Some possibilities for personal contributions include:
- **Savings.** This source is obviously very simple and easy, since it's your money, but how many of us have enough tucked away to open much more than a lemonade stand?
- **Paid-up life insurance.** The **surrender** or **cash value** of a whole life insurance policy is the equity you've built up over the years through the premiums you have paid. This is what the insurance company would pay you if you canceled the policy. You

could do that and use the proceeds for your business, but then you'd have no life insurance, perhaps at a time when your family is relying more than ever on you. A different option is to borrow against this amount from the insurance company. This cash value is money your policy has earned over and above the amount that would be paid as a death benefit. It accumulates on a tax-deferred basis; i.e., taxes are not due on this money until it is paid to you or your beneficiaries. However, if you borrow against this cash value and do not pay the loan back, you will be taxed for having received this money as income. And if you should die while any of the loan is still unpaid, the unpaid portion plus any accumulated interest will be deducted from the death benefit paid to your beneficiaries.

• **Borrowing against your retirement plan.** This is an option only if you continue to work for your employer while starting up your business and if you've built up equity (in retirement language, **vested benefits**) in your 401(k) or similar retirement plan. (But make sure you read chapter 32 discussing risks associated with continuing to work for someone else while starting your own business.) Most retirement plans allow borrowing, usually with a $50,000 maximum limit. Borrowing against this equity is relatively easy (once again, it's your money), rates are low, the repayment period can be as long as five years, and, best of all, you're repaying yourself. Remember, however, that the money can't be in two places at once: While you're using it for your business, it won't be growing in your retirement plan, and you may be shortchanging your sunset years. Your benefits person at work can explain how such a loan can be arranged. Just as with borrowing against the cash value of a whole-life insurance policy, if you do not repay the loan, the loan amount will be considered taxable, plus you will have to pay a 10 percent early withdrawal penalty if you are under 59½ years of age. (But note that you can't borrow from a Roth or traditional IRA; that's considered a **distribution** that you'll probably have to pay taxes on.)

• **Home equity loans.** This is a third way to borrow against your own money. **Home equity** simply means the difference in value between what your home is worth—its market value—and the amount of principal you still owe on your mortgage. Typically, your equity is larger the longer you've been paying down the principal, and the more property values have grown over the years since you took out the loan. If your home is worth $300,000 on the market and you owe only $100,000 in principal, your equity is $200,000. Usually, a lender will lend you 75 percent to 80 percent of the equity. A home equity loan is, in essence, a second mortgage. Rates are usually higher than first mortgages, since there is greater risk for the lender. You can usually deduct the interest you pay on your federal income tax returns. The downside is that you have to go through most of the paperwork and much of the expense and delay of a first mortgage, including paying mortgage recording taxes in some states, and your home is at risk if you can't pay the loan back. And, of course, whether and what amount of equity is available depends on home values, which can go down as well as up. If you have accumulated significant equity in your home, you may, instead, refinance your first mortgage, which also allows you to convert your equity to cash. This option is viable only if current mortgage rates are well below the interest rate on your current first mortgage (if you have one)—plus you must be willing to assume the responsibilities of your new mortgage payments for the life of the new mortgage.

• **Borrowing against the value of your stocks and bonds.** If you're fortunate enough to have such investments, this is one more way of borrowing against your own money. Instead of selling stocks or bonds and incurring taxes (and maybe missing out on some big gains), you can use them as collateral for a loan from your brokerage firm. These are known as margin loans since, as with home equity loans, you can't get the full amount of their current value (too much risk), but once again rates are low and repayment is flexible. Be careful, though; if the stocks fall far enough in value, you will be subject to a "margin call," requiring you to repay an amount equal to the drop in value, which may result in you having to sell the stocks in order to pay off some or all of the loan.

• **Credit card debt.** Every once in a while you read about a now-successful entrepreneur who rolled the dice and maxed out her credit card to get the business going. That can happen, but all in all this is not as attractive a route as the other alternatives we've listed. Credit card rates are often very high, so you'll pay a lot in interest if you can't pay off the balance quickly. Be very careful with credit card debt—the option to make only small, minimum payments leads very quickly to very large debt balances; and many credit card companies impose substantial fees for making late payments or exceeding credit limits.

Loans from Family and Friends

The next best thing to using your own money (either directly or as collateral for a loan) may be a loan from family or friends. The pluses are that you won't have to go through a lengthy application process, repayment terms could be more liberal than you'd get from a bank, and rates could be lower—maybe even nonexis-

 HOME EQUITY:
IT PAYS TO BE CAREFUL

The availability of home equity loans can vary with overall economic conditions. In general, though, if you have substantial equity, you will be able to find a loan. But it pays to be careful. Lenders compete hard to get home equity loan business, so you should shop around—you don't have to use the same lender for the home equity loan as you did for the first mortgage. The federal Truth in Lending Act requires lenders to give you the annual percentage rate (APR) upfront, which in theory enables you to compare apples to apples. Be aware, though, that you may not routinely get the *final* APR (which may include points and other charges) until the closing, when it's too late to change lenders. When shopping for a loan, don't rely solely on the advertised rate—it's not necessarily the same as the APR. Ask lenders up front about application fees, closing costs, fees for title searches and appraisals, and the like. Some of these may be negotiable.

tent. The minus is that you might strain your relationship with family and friends if the business fails and you are unable to repay the amount owed.

If you do get a loan from family or friends, it will probably be at least as much because of personal relationships as the potential of your business. But that doesn't mean that it should just be a handshake deal. It's almost always best to put the terms in writing by signing a **promissory note**. Loans that go sour are probably right up there with martini abuse as a leading source of family donnybrooks. At least with the agreement in writing you won't have two (or more!) widely different accounts of who promised what and when. And if you are unable to repay, with a promissory note Aunt Carol is in a far better position to convince tax authorities that her loan to you should be considered a tax write-off and not a gift.

A promissory note is a legally binding document in which you set out the terms of the loan: how much you received, the interest rate, how long you have to repay, and the rate of repayment. You can get forms for promissory notes in office supply stores; some personal finance computer programs have them, too. The form is just a template—you add the terms for your particular agreement by filling in the blanks.

 MANY WAYS TO REPAY

Especially with family and friends, you may be able to tailor the repayment schedule to your needs. If you anticipate not showing much income in the early stages, you can put the periodic payments closer to the end of the loan, or maybe have it all come due at the end. Or you can pay the interest periodically and repay all the principal at the end. Or you can set low periodic payments at the beginning, gradually increasing them as the term of the loan nears. It's up to you and your angels.

Loans from Financial Institutions

Commercial banks and other commercial lenders are a possibility for additional working capital, though they know very well the failure rates of new businesses and will probably take *a lot* of persuading to part with some of their money for your start-up. Don't forget to contact smaller banks, such as community banks, which may be more flexible with owners of smaller businesses. They are also frequently structured to give small business owners the attention and service that often is available only to larger businesses at larger banks and financial institutions. Expect to go through a lengthy application process. It could mean lots of time and paperwork.

If you do decide to borrow capital, the business must have collateral—something tangible the bank can take to recover its losses in case you can't pay the debt—to secure the loan. Most start-up businesses don't have a building or fleet of trucks that can be pledged as collateral, nor do they have a big stock of inventory or accounts receivable that could be pledged. As a result, banks will generally require personal guaranties and collateral from the owners of the business. This means that you will have to back up the loan with your home or other valuable property to get funding—and that you could lose this property if you fail and default on the loan.

 SIGNING UP YOUR SPOUSE

Banks always want as many places as possible to turn to in case the debt isn't repaid. That's why they often insist on a **cosigner**, someone who pledges to make good on the repayment if you can't. If your spouse co-signs, he or she puts at risk any separate property, as well as the property that you own jointly.

You also need to consider the long-term effects of paying off the debt. Most rates of profit are under 10 percent, so making the assumption of an interest-paying burden of even just 10 percent places a severe strain on a beginning business.

Loans with Government Help

If you can't get money from good old Uncle Hank, Uncle Sam might be able to help. The Small Business Administration has loan and lease guaranty programs that are designed to encourage banks and other financial institutions to lend money to small businesses. The SBA doesn't make loans itself, but by guaranteeing most of the amount lent, it encourages banks to make loans they might not normally make.

You can find out about the many SBA loan programs by checking out its Web site (www.sba.gov) or by calling the SBA at 1-800-827-5722. Through the Web site, you can also get information about the SBA office closest to you.

SBA loans can be used for most business purposes, including the purchase of real estate; construction and renovation; furniture, fixtures, and equipment; working capital; and the purchase of inventory. Franchises are eligible, too. The SBA limits the size of businesses it will help (your start-up should have no trouble meeting the requirement!), and it requires business owners to put some of their own money, including personal assets, into the business.

SBA loan programs include:

• a basic lending program (the 7 (A) **Loan Guaranty Program**) that can enable you to borrow as much as $2 million (though the SBA will guarantee only up to $1.5 million) at rates only a few points above the prime rate; you can have up to seven years to repay a loan for working capital, and up to twenty-five years to repay a loan for real estate and equipment;

• short-term loans and revolving lines of credit;

• a Prequalification Loan program targeting low-income borrowers, disabled business owners, new and emerging businesses,

HELP FROM YOUR STATE

Many states also have special loan or guaranty programs or financial assistance packages and tax relief plans for small businesses. You can get
information about such programs from the local SBA office or the office
of your equivalent state or local agency. You can also get state information over the Internet by accessing www.state.[two-letter abbreviation
of your state].us. Texas, for example, is www.state.tx.us. Once you have
accessed the state's official Web page, look for a search box and search
for "small business loans."

veterans, exporters, rural businesses, and specialized industries,
with maximum loans of $250,000; and
- microloans, up to a maximum of $35,000.

Help for Women and Minorities

The SBA has offices of advocacy to assist minority- and women-
owned businesses.

The SBA also licenses Specialized Small Business Investment Companies to make loans to socially or economically dis-
advantaged individuals. A number of private loan programs also
encourage business development by minorities, women, and people with disabilities.

 **GETTING HELP FOR AN SBA
LOAN PACKAGE**

The forms required for an SBA guaranty of a bank loan are many and
complex. The SBA provides comprehensive checklists to assist you in
gathering the information you need for a loan application. To access the
checklist, visit www.business.gov (then enter "SBA Loan Application
Checklist" in the site's search box).

IT CAN AFFECT YOUR BUSINESS'S LEGAL STRUCTURE

The decisions to bring others into the business can impact the legal structures available for your business. For example, if you have at least one other co-owner, your business will have to be either a partnership, corporation, or limited liability company (LLC). Partnerships, corporations, and LLCs—which are frequently a preferred form of organization for small businesses—and other legal forms of business will be discussed in chapters 11 through 15.

Adding Owners

If you're borrowing money, you still retain full ownership of the company. Once the loans are repaid, you have no further obligations to the lenders. If you have investors, on the other hand, you're selling them a slice of the pie. You don't have to repay what they put into the business, but you'll have to share the profits, and possibly management, with them.

"Active" Investors

Under the law, investors who are actively involved in the business (**active investors**) generally have a different status than investors who are putting up money but not taking part in how the business is run on a day-to-day basis (**passive investors**). Chapters 11 and 12 of this book get into the whys and wherefores of all this.

If you do involve other people in running the business, they might be your **general partners** (see chapter 12) or **general members** (along with you) of a limited liability company (see chapter 14).

If you have investors who aren't involved in the day-to-day operations, they might be your **limited partners, limited members** of your limited liability company, or **shareholders** of your corporation (see below).

In general, you have more flexibility in securing investments from active investors, because state and federal securities laws aren't involved. General partnership agreements, for example, can be flexible. You and your partners can negotiate as to how much of the business will belong to them in return for their financial contribution and their work in the business. You don't have to divide things equally. You do, however, need a **partnership agreement** (see chapter 12) spelling out all the terms.

"Passive" Co-Owners

If you decide to seek funding from investors who aren't actively involved in running the business, you'll face significant legal ramifications, especially with federal and state **securities laws**. These are designed to protect investors and limit fraud by people seeking investors.

The securities laws apply to the sale of any "ownership interest" in a business where the profits are expected to come from the efforts of others. Under this broad definition, virtually all types of ownership interests in a small business sold to people may be securities. For this reason, you should not contact anyone about investing in a business without fully reviewing your investment plans with a securities lawyer. This includes stock, debentures, and other similar corporate debt instruments, limited partnership interests, limited liability company membership interests, and even general partnership interests, where one or more of the general partners does not have the expertise (or authority) to participate in the management of the business.

If a particular type of ownership interest is a security, the **antifraud provisions** of the securities laws automatically apply. In addition, unless an exemption is available, a **prospectus,** which is a very technical and complex disclosure document, must be prepared, and the securities must be registered with the federal Securities and Exchange Commission and the equivalent state administration office in every state where the securities will be sold or offered for sale. If you don't comply with the prospectus and registration requirements, you'll trigger a variety of unpleasant administrative and private remedies, including money damages, rights of investors to rescind their investments, and, in extreme cases, criminal sanctions.

TALKING TO A LAWYER: GETTING STARTED

Q. *Everyone likes the stuffed dogs that my sister and I make for presents. We thought we could make a bunch of them and sell them through gift shops in the neighborhood. Do we really need all those legal papers? Can't we just do business with a handshake?*

A. You don't *really* need "all those legal papers." (We assume, of course, that you are aware of, and meeting, all Federal Trade Commission and local regulations regarding plush toys.) The answer to your question, however, will depend on how many stuffed dogs you eventually want to sell. Do you want this enterprise to grow into a business, or is it a hobby that you can make a few dollars at? If it is the former, you will naturally want to be more careful in developing and documenting your business relationships.

This is especially true if your business grows to a substantial volume. Stores may start asking about the extension of credit (e.g., "Can we pay you for these when you deliver the next ten?") to take on larger orders. The amount of money and products in play will increase, along with the number of locations where your product can be found. Then you will want to keep careful records and make sure that credit terms, times of delivery of orders, a policy for returns, and, of course, prices are spelled out in writing. Many forms that can be of use to you for this type of business are available at office supply stores and do not require a lawyer's involvement.

—Answer by Ron Coleman, attorney, Clifton, New Jersey

There is some good news—in most cases the particular ownership interest you're trying to sell will qualify for an exemption from federal and, in some cases, state registration requirements. An **exemption** is created by a statute or regulation that says certain types of securities can be sold without the expense of registration, so long as specific requirements are met. There's an exemption from federal registration requirements, for example, for a company issuing securities that are all sold to persons in one state or that are sold to investors who meet certain income and net worth tests. There are also several exemptions, many of which are incorporated into what is known as **Regulation D**, that have limitations on the number of purchasers or the total dollar amount of the offering. These exemptions restrict or prohibit advertising of the offering and also restrict resales of the acquired securities.

There is bad news, however, in that all the exemptions have very technical requirements with which you must strictly comply. Complying may be expensive, though usually less expensive than complying with the full registration requirements.

Another complicating factor is that the applicable state securities laws are frequently inconsistent with the federal securities laws, and you have to comply with both. Needless to say, no one should attempt to issue any securities without the assistance of a lawyer, accountant, and other experts.

YOU MUST REMEMBER THIS

- Find the business that's right for *you*—one that uses your particular talents and reflects your interests.
- Create a business plan that includes a comprehensive marketing plan.
- Do as thorough a financial plan as you can; try to anticipate how much money you'll need, when, and for how long.
- Be creative in looking for funding. Look to your personal circle, the commercial world, and government resources.

- Without disclosing too much about your idea or business, talk to other people about what you have in mind. The people you talk to on an everyday basis will be able to give you a "common person" approach and possible purchasers will give you a sense of the market.

CHAPTER 2

Clearing the Decks

Keeping the Legal Side in Mind
Can Save Time and Money

Okay, now Cory's done her homework and is even more sure her idea will work. Through borrowing on her own accounts and a loan from good old Uncle Charlie, she's got enough money to get started. But what about a name for her business? A license? What rules will she have to follow? And what about taxes? Help!

Of course you're eager to get started. But before actually opening your doors, you should dot some i's and cross some t's. Taking steps now will make it far less likely that you'll incur trouble and expense later. Now is the time to at least look into:

- the legal status of your business name;
- the regulations that affect your business;
- the various licenses and permits you might need; and
- getting tax identification numbers, registering for taxes, and figuring out if there are any taxes you need to pay *now*.

Many states have simplified this process, so that you only need to contact the state business development office (or comparable agency), and it will send you a packet of information that covers licenses, permits, and other regulations that apply to your business. You can also obtain this information over the Internet by accessing www.state.[two-letter abbreviation of your state].us. Texas, for example, is www.state.tx.us. Once you have accessed the state's official Web page, look for a link such as "Business Permitting" or look for a search box and enter a search for "business permits."

WHAT'S IN A NAME?

Of course, you want your business name to be catchy and compelling, hard to ignore, and impossible to forget. We can't help you there, but we can suggest a few steps that will help you avoid receiving hard-hitting letters from someone else's lawyer or being forced to trash signs and stationery you can no longer use.

Do some research. There's no point in launching a business and finding out too late that someone nearby is using the same name, or one that's very similar. The best way to avoid this is to do an informal search. Look in the telephone books and business directories in your area, or search the Internet. You can also check with the county or city clerk in your area, or your state's secretary of state (there is a good chance that your state's secretary of state runs an online searchable database). These officials maintain a list of business names that have been filed (see below).

Register your name. If you plan to do business under your name—your full, legal name—then you *may* not need to register your business name with the authorities. However, if you plan to use a business name that has no part of your name ("Comet Café") or only a part of it ("Cory's Creations"), then you need to file what's known as a **fictitious business name, assumed business name,** or **doing business as (DBA) name** with the clerk in your county or city or with your state's secretary of state.

This filing—sometimes coupled with the requirement that you publish the fact that you are doing business under this name in a newspaper in your area—puts the world on notice that "Cory's Creations" is your company. This gives you the right to conduct business under that name; you can advertise under it and use it when filing for permits, billing customers, and paying taxes, for example. In legal terms, it's your **trade name**.

But that doesn't mean you're totally off the hook. Even if your name really is Wendy, and there are no restaurants with

IF YOU WANT A TRADEMARK

Why should Wendy's and McDonald's have all the fun? Can't you protect your trademark, too? You can, and chapter 27 of this book gives you some tips. But this can be a somewhat expensive, time-consuming process, and one that probably isn't necessary for most start-ups, which are probably more concerned with surviving the first year than with conquering the world.

"Wendy" in their names in your area, and you register "Wendy's Burgers" with the county clerk, you're still going to draw the attention of Wendy's International, Inc. That's because they own the **trademark** of "Wendy's" and can very probably force you to change your business name.

You may have to register your name several times. If you take no formal steps to organize your business, you'll be a sole proprietorship and probably face no registration requirements, other than registering your business name. (See chapters 11 through 15 for the various options you have on organizing your business.) If, however, you organize your business as a corporation, you're required to incorporate formally. You might want to consider several questions before incorporating, including whether you want to incorporate in your state or in another state (e.g., Delaware) and then qualify in your state. Incorporation involves going through a formal process, the difficulty of which varies by state. Part of that process is getting approval of the name of your corporation.

Once again, you'll want to do a search to determine if your preferred business name is already being used, but this time, you'll check the official list of corporate names in your state (and any other state you plan on doing business in). You usually do this through the secretary of state's office. If the name you want to use has not been taken or is not confusingly similar to

EVEN IF YOU'RE NOT A CORPORATION

You'll probably also have to register your name (and file other paperwork) with the secretary of state if you organize as a **limited partnership** or one of the many variations of a **limited liability company** (LLC). See chapters 12 and 14.

other business names already in use, you can move to register it. Sometimes registration is good for only a set number of years, after which you must renew the registration.

Federal trademark protection is far more complete than the protections for your business name made available through the states. If your business is going to be active in several states, or if you foresee that your trademark is going to be a valuable asset, then you're well advised to register it with the federal government. Federal trademarks are registered through the United States Patent and Trademark Office. The Patent and Trademark Office provides complete step-by-step instructions for determining appropriate trademark protection and filing for a trademark. The main Internet address for the Office is: www.uspto.gov. Select the "Trademarks" link on the main Web page, then select "Where Do I Start?" Or, you can call 1-800-786-9199 (or 571-272-9250) and request printed information and forms. You can also search the trademarks database, TESS, through a link on the Office's "Where Do I Start?" Web page.

RULES, RULES, RULES . . .

It's impossible to know exactly what regulations might apply to your particular business. Regulations vary by state and locality, and they vary depending on the type of business. Some businesses, such as those that are involved in health care or food services, face complex regulations by many federal, state, and local agencies. Other businesses, conversely, may be only minimally regulated. Businesses that face regulations usually need to get permits or licenses, and we discuss the special rules they must follow below.

Other kinds of regulations affect—or potentially affect—all businesses.

• Businesses that are open to the public must comply with the **Americans with Disabilities Act (ADA)**. You may be able to get information about it through your city's or state's economic development office. The U.S. Department of Justice provides an ADA Guide for Small Businesses at www.ada.gov.

• Many types of businesses may have to be concerned with **environmental regulations**, including rules on air and water pollution, disposal of toxic materials, and use of certain products (e.g., the gas Freon, used in air-conditioning systems). For information, check out the Web site of the U.S. Environmental Protection Agency (www.epa.gov/smallbusiness).

• **Building codes** set certain standards that construction must meet; they may also require you to get a permit if you do renovations. You can get information from your locality's department of building/zoning or department of safety.

• **Zoning ordinances** regulate which types of businesses are permitted in certain areas; they're discussed fully in chapter 8 regarding home-based businesses, but obviously they affect businesses out of the home as well.

The size of the business can also affect the extent of the regulations. The laws of many states, for example, exempt businesses with fewer than four or five employees from having to carry workers' compensation insurance covering injuries to employees. (Even if your business is exempt, however, you might still decide to carry workers' compensation insurance because of the protection it will provide both you and your employees in the event one of your employees is injured while working.) A number of other workplace laws kick in at a certain number of workers. See chapters 16 through 19 for more on this topic.

LICENSES AND PERMITS

Which licenses and permits are required depends on the type and location of the business.

• **Licenses.** All states have statutes and regulations that require tests, proof of financial responsibility, and compliance with other requirements in order to obtain a license to engage in certain businesses or professions. A state license to operate a day care center is one example. Doctors, lawyers, architects, and structural engineers have to be licensed by the state before they can practice their profession. In some states, an assortment of other businesspeople have to be licensed; these include barbers, bill collectors, and funeral directors. The types of businesses

 YOU FACE MORE REGULATIONS IF . . .

In general, certain types of businesses face more regulation than others. A lot of this is common sense, with types of businesses that have the capacity to do more harm facing more scrutiny. Besides health care and anything involving food preparation, a partial list of these businesses includes:

• construction (even home repair in some places);

• anything to do with alcohol;

• anything to do with dangerous materials, chemicals, explosives, and the like;

• transportation (of freight or passengers);

• anything to do with firearms.

Some businesses are regulated by the state, some by the federal government, and some by both. Consult a trade association that covers your industry. It should be able to fill you in on the regulations that apply to you.

subject to these licensing requirements vary from state to state. Your state should be able to tell you what's required.

• **Permits.** Some businesses exempt from state licensing regulations are required to obtain a license or permit from a county or city to perform certain operations. Building contractors, for example, have to get a city or county building permit to build or remodel a house or commercial building.

• **A tax by another name.** Most cities and many counties require businesses located in their jurisdiction to have a business license. In reality, this is a tax based generally on the gross receipts of the business rather than a regulatory license designed to protect the public against shoddy work and incompetence. Avoiding this tax can be an important factor in choosing the location of a business.

TAX REQUIREMENTS

There are several federal and state tax requirements.

1. **Federal tax identification number.** Most businesses must obtain a Federal Employer Tax Identification Number (EIN) before beginning to operate. The only businesses that do not have to have an EIN are sole proprietorships with no employees. Even if you technically don't need an EIN, it's a good idea to obtain one from the beginning. Each state also requires tax registration for new businesses. In most cases the state will use the Federal Employer Tax Identification Number.

You get your EIN by filing an IRS Form SS-4. You can get one from any office that has IRS forms, or online through the IRS Web site, www.irs.gov. If you mail in the form, you'll get your EIN in four to six weeks. You can fax the SS-4 to the IRS office located in your state and the number will be issued within twenty-four hours (the IRS Web site has a "Where to File Tax Returns" section from which you can obtain the appropriate fax number), or you can call direct (800-829-4933) and receive the EIN number verbally. If you phone, you must place the number on the SS-4 and mail it to the IRS for processing.

2. **State sales tax registration.** All states that have sales taxes also require any business not exempt from the tax to register with the appropriate state agency. You'll be required to collect the tax and send it to the state regularly (monthly or more frequently). However, as long as you sell the product to the public and collect the tax at that time, you shouldn't have to pay taxes to get the product in the first place. To avoid paying taxes on the materials you buy from wholesalers, you should get a **resale tax certificate** from the state tax authorities.

3. **Federal and state income tax returns.** As if all this weren't enough, all businesses must file annual federal and state income tax returns. The applicable forms vary with the type of business. Further, some types of businesses must pay income tax if they have sufficient taxable income. Other types of businesses must file a tax return, but they do not pay taxes. Partnerships, S corporations, limited liability companies, and other businesses that as a general rule pass the tax consequences of their operations to their owners file a different type of return than do businesses that are operated as C corporations. The differences in the way various types of business organizations are taxed are discussed in part VI.

4. **Withholding requirements.** If you have employees (including yourself if your business is a corporation), you'll be required to withhold from their wages federal and state income taxes and FICA (Social Security and Medicare) taxes. You have to regularly send these funds to the IRS (in the case of federal withholding and FICA) and the applicable state tax agency. Since your business is just getting started, initially you will have to deposit payroll taxes in a special account on a monthly basis—by the fifteenth day of the month after the taxes are withheld. After a few years, if your annual payroll taxes exceed $50,000, you will have to begin depositing the tax money semiweekly—every three banking days. The state requirements may or may not be the same as the federal deposit requirements. All of this

WHAT YOU'LL NEED, TAX-WISE

The Internal Revenue Service (IRS) publishes a wealth of information for small businesses that is available at any IRS office, as well as on the IRS Web site (www.irs.gov). On the IRS Web site, select the "Businesses" link, then select the "Starting a Business" link. Also obtain, in print or on-line, Publication 583, "Starting a Business and Keeping Records." It contains all the information you need from the IRS's perspective. You should also look for a "Recommended Reading for Small Businesses" link on the IRS Starting a Business Web page. Many state tax commissions have similar publications describing the state taxes that apply to a business. Both types of publications contain samples of the tax registration and other forms that must be filed.

is very confusing, but it's important to know the requirements and follow them, since there may be heavy penalties for late payment. Remember that the principal officers of the company may be *personally* liable for payroll taxes that are not paid to the IRS. You may find it pays to use a payroll service for this job. And any business, no matter its size, should have a tax adviser.

5. **Unemployment insurance tax.** Most states require your business to register, or at least periodically file, with the state agency that administers the state unemployment insurance tax. This is a tax based on the business's payroll. A business must also periodically pay the federal Unemployment Insurance Tax, which is also based on its total payroll.

YOU MUST REMEMBER THIS

• You'll very probably have to register your business name; this isn't the same as registering a trademark, but you probably won't be ready for that step right away in any event.

• You'll also probably need some licenses and permits.

• At the very least, it pays to look into zoning laws, building codes, and other regulations that might affect you.

TALKING TO A LAWYER: INTERNET NAMES

Q. *I think my business can do well on the Internet, but how do I choose an Internet name? Is it the same as my business name? How do I register an Internet name?*

A. Your Internet service provider can help you apply for an Internet domain name. Domain names commonly include shortened versions of business names or brand names, followed by ".com." Your Internet service provider will charge a small fee for registering the name and for hosting your Web site and e-mail on its servers, and the domain name authority will also charge a small fee. The fact that a domain name is available and can be registered is not the end of the story, however. Domain names can be confusingly similar to one another, or they may differ only by the fact that they end in ".gov" or ".org" rather than ".com," or they may end in a country designation, such as ".uk," rather than ".com." The owner of a domain name that is very similar to yours may object to your use of the domain name, and your use might even constitute trademark infringement. The similarity may not come to light until after you have started using the new domain name. Unless you are confident that your domain name is unique, it might be a good idea to have your attorney order a full trademark search that includes Internet domain names.

—Answer by Thomas M. Pitegoff, attorney,
Pitegoff Law Office, White Plains, New York

• Uncle Sam and the state make you start going through tax hoops right away, but there are usually packets of information that will guide you.

• These requirements are not terribly burdensome. They may take some time, but you can, and must, meet them.

CHAPTER 3

Do You Need a Lawyer?

A Quick Guide to When You Need Legal Help—and When You Don't

Cory has a good idea about the office and sales help she'll need to run her business, but she is certainly not a lawyer—how is she supposed to know if and when she needs legal help? How does she even recognize a legal issue, let alone one that's hot (she needs legal help), that's semi-hot (she can take steps with her lawyer reviewing what she's done), or that's not (she can handle it on her own, unless it becomes more complicated)?

It's impossible to give hard-and-fast answers to these questions. Everyone's business is different. Even more important, the kinds of legal matters that pop up from day to day are different, even for the same types of businesses.

What you're weighing is the cost of the various ways of getting the legal job done, along with the risks involved in the choices you make. A good basic rule of thumb is that (1) getting help early might save you time, trouble, and money down the line, and (2) the more money that's at stake and the higher the risk, the more you want to be sure you're doing it right. In that regard, the calculation is a lot like the mental gymnastics you go through in deciding whether to buy insurance. You probably don't want (and can't afford) to insure against every risk, but at the same time, it's very scary to have no insurance at all. Most of us sort through the options, look at the risks we face, peer into a cloudy crystal ball, and select the insurance that seems to cover the risks that would hurt us the most and that we're likeliest to face.

With legal services, the trick is to recognize which of the many things that cross your desk have a large legal dimension and have enough at stake to make the "insurance" of working with a lawyer a good idea. Even better than "insurance," a good lawyer can help prevent problems from happening or better enable you to reach a good outcome if they do. An ounce of prevention is better than a pound of cure every time.

LEGAL LIGHT FLASHERS

The chapters of this book cover most of the areas that have a legal dimension associated with a small business. Most of these topics don't erupt into full-fledged legal matters the majority of the time. But here's a list of major actions/transactions where you should at least strongly consider getting legal help:

- assessing and negotiating franchise agreements;
- creating standardized forms, such as purchase orders and contract confirmations, that the company will use in the business;
- buying or selling a business;
- negotiating loan terms;
- negotiating leases of land or equipment;
- buying or selling property;
- negotiating agreements to license others to use patents, trademarks, or other intellectual property rights that you own, or negotiating to obtain a license to use rights from someone else;
- negotiating other types of contracts;
- responding to a lawsuit that's been filed or one that is seriously threatened (responses might involve negotiating with the other side, coming up with legal strategies, filing appropriate motions in response to the other side's motions, conducting pretrial steps, and so forth);
- filing a lawsuit on behalf of the business;
- dealing with the government on a serious issue (e.g., how the business is regulated);
- dealing with tax authorities on a serious issue;
- seeking new investors (raises issues under securities laws);
- opening offices or beginning to do business in other states or countries;

WHEN THE "LEGAL" LIGHT FLASHES

A lot of businesses are sensitive to problems that *might* have a legal dimension. They make it a practice to call their lawyers, set out the facts, and ask for guidance. Most of the time, at the cost of a few minutes of their lawyer's time, they'll learn it's either nothing to worry about or something they can deal with by taking a few precautions. Sometimes they'll be told it is a problem and will work with their lawyer to solve it before it becomes bigger.

- devising strategies for dealing with a business in trouble (bankruptcy and other options);
- making provisions for a strategy in the event of your disability or retirement; and
- making provisions to pass along your business interests to family members and minimize taxes upon death (estate planning).

Not Just Problems

There's a tendency to think about legal matters as being "problems," but notice that a lot of the events in the list above deal with opportunities—buying a new business, getting a loan to expand the business, signing up new investors, and buying or leasing a new place of business.

The point is that the legal side of your business is much more than putting out fires and suing or being sued. The vast majority of business lawyers spend their time outside of court. They negotiate on behalf of clients, conduct research, deal with government agencies, counsel clients, draft documents (especially contracts), and otherwise advance transactions. A big part of their work is keeping you away from court and from the fuss and expense of being embroiled in legal matters. You could benefit from their help whenever a lot is at stake, not just when trouble is brewing.

UNBUNDLING CAN SAVE YOU MONEY

Unbundling is an awkward word for a good thing—a way to save you money on some of your legal needs. Many times, lawyers tend to handle a legal matter from beginning to end. They track down all the required information, write all the documents, and file them with the appropriate agencies.

Unbundling simply means that, if you so desire, your lawyer can untie that legal bundle and suggest how the work can be split up. Maybe you can gather some of the information, fill out some of the forms, write some of the letters—with the lawyer's job merely to review what you've done and offer suggestions. He or she is your coach but might not be an active player, except for court appearances or handling more difficult technical matters. Yes, you or your staff do more work—but you save money with unbundling. The choice is yours.

DO NEW BUSINESSES NEED A LAWYER?

Up to this point, this chapter has dealt with generalities. Here's a more detailed look at law in the real world. We focus on setting up your business, since that's something all businesses go through. We can't definitely answer whether you'll need a lawyer to help you at this stage, but we examine the considerations that come into play in making that decision.

Do It Yourself?

The basic legal and tax forms that have to be prepared and filed to get a new business properly operational are quite simple and straightforward. Except in a few states, there is no requirement that a lawyer prepare or sign any documents that have to be filed.

With this being the case, do you need to use a lawyer when a new business is organized, and afterward when the business makes a major organizational change? As your business grows in terms of revenue, number of clients, and number of employees, do you need a lawyer to help you change the structure and infrastructure of the business as it deals with new circumstances? Handling one employee is very different from dealing with ten, fifty, or one hundred. Are you and your business prepared for success?

On simple matters, where not much risk or money is riding on the outcome, you might not need a lawyer. If you're simply going to begin a sole proprietorship, operating out of your home, and you understand and can deal with the risks of exposing yourself to personal liability then there might be little to the legal side of opening the business.

A lot of businesses begin this way. If your business is one of them, many of the scenarios that we set out in the rest of this chapter won't apply to you—at least at first. If your business prospers, and you expand and bring in other investors, you'll very likely need a different form of business organization. Then you'll want to return to this chapter.

Get a Lawyer's Help?

The more complicated things get and the more that's at stake, the more you probably need a lawyer. For certain kinds of matters, only a business lawyer has the necessary training and experience to provide expert advice.

Let's say that your start-up is more substantial than a sole proprietorship, with bigger capital needs, outside investors, the possibility of doing business in several locations, and the need for specialized documents between the investors to set out their rights and responsibilities. You would benefit from legal advice on the critical issues, such as:

• what type of business entity to form (should your business be a partnership, a limited liability company, a corporation?);

• the proper state where the business should be legally organized;

• the kinds of documents that are appropriate for that type of business and its investors;

• the appropriate documentation for major transactions; and

OTHER FORMS OF BUSINESS

Many people think you get legal help only for setting up a corporation, but employing a lawyer is just as important when a partnership or limited liability company (LLC) is your form of business. In many of these businesses, the same issues have to be resolved. The only real differences are the names of the principal documents and the statutory framework that governs the business entity.

A well-drafted partnership agreement or LLC operating agreement could be as complex and difficult to draft as the articles of incorporation, by-laws, and other basic corporate documents. Although preprinted agreements are commercially available for these business forms, they provide only general, or "boilerplate," direction and are inadequate in one or more important respects in almost every case.

- advice on the myriad of other questions and issues you, as the owner or manager of a business, may have from time to time.

THE ROLE OF A LAWYER IN AN EXISTING BUSINESS

The first few years were rough, and it's not all that easy now, but Tom's got his remodeling business going. Yes, there are a lot of other remodelers out there, but offering fair prices and reliability really does result in happier customers, word-of-mouth advertising, and a growing business. Tom wants to concentrate on his business, but he knows he can't just ignore the legal side of things. How can he make sure he's keeping up with legal developments yet spend as little time and money as possible?

If Tom's business is like most, there are four general types of legal matters that typically come up:
- major transactions, such as a bank loan or a purchase or lease of equipment or real estate, which can involve drafting or

USE *YOUR* LAWYER

Often a lawyer is involved in a transaction, but you can't be sure your interest will be represented unless he or she is *your* lawyer. Even if the law firm representing a bank prepares the loan documents and the borrower has to pay for this work (which is customary), the borrower's attorney should review all the documents before they are signed.

reviewing various legal documents and preparing minutes to authorize these transactions;

• changes in statutes and regulations that require changes in the company's standard contracts and other documents, internal manuals, and filings;

• ongoing compliance with government regulations—for example, timely filing of corporate annual reports, assumed name refiling, and the like; and

• the need to periodically review and update the company's legal structure.

Annual Legal Audit

One way for Tom to save money, minimize risk, and generally get on top of potential problems is to ask his lawyer to sit down and do a review of the legal side of the business every year. This annual legal audit can uncover omissions, such as the absence of corporate minutes. It can point out needed changes in documents brought about by new laws and regulations. It can provide Tom with the opportunity to discuss potential problems and be better able to resolve them efficiently and cost effectively.

The best time for this annual legal audit is a month or so before the end of the company's taxable year. This enables the audit to include year-end tax planning issues. Frequently, you can save substantially on taxes by either completing a transaction during the current tax year or deferring the transaction until the next taxable year.

Many businesses that are corporations have audits done a month or so before the company's annual meeting and use the audit as a planning vehicle for action that needs to be approved at the annual meeting. Most small businesses, however, operate on a very informal basis and do not hold regular annual meetings. This informality is built into many state corporate statutes, which require an annual meeting but allow the requirement to be met by the use of consent minutes signed by all the shareholders and directors. Consent minutes ratify the action taken even though no meeting is held. Although it is legally possible to avoid having an annual meeting, one should be held if for no other reason than to review the annual legal audit.

The following is a partial list of the issues to be reviewed in an annual legal audit:

- basic documents related to the business itself—for example, if the business is a corporation, articles of incorporation, bylaws, stock transfer records, and procedures for keeping minutes of meetings and corporation actions; the articles of organization and operating agreement of a limited liability company; the partnership agreement of a general partnership, limited liability partnership, or limited partnership; in a limited liability partnership, the statement of limited partnership;

- employment agreements;

- all leases, licensing agreements, and other contracts with third parties, with particular emphasis on termination dates, renewal options, and the like;

- insurance policies;

- all standardized contract forms used by the business—for example, purchase order forms, warranties, brochures, and so forth;

- internal policy and procedural manuals, such as employee policy and procedure manuals and antitrust compliance handbooks;

- transactions that require additional documentation, such as official minutes;

- regulatory compliance—for example, assumed or trade name filings, environmental regulations, ERISA (pension law) problems, and SEC requirements;

- structural changes in the business organization, such as

TALKING TO A LAWYER: KNOWING WHEN YOU NEED LEGAL HELP

Q. When do I really need a lawyer, and when can I use one of those "lawyers-in-a-box" products or software?

A. You clearly should use a lawyer when you are undertaking a significant transaction for the first time. If it is the type of contractual relationship with which you have become very familiar, you might call the lawyer only if you are confronted with unusual provisions.

—Answer by Michael E. Flowers, partner,
Bricker and Eckler, LLP, Columbus, Ohio

conversion to another business form or adoption of a retirement plan or a fringe benefit plan;

• filing of annual reports with the secretary of state and other regulatory bodies;

• tax planning issues, such as S corporation status, legal audit, and alternative minimum tax review;

• filing of tax returns, licenses, and reports;

• pending and potential litigation involving the company; and

• recent legal developments affecting the business.

YOU MUST REMEMBER THIS

• The more that's at stake—in money and risk—the more you're likely to need a lawyer's help.

• Early help is better than late; after you've signed a contract your lawyer might not be able to do much for you.

• Legal help is important not just when trouble's brewing, but when you want to make the most of opportunities.

• You might be able to save money by doing some of the work yourself and having your lawyer review what you've done.

CHAPTER 4

Choosing a Business Lawyer

How to Find the Right Lawyer for Your Company

After thinking about her commercial lease and trying to file her corporate documents, Cory has decided that she'll save money and avoid headaches by having a good business lawyer to advise her on her most important transactions. But how does she find someone with the right kind of background? How can she keep a lid on costs?

HELP WANTED: LAWYER

There's probably no substitute for experience. Look for someone who has organized and represented businesses. When you're just beginning, a good, experienced lawyer will probably be able to fill all your needs. When you're larger, you might also need to seek the help of specialists (labor lawyers, tax lawyers, trademark and intellectual property specialists), but that's down the line.

Fortunately, there are many ways of finding someone who's good. Here, we list a few places to start.

Referrals from other businesspeople. The chamber of commerce in your area might be able to recommend good business lawyers. You might also get good recommendations from bankers, accountants, insurance agents, and others you're working with. Is your type of business unusual? It might be helpful to get recommendations for a lawyer who already knows about representing *your* kind of business, especially if it presents particular legal problems. Ask other people in your line of work or get recommendations from trade organizations you belong to.

Referrals from other lawyers. If you know some lawyers and they do not practice business law, they may be able to recommend lawyers who do. Many trustworthy lawyers make a habit of referring more than one attorney so you can choose the right one for you.

Referrals from bar associations. Your local bar association may have a lawyer referral program or be able to give you a list of lawyers who are members of committees that deal with business law.

Referrals from friends. Any friends or relatives in business for themselves? Ask them about what kinds of legal help they've had and how satisfied they were. Take their recommendations seriously, especially if the work they've had done is similar to the work you have in mind.

Referrals from state and national certification programs. Certification is not as widespread among lawyers as it is in the medical profession, and there is no general specialty program for business lawyers. However, quite a few state and national programs certify lawyers as specialists in a variety of areas that involve the business enterprise, including commercial and corporate law, bankruptcy law, creditors' rights, tax law, and so forth.

To be certified, a lawyer must show that he or she has substantial experience in the area in which certification is sought and must also fulfill specific continuing education and peer reference requirements. In addition, almost all lawyer certification programs require applicants to pass a written examination in the particular specialty field of practice. Lawyers don't have to seek such certification to practice, and many good lawyers don't.

You can get directories of certified lawyers from the national organizations listed in the appendix. A number of states offer certification programs in various areas that touch on business, such as taxation and workers' compensation.

 TYPES OF FIRMS

Many lawyers who practice by themselves or in small law firms practice business law. Virtually all medium and large law firms will have one or more lawyers who represent business clients on a regular basis.

Advertising. Since many lawyers now advertise their practice areas, you should be able to locate a number of local lawyers who practice business law by looking in the Yellow Pages or searching online. Be aware, though, that in most states lawyers aren't certified as specialists in anything. Thus, in many of the states that do not certify lawyers as specialists, the credentials that lawyers advertise (such as concentration in a particular area) may be self-proclaimed without any independent verification. Conversely, the absence of such credentials in advertising may be attributable to ethics rules and does not necessarily mean the lawyer is inexperienced.

Lawyer referral services. In most communities you can find bar-sponsored lawyer referral services. Often these services maintain specialty panels to help you find a lawyer who has experience and focuses on business matters. The ABA maintains an online directory of lawyer referral services at www.abanet.org/legalservices/lris/directory.

So, finding a competent business lawyer to represent you should not be a problem. Remember also that if your particular situation calls for some special tax, securities, or other expertise that the lawyer you have chosen does not have, he or she must disclose this fact to you and, with your consent, consult with another lawyer with the requisite knowledge to assist with those issues.

MEET THE LAWYER *FIRST*

Many lawyers are willing to meet with you briefly, free of charge, so the two of you can get acquainted. You can meet with several lawyers and do some comparison shopping, then hire the one you feel would do the best job for you.

First Steps

No matter what areas a lawyer says he or she specializes in, it's best to verify for yourself whether he or she will be able to meet

ARE YOU COMFORTABLE WITH
THIS PERSON?

When you're making your hiring decision, don't forget to consider your comfort level with each attorney you're considering. This involves personal style or personality, physical environment, office organization and staffing, and convenience (e.g., office hours, availability by phone or e-mail). You want to feel comfortable confiding in your lawyer, and you want to feel that he or she will return your calls promptly and will be able to give you the time and attention you need.

your needs. A good reliable lawyer will not be offended by any such questions. During your first call, ask the attorney or the attorney's secretary or office manager:

- How long has the lawyer been in practice?
- What percentage of the lawyer's practice is devoted to your type of legal matter?
- If the lawyer is a specialist in the area of law you are seeking, how long has the attorney specialized? What specialty memberships or certifications does he or she have?
- Can the lawyer provide you with references to clients he or she served with similar needs?
- Is there a fee for the first consultation, and if so, how much is it?
- If you make an appointment, what information should you bring with you to the initial consultation?
- It is important to inform the lawyer of your expectations. Is the lawyer willing and able to meet your expectations? If you are new at this, ask the lawyer what the nature of the attorney-client relationship would be with a case such as yours.

What Questions to Ask

Once you have an appointment, and if you are seeking help with a particular legal matter, come prepared to summarize the facts of your situation briefly and accurately. Providing a written summary really helps. After you have explained your situation, ask:

• What steps will be necessary to handle the matter, and how long will they take? Are there alternative courses of action? What are the advantages and disadvantages of each?

• What experience does the lawyer have in handling this particular type of matter? (This is the same as the initial inquiry, suggested above, but this time it is based upon your particular circumstance, which the lawyer now knows in detail.)

 EVALUATING YOUR ATTORNEY

How do you know your lawyer is doing a good job representing you? A former chair of the ABA's Business Law Section, Maury Poscover, suggested the following criteria in an article in *Industry Week* magazine.

• **Has my lawyer learned my business?** He or she should understand your operation, and perhaps know your key employees. "House calls" to visit your facility can make your lawyer better prepared to provide preventive advice and good judgment.

• **Does my lawyer have my trust?** The relationship should be one of great trust and sharing. Your lawyer should have your best interests in mind, take a personal interest in your success, and call you periodically to assess your company's progress.

• **Does my lawyer add value?** That involves:

  o providing high-quality, cost-effective services;

  o using technology effectively—including computers, e-mail, and the Internet;

  o having access to support staff, including specialized legal help and well-trained paralegals, who may be able to handle a substantial amount of work at a lower rate;

  o being receptive to billing arrangements that accommodate your changing and growing needs and expectations.

• If the matter involves a dispute, what are the outcomes the lawyer expects (including time involved, costs, size of awards, and burdens on you personally)?

• Exactly who will be involved in working on your case and how? What experience and expertise do these others have?

• How can you participate—what can you do, under the lawyer's guidance?

• What will it cost, and how will you be billed?

If you're seeking someone to handle a wide range of issues that come up, ask about experience the lawyer has had with businesses in your line of work, or with businesses about your size. Ask who else in the firm is available to work with you, how the times of the various lawyers will be billed, and how you can save money by gathering information, preparing documents, and so forth.

ATTORNEYS' FEES

Organizing a Business

The fees a lawyer will charge for organizing a business vary depending on the complexity of the business arrangement and the number and overall length of the documents that are required.

Although many lawyers will advertise or quote a set dollar fee for organizing a corporation, LLC, partnership, or other business form, this fee does not normally include any filing fees and the like. Generally, it covers only "plain vanilla," simple deals in which standardized form documents can be used with just a few modifications. This approach may not adequately meet the needs of your business and its investors. In many cases, you'll need very sophisticated customized documents, and that will cost more.

Because customized documents are so often required, most lawyers want legal fees to be charged on an hourly basis. Increasingly, however, lawyers who charge hourly are willing to

ONCE A BUSINESS IS RUNNING

Usually, lawyers charge a per-hour fee for representing an existing business. Often a business will work out an arrangement whereby it will pay a law firm a monthly or quarterly **retainer**, which is based on the estimated fees, with the understanding that there will be an adjustment at the end of the year, based on the actual time expended. Sometimes the retainer is merely an availability fee that guarantees the law firm will give the business's legal work priority. Under this type of fee arrangement, each legal matter will be billed on whatever basis the client and firm have to agree to.

---

quote a per-hour charge *and* a maximum fee that will not be exceeded, regardless of the number of hours that are spent.

There is really no standard per-hour charge. Generally, the more experience the lawyer has, the higher the per-hour fee. That doesn't necessarily mean you'll spend more, however. A more experienced lawyer, because of greater expertise, may be able to complete the legal work involved in organizing the business in far fewer hours and therefore at a lesser overall fee than a less experienced lawyer.

The total amount of legal fees will almost surely be less for work conducted on a sole proprietorship. They may be about the same regardless of the other business forms chosen. The fees for drafting the organizational documents for a non-corporate business form (for example, an LLC) may be slightly lower than for a corporation in some cases because fewer separate documents may be required.

Keeping Fees Down

You can do a lot to minimize your legal fees.

1. Do some things yourself. There are plenty of tasks you can perform that need to be completed as part of the organizational

process. Most lawyers will provide a list of those tasks clients can perform themselves. Examples include obtaining

- business licenses;
- the business's federal tax ID number;
- the sales tax registration number; and
- various types of business insurance.

2. You can cut down on the amount of billable time by filling out various required forms, for example Form 2553, which is required if a business formed as a corporation is to be taxed as a subchapter S corporation. The attorney then only has to review the completed paperwork.

3. Be organized. Make sure your lawyer has the basic information about any legal matter that's cooking—the people, the documents, the background. If possible, gather several legal matters together, and consult with your lawyer about all of them. That should save the lawyer time and you money.

4. Replying right away to your lawyer's requests for information will help reduce billable time. Don't waste money making your lawyer follow up on prior requests or correct errors caused by your incomplete answers to requests for information.

5. Be brief. Keep your phone calls or visits as short as possible and to the point. Don't schmooze about the basketball game. Don't involve the lawyer in business matters that don't raise legal issues—you might well find more qualified people to give you advice and save yourself money.

6. Do an annual legal audit. Fees for the legal audit and any follow-up legal work resulting from it will be far less than the fees incurred in cleaning up a legal disaster that could have been prevented if timely corrective or preventive actions had been taken.

7. Calling your lawyer *before* committing to a transaction that is not in the ordinary course of business is a very cost-effective way to reduce legal fees. A ten- to fifteen-minute discussion with the lawyer for the business will often suffice. The bill for this conversation will be far less than the bill for trying to get out of a transaction that should never have been entered into in the first place.

A simple example will illustrate this point. Assume a small corporation wants to issue some additional stock. If the corporation's lawyer is called before the stock is issued, the lawyer will be in a position to ask the right questions to determine whether there are any significant securities law issues that might be triggered by the proposed issuance. It may turn out that none exist and the only concern is to be sure that the same legends on the share certifications already issued are on the new share certificates. On the other hand, it may turn out that certain documentation to qualify the new shares for an available securities registration exemption may be necessary under the circumstances. If the offering circular and other documents are not drafted, very serious and very expensive legal problems are likely to arise months or even years after the stock is issued. The total fees for resolving these problems will be far higher than the fees incurred for the legal advice and document drafting.

YOU MUST REMEMBER THIS

- Personal recommendations from people you trust are a good way to find a good lawyer.
- Recommendations from people whose businesses are like yours are especially good.
- Try to interview several lawyers before making hiring decisions, and ask them the same questions about their experience, availability, and fees.
- Remember, the lawyer charges you for his or her time; there might be a great deal you can do to reduce the lawyer's time spent on your legal matters—and thus the fees you'll pay.

CHAPTER 5

Buying a Business

The Basics, Including How You Can Maximize Your Advantage

Tom, like Cory, has decided that he wants to be his own boss. But he doesn't want to start from scratch (too scary) or through a franchise (possibly increased costs and diminished upside). There's another option—he could buy an existing business (which may or may not be a franchise). There are plenty of successful existing businesses out there that might be just right for him. But how will he know if he has found the right one and then make sure that his rights are protected when he negotiates to buy? Read on for some expert tips.

This chapter deals with just some of the issues you'll face if you decide to purchase a business. Have a look at chapter 32 too, which discusses business sales from the standpoint of the seller and gets into the specifics of the sales contract. (It's always good to appreciate the other person's point of view in negotiations, and, of course, the sales contract is equally important to both parties.)

First of all, understand that the process of buying and selling a business is heavily dependent on exchanging information. Naturally, as a buyer you'll want to know as much as possible about the company you're thinking of purchasing. And the seller will want to know a good deal about you, too—your financing, your creditworthiness, your ability to live up to the obligations of the sales contract, and especially your ability to meet the payments if you're not paying in a lump sum.

The law can be heavily involved in all these exchanges of information and is of course involved in the legal documents that formalize the various stages of the process.

FIRST QUESTION:
BUY A BUSINESS OR ASSETS ONLY?

To the layperson, this seems like a no-brainer. When you buy a business, you buy it—lock, stock, and barrel. But often it's best to buy just part of the business—the part with the greatest potential benefit and least potential risk.

Let's look at your choices. When you buy from a corporation, you could buy the entire business or just the **assets** of the corporation and leave the corporate shell behind, kind of like a crab in molting season.

What assets are we talking about? That varies with the business, of course, but it could be:

• tangible property, such as manufacturing facilities or an office;

• equipment; trucks, cars, and other vehicles; inventory; and so forth; or

• intangible property, such as patents and trademarks; goodwill; or the seller's noncompetition agreement.

One advantage of just getting the assets is that you have less chance of picking up the corporation's existing or future liabilities, including:

• lawsuits by customers, employees, or suppliers, some of which might not even be filed for months, if not years;

• violations of government regulations; and

• long-term contracts that you want no part of.

On the other hand, if the corporation benefited strongly from existing contracts, including perhaps several years of guaranteed peace through a union contract, you might want to buy the corporation as such and continue the contracts.

Another advantage of buying only the assets is that you may well get significant tax breaks, including the opportunity to depreciate anew some assets that may have already been depreciated by the corporation. This essentially enables you to show a "paper" cost, and thus show less earnings and possibly

SHOULD YOU USE A BUSINESS BROKER?

A business broker, like a real estate broker, could make your search easier. A business broker can help you identify potential existing businesses that fit your specific needs, and provide services from just identifying potential business all the way to handling the negotiation and sales transaction. However, this service isn't free. Just as in real estate transactions, the buyer's broker generally gets a percentage of the sale price, usually as a percentage of the commission paid to the seller's broker (typically in the 10 to 12 percent range). The good news is that you do not have to pay the fee directly; the bad news is that you don't have someone in *your* corner and may wind up paying indirectly. The broker has no legal duties to you and may not be the best person to advise you or to negotiate the agreement with the seller.

You could negotiate with a broker to represent you as a buyer's broker, paying the broker directly so that you have his or her loyalty. The discussion of brokers' contracts in chapter 32 may help you negotiate a good agreement with a buyer's broker.

---

pay less in taxes. You'll also start off with a higher tax basis for the assets, and thus pay less in capital gains when you eventually sell them.

Because of considerations such as these, most small business sales are of assets rather than the entire business.

THE SELLING PROSPECTUS

Whether you use a broker or not, your first detailed look at a business for sale will be something called a **selling prospectus**. You may not learn the name of the business in this document—sellers often want to maintain confidentiality, so that their customers and business contacts don't know the business is for sale. However, you will learn:

- the basic story of the business, including its history and current status, its location, assets, operations, competition, and profit-and-loss picture;
- the role of the owner, including the part the owner plays in day-to-day operations and his or her role in making the operation successful;
- the owner's reasons for selling;
- at least a summary of the business's finances; and
- the asking price and terms.

Chapter 32 discusses these statements more fully, but this should give you a rough idea of what to expect.

BUYER'S INVESTIGATION

If the prospectus interests you, you'll want to have a personal interview with the owner and review detailed accounting information. The interview should include a disclosure of more difficult information and an immediate review of the accounting in place.

You'll have to make a determination with respect to the accuracy and validity of the accounting. You'll very likely want to have expert advice at this stage, but here are a few general tips. Look at such documents as:

- the company's "books"—its profit-and-loss statements and balance sheets, not for just the current year but for several previous years as well;
- tax returns going back at least several years;
- other important documents, such as loan documents, pending lawsuits, and regulatory tangles, if you're going to acquire the whole business; and
- all accountants' documents.

In considering these accounting reports, remember that **compiled reports** are balance sheets based on information provided by the business. They represent the owner's view of things

DUE DILIGENCE CHECKLISTS

Due diligence checklists can be found on the Internet.

Try smallbusiness.findlaw.com and click on "Business Form & Contracts" and then select "Contracts A to Z" and then "Due Diligence Checklist—Purchasing a Business"; or visit www.sba.gov/smallbusinessplanner/start, then select "Buy a Business."

and thus aren't at all independent or of much use to you. Far better are **review reports** (in which there is some independent investigation by an auditor) and **audited reports** (in which a certified public accountant conducts a fuller independent examination of the company and determines whether its statements are in keeping with generally accepted accounting principles). An important caveat: Even audited reports are based on seller-provided information!

Often buyers use certain due diligence checklists so that they can be sure a thorough investigation will be accomplished. It is a good idea for you and the seller to review the checklist to agree on the procedure to be used for the disclosures.

 GETTING TO KNOW YOU

Running an owner-managed business will often require a certain personality, and it's often a good idea for you and the seller to use at least part of your meeting to determine if you have the qualities needed to succeed in the business. This is especially true if the seller will finance a part of the purchase price, because he or she will then have a direct stake in your success. At the very least, you and the seller should be able to establish a working relationship.

STATEMENT OF INTENT

It is generally difficult for the parties to determine if the deal can be done without discussing the major terms of the transaction, including overall structure and price. Whether the discussion is detailed or general, you and the seller will want to document the status of your evolving understanding before you get to the point of negotiating an actual contract.

This desire will often result in a statement of intent document. The **statement of intent** is by definition an agreement to agree and is not traditionally enforceable as a contract. It is important that this fact be repeated in the language of the document and that you and the seller fully understand the limitations of the document.

Don't place agreements that *are* intended to be enforceable in the statement of intent document. Experience has shown that many of the problems that have ensued from using statements of intent come when one party assumes that the statement is an enforceable contract.

As long as you and the seller understand that the statement of intent is designed just to clarify your thinking and points of agreement during the negotiation process, it can be very helpful in drafting the contract for purchase and sale of a business.

THE CONTRACT

The contract for purchase or sale of a business is absolutely central to the transaction. Like a contract to sell a home, it will determine the basis upon which the business is sold. We discuss the sales contract in some detail in chapter 32, but here are a few general points to be aware of.

What, exactly, are you buying? The structure of the contract will depend upon whether you're purchasing specific assets of the business or the entity conducting the business. If it's an asset purchase, the assets should be specified, along with any liability of the business you've agreed to assume. If it's an entity purchase, the contract should specify that the buyer will not assume any undisclosed liabilities. This is usually accomplished by a **warranty** from seller to buyer, which essentially gives you the legal right to come after the seller should an undisclosed claim against the business surface. Note, though, that initially the buyer will be responsible to the person or entity that is claiming a contract or tort-based wrong.

While it is more obvious in the asset purchase agreement, even in the entity purchase situation there must be a method to define exactly what is being purchased. This is frequently accomplished by attaching detailed schedules to the contract that specifically identify the assets and liabilities or specifically define the balance sheet of the entity, so that the exact nature of what constitutes the business and what is being transferred can be identified, item by item.

Contingencies. If you haven't been able to fully investigate the purchase before preparing the contract, the contract might provide that it is contingent on certain factors (i.e., that facts about the business as asserted by the seller can be verified). That way, you can have an additional period to investigate without irreversibly committing yourself.

Access to the business. If there will be a period between the execution of the contract and the closing (**interim period**), the contract can specify that you will be allowed, to a certain extent, to come onto the business premises, access business records, and otherwise be informed about the nature of the business. Don't expect total access; it's not your business yet and the seller still needs to operate the business without too much distraction.

Cash. Generally, don't look to get an infusion of cash from the business. Cash is not normally transferred. In an entity purchase, cash accounts will usually have minimal balances. In an asset purchase, cash accounts will normally not be transferred. Accounts receivable will usually be treated similarly to cash except where collection of an account receivable is linked to future performance.

There are many other important terms of the contract, including selling price, schedule of installments to complete the sale, and tax considerations. These are discussed more fully in chapter 32 on selling a business.

NONCOMPETE AGREEMENTS

The last thing you want is to buy a business and have the old owner pop up a few months later as a competitor. That's why you'll want the seller to provide you with an assurance that after the sale of the business, he or she will not compete with or remove personnel from the business. Sometimes these agreements are included in the sales contract (where they become part of the intangible assets you acquire) and sometimes they are handled in a separate document.

Either way, you have to make sure that the courts will enforce the agreement. In general, that means it must be reasonable both in terms of duration (how long it will last) and geographic area (what region it will cover). What is reasonable for such agreements? In many states, three years is an outer time limit. Geographic restraints will of course vary depending on circumstances. Fifty miles might be reasonable in a very sparsely settled region, but twenty-five miles might be too many in the heart of a huge metropolitan region. Have your lawyer look into the statutes and cases in your state and any other state that might have jurisdiction.

The tax effects vary for seller and buyer. For you as buyer, the payment for the noncompetition agreement is spread over (**amortized for**) the period of the agreement and deducted according to the amortization.

What happens if the seller violates the agreement? You can take him or her to court and seek money damages. However, damages are often difficult to prove (can you really determine how much business he or she has taken from you?), and so you might be better off to specify a dollar figure for damages in the agreement (in legal terminology, these are **liquidated damages**).

SELLER TO STAY ON AS A CONSULTANT?

The flip side of noncompete agreements are provisions for the seller staying on as a member of your team—at least for a while. Your contract can include a section specifying that the seller will stay on as a consultant for a specified term, at a specified salary. You get the value of what should be very good advice, and you can deduct the cost as a business expense.

CLOSING

Just as in a real estate transaction, the closing process involves signing the final papers of the purchase and sale. Here's what may take place:

• Often, the buyer won't know the final purchase price until closing, when it will be determined in accordance with procedures set forth in the contract. The actual purchase price may depend on such procedures or events identified in the contract as inventories of assets, final accounting for payments received for accounts receivable, and identification of certain receipts after initial periods of operation under the new owner.

• At closing, the seller (and often the buyer) will be required to certify that the warranties and representations given in the contract, which will remain the basis for a legal action after the closing, were and are true and accurate.

• The buyer and the seller will sign the documents of transfer, and the buyer will sign documents relating to payments and will usually make a payment.

• The contract may provide for certain allocations of payments or deposits between the buyer and the seller.

Typically, at the end of the closing process, the seller will have accomplished the transfer of the business to you, the buyer. You will have paid for the business and will take possession of it.

YOU MUST REMEMBER THIS

• Buying a business is a huge decision. Make sure you investigate every important aspect thoroughly, and be sure to get expert help in evaluating the opportunity, valuing the business, and negotiating.

• Try to buy the assets of the business; try not to buy the problems.

• Don't be offended if the seller needs to learn a good deal about you—communication is the key for both parties.

CHAPTER 6

Is Franchising for You?

Practical, Hands-on Tips for Evaluating a Franchise Opportunity

Sam is fed up with working for someone else. He's got some money saved up. He has heard about how some people got in on the ground floor with the right franchise and are now driving around in Porsches. Is it that easy? How can he tell a good opportunity from a disaster in the making? How can Sam protect his hard-earned money (and his sanity)? The law can be a big help.

Franchises are everywhere, from the sub shop in the strip mall to the motels and the car dealership on the highway. They can be an attractive way for you to go into business, since they come in all sizes and let you tie into a going business, or get in on the launch of a new one.

Starting a new business can be scary. There are so many unknowns, from how to market to where to locate and how to figure (and control) costs. Buying a franchise helps you get a handle on the business, because you're not starting from scratch but rather building on the experiences of hundreds or thousands of other people.

As of 2005, there were at least half a million franchises, and they accounted for more than one-third of all U.S. retail sales (including motor vehicles and motor vehicle fuel). Fast-food restaurants, hotels, motels, auto dealerships, soft drink bottlers, and accounting services are fertile grounds for franchises.

But franchises aren't a panacea. Though they're widely thought to be a better bet in general than a start-up from scratch, this isn't always true. Sometimes they come with high start-up costs. And with a franchise, you're not exactly your own boss. You have to stick to your contract with the franchisor, which means you don't have complete control over many aspects of the business.

This chapter highlights the strengths and weaknesses of franchises. It tells how you can protect yourself in franchising and make the best decision about whether to buy a franchise.

WHY FRANCHISING IS POPULAR

A franchise is a way of doing business. The **franchisor**, be it McDonald's®, Ford Motor Company®, or Motel 6®, grants you, the **franchisee**, the rights to sell the company's products and services. You become a part of the franchisor's business by using its name and logos. Franchising can involve anything from peddling humble burgers and subs to offering a sophisticated service such as tax preparation. No matter what you're selling, though, it involves the licensing of an established trademark or trade name.

Why are big companies eager to let little ol' you have a slice of the pie? From their standpoint, the logic behind franchising is simple: It costs them much less money to build a network of outlets to distribute goods and services by using franchises than by operating company-owned units. And they get extra money from licensing trademarks and trade names and from other services they provide to franchise holders.

What do you get? You always get the goodwill of the

 FINDING FRANCHISE OPPORTUNITIES

Every year, the January issue of *Entrepreneur* magazine lists its "Franchise 500," the best franchise opportunities. Check it out on the Internet at www.entrepreneur.com/franchise. The International Franchise Association also provides help in locating franchise opportunities at www.franchise.org. If you live in or near a large metropolitan area, there will also usually be a franchise exhibition at least once per year.

STRUCTURING A FRANCHISE

If you go ahead and purchase a franchise, does the fact that it's a franchise affect whether your business should be a sole proprietorship, a partnership, a corporation, or a limited liability company? Not really; it can be any of these. Key factors are the size and financial success of the business, tax considerations, and your potential exposure to liabilities from operating the business. If you set up a corporation or limited liability company to be the franchisee, however, it is likely that the franchisor will ask the owner or owners to sign personal guaranties of the franchisee's obligations to the franchisor.

---

franchisor's trademarks and trade name, and you usually get expert guidance in such matters as site selection, training of employees, bookkeeping, and other managerial services. This help is particularly valuable to businesspeople with little or no prior experience.

WHAT IT COSTS YOU

Usually you pay a franchise fee for the right to use the trademarks, trade names, and trade secrets of the franchisor and for managerial services involved in getting the franchise established. Frequently, you'll also be required to purchase all of the franchise's initial equipment, including signs and trade fixtures, from the franchisor. You may also be required to purchase many of your supplies from the franchisor or from franchisor-approved sources.

And that's not all. You'll normally pay the franchisor a royalty based on a percentage of your gross receipts. It's usually about 5 percent, but the percentage can vary widely, especially among industries. The royalty covers continuing support services, as well as a licensing fee for use of the franchisor's trademarks and trade names. If the franchisor owns the franchised location, you'll obviously have to pay rent to the franchisor.

THE PROS AND CONS OF A FRANCHISE

A franchise is not a guaranty of success. Franchises generally have pros and cons as compared to owning a similar but independent business, and every franchise has its own unique set of trade-offs.

Advantages of a Franchise

- You can reap the benefits of the franchisor's knowledge and experience. If you're a rookie in the business, you'll especially need the franchisor's help with training and site selection.
- Because the franchisor is promoting its business, usually vigorously, your business will often receive a boost from the franchisor's advertising.
- As a franchisee you do not need years to establish a reputation for quality goods or services, because the franchisor has provided you with a proven, recognized brand, assuming that the franchisor is not a fledging company.
- Because some franchisors offer the products, supplies, services, and equipment used in your business for sale at a reduced rate, your operating costs could be reduced.
- Some franchisors are skilled at site evaluation, helping you find a specific, optimal location for your business.

Disadvantages of a Franchise

- You lose control: The franchisor sets the rules, and you must follow standardized procedures and offer certain products.
- The franchise agreement is prepared by the franchisor and naturally favors the franchisor. If you're buying from a well-established franchisor, you have unequal bargaining power and sometimes little room to negotiate the terms.

• The royalty fees you pay are based on a percentage of monthly gross sales, not profits. You must pay them, even if you're losing money.

• The standard franchise agreement may restrict your transfer of ownership, preventing you from selling the business to the highest bidder or giving it through your will to your spouse without the franchisor's prior approval.

• You may not be able to relocate a franchise if your site becomes unsatisfactory.

• The termination clause in your contract may let the franchisor terminate the relationship by canceling the contract or not renewing it. This can punish franchisees who don't toe the line.

• Because you're buying into a name, you're also getting any problems associated with that name. If there's bad publicity about the national company, or even if your customers get lousy service from another franchisee, you'll be socked with guilt by association.

• Your own franchisor could be your worst competitive threat if it establishes other outlets nearby or sells products through other channels of distribution.

• The franchise agreement may be only for a period of years—e.g., five or ten. After that, you may not be able to continue your business, or the conditions to renewing your franchise may not be to your liking.

• Your sources of supply may be tightly regulated, or you may have to pay "fees" to your franchisor, thereby increasing your costs.

• Finally, you may have to file monthly or even weekly reports with the franchisor, which involve voluminous, cumbersome paperwork.

HOW THE LAW PROTECTS YOU

The law requires pre-sale disclosure in many—but not all—franchise sales. Thanks to federal law and the laws of many states, you have a right to key information that will help you avoid picking a lemon.

The Federal Trade Commission (FTC) has a Franchise Rule. It requires franchisors to give you information *before* you commit to buy a new franchise that will enable you to decide whether the deal is one you should accept or run away from. A number of state laws require somewhat more stringent disclosures, and usually franchisors meet both requirements at once with a Franchise Disclosure Document (FDD).

Under FTC rules, you have a right to this document at least fourteen days before you legally commit yourself to the purchase or pay any money. The FDD is a detailed disclosure statement. It's not fun reading, and neither is the proposed **franchise agreement** (contract) that has to accompany it. (See chapter 7 for more on franchise contracts and how you might be able to negotiate for better terms.) But if your life savings are on the line, you have plenty of incentive to check this opportunity out. Remember, the government doesn't vouch for the accuracy of these documents. It's up to you to verify the information and use it wisely.

The law does not require an FDD when you buy an existing franchise from another franchisee.

 HELP FROM OTHERS

Don't be penny-wise and dollar-foolish. Getting professional help at the front end can save big bucks at the back end. Your accountant can look at the franchisor's figures with an expert eye. Your accountant or your lawyer can help you get information on the franchisor from financial services companies such as Dun and Bradstreet. They can also help you evaluate the economic risks of the particular venture compared with similar franchised and non-franchised ventures. Careful investigation may even uncover improper hidden charges and kickbacks. Be sure your advisers are solidly experienced in evaluating franchise opportunities.

The FDD has twenty-three categories of information. Here are some of the most important ones, along with some tips on how to use the information presented:

1. Basic information about the company, including names under which it does business, a description of the business, its business experience, how long it has operated this type of business, number of franchises sold, and so forth.

    a. Does the franchisor have a long-established, good reputation?

    b. Have you consulted the Better Business Bureau, the chamber of commerce, or your banker to inquire about the franchisor's business reputation and credit rating?

2. Experience and background of the key executives in the business.

3. Whether the franchisor has previously filed for bankruptcy.

4. Recent litigation involving the franchisor and its key people, including pending cases. Don't necessarily be scared off by some litigation—hardly any business is involved in *no* lawsuit—but:

    a. Watch out for cases involving fraud, deceptive trade practices, violations of franchise laws, etc.

    b. A pattern of litigation or even a large number of cases can be a red flag.

5. Costs required to start the business, including initial franchise fee, and an estimate of the initial investment you'll have to make. Restrictions on sourcing—look for these. If you can't shop for equipment and supplies from competitive sources, it could cost you dearly. And watch for later re-investment obligations.

6. Responsibilities you and the franchisor will have to each other.

7. Your territory (if any). Do you have exclusive rights, how big is it, do you have to achieve a certain sales volume to keep it exclusive? How many franchises are there in your general area? How can your franchisor compete against your franchise?

8. Additional important aspects of the franchise relationship,

such as termination, renewal, and transfer rights, and how disputes may be settled.

9. Names, addresses, and telephone numbers of other franchisees in your state and in neighboring states. Also included are names and addresses of those franchisees that left the system in the prior fiscal year. By all means, use this information. Don't just contact franchises that the franchisor steers you toward. Visit a good cross section of the going concerns, and make sure you find out why the "gone" franchises aren't around anymore.

10. A fully audited financial statement of the seller.

   a. Have your accountant analyze these figures to get an idea of the financial strength of the company—you want it to be around for a long while.

   b. Be wary if figures show that investors are paying their upfront money but not their royalties. This may indicate that units aren't doing well.

11. Statistical data about the system. Is it growing or shrinking? Are locations being "churned"?

Some businesses are exempt from the FTC rule. If your prospective franchisor says he or she did not provide a disclosure statement because he or she is not covered, verify this with the

 SOME BASIC QUESTIONS

Before you decide on a particular franchise opportunity, ask yourself these questions:

- Have consumers had a chance to accept the product or service?

- Would you purchase the product or service?

- Does the territory provide adequate sales potential?

- Have *you* determined whether there is a market for the product or service in your territory at the price you will have to charge?

- Is this a product or service that's apt to stay in demand, or is it a flash in the pan?

PROTECT YOURSELF

Compare, compare, compare. Contact other sellers of franchise opportunities, request their disclosure statements, and compare them to your
seller's information. Does this system have an independent franchisee
association (check FDD Item 20)? Ask the officers of the association
what role franchisees play in system decision making. What is the level
of cooperation and mutual respect in the system?

FTC, an attorney, or a business adviser. Even if the prospective
franchisor is not legally required to give you the document, you
can still request the information that is contained within it. The
data will really help you in making your decision.

DO YOUR HOMEWORK

Retain the services of an attorney who concentrates in franchising. He or she can help in almost every step of the process. But
you should do some legwork, too: It'll save you in legal fees, and
you'll get a better sense of the business.

   Contact other franchise owners. They can help you match
the disclosure statement information with their own experiences. Spend some time with them during the workday to see
the operation in action. Ask what help they got from the company, and how it followed up on its promises. Did it give them
the tools they needed to get the business up and running? Are
they getting enough advertising and support for their royalty payments? You should also ask about problems. Would they make
the same investment again, knowing what they do today?

   Be skeptical of the franchisor's sales presentations. A
franchisor who has a legitimate offer does not need to use high-
pressure tactics such as "better hurry, another buyer wants this
deal" or "do this today because who knows how much it will cost
tomorrow." Such language should raise a red flag. Remember,

ADDITIONAL SOURCES OF INFORMATION

The FTC provides helpful information. Visit the FTC Web site at www.ftc.gov and enter a search for "Buying a Franchise." The SBA also provides a wealth of information for prospective franchisees as part of its information for starting a business. Visit www.sba.gov/smallbusinessplanner/start and select the "Buy a Franchise" option. Franchisees of large franchises often form their own associations. Use the Internet to search for franchisee associations for any franchise you are considering. This information may also be available in the FDD. See how much support franchisees offer each other. You may also learn of significant problems franchisees are having with their franchisor.

the FTC rule requires that the franchisor *must* wait fourteen days after giving you the required documents before you may pay any money or sign any agreement. And while you're being skeptical, also disregard any franchisor's claims that the job will be easy. Success requires hard work.

YOU MUST REMEMBER THIS

- Franchising has advantages, but success is not automatic.
- Get as much information as you can—before you commit.
- Don't be pressured—the law gives you at least fourteen days' breathing room, and there are few if any great deals that you'll miss by not rushing into a commitment.

CHAPTER 7

Understanding and Negotiating the Franchise Agreement

Don't Be Intimidated When Confronted by Those Bulky Legal Documents

Sam has decided to buy a franchise after coming to the conclusion that for him franchising will provide a shortcut to success. He has now targeted one or two prospective concepts that he finds appealing. He's even investigated the concept and completed the due diligence process. But that bulky contract they've presented to Sam is really daunting. How can he understand this franchise agreement? Is it possible to negotiate the agreement to his satisfaction?

NEGOTIATING THE FRANCHISE AGREEMENT

Are franchise agreements negotiable? In some instances, they may be very negotiable; in others, your ability to negotiate may be very limited.

Negotiation is a function of many factors, and it's a mistake simply to assume that the franchisor's franchise agreement is fixed in concrete. As a general principle, assume that every franchise agreement is negotiable, giving due regard to the franchisor's economic and legal interests.

With limited exceptions, there are no legal prohibitions on franchise agreement negotiations. However, a franchisor may have sound business reasons why it does not want to negotiate a franchise agreement (in addition to the obvious ones). For example, a franchise system that has different forms of agreements in effect will be more difficult to administer. Moreover, some franchisees may become resentful if they find that another franchisee has negotiated a better deal.

Negotiability will normally be a function of bargaining power, which, in turn, will be a function of supply and demand, and the life cycle of the franchisor.

Negotiating with a Well-Established Franchisor

A highly respected, successful, fully developed franchisor can write its own ticket. It will have prospective franchisees lined up outside its door and will be able to pick and choose from among them. In this circumstance, there is little reason for the franchisor to sit down at the negotiating table.

Even here, however, the franchisor will sometimes be willing to discuss matters that are unique to the franchisee or the market. For example, a franchisor may be willing to waive a provision that prohibits ownership of a competing operation if the prospective franchisee already owns such an operation.

When exceptions to the standard franchise arrangement are necessary, the franchisor may be willing to modify the terms of the franchise agreement or provide the prospective franchisee with a side letter that states what the understanding is.

 BEWARE THE INTEGRATION CLAUSE

Be careful to make sure that any side letter specifically provides that it is a supplement to the franchise agreement, for franchise agreements typically have a so-called **integration clause**, which provides that there are no written or oral side agreements or understandings that modify the written franchise agreement. It is also a good idea to add a sentence like the following at the end of the franchise agreement, before the signatures: "This agreement is modified by an amendment [or letter agreement] dated as of the date hereof."

NEGOTIATING WITH OTHER FRANCHISORS

While the well-established franchisor may be reluctant to modify the terms of its agreement, many franchisors are start-ups or at least at a much earlier stage of their life cycles.

A new or untried franchisor may have sold few, or even no, franchises; start-up costs may have exceeded projections; and cash (especially yours) may be very attractive. In this case, you may have significant leverage, especially if you're well-heeled. It may be difficult for the franchisor to turn down reasonable requests when there is cash on the table.

What you may not realize is that you can bring many things to the bargaining table besides money:

• Do you have a reputation or track record of past success in developing new businesses? If you're known for your prowess as a businessperson, you might be an attractive catch to a new franchisor.

• Are you a celebrity, or at least well-known in your community? That too can make you a good find.

• Often numbers in themselves can be attractive to a franchisor, so that a commitment to enter into a multi-unit development contract can be a strong incentive for a "younger" franchisor to negotiate various points.

IT'S THEIR AGREEMENT—UNLESS YOU NEGOTIATE

From your perspective, franchise agreements are rarely friendly. The franchisor and its attorneys draft them, and they're intended to protect the franchisor's interests. They are typically very lengthy (more than thirty pages) and very detailed when spelling out the franchisor's rights and your obligations, but sketchy as to what are *your* rights and *the franchisor's* obligations.

- Willingness to pioneer a new or remote market may carry some weight.
- Fluency in a foreign language could be important to a company seeking to develop franchises in an ethnic area.

WHAT ARE THE CRITICAL TERMS OF THE FRANCHISE AGREEMENT?

Most often, you're probably not going to be entering into an agreement with a franchisor on either extreme of the "well-established/just getting started" spectrum. In such cases, some elements of a franchise agreement probably represent core system values that the franchisor just will not sacrifice in any circumstances, while other elements may be a little more adaptable.

It is also important to note that franchising is not an industry, but rather a way of doing business. Therefore, important provisions found in franchise agreements for one industry (such as **noncompete agreements**) may be unnecessary in another.

What are some of the typical subjects that a prospective franchisee should look for and understand?

1. **All fee payments.** More specifically, are the requirements for fee payments well-defined, and are the amounts of fees or the formula for calculating them fixed or subject to unilateral change by the franchisor? Can your franchisor impose additional fees after the franchise agreement has been signed?

2. **The term and renewal rights.** How long is the initial **term** of the franchise (i.e., for how many years will you be able to operate the franchise under this agreement)? Is that term typical for the industry? Do you have the right to renew on substantially the same terms, or may you renew only on the "then-current" terms at the time of renewal (i.e., those terms being offered to new franchisees at renewal time)? Can you limit the circumstances under which the franchisor can refuse to renew the franchise?

3. **Personal participation by the franchisee.** Must you devote all your time to the endeavor, or may you delegate this responsibility to a manager?

CAN YOU NEGOTIATE INITIAL FEES?

Some possible questions for negotiation include: Is there flexibility in the initial fee you'll be required to pay? Can you reduce it, or at least spread it out over a longer term? Can you get some of it back if the franchise is terminated before the contract expires? What exactly does it cover (training costs, start-up promotional costs, inventory, equipment, etc.)?

4. **Supply sources.** Must you purchase from designated sources, some of which may be affiliates of the franchisor or may be paying the franchisor a rebate? If so, are there any limits on how the products or services will be priced? Are these products or services being sold at competitive prices? Can you have an independent, competitive source of supply approved?

5. **Noncompetition provisions.** Can you engage in an outside business, or even competing business, during or after the term of the franchise? What will happen to your fixed assets if you cannot compete after the franchise relationship ends?

6. **Breaches.** If you breach the franchise agreement, will you be given the opportunity to correct your breach, and if so, has an adequate amount of time (a **cure period**) been provided?

7. **Transfers.** What restrictions has the franchisor placed on your ability to sell or transfer your franchise? Do your spouse or children have to qualify or otherwise complete a training program in order to become your successor? Can you buy out, or sell to, a partner? Must you first offer to sell your franchise to the franchisor before completing a deal with a third party? (This will frequently discourage third parties from entering into negotiations to buy your franchise.) Must the business be sold to someone who must agree to continue its operations as part of the franchise system? Will you be subject to a noncompetition provision?

8. **Territorial protection.** Will you have any protected territory? Are there any restrictions on where the franchisor may place new company-owned or franchised units? If not, will you

have a right of first refusal with respect to any new unit placed in your trade area? Can the franchisor distribute competing goods or services through other channels of distribution?

9. **Franchisor's service obligations.** What *firm* commitments has your franchisor made—in the franchise agreement—to provide you services before or after you commence business? Are these sufficient? One of the most common complaints of franchisees is that once the business is open, the franchisor has no real commitment to support the business.

10. **Trademark protection.** Has your franchisor guaranteed that it owns the primary trademark and will defend you and the mark if someone claims that this is not the case? If your franchisor wants to change the mark, will you have to pay the costs to change your signs and other tangible property on which the mark appears?

11. **Use of advertising fees.** What assurances do you have that funds paid to your franchisor and intended for advertising will be so used? Will these funds be paid into a segregated bank account? Who decides how these funds will be spent? Do franchisees have any input into this process? Can the franchisor use advertising funds for costs of producing advertising or administering the ad fund? Are there any restrictions on the amounts that can be paid to your franchisor to recoup these costs and expenses? Can you or the franchisee community have the ad fund audited?

12. **Waiver of legal rights.** If a dispute arises, where must lawsuits be brought? Do you waive your right to a jury trial, or to punitive or exemplary damages? Alternatively, does the franchise agreement provide for mandatory, binding arbitration? If so, where and under which circumstances? Is there a short period of time during which claims must be asserted before they are barred?

Every franchise involves trade-offs of risks and rewards. The bottom-line inquiry with any franchise offering is: Does this franchise represent a reasonable price/value relationship?

• **Price** is a combination of the fees, initial investment, contractual restraints, inherent franchise risks, and time commitment by you.

TERMINATION PROVISIONS

Provisions in the franchise agreement may cover circumstances that can trigger a termination, standards that apply before a franchisor can terminate (**good cause, just cause, reasonable cause**—these small distinctions can make a big difference), the amount of notice that must be given, and opportunities for the franchisee to cure the breach and stop the termination. Fifteen states have laws that prevent the franchisor from terminating unless it is for good cause; i.e., because the franchisee has failed to comply with the franchise agreement. All of these topics can be part of the negotiations of the franchise agreement in all states, even those that don't regulate termination. In states where some protection for franchisees exists, you can attempt to make these protections stronger in your contract; and in states without protection provided by statute, you can attempt to get some of these provisions into the contract.

• **Value** is a combination of economic opportunities and leveraging the value of system brands, training, operating support, advertising, and the like.

Obviously, you want the value to outweigh the price—and being shrewd and persistent (and fortunate) in negotiations can tip the balance in your favor.

YOU MUST REMEMBER THIS

• The franchise agreement is one of the most important documents you will ever sign. Make sure you understand it fully and have good legal advice before you sign.

• Any promises the seller makes to you must be included in the contract. If some are missing in the final contract, ask why. If you sign the contract without the promise there, the seller will not have to do it.

• Don't be afraid to negotiate. You'll never know what concessions you can get unless you try.

PART II

Setting Up Shop

Whether you're manufacturing lawn furniture, selling stuffed animals, or offering high-tech computer consulting, you'll have to face certain basic issues, all of which have legal dimensions:

- Do you need any permits or licenses?
- Do you have any unique ideas or concepts that you want to protect from your competition?
- Do you need any extra capital? How can you get it?
- Should you have an office in your home?
- If not, should you lease or buy space, and where will you be located?
- Is zoning an issue?
- What risks do you face in the day-to-day operation of your business, and how can insurance help?

CHAPTER 8

If Your Business Is Ten Feet from the Kitchen

Be Worry-Free by Taking Care of These Legal Wrinkles Affecting Home-Based Businesses

Where should Cory locate her business? Maybe in a space she's very comfortable with—her house. More and more entrepreneurs are starting off right at home. For David and Theresa, running their separate businesses from home is great. He's a graphic designer; she's an illustrator. Each has turned a bedroom of their roomy old Chicago condo into an office. They have no employees, rarely see clients at their home office, and don't even use messengers much (you can send art by e-mail). But not all home businesses are this discreet, and even David and Theresa have to mind a few p's and q's. This chapter tells you how to make the most of your home office and face the least problems—legally.

Sometimes it seems that home-based offices are as common as snowflakes in Alaska. Corporate downsizing has played a role. So has the trend toward two-income families (sometimes, one works out of the home, one in). Personal computers, e-mail, and handheld devices have made it easy to communicate all over the world just by pushing a button.

The Bureau of Labor Statistics reported in 2006 that more than 21 percent of people did some or all work from home. The number is expected to rise dramatically in the years to come.

Certified public accountants and management consultants often run such businesses, as do technicians, contractors, and folks in sales and services such as insurance and real estate.

Obviously, starting a business at home has lots of pluses: You are probably comfortable there, the price is right, and you can dress as casually as you like. But just because it's your PC in your den, you don't necessarily have the right to do whatever you want. There are a few legal hurdles to clear if you're starting a home-based business, as well as tax and insurance considerations that you should be aware of. As usual, it's better to deal with these earlier rather than later. Shuffling them off to the back of your mind or the bottom of the to-do pile might lead to trouble and hassles later on.

ZONING

You've probably spent as much time thinking about Pluto as you do about zoning. (More if you add in Pluto the dog.) But depending on what you're doing and where you're doing it, your home-based business might make you acquainted with the obscure little corner of local government called the zoning department.

Zoning is a way of keeping neighborhoods from getting cluttered with all sorts of things. Property values in your nice suburb would plummet if your next-door neighbor opened a combination mink farm/roller rink in the backyard. That's why your town or city probably has zones for heavy industry, commercial space, and residential space, as well as some for mixed use.

 BUT IT'S NOT REALLY A BUSINESS . . .

Don't be lulled into thinking that just because you work out of your home you're not in business. David, the graphic designer, bills more than $100,000 a year but thinks of himself as a freelancer who works today for this client, tomorrow for that. From the law's standpoint, though, he's not a temporary employee of those clients—he's a business. He has to be concerned with credit, collections, contracts, taxes, insurance, how to structure the business, and a lot more, just as if he worked out of commercial space.

The problem, or at least potential problem, is that your neighborhood might be zoned strictly for residential use only. You can find out by tracking down your zoning office (it might not be easy to find) and asking some questions based loosely on the business you're thinking of starting. The quieter and less obtrusive it is, the more likely you're okay with the law (or that no one will even discover that you're running the business in the first place).

Red flags are apt to be raised by:

- visibility (don't try to repair cars in your front yard);
- noise (no printing press in your condo's extra bedroom);
- smell (a tannery in the garage just won't make it);
- signs (maybe the law will mandate none, or specify a maximum size);
- traffic (perhaps caused by plenty of clients visiting the business and taking up parking spaces, or by a steady stream of deliveries and messengers);
- employees (the zoning laws might limit you to a certain number; again, controlling the number of people in the neighborhood is the primary concern).

If your preliminary inquiries indicate that there might be trouble (or if trouble comes after you've started, perhaps because the business has grown), you may have several good options.

 TAKING CARE OF WEE ONES

Lots of folks operate day care centers from their homes. These businesses are often regulated by the state and localities. Many states have special license requirements for day care centers. You may get a break, though, if you're caring for only a small group of children. In some states, the licensing and other requirements for day care centers in private homes that care for only a few children are less rigorous than larger group day care centers. Either way, find out what regulations apply and deal with them early in the process.

1. Adapt the business so you comply—make sure that your signs are the right size, that you don't use too many parking spaces, that you have no more than the maximum number of employees (but maybe your locality's law limits *full-time* employees, so you can have a larger number of employees if they are actually in your home office less than full time).

2. Try to get the law to adapt to your business. The zoning language may go back decades, long before your type of business ever existed. It may be enough to convince the bureaucrats in charge of enforcement that your business does not violate the spirit of the law.

3. If that fails, your zoning laws probably let you petition the powers that be for either a **special use exemption** or a **variance**. Either one essentially creates an exception for you. You'll have to make a formal request to the zoning board or a similar governmental body. There probably will be hearings to let your neighbors voice opposition if they're so disposed. It's probably a good idea to hire a lawyer experienced in zoning to represent you. Be prepared to show that the business causes minimal problems, and try to secure testimony from neighbors who aren't bothered.

4. If you're on the edge of a zone, you could try to have the small area covering your home rezoned slightly so you're in a permissible zone, rather than one in which you're violating the law, however technically. This probably requires a vote by city council (or whatever your local legislature is called), and going this route might end up taking a lot of time and effort.

PRIVATE REGULATIONS

Even if the zoning folks don't raise any problems, you might run afoul of other regulations. If you live in a condo or co-op, there is certainly a governing document (the **declaration** or **master deed**) that spells out the rules and regulations of living there. If you rent, there's probably a lease that tells you what you can and cannot do. Sometimes residential developments have **declara-**

tions of covenants and restrictions put in by the builder to assure buyers that the quality of living there won't deteriorate. Many of these covenants can have the same restrictions as the residential zoning ordinances discussed above.

All of these probably include some standard language designed to deter (or at least limit) the business use of the property. And in principle these aren't bad ideas. With most of your life savings tied up in your house, you're probably very happy that the guy down the block can't open up a rifle range.

A good first step when you're thinking about starting up a business in your apartment or house is to look at whatever document sets the rules. Maybe what you're thinking of isn't prohibited.

If it is verboten but so quiet that no one would notice, you might decide to go ahead and take your chances. Unfortunately, you might run a real risk—breaking the lease, angering the neighbors, or getting the condo board involved.

It might be possible to resolve any potential problems from the get-go with a little negotiation. Some of the language may be ridiculously restrictive. Some leases, for example, read like they haven't been changed since the Coolidge administration, when they were written by lawyers determined to stamp out *anything* a tenant might conceivably do that had the remotest chance of damaging the property. And maybe the landlord or the condo board won't really care about your little business once you've explained it to them, even though it might be technically outlawed by draconian language.

Put yourself in their shoes. What the landlord really cares about is that you don't damage the property, disturb the other tenants, or open the landlord up to liability claims (there goes your idea of making fireworks on the back porch). If your business is really inoffensive, reassure them: Let them know that the business will be run during normal hours, with little extra noise and traffic. It's far better to have it recognized by a rider in the lease or a waiver in the declaration. That way you're spared nasty surprises after you've sunk money into the home office. Moving would be a pain.

TAXES

The good news first: You can deduct many of the expenses of your home office if you satisfy IRS requirements. (And you can deduct other expenses such as business supplies and equipment just as if you had a business not based in the home.)

The bad news? Satisfying the IRS is not easy. After all, almost everyone has a home, and it's tempting to create a little home business (at least on your tax forms) that would enable you to save on taxes. You might want to consult with a lawyer or accountant before deciding to operate your business from your home to be sure that you will meet all the requirements and the deduction will be upheld, even if challenged by the IRS.

IRS Publication 587 provides information on figuring and claiming the deduction for business use of your home.

Besides the "business-not-a-hobby" test, here are some of the IRS hurdles you might have to jump through.

Exclusive and regular use test. This test requires that the portion of your home used for the business be used solely for the business, as well as regularly. Now, this doesn't have to be a whole room. It can be just a portion, as long as the space is clearly demarcated. So a portion of the spare bedroom that houses your desk, PC, and business phone would be okay as a deduction, as long as the kids didn't do their homework on the desk, and as long as you used it regularly for work. If you tried to deduct the whole room, however, you'd have to show that it was strictly an office—not a second TV room for the family. (If you're running a day care business out of the home, you don't have to meet the exclusive use test—on the ground that the kids are apt to be everywhere, even if you don't want them to be. But you can't deduct the whole house either. There's a complicated test that balances the square footage you use regularly for day care by the number of hours the business is in operation. See IRS Form 8829 for details.)

Principal place of business test. Historically, this has been a sticking point for many home-based business owners who also

YOU'LL NEED OTHER INSURANCE, TOO

Even though your world headquarters is just to the left of the toaster, you probably need a lot of the same kinds of insurance bigger businesses do (see chapter 10 for more on insuring your business). In fact, because your business may be totally dependent on *you*, it might be a good idea to check out a disability policy for yourself, as well as a business interruption policy in case a fire or natural disaster shuts you down.

worked on the road (contractors and sales reps, for example). Nowadays, if you can show that your home office is the main place you do your administrative work you should be fine—the fact that you're out selling 90 percent of the time won't matter if you do your paperwork at home.

If you pass the tests, then you can deduct all your **direct expenses** (i.e., money you spent to convert the space to business use), as well as a portion of the indirect expenses like rent, mortgage payments, real estate taxes, insurance, utilities, etc. To figure your deduction for indirect expenses, you normally figure what percentage of the square footage in your home is used for the business, then take that percentage of the indirect expenses as a deduction. So if you use 200 square fee of a 2,000-square-foot house for your home office, you could deduct 10 percent of all of your indirect expenses. IRS Form 8829 takes you through the calculations.

INSURANCE

If you own your home, you ought to have homeowner's insurance; if you rent, you need renter's insurance. These policies protect you from loss if there's a fire. Sometimes they cover certain natural disasters, too. They also protect you if you're sued for negligently causing an injury to someone on your property. If the meter reader falls down the stairs or your neighbor slips on a freshly waxed floor, the insurance company will defend you in court and cover your losses up to the amount on the policy.

But what if you're running a business out of the home? Are your business activities and property covered? Not necessarily. You'll have to read your policy to be sure. Often the policies exclude business use. You can probably upgrade your policy to cover the increased risks caused by the business. You'll pay a little more for a business rider, but the peace of mind will be worth it.

Certain home businesses—for example, those that store a pricey inventory or attract a lot of people coming and going through the premises—might have to get a special policy. Some companies offer a "homework" policy that combines homeowner's insurance with business protection. If that's not available, work through your insurance agent to get your business protection through the same company as your homeowner's or tenant's policy. That should enable you to tailor the business policy to cover only the increased risk caused by the business, so you won't have to pay double for the same protection.

YOU MUST REMEMBER THIS

• Don't assume your business won't run afoul of zoning laws or the rules of your condo or development—it's better to check it out first and avoid unpleasant surprises later.

• A lot of the problems of running a business out of the home can be solved by being flexible, using a little common sense, and negotiating with neighbors or the authorities.

• Even if you have to spend a little more, make sure your insurance covers the increased risks your business brings to the home.

CHAPTER 9

Location, Location, Location

Your Guide to Protecting Yourself in Leasing Property—and More

Let's say Cory's business is retail—Cory's Creations. Then working at home probably won't cut it. She will need to find some space where the public can find her and the wonderful stuff she makes. That will put her into the world of commercial real estate, where the law is a very big player.

An old question goes, what are the three most important factors in real estate? Location, location, location. The law can't help Cory find the best location for her business, but if she's savvy and a good negotiator, it can help her make and enforce the best possible deal for that space. Here are some quick tips.

LEASE OR BUY?

One of your first decisions will be whether to own your space or rent it. A lot of start-up businesses won't have the capital to buy existing space or build their own new space, so that won't even be an option. If you're one of the lucky ones who does have that much capital, consider the changes you're anticipating for your business, such as future growth and other financial needs. Is buying or building better than leasing for your particular business? If the building is mortgaged, the term of the mortgage will frequently be longer than the lease term of a similar space, so you're making more of a commitment.

You can try to have the best of both worlds by negotiating for a lease with an option to purchase or a "right of first refusal" if the owner decides to sell. (This would give you the right to purchase the property before it is offered to anyone else.)

LEGAL HELP PAYS HERE

Whatever you decide is right for your business, you can be sure it will involve numerous long and complex documents. Even with just a one-year
lease, you're probably looking at a big outlay. With so much at stake, this
is one of those times when legal help is strongly recommended, if not
absolutely necessary. Have your lawyer review all documents involved in
purchasing, building, leasing, or remodeling a building or other space.
Your lawyer might even do the negotiating, though a good broker may be
more familiar with the going lease rates and building costs.

THE SMALL PRINT: UNDERSTANDING COMMERCIAL LEASES

The saying "don't sweat the small stuff" does not apply to commercial leases. Leases are binding legal contracts. What you
agree to today will affect you and your business where it counts
most—the bottom line—for years. This chapter will help you
recognize the red flags in commercial leases. In the meantime,
here are some tips to keep in mind.

First, read the lease. All of it. Even the small print. *Especially*
the small print. Now is the time to be picky. Be clear on exactly
what is included in the lease. Is parking included? Who is responsible for keeping the sidewalk and parking lot cleared of ice
and snow? If the phones go down, who is responsible for getting
them fixed? Who pays for the cleaning crew? Elevator repairs?
Security? Minor repairs? Bathroom supplies? Garbage removal?
Double check the obvious: square footage, the name of the company, the length of the lease.

Most landlords will provide you with their standard lease
form. This is probably a "one size fits all" type of lease, which
may be inappropriate for your business. Remember, the landlord's attorneys probably drafted this lease for the benefit of the

landlord. Just because they call it "standard" doesn't mean it's fair or that you can't negotiate the terms.

How much leverage you'll have in the negotiations depends on the market you're considering. If there is a shortage of commercial real estate, you may have to do more compromising than if there is an abundance of space available. Nevertheless, these are the terms by which you and the landlord will have to live, so if something in the lease worries you, flag it.

Second, if it isn't in the lease, it doesn't exist. Forget what the landlord promises you as you're negotiating the lease. If it isn't in writing, it isn't yours. For example, the building might be patrolled by security guards hired by the landlord. But if your lease does not include language that the landlord will provide security for the customers and tenants, the landlord has the right to stop providing security, and there's nothing you can do about it. On the other hand, if your lease states that the landlord will provide a certain number of security guards to patrol the building during business hours, the landlord must do so.

The Basics

A basic lease will require you, the tenant, to pay the landlord a sum of money for the privilege of operating your business in the landlord's building. This will generally be referred to as a base rent. **Base rent** is calculated by taking the square footage of the space and multiplying it by a set dollar amount (e.g., 5,000 square feet × $2.25 per square foot = annual base rent). The square footage used in the lease is not the same as the **usable** square footage, which is always less than what you pay rent on. The rent-per-square-foot and the way the square footage is figured may or may not be negotiable, depending on supply and demand.

Additional Rent

Here comes the tricky part: The base rent is only part of what you have to pay the landlord. Be aware that there will be another clause to cover **additional rent** or **excess use**. This section *is* very negotiable, and you should pay extra attention to every word. This catchall can be a blank check for the landlord's benefit if you're not careful.

Have the landlord define, in great detail, "additional rent." Find out whether the base rent includes taxes, insurance on the building, and utilities, or whether this is part of the additional rent. This is where the landlord will charge you for items such as after-hours heating, ventilation, and air-conditioning (HVAC) or improvements made to the building that may not even benefit you. These items can add up quickly to several hundred dollars per month. Find out if the cost is shared among all the tenants in the building. In some cases, the landlord may try to collect the full cost from *each* tenant. Try to negotiate the right to challenge the landlord's calculation of additional rent and operating expenses (see below) and try to add a provision requiring the landlord to submit details of the charges.

Operating Expenses

Another clause that can cost you a bundle is **operating expenses.** A standard landlord lease will require you to pay for all costs of owning, managing, maintaining, and operating the complex. This will usually include the key phrase "without limitation." Experienced commercial landlords do not expect you to agree to this clause, although they will be quite happy if you do.

At the very least, you will want to exclude from operating costs:
- capital costs for the building;
- the costs of any debt financing;
- construction costs for improvement to the space of other tenants;
- costs covered by the landlord's insurance; and
- costs covered by warranties under the landlord's construction or equipment contracts.

Sophisticated tenants won't stop there, however. You will also want to exclude:

- costs of disputes between the landlord and other tenants;
- costs connected to concessions operated by the landlord; and
- costs of obtaining and installing art or decor for the complex.

Find out how the common area charges are calculated. If the cost is shared, find out whether it is calculated on a pro rata basis. In most shopping complexes, large retailers (often called "anchors") are given cost reductions to encourage them to lease space in the center. One concession is that the large retailer will pay a flat rate, rather than a pro rata share, toward common area costs or operating expenses. The landlord deducts this amount from the overall operating expenses and *then* divides up the remaining operating costs on a pro rata basis among the smaller tenants.

If your business is the smallest in the mall, you don't want to be required to pay as much or more toward operating expenses as the behemoth department store. Bargain for language that protects you from paying more because of disproportionately low contributions from the larger retailers. As with additional rent, your share of operating expenses should be based on the percentage your space is of the total square footage of the building. If your square footage is 5 percent of the building, then you should pay no more than 5 percent.

WHAT CLAUSES SHOULD BE INCLUDED IN A COMMERCIAL LEASE?

The lease should state the full name and legal address of the building, owners, and management company. It should give the exact size of both the building and the space to be rented, in square footage. Find out how the space is measured to prevent surprises later on. Or ask the landlord to make an **exhibit**—a diagram of the space showing dimensions—part of the lease. The lease might also clarify whom the brokers represent. Many tenants are surprised to learn the broker actually represents the landlord.

Parking

How many parking spaces are provided per thousand square feet? Are there designated parking spots that go with your property? Who pays the costs for maintaining the parking lot? Whatever the cost to you for parking—even if it's free—put it in the lease and make sure the price of parking is fixed for the duration of your lease. Just because parking is free now doesn't mean it's going to be free in five years.

Competition

In some types of businesses it is important to have a provision in the lease prohibiting the landlord from leasing space to a competitor. If the landlord will not agree to this, include a provision stating that space leased to any competitor must be located on a different floor or in a different wing of the building.

Option to Renew

Always include a **renewal option**. This will give you the right to renew your lease for one or more additional terms and may be based on the fair market value of the property at the time of the renewal. The key here is to come to an agreement with the landlord as to the definition of fair market value or the formula for how the future rent will be determined. You will be required to notify the landlord in writing within a specified time period if you wish to renew your lease. Without this option, you could be forced to move or pay higher rent to remain in your current location.

Option to Expand

An **option to expand** will give you the option of leasing additional space and will determine how the rent for that space will be calculated. This way you can lease only the amount of space you need right now, with the protection of being able to increase the amount of space when and if it is needed. The advantage is that you are not obligated to rent the additional space unless you want it. The disadvantage is that there is no guarantee the additional space will be available when you want it.

Terminating the Lease

Landlords loathe termination clauses. Smart tenants insist on them. A **termination clause** will allow you to cancel your lease if your business suffers a significant decline in trade or business. Do not take this right lightly.

This provision could cause some difficulties. It will allow the landlord to audit your books and records to determine if indeed you have suffered a significant decline. You will probably be required to pay the landlord's out-of-pocket costs, such as the tenant improvement allowance and legal fees. In addition, you will no doubt be prohibited from leasing space for a similar purpose in your geographic area for the remainder of the lease. If you do lease new space during that time, this clause will most likely give your former landlord the right to collect the rent you would have owed had you stayed.

Nonetheless, if it gets you out of a lease that is no longer profitable for you, the hassle will be well worth it.

Security Deposit

If you are required to make a security deposit, try to have the initial security deposit reduced during the term of the lease. If this is not available, talk to your broker about having a letter of credit (which is essentially a guarantee of payment by a bank) issued to cover the security deposit.

Stipulate that the landlord must return this to you within thirty days after the lease terminates, unless you are in default. State that the landlord must return the full security deposit, minus the cost to repair any damage other than normal wear and tear. The lease should address whether your security deposit will be collecting interest and whether you or the landlord keeps the interest. Laws regarding interest on security deposits vary from state to state.

Use

The lease will most likely require you to state how you will use the space. Be as general as possible. Being too specific will prevent you from possible expansion in the future or from subleasing extra space. Avoid the words *solely*, *only*, and *for no other purpose*. *Primarily* and *principally* will give tenants greater leeway but should be avoided if possible.

Occupancy and Commencement

Note the difference between *occupancy* and *commencement*. **Occupancy** is when you can get into the space to install computers and telephone systems or move in furniture: It does not necessarily mean you are open for business. **Commencement** is when the rent actually starts. You want the commencement date to be the date you are open for business. Include a clause stating that if the space is not available for commencement within thirty days of the agreed-upon date, you may, at your sole discretion, cancel the lease by notifying the landlord in writing.

Tenant Improvements

Tenant improvements are improvements that the tenant wants made to the space to accommodate the business. For example, if you've got a retail store in a mall, you might need a tile floor laid for the main area and walls put up for dressing rooms. But what happens when the landlord lays tile that you consider inferior or the wrong color? The landlord might expect you to pay for the materials or expenses, while you assume the landlord will pay for this.

Your goal is to make sure the work is done on time and to your specifications. If the landlord is to make tenant improvements to your space, draft a letter to him or her specifying the work to be done. This should be very specific. Tenant improvements can be a major source of cost overruns. Include the work to be done and the materials to be used, from re-carpeting and repainting to repairing ceiling tiles, all the way down to the outlets. The lease should state that your acceptance of the space is subject to the mutually agreed-upon improvements and the clean-up afterward, which will be paid for solely by the landlord. The lease should specify that the landlord will pay for the improvements, how such payments are to be made, and who has authority to make changes to the plans.

If the landlord says the space will be improved to the building standard, get a definition of *building standard*. Keep an eye out for any language in this clause that mentions an **administration fee** for the landlord or the management company—this would be a percentage of the tenant improvement costs. Negotiate these fees down or eliminate them altogether.

Building Services

Specify what the landlord will provide in the way of building services and landscaping. This should include such items as air-conditioning, heat, power, and telephone wiring. In some parts of the country, it should include snow and ice removal. The sophisticated tenant will always find out the cost per hour for after-hours heating, ventilation, and air-conditioning (HVAC).

Americans with Disabilities Act

The lease should state whether the landlord is in compliance with the Americans with Disabilities Act (ADA). This is very important. If the building is not in compliance, the landlord may try to pass the costs on to you. Include a provision stating that if the building is not in compliance with the ADA, any costs to bring it into compliance will be borne solely by the landlord.

Signage

Does the lease allow you to put a sign above your door? Find out where you can put your business signs and what the size requirements are. Find out whether you or the landlord bears this cost. Make sure there is no extra charge to have your business included on the mall or lobby directory. (Some landlords limit the number of names a tenant may list in the directory.)

Relocation

Most leases give the landlord the right to move you to another location, or similar space, during your lease term. The lease will probably require the landlord to pay for some of the moving costs. Make sure these costs include, but are not limited to, the installation of computers and phones and the replacement of all your printed materials (business cards, brochures, stationery, and invoices). You will also want to:

• Specify that the total cost of the new space will not be greater than what you would have paid in your former space during the rest of your lease.

• Require that the landlord pay any additional cost involved if your business uses sophisticated equipment that will be expensive to move and install.

• Determine how much time you will need to notify the landlord as to whether you'll accept the move, and find out whether you have the right to refuse to relocate. If you do not accept the move, reserve the right to cancel the lease.

• Bargain for the right to refuse any relocation in the last year of the lease.

SUBLEASING

You as Sublessor

If you rent more space than you need, a clause in your lease giving you the right to sublease the excess space will give you some options for using that space. A **sublease** is a new lease between you (the tenant) and a third party (**sublessee**). The original lease between you and the landlord is not affected by the sublease.

You must still pay the full rent to your landlord under the lease, while collecting rent from the sublessee. The term of any sublease should be short enough (e.g., six months or one year) so that you can regain possession of the leased space in a reasonable amount of time.

TALKING TO A LAWYER: HOW TO SOLVE LANDLORD PROBLEMS

Q. *It's one hassle after another with our landlord, with both of us always complaining about the other. What can I do to resolve things without going to court?*

A. The first thing you want to do is figure out if you are really dealing with the landlord or with a management company hired by the landlord. If you don't feel comfortable asking the person you normally deal with, you can call the county recorder's office and ask who the taxpayer is for the property. The taxpayer is the owner of the building and is your true landlord.

If you are dealing with the management company, the person you regularly deal with is probably a leasing agent. Ask to speak with the leasing agent's superior or go directly to the owner and ask that another agent be assigned to your file.

You can also turn to mediation. Check your lease to see if there are any mediation clauses. Every state—and most counties—has professional organizations that offer mediation services. You can find these organizations by looking through advertisements in real estate journals or by calling your state bar association. Every state bar association has a real estate section that can steer you toward potential mediators.

—Answer by Cindy Moy, attorney and author,
Golden Valley, Minnesota

Another way to achieve the same result is to include in the sublease a provision that allows you to terminate the sublease at any time by giving reasonable advance notice, such as ninety days. One disadvantage of these arrangements is that the sublessees may demand similar rights.

One thing to keep in mind when subleasing: You do not want your business to suffer financially if your sublessee cancels the lease at an inconvenient time. In other words, don't bet your business's success on profits from subleasing.

You as Sublessee

If you are the sublessee, request to see the main lease so that you understand the terms the tenant is under. It may be that that lease does not allow him or her to sublease to particular types of businesses. The fact that you're an innocent party will be small consolation if you have to relocate your business and lose time, customers, and money.

LEASE CLAUSES THAT WILL COST YOU MONEY

The additional rent clause discussed earlier can leak major money from your pocket to that of the landlord, but that's not the only clause that can end up costing you big bucks. Beware the following clauses—often buried in standard landlord leases—that could drain your pocketbook.

Landlord's Management Costs

Landlords generally reserve the right to hire a management company to manage their properties. Look out, though, for language that allows the landlord to pass these costs on to the tenants, probably as operating costs. Such language will probably refer to these expenses as managerial or administrative costs relating to the building or parking facilities.

TALKING TO A LAWYER: WHAT A LANDLORD CAN—AND CANNOT—DO

Q. My landlord keeps threatening to come over with some guys and toss me out on the street if I don't pay the rent. (I admit I'm late a lot of the time.) Can he do this?

A. Sure, he can toss you as far as he wants—but it would be illegal. Your landlord has plenty of legal ways to toss you out, though, as well as to get the rent you owe. There are two legal issues here. The first is regaining possession of the premises. The landlord will go to court and have you served notice for breach of your lease for nonpayment of the rent. You have to be properly served, and that may take a little time. ("Serving" is the process of official notification of court documents.) Then, the court will hold a hearing, usually between seven and fourteen days after notice is served. The court will issue a decision, and you will have to pay the rent you owe, as well as the court filing fees and the costs of serving you with notice. If you do not pay the money at that point, the landlord will receive a *writ of restitution* from the court, an order giving rights to the landlord to have you physically removed from the property. The landlord will take that *writ* to the sheriff's office in the county in which the property is located and pay the sheriff to serve you with the *writ*. If you are not there to receive the service, the sheriff will post it on the premises. At that point you have twenty-four hours to abandon the property. If you do not abandon the property within that time frame, the landlord can enter the property and have all your goods removed.

The second issue is the back rent and other costs associated with regaining possession of the property. The landlord will have to sue you in order to get a judgment against you. The judgment will include the rent you owe, future rent you would have owed under the lease (if the landlord is unable to rent the property to someone else), and any other costs associated with leasing the premises to another business. You may even have to pay for any improvements or modifications the landlord has to make to the property to rent it to the new tenant. If you do not pay this judgment, the sheriff will hold an auction to sell the goods from your premises, if any. The judgment will also go on your credit report, making it difficult for you to rent from any other landlord and affecting any other instances in which you may seek credit, such as for a mortgage, car loan, or business financing.

Perhaps it would be safer and less costly to pay your rent on time.

—Answer by Cindy Moy, attorney and author,
Golden Valley, Minnesota

Reimbursing the Landlord for Costs Associated with Tenant's Sublease

The clause will require you to get the landlord's approval to sublease your premises. Be alert for any language that also requires you to reimburse the landlord for any fees incurred while reviewing the sublease, including attorneys' fees and accounting costs.

 ## TALKING TO A LAWYER: MODIFYING A LEASE

Q. We've been open six months and already I'm seeing that some changes to the property could really help business. Can I ask the landlord to modify the lease so we can modify the premises?

A. Yes. Typically, landlords will help. However, you can expect the landlord to add the costs of any improvements to the lease costs. Tenant-paid improvements will need to be approved, and the landlord may ask that the premises be returned to its original condition at the end of the term. Changes or modifications that can't be removed belong to the landlord.

—Answer by G. Lane Ware, attorney,
Ruder, Ware & Michler, Wausau, Wisconsin

ADDITIONAL INFORMATION

The Small Business Administration provides information regarding commercial leases as part of its small business start-up planner. Visit www.sba.gov/smallbusinessplanner/start, then select "Pick a Location" to find links regarding commercial leases and a leasing checklist.

Limiting the Tenant's Right to Market Space Available for Sublease

When you open up your premises for sublease, you may be competing with your landlord, who also has space to lease. To reduce such competition, the landlord may include a clause that limits your ability to advertise your available space. The clause may also prohibit offering your space at rent lower than that offered by the landlord for comparable space in the same building. Thus, potential sublessees have less incentive to lease from you when they have to pay the same rent as they would if they were to get their own space from the landlord.

YOU MUST REMEMBER THIS

• A commercial lease can be quite intimidating, but don't forget that you have every right to understand it and to try to negotiate the best deal you can.

• Take your time while you make your way through the clauses, and don't be discouraged by complicated language. If something seems ambiguous, make the landlord clarify it so that you aren't caught off guard by added expenses later on.

• The bottom line: Know what you're signing.

CHAPTER 10

Buying Peace of Mind

*That's What Insurance Is for—but Don't Forget
the Legal Dimensions*

> *Cory has gotten started: She has her location picked out and has
> worked with her business attorney to make sure everything is in
> order. She is getting her first orders and working with her
> venders. As if she hasn't got enough worries as a small-business
> owner—keeping customers happy, getting good employees,
> making sure the check is in the mail—sometimes in the middle
> of the night she is hit by more exotic worries. What if her busi-
> ness is destroyed by a fire? An earthquake? A plague of locusts?
> What if she is sued by someone who walked through her plate
> glass door?*

The good news is that you can get insurance against all these
perils (maybe even the locusts). And insurance companies
also provide a myriad of other benefits for you, including legal
counsel to advise and even to represent you at trial if a case goes
that far. Insurance coverage may not cost much either. But it
helps to do some serious thinking—as opposed to late-night free
associating—about what you really need to protect yourself
against. You can also reduce costs by taking steps to reduce risk,
shopping carefully for policies, and following some cost-saving
tips in how you structure policies.

This is a good example of preventive law—taking small steps
now to ensure that you won't face big problems down the road.

FINDING BUSINESS INSURANCE

You'd probably do best to buy all of your business insurance from
one source, so you don't duplicate coverage. Ask other business
owners which insurance agents or brokers they'd recommend. It's

ANOTHER CHEAP FORM OF "INSURANCE"

From your perspective as the owner of the business, you should consider whether you need personal protection from business liabilities. While not strictly a form of insurance, a limited liability entity (e.g., corporation, limited liability company) will shield you from most personal liabilities of a sole proprietorship or general partnership business. You might lose the business in a disaster, either of Mother Nature's making or your own management failures, but saving your home and personal assets from that disaster might leave you in a better frame of mind. Chapters 11 through 15 of this book examine various forms of business organizations and how they affect your personal liability.

best to work with an insurance agent who represents a number of insurance companies. Because of this, he or she is not tied to a particular company and is in a position to select advantageous coverage for you from a wide range of vendors. If your business has special insurance needs, your business association or an owner of a similar kind of business might be able to suggest agents with experience in insuring businesses such as yours. Usually it's a good idea to discuss your needs with several agents. Not only will you be able to compare quotes, but from each you will get a perspective on which types of insurance your business needs.

MORE ON AGENTS

You can get the name of independent insurance agents in your area from Independent Insurance Agents and Brokers of America, 127 S. Peyton Street, Alexandria, VA 22314; phone: 800-221-7917; Web site: www.iiaba.net.

INSURING YOUR BUSINESS LIKE YOU INSURE YOUR HOME

One big part of business insurance is not new at all. You have homeowner's insurance to protect your home from fire and other hazards, and to protect you from lawsuits if someone is injured on your property. You can get a **business owner's policy (BOP)** to cover similar risks to your business, as well as some others that are unique to the business situation. The insurance industry has come up with standard packages for certain kinds of businesses (stores, contractors, etc.) and they're a good place to start. Make sure, however, that your agent truly understands your business—it may be that the standard policy she so quickly whipped out really doesn't fit what you're doing.

Not all BOPs cover the same risks. You'll want to look at coverage carefully to make sure you're getting what you need. Here are a few good tips:

• **Coverage for property loss** should include the basic perils that can destroy your property (fire, theft, etc.), as well as any special perils that you're aware of. (Are you in an earthquake-prone area, a flood plain, a high-locust zone?) In assessing "such risks as" earthquakes and floods, you'll have to weigh the likelihood of their happening (does the river rise every five years? every fifty?) against the extra cost of the insurance. Also, given your situation, it may be important that the policy cover some other perils, such as damage from a burst pipe or smoke damage from a malfunctioning furnace.

As in homeowner's insurance, there are general levels of coverage built into policies, with the more expensive covering the broadest range of hazards to your property. **Specific form** policies are the most comprehensive and don't cost that much more.

At the same time, you'll want to double check exactly what property is covered. If you own your property, you'll want the coverage to cover everything you own, including the business property on the premises. You can try to negotiate to have the policy broadly written to cover some kinds of equipment and other

WHAT IF YOU'RE LEASING SPACE?

If you're renting space, you'll need insurance for your business's possessions—computers, furniture, and so forth—as well as improvements you've made to the space (such as paneling or carpets). Whether you need more than that may depend on the terms of your lease. Often landlords require you to take out insurance against certain hazards (such as liability for an accident on the premises) as a way of lessening their own risk. Be aware of such clauses; they may be negotiable.

property that you don't have now but might have in the future. Also, make sure the policy covers leased equipment, if the risk of loss would fall on you. (Your lease might require you to insure it.)

Get a policy that gives you **replacement value coverage**. That way, you'll get what you need to buy new property to replace the old, not just enough to let you buy property as old as what you lost.

• **Protection from liability** protects you if someone does a swan dive in aisle three or steps in a hole in your parking lot. As in your homeowner's policy, the insurance company will defend you in court and pay damages up to the amount of insurance purchased.

Unfortunately, a BOP does not cover you against all risks. It *may* cover you against business interruption (check carefully), but it will not cover your business for workers' compensation, health insurance, and many other kinds of insurance that might well be desirable. Read on to decide whether they're for you.

BUSINESS INTERRUPTION INSURANCE

You carry **business interruption insurance** (often referred to as **business continuation insurance**) to offset losses if the business is forced to shut down for a substantial period because of a fire, flood, or other catastrophe. Yes, your **property insurance** will enable you to replace whatever's been burned or blown away, but you still may be out of business until the replacement property is ready. You'll want this insurance to cover lost profit, as well as taxes and salaries.

How long will this period be, and how much insurance should you take? Everyone's crystal ball is probably cloudy on these points, but you can consider the kind of business you're in and the resources of your community. If you could restock in a few weeks and know that you'd have no problem renting space in the neighborhood, then maybe you need to buy only enough coverage to get you through a brief period.

EXTENDED PERIOD OF INDEMNITY

Even if you're covered until the repairs are made, you may still suffer through a slower period as you build your business back up. You might consider purchasing additional insurance to carry you through the lean times until your customer base is fully regained.

PRODUCT LIABILITY INSURANCE

Product liability insurance protects you against damage claims filed by third parties injured by a product of your business. It's

---

 MAKE SURE YOUR DOCUMENTS ARE SAVED

Ever try to recover an insurance claim missing all evidence of what the property is worth? Ever try restarting a business when all your databases are kaput? Don't let it happen to you. Store backups of both your paper records and computer files on digital files or hard drives stored off-site.

---

sometimes included with the BOP: Check to make sure, and get it separately if it's not. This type of insurance is particularly important if you sell imported goods or food or any product that you make.

MALPRACTICE INSURANCE

Malpractice and **errors and omissions insurance** are ultra important for certain kinds of professional businesses. Doctors, lawyers, architects, accountants, computer technicians, and other professionals, by the very nature of their work, have the capacity to cause major losses—and sometimes big lawsuits—if things don't pan out. This type of insurance protects you against claims based on your negligence, errors, omissions, or plain old wrongful acts. Warning: It might be expensive, though getting a high deductible is one way of limiting costs.

VEHICLE INSURANCE

If you use your personal car for your business and don't usually have customers in the car or carry around a dangerous product (you're not in the dynamite business, for example), then for a very modest additional cost you should be able to add coverage for your business to your existing personal policy. If you have vehicles just for the business, however, you'll need separate business coverage.

WORKERS' COMPENSATION INSURANCE

Workers' compensation insurance is a great benefit to businesspeople: It protects you against damages that arise under your state's **workers' compensation system.** All states have such a system. It requires that workers be paid for injuries they suffer on the job, no matter what the cause. Even if they're clearly at

INSURANCE BY ANOTHER NAME

There are a few types of specialized business insurance products that go by the name of bonds. **Employee fidelity bonds** are a form of insurance to protect against embezzlement. Some businesses are required to have fidelity bonds for employees, such as bookkeepers, who handle money. Most businesses, however, can choose whether to bond all or some of their employees to protect clients from employees' theft or vandalism. **Performance bonds** exist in the world of contracting. A contractor who has taken out a performance bond on a job has insured the customer that the job will be completed on time as stated in the contract. If the contractor fails to perform according to the contract, the bonding company must complete the contract or pay another contractor to finish the work. **Payment bonds** guarantee payment to a general contractor or a subcontractor if the owner or general contractor fails to pay, and may be required by contract on certain types of work or projects. A payment bond is a security device for an owner or general contractor to insulate against suits for payment on the contract, especially if there is the possibility of the bonded party becoming insolvent or filing for bankruptcy.

fault, you'll have to pay, though under state law, the benefits are set according to a preexisting schedule and are relatively low. And there are very rarely any **pain and suffering** or **punitive damages** under workers' compensation. Nonetheless, you're well advised to carry insurance against this risk.

Many states require you to have it, though some exclude businesses with just a few employees. It's available from the state or privately. Rates reflect the kind of business you're in, your safety record, etc. There may be some cost-saving possibilities with workers' compensation insurance, besides maintaining a good safety record. For example, you're not required to have workers' compensation for independent contractors (since they're not employees). Beware, however, that establishing that

A TAX BY ANOTHER NAME

You've probably heard of **unemployment insurance**. This is one form of insurance that, for better or worse, you don't have to worry about. It's not insurance at all but really a tax based on the payroll of a business used to pay benefits to all long-term unemployed workers in a state. You can't save money by shopping for it, and you can't simply not have it. It's a tax, and you have to pay it.

a person is an independent contractor can be difficult. See chapter 16 for a discussion of how workers are classified as independent contractors.

EMPLOYMENT PRACTICE LIABILITY INSURANCE

Here's a new form of insurance that's selling very well to big businesses. It covers an employer sued over things like sexual harassment, discrimination, and wrongful discharge. News stories about big verdicts in such cases are probably driving up demand. It may be too pricey for small businesses, and the risk may not be great enough.

INSURANCE FOR CORPORATE EXECUTIVES

If your business is incorporated, at least look into **director and officers liability insurance**. This will pay your expenses and damage awards as a result of suits filed against you by shareholders of the corporation.

PENDING HEALTHCARE LEGISLATION

As the updated version of this Guide goes to press, Congress is debating significant changes to how healthcare may be provided in the U.S. in the future. At this time, it is uncertain what may be required of or available to businesses in terms of healthcare coverage.

IF YOU'RE NOT THERE . . .

You can insure your health and that of your employees through your business (see below), but if your business is small, its success probably depends totally on you, and it provides most of the income for your family. Health insurance alone is probably not enough. Consider

- **disability** (or **loss of income**) insurance, which pays a portion of your gross income if you have a long-term disability and cannot work; and
- **life insurance** that will provide a death benefit to your family. If you have co-owners, you can take out a policy that names them as beneficiaries and provides funds to compensate the business for your loss and funds to purchase your interest in the company. This **key person** insurance thus benefits your family *and* keeps the business going.

HEALTH INSURANCE

This is a subject perennially in the news. It's a big concern to workers and to employers. (And thus a double concern to you, because you may be an employer and an employee at the same time.) The field is changing fast, what with HMOs, PPOs, and a host of other alternatives to old-fashioned choose-your-own-doctor, pay-as-you-go plans. Here are a few general tips:

- Don't pick a plan out of the blue. Meet with employees to see what's important to them, explaining that you may not be able to afford what they want and they might have to share some of the costs.
- Meet with several agents to get ideas about alternatives. Comparison shop. This kind of insurance doesn't have to be prohibitively expensive. Look into whether your business association offers group rates.
- For any policy you're considering, look into the:

    o coverage (make sure you understand what is and is not covered; be wary of policies that pay only for hospital care or leave out many medical treatments);

    o stability and financial strength of the carrier;

    o ability to renew the policy (can the company cancel it? is renewability guaranteed?);

    o ease of administering the policy (is there an 800-number you can call to get your questions answered?); and

    o reputation of the carrier for processing and paying claims quickly.

 MORE ON HEALTH INSURANCE

- Insure.com (www.insure.com; 800-324-6370) has a free database of health insurance providers and articles on different types of insurance and the needs of small businesses.

- Many small business groups (like the National Association for the Self-Employed—www.nase.org; 800-232-6273) offer health insurance packages.

- The Small Business Administration may be able to help. Call its answer desk at 800-U-ASK-SBA (800-827-5722) or access its Web site at www.sba.gov.

MONEY-SAVING TIPS

- Consider taking high deductibles. Yes, you'll be forced to pay more of the share of each claim, but your premiums will go way down. Unless you're constantly filing small claims, you should save money overall.
- Minimize the claims you may have to make by taking steps to make your business safer for all concerned. Limit the hazards that might lead to lawsuits by performing a risk assessment: Install sprinklers, fire extinguishers, a fire alarm system (which will lessen the risk of fire and lower premiums), high-quality locks, and antitheft devices. The Department of Homeland Security provides a wide range of information to help prepare for and deal with disasters and emergencies at www.ready.gov. Preventive steps like this make your business a better risk, so you're a candidate to save on insurance.

YOU MUST REMEMBER THIS

- It's a bad idea to have no insurance—you have too much to lose.
- Comparison shop, find a good agent, and insure against *likely* hazards.
- Making sure your business is safe makes sense—and will save you money.
- If you borrow money to operate your business, the lender will require insurance on the collateral (e.g., machinery or inventory) and maybe even key person insurance.

PART III

Types of Business Organizations:

Which Legal Form Should You Choose?

When you started your business, you probably gave a lot of thought to sales and suppliers, customers, and competition. You probably didn't think much about the legal structure of your business—about how the choice you made could save you lots of money and hassle down the line.

You could be a sole proprietorship or a corporation. Maybe you want to take in partners. Maybe you want to explore the newer and very popular form of business organization, the limited liability company. We explore the pros and cons of all these options in this part.

If you're like most business owners, you want:

- protection against being personally liable for judgments against the company, its debts, etc.;
- the ability to transfer ownership as you wish, especially if you want to keep the business in the family or want it to continue after you or one of the other principals leaves;
- a simple, workable management structure;
- low organizational and administrative costs;

- the ability to do business in more than one state, without complications (maybe not relevant now, but you can dream); and
- the ability to take advantage of tax laws and keep taxes as low as possible.

Guess what—in all these areas your choice of how your business is organized legally makes a big difference.

You can get most or all of these features in most types of business organizations, but often you have to do some juggling and weigh one factor against another. This part gives you the skinny on each alternative.

By the way, you're not stuck forever with the choice you make when you're just starting out. This part also gives you the legal scoop about going from one form of organization to another.

CHAPTER 11

Sole Proprietorships

It's Easy, It's Popular—but Know What You're Getting Into

Lisa doesn't think she's a businessperson, and she certainly doesn't think she has a "company." She gives saxophone lessons at home and makes a few bucks. It doesn't sound like much, but legally she does have a business and must comply with tax, licensing, and other regulations. If she doesn't take legal steps to choose a structure for her business, she's defaulted to the most common kind of business, the sole proprietorship. That's not necessarily a bad thing—if it were, millions of us would be unhappy campers—but different legal forms may lead to different consequences for her business. Maybe something besides a sole proprietorship would work better for Lisa.

If you're the sole owner of your company and you don't create a corporation or some other form of business, then, know it or not, like it or not, you're a sole proprietorship. If there is more than one owner or the business is incorporated as a corporation (a process that is described in later chapters), it cannot be a sole proprietorship.

A sole proprietorship can have employees, however. And, except for a few restrictions that vary from state to state, it can operate any type of business.

Sole proprietorships are the most prevalent form of business in this country. Recent statistics indicate that there are over 21 million sole proprietorships, compared with 5.6 million corporations and 2.7 million partnerships.

THE PROS AND CONS OF A SOLE PROPRIETORSHIP

The essential legal distinction between a sole proprietorship and a corporation, limited liability company, and most other forms of business organizations is that the sole proprietorship does not have a separate legal identity from the individual starting/running the business. All of the advantages and disadvantages stem from this fact.

Not having a separate legal identity means that the sole proprietorship probably does not have

- limited liability,
- perpetual existence,
- free transferability of shares of ownership,
- the ability to own property in its own name, and
- the ability to bring suit and be sued in the business name.

Chapter 13 has more on each of these topics, from the standpoint of corporations.

Advantages of a Sole Proprietorship

A sole proprietorship is an inexpensive and informal way of conducting a small business. In fact, it's the simplest form of busi-

 ### NO SEPARATE TAX STATUS

Since the assets of the sole proprietorship are deemed to be owned by the proprietor, a sole proprietorship has no separate tax status. You must report the taxable income, credits, and deductions of the business on your individual income tax return. This may or may not be a good thing. One clear advantage is that it avoids the double taxation (of corporate income and dividends paid to shareholders) that is a feature of some (but by no means all) corporations. See chapter 15 for more on the ins and outs of business taxation.

ORGANIZING A SOLE PROPRIETORSHIP

It could hardly be easier. Depending on the laws of your state and locality, you may have to apply for one or more business permits and licenses, but you'd have to do that no matter what business form you chose. If your business is to operate in a name other than your own, you may have to comply with a state or local assumed named statute and file a "Doing Business as Certificate" or "Assumed Name Certificate." Again, you'd have to do that in any event. Other than that, no special written documents will be necessary for your sole proprietorship unless you are buying or leasing property or will operate a franchise. About the only thing you may do differently is file a Schedule C as part of your personal tax return. Just make sure you check with your local and state authorities to determine exactly what is required for your business.

---

ness organization. Few statutes deal with its organization or operation, and those that do (like assumed name statutes) apply to all businesses. In contrast, many laws spell out the legal requirements of a corporation, limited liability company, or partnership. A sole proprietorship gives you an opportunity to own your own business without the formalities and expense of incorporation or the necessity of sharing control of the business with partners or shareholders in a corporation.

Disadvantages of a Sole Proprietorship

• The biggest problem is that your business assets and obligations are not separate from your personal ones. This means you're fully liable for the debts and other liabilities of your sole proprietorship. Your home, car, personal savings, and other property could be taken away to pay a court judgment. Insurance can protect against some of the potential exposure to personal liability (see chapter 10), but it cannot protect you from claims of creditors and some other types of liability claims. Moreover, adequate insurance coverage may be too expensive for the sole proprietor.

TALKING TO A LAWYER:
CAN I COMMINGLE?

Q. I have a small business doing technology consulting. I have an office in my home. I established a separate bank account for the money I make, and I pay myself a salary. I also have a bank account for my regular life. I pay my normal living expenses out of that account. Sometimes I use my business account to pay my regular bills when I'm short on funds. Since it's all my money anyway, should I be concerned about any legal problems? I always pay my business account back for any money I have to borrow.

A. You have a right to commingle funds, but be sure to keep adequate records. The IRS and state income and sales tax auditors may want to see a clear paper trail of your funds. It is also difficult to measure your business's performance without proper accounting.

—Answer by David L. Haron, attorney,
Frank, Stefani, Haron & Hall, Troy, Michigan

TALKING TO A LAWYER:
DIVORCE ON THE HORIZON

Q. I'm headed for a divorce. What's going to happen to my small business? Everything is in my name.

A. The value of the business would be a marital asset and generally subject to division in the divorce. If you and your spouse couldn't agree on how to divide your property (including the business), the divorce court would do so as part of its decision.

—Answer by David L. Haron, attorney,
Frank, Stefani, Haron & Hall, Troy, Michigan

TALKING TO A LAWYER: WHAT ABOUT DEATH AND DEBTS?

Q. *I am a sole proprietor and my spouse passed away nearly a decade ago. Would my children be responsible for my business debts upon my death? Could my children collect any outstanding invoices?*

A. Your estate, to the extent it is solvent, would be responsible and could collect invoices. That is one of the jobs of the executor of your estate, whom you name in your will. Your children aren't directly responsible for your debts, but the debts will follow any account or assets passed through the estate to the children, so in that way they might have to deal with your creditors.

—Answer by David L. Haron, attorney,
Frank, Stefani, Haron & Hall, Troy, Michigan

Protection against personal liability is one reason that many entrepreneurs choose to operate as a corporation or other form of business that has limited liability.

• The single-ownership principle, combined with the lack of separate entity status, creates severe problems when you die. Legally, a sole proprietorship ceases to exist at the proprietor's death. Unless the executor of your will is authorized to continue the business during the administration of the estate, a new owner is found, or the business is incorporated, the sole proprietorship will have to be liquidated. This means your family will lose the going-concern value of the business. Providing an optimum estate plan may, therefore, be more difficult for a sole proprietorship than for other forms of business organizations.

• A sole proprietorship also has the least flexibility of all the business forms in raising capital. You can't sell ownership interests to other persons, and your ability to borrow money for the business depends on your net assets.

**TALKING TO A LAWYER:
CAN I SHIELD MY SPOUSE?**

Q. *I'm just a small-business owner, but I don't want my business to ever cause problems for my spouse. If I stay a sole proprietor, can I make sure she'll never be liable for my debts?*

A. The simple answer is "no!" In a community property state, it is almost certain creditors would go after her if the business failed. (In community property states, the law holds that each spouse owns equally the income earned and the property acquired during the marriage. The community property states are Arizona, California, Idaho, Louisiana, Nevada, New Mexico, Texas, Washington, and Wisconsin.)

Even in other states, it would be cumbersome, to say the least, to establish that the business is your sole and separate property—and responsibility. In any case, the record-keeping costs and legal exposure for her would far outweigh the costs of setting up a corporation or limited liability company, which would protect both her and you from the business debts.

—Answer by Gerald V. Niesar, attorney,
Niesar & Diamond, LLP, San Francisco, California

YOU MUST REMEMBER THIS

• A sole proprietorship has no red tape—it's simple and cheap.
• Everything you own could be at risk if something bad happens to your sole proprietorship.
• You might find it hard to raise capital, and your death may cause real trouble if your business is a sole proprietorship.

CHAPTER 12

Partnerships

They Come in Many Flavors, Including General and Limited—Which One's for You?

Fred and Ethel have just had a great idea. Their revolutionary new gadget is going to set them up for life. But first, they've got to set up their company. It can't be a sole proprietorship (there are two of them), but it could be a general partnership, a limited partnership, a corporation, or a limited liability company. If they decide on the partnership route, what do they have to do? And how can they keep a friendship that's lasted since second grade from crashing before the second quarter of the partnership?

The legal definition of a partnership is pretty simple. One exists if:

1. an association of two or more persons
2. who have not incorporated
3. carry on a business for profit as co-owners.

A partnership exists if these conditions are met, even though the persons involved may not know it or even intend that the business be a partnership—and even if they don't actually make a profit.

Kinds of Partnerships

There are two main types of partnerships recognized in the United States: **general partnerships** and **limited partnerships**.

While a general partnership can exist with no formalities at all—as in our example with Fred and Ethel—some formalities are usually a good idea. In a general partnership, each partner has unlimited liability for the debts and obligations of the general partnership. Moreover, any partner can bind the partnership contractually to third parties. This means that Fred could be responsible for a contract for a new car signed by Ethel on behalf of the partnership, even if Fred disagreed with the purchase.

For these reasons, it is important to define in a written agreement what decisions partners can make individually and which ones require a vote of the partners. (For other ideas of what can be in the partnership agreement, see page 126.) In addition, most states require that the partnership file a certificate in the county in which it will do business.

Unlimited liability means that if you're a general partner, not only can you lose whatever money or other property you have put into the partnership, but also your house, boat, and stock portfolio might go to pay the claims of the partnership's creditors. In terms of management responsibility, general partners carry the load—they actively run the business on a day-to-day basis, while limited partners (see next paragraph) sit on the sidelines.

In a limited partnership, there must be at least one limited partner and one general partner. The advantage of being a limited partner is that if the business is unsuccessful, the limited partner may lose the amount of money invested in the partnership but has no additional financial risk. So if you are the limited partner, you'll bear the same risk of loss as a shareholder in a corporation or a member of a limited liability company. That's why limited partners are said to have limited liability. Limited partners also have no management responsibilities within the company and are in fact forbidden from managing company business.

In terms of the business's stability, adding or subtracting lim-

 PARTNERS INDEED

Fred and Ethel are husband and wife. They jointly operate a retail shoe store that they've never incorporated. Guess what? They're probably partners in business, as well as in life. Unless it is clear from their financial records that one of them is the true owner and the other is merely an employee (in which case the company would be classified as a sole proprietorship), the business will be a partnership, and both the husband and wife will be considered partners and co-owners of the business.

ited partners is not potentially as disruptive as the retirement, death, or disability of a general partner. In terms of paperwork, there's more if you set up a limited partnership. In fact, a limited partnership cannot exist until a certificate of limited partnership is filed with and approved by the secretary of state's office in the state in which the limited partnership is based.

Partnership harmony doesn't demand that Fred and Ethel be treated exactly equal. If each of them can afford to put $25,000 into the new company, and both had about the same amount of other property, then being general partners would make sense. But if Fred just inherited a chunk of money, it might make sense for him to be a limited partner, because he has more to lose if the business short-circuits. (Of course, he'd have to step back and not take an active role in management to retain his status as a limited partner.)

There is a special type of limited partnership, the **limited liability partnership** (LLP). This form of partnership was created for professionals (such as doctors, lawyers, accountants, and architects) who could not form corporations because states did not want the professionals to have limited liability related to the services they provided. LLP partners have unlimited liability just like general partners, but are shielded from liability for the malpractice of their partners (as long as they were not involved in the malpractice or supervising the partner who committed the malpractice). Some states, such as Colorado and Delaware, have opened the LLP form to nonprofessionals, allowing partners to be shielded from liability for torts committed by fellow partners. A tort is a form of wrongful conduct that causes harm to an innocent third party, who can then sue the "tortfeasor" in court to recover damages.

THE PROS AND CONS OF A PARTNERSHIP

Advantages of a Partnership

• Partnerships can be flexible; partners have the ability to make virtually any arrangements defining their relationship to each

YOU CAN LOSE YOUR LIMITS

Limited partners can lose their limited liability if they take part in management of the business and if creditors and other third parties reasonably believe them to be general partners.

other that they desire. In a corporation, the ownership interest and profits have to be proportionate to the investment made. In a partnership, the partners can agree to split the ownership and profits in more flexible ways, and losses can be allocated on a different basis from profits.

• You'll probably find it easier to come up with a more flexible way to control the business in a partnership than in a corporation, since the control of a corporation, which is based on ownership of voting stock, is much more difficult to alter.

• Because you can sell **equity interests** (ownership) in a partnership, it's easier to raise capital in a partnership than in a sole proprietorship. (However, because investors are more familiar with the corporate form, a corporation may have a greater ability to raise capital than a partnership.)

• With careful advance planning, a partnership can avoid some of the problems inherent in a sole proprietorship when an owner dies, retires, or becomes disabled. In fact, many believe that a limited partnership is the ideal vehicle to provide for continuity and succession in a family-owned business (see page 128 of this chapter and chapters 33 and 34 for more information).

 WHAT'S IN A NAME?

A partnership's name doesn't have to include the names of the partners. Like any business, the partners could simply register an assumed name with the appropriate office and do business under it.

Disadvantages of a Partnership

• The major disadvantage is that in both limited and general partnerships, general partners have unlimited liability. This means that to protect their personal assets they have to take some additional (and maybe costly) steps. For example, a general partner doesn't have to be a person. Often the general partner is a corporation or limited liability company, and this form of business then provides liability protection for the owners. In these ways, the threat to a general partner's assets can often be minimized or eliminated.

• Another important disadvantage is that a partnership is not as stable as a corporation. If a partner dies, retires, or otherwise no longer wants to be involved in the partnership, or, in some cases, files for bankruptcy, the partnership will have to dissolve if the remaining partners do not wish to continue the business or if there are not enough partners remaining (at least two partners for a general partnership, and at least one general and one limited partner for a limited partnership). In contrast, a corporation, under most statutes, continues forever, as long as there is at least one owner, until some specific action is taken to dissolve it.

• As compared to a corporation it may be more difficult in a partnership to have a hierarchy of management and to raise capital from outside sources. But creative agreements can provide for specific management arrangements and variations in capital ownership in the partnership.

TAXATION OF PARTNERSHIPS

Partnerships are taxed on a conduit or flow-through basis. This means that the partnership itself does not pay any taxes. Instead, the income and various deductions and tax credits from the partnership are passed through to the partners based on their percentage of interest in the profits and losses of the partnership. Then the partners include the income and deductions in their individual tax returns.

YOU COULD LOSE YOUR SHIRT

If your partnership agreement doesn't limit the authority of the partners to make deals (see below), the alternative is to be very sure of your partners. A partner's brainstorm to buy a lifetime supply of product or launch a megabucks ad campaign commits the company. Even if you weren't informed, you could be liable for the debts. In the absence of an agreement to the contrary, partners act simultaneously as agents and principals in all partnerships business, and they can therefore bind their copartners to contracts without explicit approval of the copartners.

ORGANIZING A GENERAL PARTNERSHIP

Although general partnerships aren't required to have any kind of written agreement, it would be foolish not to have one, if for no other reason than to provide concrete evidence of the partners' agreement.

A written partnership agreement will typically cover:
• duration of the partnership;
• how much money each partner is contributing;
• partner salaries;
• sharing of profits and losses (for example, the partners can decide how to split profits if one partner has put up all the money, but the other partner has supplied the essential ideas);
• reimbursement of expenses;
• vacations and fringe benefits;
• voting rights;
• duties and responsibilities of each partner;
• which partners have check-writing authority;
• which partners have authority to make agreements;
• the rights of the remaining partners when one of the partners leaves the partnership or dies;
• what happens if a partner becomes disabled or dies;

- admission of new partners; and
- what happens if the partnership liquidates.

Your agreement should be carefully tailored to the particular needs of the partners. It will probably be a lengthy and very complex document. It's almost certainly best that a lawyer draft the agreement.

ORGANIZING A LIMITED PARTNERSHIP

Organizing a limited partnership takes more paperwork. State laws require you to file a document known as a certificate of limited partnership in the secretary of state's office. You'll also have to pay a filing fee. Some states also require that you file a copy of the limited partnership certificate in a local filing office, usually in the county where the company's principal place of business is located. While the information required in the certificate varies, all laws require:

- the name of the limited partnership;
- the address of its principal place of business;
- the name and address of the person who is to be served with legal documents;
- the name and business address of each general partner; and
- the latest date when the partnership will dissolve.

Some of the laws also require the business purpose to be specified as well as the circumstances under which additional capital may be required. All laws also let the partners include any other information they wish in their certificate.

Of course, you should have a limited partnership agreement. In general, it's very similar to a general partnership agreement, except that it will have specific provisions setting out the rights and obligations of limited partners as well as general partners. Sometimes, state laws require you to put certain obligations into the agreement if it is to be enforceable. Examples include the obligation of partners to contribute additional capital and the circumstances when a capital call is triggered.

Whether you own a general partnership interest or a limited

WITHOUT AN AGREEMENT

Almost every state has adopted the **Uniform Partnership Act (UPA)** or the **Revised Uniform Partnership Act (RUPA)** to kick in should your partnership have no written agreement. In the event of a dispute, a court would apply whichever law was adopted in your state in lieu of an agreement. Even with an agreement, the court may use the law to fill in the blanks if the partners failed to specify important terms—for example, how profits are to be shared among partners. It is also possible that the terms supplied by your state's law (equal management, equal share of the profits, etc.) were not what you had in mind. It's always best to put partnership agreements in writing.

partnership interest, if you have an estate plan that includes a living trust, discuss having your business interest held by your living trust. This can avoid a number of problems in the event of disability and at death. However, such an arrangement may create problems with your business plan so be sure your personal estate plan and your business plan are properly established and coordinated to protect your interests and those of your loved ones.

PASSING ON THE BUSINESS

The mechanics of succession vary with the situation. If you want to pass your share of the business to other family members (usually a spouse or children), it is relatively simple to transfer your interest to them, perhaps by leaving the family members enough cash (possibly through life insurance proceeds) to buy out the other partners at your death and thus avoid conflicts. Limited partnership interests can be given to family members who are not going to be actively involved in the management of the business. (In a small corporation, you can achieve the same purpose by leaving voting stock to family who will operate the business and leaving nonvoting stock to others.) There are certain tax advantages, however, to having a limited partnership rather than a corporation as an owner of a family-owned business. (Your lawyer or tax accountant can provide you with details of the differences between these alternatives.)

If some family members are active in the business and others are not, it is important to consider how you will leave your business and other parts of your estate to the family. Also, while many business owners want to pass the value of their businesses to family members, who will handle the responsibility? What is the nature of the relationship between family members and your employees and other business participants? Experienced counsel can help you deal with some issues that are critical to the success of your business and the well-being of your family.

Things get slightly more complicated if you decide to pass ownership on to people who are not beneficiaries of your will, or to a combination of those who are beneficiaries and those who are not. If your business is a partnership, you will usually want your partners to remain in operational control. A **buy-sell agreement** is the most common device for transferring ownership of a business on the death of a partner. Under such an agreement, the remaining partners agree to purchase your interest when you die. This allows the business to continue running smoothly with the same people in charge, minus one.

Do you want to start to transfer ownership interests while you are alive? The nature of partnerships allows owners to transfer ownership at a reduced cost while maintaining control of the business and reducing potential estate tax liability. These techniques are sophisticated and you should discuss your options with an attorney.

Buy-sell agreements typically provide that upon the partner's death, his or her interest in the business will be acquired by the remaining partners or by the business itself, leaving the deceased partner's relatives with the proceeds of the sale. Life insurance is usually the vehicle used to finance these arrangements, which lets the business avoid a drain on its capital. The partners buy life insurance on each other's lives, and the proceeds go to the surviving spouse, children, or other designated beneficiaries, in return for the deceased owner's share of the business. Alternatively, the partnership can own the insurance and use the insurance proceeds to buy the deceased partner's interest, which is then retired or allocated to the other partners.

YOU MUST REMEMBER THIS

• Partnerships can be a very effective way for two or more people to be in business together.

• All partners in a general partnership and general partners in a limited partnership are each potentially 100 percent personally liable for the debts and obligations of the partnership.

• A limited partnership permits limited partners—those who invest in a company but do not take part in its day-to-day management—to protect themselves from unlimited liability; generally, they can lose only what they invested in the business.

• Partners should agree in advance about how the company will be run, how profits will be split, etc.

• A written partnership agreement will help make everyone clearer on what's been agreed to.

CHAPTER 13

Is a Corporation for You?

They're Persons Under the Law, Which Opens Up Many Intriguing Possibilities

Alan, Bob, and Charlie are cousins who've just realized their lifelong dream of going into business together. They think that "ABC, Inc." would be a great name for their business—until they find out that they can't be an "Inc." (that is, they can't be a corporation) unless they're actually incorporated. That starts them thinking. What is incorporation? It must be a good idea for bigger businesses, since they all do it, but is incorporation for them? Are there different kinds of corporations? How does being a corporation affect the day-to-day operations of a business?

The basic legal point about corporations is that they are a **separate legal entity**. Pretty much all of the advantages of incorporating a business—and the drawbacks too—stem from this fact.

The term *separate legal identity* simply means that a corporation has a legal status that is independent of its owners (shareholders). The corporation's independent existence undergirds the basic corporate attributes of:

• limited liability of corporate actors (including owners, directors, and officers);

• perpetual existence (a life independent of the life of the owners, directors, and officers);

• free transferability of shares;

• the ability to own property in the corporation's name;

• the ability to bring suit and be sued in the corporate name; and

• status as a separate taxpayer.

All but the last of these are good things, and the taxpayer status can be a benefit in certain circumstances. This helps explain why the corporate form is popular. However, the separate legal

OTHER WAYS OF BEING "SEPARATE"

Partnerships and limited liability companies are also legal entities for some purposes. The separate entity status of partnerships is, however, less complete than in corporations. The entity status of limited liability companies, on the other hand, is virtually the same as corporations, without many of the cumbersome requirements (see chapter 14).

identity also accounts for the tripartite system of corporate management, consisting of shareholders, directors, and officers. This can be cumbersome, especially for a small business, which is why corporations are not the best form for all businesses.

Corporations in a Nutshell

A corporation is a legal entity that you form by filing **articles of incorporation** (or, in some states, a **certificate of incorporation**) with the secretary of state of the state in which you have chosen to organize the corporation, along with the required filing and license fees.

One or more persons can form a corporation. Thus, a sole proprietor can incorporate if he or she wants to. With some exceptions (doctors and lawyers are prohibited by ethical and regulatory constraints from operating in certain types of corporations), corporations can generally operate any type of business.

The people who file the articles or certificate of incorporation are called **incorporators**. The ownership interest in a corporation (equity) is called **stock**, and the owners of shares of stock are called **shareholders** or **stockholders**. There are two types of stock, **common** and **preferred**. Voting rights typically belong to common stockholders. Corporate profits are distributed to the shareholders in the form of dividends, but dividends generally must be paid to the preferred stockholders before the common stockholders receive dividends.

Corporations traditionally have a tripartite management structure: shareholders elect directors who are responsible for the overall management of the business and who hire officers to handle the day-to-day affairs of the business. Most states require a minimum of three directors, and in small, closely held corporations directors usually serve one-year terms. It is very common in small corporations for most, if not all, shareholders to also serve as the directors and as officers. Many states have loosened the requirements regarding directors; for example, by allowing fewer than three directors if there are fewer than three shareholders (and some states have eliminated the requirement for directors where there are very few shareholders). Regardless of how many directors your corporation may have, it is always a good idea to have an odd number of directors to avoid deadlock on important issues.

One last point: To achieve the benefits of incorporation—limited personal liability and all the others—you have to be sure to adhere to your state's laws regarding how the corporation is to be formed. (Ditto if you're forming a limited partnership, limited liability company, etc.) If you don't comply with all the requirements, you may fail to form the corporation legally and thus default to a general partnership or sole proprietorship, depriving you of the benefits you sought. We talk more about this later in this chapter.

THE ADVANTAGES OF CORPORATE LIMITED LIABILITY

Shareholders generally are at risk only for the amount of money or other property they invest in the corporation, though some state laws make shareholders of small corporations liable for unpaid wages. So Alan, Bob, and Charlie could each put up $5,000 in return for stock in the company and know that creditors of the corporation couldn't come after them personally for payment. Even if the business is deader than a three-day-old halibut, they can lose only their investment.

This ability to shield personal assets from the creditors of a corporation is attractive to investors. Given a choice, an investor will always choose limited liability to unlimited liability.

When shareholders of a corporation guarantee its debts, co-sign its notes in their individual capacity, or pledge their own assets as security for loans to the corporation (which frequently occurs because of creditors' demands), the shareholders waive (or give up) their limited liability with respect to those debts, notes, or assets. But this is a limited waiver. The shareholders in question still have limited liability with respect to any other debts or obligations of the corporation.

The following example will help illustrate this distinction. Suppose Bill is the sole shareholder in Bill's Bakeries, Inc. He personally guaranties payment of a $20,000 bank loan that is used to purchase a new delivery truck for the corporation. Alas, people don't want Bill's buns, and the corporation ceases doing business and is liquidated. At the time of liquidation, the corporation has $50,000 of assets, and the creditors of the corporation other than the bank that made the truck loan have valid claims of $75,000. The bank can recover whatever is still owed on the truck loan directly from Bill because of the personal guaranty. The other creditors, however, can recover only $50,000 from the

 ## LIMITED LIABILITY IN THE REAL WORLD

Shareholders are limited in their liability, but if you invest in a small corporation you might very well have to give your creditors another way to get at your personal assets. Banks and others who lend money to small, new corporations know very well that they can't routinely get their money back if their claims are greater than the assets of the corporation. Therefore, they often require investors to obligate their personal assets by personal guaranties or by co-signing a note or other obligation in their *individual* capacity. Some federal tax obligations may also be asserted against controlling shareholders.

corporation. They cannot recover the additional $25,000 they are owed from either the corporation, because it does not have any more assets, or from the shareholder, because the shareholder's other assets are protected by the limited liability doctrine.

The Importance of Perpetual Existence

Probably most new businesses aren't thinking enough ahead to care about this advantage—heck, a lot of them would be happy to be guaranteed that they'd be in existence five years from now—but this can be a big problem if a business is *not* incorporated. If Alan, Bob, and Charlie are all general partners, for example, when any one of them ceases to be a partner, for any reason, the partnership will end up being dissolved and liquidated *unless the remaining partners agree to continue the business, or unless their partnership agreement included a continuation clause, in which case no new agreement is necessary to preserve the partnership.* If there is no continuation clause, getting necessary consent from the partners to continue the business can be very difficult, perhaps impossible. This is true even if liquidation may result in significant losses to all the partners. The risk of losing the business is one of the principal drawbacks of operating as a partnership.

In a corporation, on the other hand, if a shareholder leaves, there is no risk of liquidation because the life of a corporation is indefinite (as long as there is at least one shareholder). Thus, perpetual existence gives a corporation permanence, and this in turn may make investments in a corporation somewhat safer than investments in other less permanent business organizations.

The Importance of Being Able to Freely Transfer Shares

Being able to freely transfer shares to anyone gives an investor the right to liquidate his or her investment at any time. This right to transfer makes shares of the stock very marketable—provided, of course, there is someone who wants to buy them. The shares of all the corporations where stock is registered with a stock exchange like the New York Stock Exchange are, for example, freely transferable.

But in a small corporation with only a few shareholders, free transferability of stock can often be a detriment. Let's say, for example, that Alan, Bob, and Charlie are three founding shareholders of a corporation that operates a camera store. After a lean period at the beginning, they've become successful. Now Bob wants to sell his shares to someone Alan and Charlie intensely dislike. But for the store to be successful, all three shareholders have to work there regularly without undue friction between them. If Bob can freely transfer his shares to anyone, and Alan and Charlie can't prevent the sale, it could be a disaster.

In many states, a complete prohibition against the transferability of stock is not possible. That's why in most small corporations, the shareholders enter into what is known as a **shareholders' agreement** or a **share transfer restriction agreement**, which will impose restrictions on the sale of stock (usually meaning that Bob would have to offer his shares to Alan and Charlie or the corporation before he could sell them to an outsider). These agreements have to conform to your state's corporation laws, as well as to precedents established by case law. It's a good idea to get legal advice when drafting such an agreement.

The Importance of Being a Separate Legal Entity

As a separate legal entity, a corporation has the right to own and dispose of property in its own name and to sue and be sued in its own name. This makes things a lot easier for everyone doing business with the company, since it does not require action by all the shareholders.

A limited liability company, like a corporation, may own property and sue and be sued in its own name. A sole proprietorship, on the other hand, does not have separate entity status, but this does not cause any practical problems because there is only one person, the sole proprietor, in whose name title to property belonging to the proprietorship is taken. Moreover, suits by and against a proprietorship must be in the name of the sole proprietor, even if the proprietorship operates under a name different from that of the proprietor.

TYPES OF CORPORATIONS

There is more than one kind of corporation, just as there is more than one kind of partnership. The various types of corporations, however, are not as distinct as general and limited partnerships are.

From a nontax perspective there are three main forms of a corporation:

1. the general business corporation,
2. the close corporation, and
3. the professional corporation.

The last two are specialized forms of the general business corporation.

From a tax standpoint, any of these corporations can be taxed as a C corporation or, if they qualify and choose to be taxed as such, an S corporation. (These are designations that refer to sections of the federal tax code and are discussed below.) As the next section explains, being taxed as an S corporation may well save on taxes overall.

General Business Corporations

A **general business corporation** is a corporation, usually organized for profit, that is formed under a state's corporation act. Shares of stock in a business corporation are **securities**. This means they have to be registered with the state or federal government, unless they or the transactions in which they are sold are exempted from such laws. The good news is that the securities of most small businesses are typically exempt from registration.

Close Corporations

A **close corporation** is usually one in which all or most of the shareholders are actively involved in managing the business, and the shares have not been offered to the public. Most start-up corporations, and plenty of existing small businesses that are incorporated, are close corporations.

Because they're so common, many state laws have special provisions designed to meet the needs of close corporations. These special statutes vary from state to state but generally provide that:

• the shareholders may manage the corporation directly rather than through directors or officers; and

• the shareholders may make other agreements for management that are not available to other corporations.

Professional Corporations

This kind of corporation is limited to the practice of a profession with professionals licensed in that field as its only shareholders— a requirement that necessitates a mandatory buy-out plan if a professional retires, dies, or has his or her license to practice suspended or revoked.

The kinds of professionals that can take advantage of this type of corporation vary from state to state. Usually, though, they include lawyers, accountants, and doctors. In some states, the list might also include psychologists, social workers, dentists, and engineers. These corporations generally offer better protection than partnerships from malpractice awards. Although a professional is individually liable for his or her own malpractice, in most states there is no liability for the malpractice of other professionals in the professional corporation.

TAXATION OF CORPORATIONS

Those thinking of setting up a corporation—or any other form of business—ought to be concerned with how their choice of business form affects the taxes they'll have to pay. For partnerships and sole proprietorships, the company isn't taxed per se, but rather taxes are simply passed through to the owners. This results in income being taxed only once.

A corporation is a legal entity, which is swell in itself and confers many benefits. It does, however, open itself up to the unwelcome possibility of **double taxation**: a tax on the earnings of the corporation as an entity, and a tax paid by the shareholders on dividends (profits) paid by the corporation.

Fortunately, there's a way around this for most small corporations—meeting the requirements of subchapter S of the Internal Revenue Code and choosing to be taxed under this section. There are two subchapters in the Internal Revenue Code that govern corporations. One is subchapter C, under which many corporations, including large ones, operate (**C corporations**). The other is subchapter S, which small corporations meeting certain criteria can choose (**S corporations**).

C Corporations

Unless your corporation has chosen to be taxed as an S corporation, it's automatically taxed as a C corporation. This means it must pay tax on its net taxable income, and then the shareholders must pay a second tax on any of the corporation's net earnings that are distributed as taxable dividends.

But in a small corporation, where all the shareholders work in the business, it may be possible to avoid taxation on profits by avoiding the profits all together! If the owner-employees pay themselves enough (while still satisfying IRS rules that the compensation be "reasonable") there would be no profit, and thus no tax on the business or on dividends.

In such a situation, a C corporation might enjoy some tax *advantages* over the other forms. Once again, the key is the separate legal identity of the corporation. Shareholders who are employed by a corporation in some capacity can qualify as employees of the company. As a result, they're eligible for special life and medical insurance programs and other fringe benefits. These can result in tax deductions to the company for the cost of these business expenses. These breaks aren't available to sole proprietors, partners, or the members (owners) of a limited liability company, who are regarded as self-employed.

S Corporations

An S corporation is a business corporation (including a professional corporation, a close corporation, or both) that has chosen to be taxed under subchapter S rather than under subchapter C, the normal corporate tax section. This avoids double taxation at the corporate and the shareholder level.

S corporations are taxed like partnerships. Except in a limited number of circumstances, an S corporation itself does not pay any taxes. Rather, the income and deductions generated by the S corporation are passed through to the shareholders, who report their share on their individual tax returns.

The basic eligibility requirements are that the corporation be a domestic corporation (i.e., one formed under the laws of a state or territory of the United States) and:

- not have more than one class of stock; and
- not have more than 100 shareholders who are individuals, estates, or certain trusts, none of whom are nonresident aliens.

You can choose to be taxed as an S corporation by filing **IRS Form 2553**, which must be signed by all the shareholders. The Form 2553 must be filed not later than two months and fifteen days after the beginning of the taxable year in which it is to be effective. For newly formed corporations that wish to have sub-

 TAX TIP—CHOOSE NOW

Any corporation, including a professional corporation and an existing C corporation, can choose to be taxed under subchapter S if it meets the eligibility requirements. However if you think that at some point you might want to be an S corporation, you're generally better off, because of some very complex potential adverse tax consequences, starting off as an S corporation, rather than converting from a C to an S corporation sometime after incorporation.

ADVANTAGES OF HAVING FEW EMPLOYEES

One way of making these fringe benefits more attractive to shareholders working in the business is to spread them over relatively few employees. Yes, you have to make them available to at least 70 percent of your employees, but what if you use temps, part-timers, independent consultants, and outside contractors so much that the number of actual employees isn't much larger than the number of shareholders who work in the business? Then the shareholders can benefit without unduly adding to the cost of doing business.

chapter S apply right from the start, the taxable year begins when the corporation:

- has shareholders,
- acquires property, or
- begins doing business.

The clock starts ticking when any one of these happens. This technicality can be a trap for the unaware. For example, the period for filing Form 2553 begins to run from the day the corporation enters into a lease, even though it is not at that time conducting any business operations and even though the incorporation process is incomplete and no shares have been issued to shareholders.

Many new businesses are now selecting the limited liability company as their form of business because it offers limited liability for the owners, but can avoid the double taxation of C corporations. See chapter 14 for more information.

RUNNING A CORPORATION

The day-to-day life of your company won't be much different if it's a corporation—except that you have to adhere to the corporate formalities to get the benefits of incorporation. If you ignore the formalities and simply run the business as if it were a sole proprietorship, you'll also run the risk of exposing yourself to personal liability if a court decides to **pierce the corporate veil**. A court may pierce the corporate veil if, in response to a claim, it closely examines the inner workings of a corporation and determines that the corporation has not met the necessary legal formalities for its directors to benefit from the personal liability shield.

Corporations at Work

The key to business is taking in more money than you spend, and that won't change no matter what form your business has. Most of your time will probably be spent dealing with customers, marketing, suppliers, and inventory.

But from time to time you'll have to do things differently because you're a corporation. Here's a brief checklist—but when in doubt, err on the side of caution.

- Issue share certificates.
- Be sure to use the correct, full corporate name on your letterhead, ads, contracts, etc.
- Make sure everyone who deals with your company knows that you—or the other officers—are acting in your capacity as agents of the corporation, not personally. That means using appropriate titles—president, secretary, treasurer—when signing everything from checks and contracts to ordinary correspondence.
- Don't mingle—money, that is. Keep your personal finances separate from the corporation's. If you dip into corporate money, don't just reach into your pocket: Establish a paper trail that shows that you received dividends, took a salary, or took out a loan.
- Maintain the appropriate corporate records, including your bylaws, resolutions, and minutes of meetings. Document that all major actions were taken by the corporation, not by you personally.
- Hold the meetings required by law. You'll usually have to hold annual meetings of shareholders, at which you'll probably elect directors.

SOME INFORMALITY IS OKAY

It's not necessary that the board or shareholders of a small corporation always meet to take action. Corporate statutes and the bylaws of most corporations allow for meetings to be held by telephone conference call and allow shareholders and directors to take action by means of unanimous written consent.

ORGANIZING A CORPORATION

Let's say that after reading this far, you've decided the corporate form is for you. The legal formalities for setting up a corporation can be complicated, but not necessarily more complicated than for a limited partnership (chapter 12) or a limited liability company (chapter 14). You might even have to do less than you would to properly set up these other forms of business organizations.

Corporate codes require:

- filing a document generally known as either **articles of incorporation** or a **certificate of incorporation** (either of these may also be known as the **corporate charter**);
- establishing bylaws;
- issuing share certificates; and
- holding an organizational meeting.

Articles of Incorporation

The **incorporator** is the person who gets the wheels going. The incorporator (sometimes called the **promoter**) can be you alone in almost all states or can be two or more people. Either way, the only document that the law requires you to file is the articles of incorporation. The corporation is legally formed once you've filed it, along with the appropriate fee, in the office of the secretary of state in the state where the business is to be incorporated.

In most states, the secretary of state's office has official printed forms for articles of incorporation available online. These require five or six types of information:

- the name of the corporation (which cannot be in conflict with the name of other corporations already incorporated in the state);
- the name of the corporation's registered agent and the address of the corporation's registered office;
- the business purpose (not necessary in some states);
- the initial capitalization (how many shares of what type of stock will be *authorized*—the number to be *issued* is decided later by the directors);
- the names and signatures of the incorporator(s); and
- the names and addresses of the initial directors (not all states require that the certificate of incorporation name the initial directors, and often they are named by the incorporators).

Simple? Well, yes and no. The devil is in the details. You must select a state in which to file your articles of incorporation. Technically, you can select any state you prefer. Many large corporations file their articles in the state of Delaware because it has long-established corporate laws and a special corporate court. For most small, new businesses, it usually makes sense to file in the state in which the company is doing business. However, if you begin to regularly conduct business outside your state of incorporation (your "domestic" state), you will have to file a certificate of authority in every state in which you conduct that business. This will authorize you to act as a corporation in those other ("foreign") states.

Every corporation must designate a registered agent, and the registered agent must have a physical address in the state of incorporation. The registered agent accepts legal documents on behalf of the corporation. There are a number of businesses that will provide registered agent services for a fee.

Most states request that you state a business purpose and the duration of the corporation. Most articles of incorporation state "any lawful purpose" as the business purpose and "perpetual" as the duration.

PROMOTER LIABILITY

A "promoter" is someone who deals with preincorporation issues, often by entering initial contracts on behalf of the soon-to-be-formed corporation. But there's a problem: Since the corporation does not yet exist, it legally cannot be bound on these preincorporation contracts. As a result, there is chance the promoter may wind up personally liable on the preincorporation contracts. To protect the promoter, the effectiveness of these preincorporation contracts should be made conditioned upon (1) the corporation actually being formed, (2) the corporation adopting (ratifying) the contract, and (3) both the corporation and the other party to the contract releasing the promoter from personal liability on the contract.

Is Capitalization a Problem?

Determining the appropriate capitalization may or may not be a difficult task. Attorney Thomas Pitegoff writes, "It is often quite simple. In my own practice, unless there is good reason to do otherwise, I recommend that my clients

• authorize the largest number of shares that can be authorized for the lowest possible tax;
• authorize only one class of stock;
• set no par value on the stock; and
• issue a small number of shares for a small investment, with any additional investment being a loan to the corporation rather than capital."

Historically, all stock had to have a stated par value, which is the absolute minimum price a share of stock could be sold for. Many states no longer require a stated par value and in states that still do, many allow the articles to state "no par value." Where a par value must be stated, it is common to state a par value of $0.001 (one-tenth of a cent per share).

The key variables are how much capital your corporation needs and what you have to do (or promise) to attract investors.

TYPES OF STOCK

There are two basic types of stock, **common** and **preferred**. Common stock is the most, ahem, common type of stock. It usually includes voting rights—one share = one vote. Preferred stock often does not have voting rights but is given a higher preference for dividends. Preferred stock usually requires that its holders be paid a dividend before the holders of common stock can be paid one. Also, in the event the corporation ceases to operate and liquidates, preferred shareholders are paid from the assets of the corporation before common shareholders. Preferred shareholders are usually investors in the corporation who do not have an immediate interest in managing the company—hence, the lack of voting power. However, many preferred shares have a clause that permits them to be converted into common shares (at a ratio, for example, of ten shares of common for each share of preferred stock), in the event the preferred shareholders do want to become more involved in how the business is run. Finally, you can have multiple classes of common and preferred stock; each class would then have rights that are different from the other classes.

Obviously, if all your investors are close family members who are mainly interested in helping you get started (as opposed to making a bundle), then one class of stock will probably be enough. The more people you bring in, however, the more you'll want to explore these various ways of meeting investors' demands.

Other Necessary Documents

Although a corporation begins its existence at the time its articles of incorporation are filed, there are a minimum of three other documents that usually have to be prepared before the corporation can legally begin to conduct business: the bylaws, stock certificates, and organizational meeting minutes.

OFF-THE-SHELF OR CUSTOM?

Although it is possible to buy inexpensive standardized forms for organizing a corporation from a number of sources, these off-the-shelf forms are often inappropriate. They may contain provisions—or more likely omit provisions—that can create serious legal and practical problems down the road.

Bylaws

Think of the articles of incorporation as the birth certificate of the corporation. And then the bylaws are its constitution. The purpose of bylaws is to provide guidelines for regulating the internal affairs of a corporation. Typically, corporate bylaws deal with:

• the mechanisms of shareholder, director, and committee meetings;

• how stock and dividends are issued; and

• the appointment, duties, and removal of the officers and directors.

All may be well and good if you have a plain vanilla corporation, with no unusual arrangements. But if the corporation has more than one class of stock, each having the right to elect a separate class of directors, or wants to have directors and shareholder supermajority voting or quorum rights that are intended to protect minority shareholders, then, at the least, you will have

 ## IT MEANS YOU OWN THEM

Stock certificates are documented proof that you own shares in the corporation. A stock certificate is like the title certificate you receive when you buy a car.

to modify a number of provisions in standardized bylaws forms, or create your own. The more complex the corporation, the more you should use a lawyer.

As your business grows, you may find it necessary and prudent to modify your bylaws to reflect the new realities of your business.

Stock Certificates

Corporations must issue stock to the owners. You can easily get standardized, beautifully printed certificates for both common and preferred stock that conform to the minimum requirements under state law. These often contain easy-to-fill-in blanks for items like the name of the corporation (which is often printed on the certificates), and the number and par value of the shares. If you have an estate plan that includes a revocable trust, talk with your attorney about having the certificates that you own titled in the name of your trust. This will allow your business interests to avoid the pitfalls of probate, which include the lack of privacy about your business's affairs.

The problem is that these forms are generally inappropriate when there is more than one class of common or preferred stock. Moreover, they do not contain various notices, or **legends** as they are commonly called, that may be required for enforceability, or at least may be highly desirable even if they are not legally required. Share certificates of small or closely held corporations may include one or more of the following legends (statements):

• a legend that the shares represented by the certificate are not registered under the federal and state securities laws and cannot be transferred without compliance with these laws;

• a legend that the shares are subject to contractual transfer restrictions under which the corporation and/or the other shareholders may have a first refusal or mandatory right to purchase the shares (If your corporation will be closely held—with all or most of the shareholders actively involved in managing the business—you'll probably want to have share transfer restric-

COMPLYING WITH SECURITIES LAWS

During the organizational phase, you and any other co-owners must be very careful *not* to contact anyone else about investing in the business without first consulting the lawyer representing the business. You first need to get advice on whom you can contact and what you can say or not say about investing in your business. If you don't follow this advice, you could face serious fines and other court-imposed sanctions for not complying with federal and state securities laws. And these improper contacts, although made in good faith, could also jeopardize the ability of your company to qualify a later securities offering under one or more of the relatively inexpensive registration exemptions.

---

tions noted on all stock certificates, so that you'll have some control over whom you'll be in business with.);

• a legend to the effect that the voting and management rights of the corporation are significantly different from the standard rules specified in the corporation code and are set forth in a shareholder management agreement. (You'll want this if you have agreements protecting the rights of minority shareholders.)

Organizational Meeting Minutes

Some state corporation codes require two organizational meetings, one by shareholders to elect the directors and a second by the directors to approve everything else, but the requirements vary by state. In Delaware and New York, for example, the corporation typically adopts the bylaws and appoints the initial directors. The directors then appoint officers, authorize the issuance of the initial shares to specific persons and the consideration (money, equipment, etc.) to be paid for those shares, and authorize the opening of a bank account or accounts. Thus, in those states the two organizational meetings are for the incorporator(s) and directors, not the shareholders and directors.

**TALKING TO A LAWYER:
WHO RUNS A CORPORATION?**

*Q. I'm thinking of expanding my business and making it a corporation.
Who owns a corporation? How can I be sure I'll still be running
things?*

A. When you organize the corporation, you should consider what assets
the corporation will initially own. Will it simply have a bank account
with some cash in it? Will it own your inventions? Will it have inventory, contracts, and accounts from a business you had been running
as a sole proprietor?

The likelihood is that you will want to contribute these assets to
the corporation in exchange for shares of stock of the corporation. If
more than one person is involved, you will have to determine who
contributes what, and how many shares of stock the corporation will
issue in exchange for that contribution. These decisions should be reflected in a resolution of the directors of the corporation and entered
in the corporate minutes. The corporation would then issue the stock
to the new stockholders.

If you have set up the corporation with one class of stock, the majority owners will have control of the corporation. They elect directors,
who manage the business of the corporation. Directors, however,
cannot act alone. They take action only through formal meetings (in
person or by telephone conference call) or by written consent.

The directors hire officers (at least a president and secretary, and
possibly a treasurer and one or more vice presidents and others), who
manage the day-to-day affairs of the business. In a corporation owned
by one person, that owner can in most states also be the sole director
and the president. Control involves many other considerations, which
you should discuss with your attorney.

—Answer by Thomas M. Pitegoff, attorney,
Pitegoff Law Office, White Plains, New York

Many state statutes, however, require only one meeting, at which the corporation will typically

- ratify all the actions taken by the promoters and incorporators and approve reimbursing them for any expenses they have incurred;
- adopt the bylaws and the corporate seal;
- select and set the salaries of the officers;
- indemnify the directors and officers from personal liability;
- authorize issuing shares and the consideration for the shares that are to be issued;
- approve resolutions designating one or more banks as depositories and establishing check-signing authority; and
- authorize designated officers to take the appropriate action to complete the incorporation process, including, if necessary, qualifying as a foreign corporation in another state.

The minutes of this organizational meeting are necessary to

TALKING TO A LAWYER: WHY INCORPORATE?

Q. What do you think the main advantages of incorporation are?

A. A corporation affords limited liability to its owners. Many advisers prefer the corporate form to limited liability companies because the corporation is a known entity. Corporate statutes have existed for decades in substantially the form in which they exist today. There is well-developed case law defining the rights and obligations of shareholders, directors, and officers. The same cannot be said for limited liability companies, which are entirely created by statutes. In some cases, the cost of setting up a corporation can be less than that for setting up a limited liability company. If your eventual goal is to go public (i.e., offer stock in the corporation to the general public), the corporate form is usually preferable.

—Answer by Thomas M. Pitegoff, attorney,
Pitegoff Law Office, White Plains, New York

complete the organizing phase of a corporation from a legal perspective. They also can give you headaches. The resolutions listed above are almost always included in organizational minutes, and they are generally in preprinted organizational minutes forms that you can buy.

The problem is that some of these standardized resolutions may need to be modified. This is frequently the case, for example, with standard form resolutions authorizing indemnification of the directors and officers and the purchase of directors' and officers' liability insurance.

Moreover, other approval resolutions may be necessary, and these may or may not be included in the preprinted forms. For

TALKING TO A LAWYER: WHAT'S SPECIAL ABOUT DELAWARE?

Q. I hear a lot about Delaware corporations. Is it worth my while to organize my corporation in Delaware?

A. It may depend on the size of your business. Many public companies (i.e., companies that sell their stock to the general public) are Delaware corporations. The reason is that Delaware took an early lead in making it easy for corporate managers to run their companies. Because so many corporations were organized in Delaware, that state has well-developed corporate case law, which means that officers, directors, and shareholders can more easily predict the outcome of difficult corporate issues there than in most other states.

Today, the differences among state corporation laws are not great, but differences still exist, and these may be significant in specific situations. Delaware still has one of the most favorable corporate statutes from the point of view of management, and the Delaware office of the secretary of state acts very much with the customer in mind, usually responding quickly rather than bureaucratically.

—Answer by Thomas M. Pitegoff, attorney,
Pitegoff Law Office, White Plains, New York

**TALKING TO A LAWYER:
WHAT ABOUT SMALL
CORPORATIONS?**

*Q. Is incorporating in Delaware (or Nevada or another state said to be
friendly to corporations) advisable if the business is small and closely
held?*

A. In a great majority of cases, the differences in state laws will not really
affect small businesses that are closely held. So, if you incorporate in
another state, you are asking for *two* states to look into your affairs.
Why two? Because, if you are in Ohio but form your corporation under
Nevada law, you still have to qualify to do business in Ohio, where you
are actually located. The costs of qualifications will be almost as great
as the original filing fees for a new corporation. And because you are
doing business in Ohio, you will be subject to all of the taxes and other
regulations that would apply if you had incorporated under Ohio law in
the first place. As a general rule for small businesses, incorporate only
in the state in which you will do business to avoid extra taxes and regulations.

—Answer by Gerald V. Niesar, attorney,
Niesar & Diamond, LLP, San Francisco, California

example, since the corporation as well as the shareholders must
approve taxation as a subchapter S corporation, a resolution to
this effect should be adopted at the organizational meeting if
you've decided to go that route.

YOU MUST REMEMBER THIS

• Corporations have a separate legal status, apart from you
and any other investors.

• Investors can freely buy and sell shares, are shielded from
personal liability, yet can control the business.

**TALKING TO A LAWYER:
WHERE TO INCORPORATE?**

Q. Do I have to incorporate in every state I do business in?

A. No. A corporation has one state of incorporation. When the corporation's activities in another state rise to a certain level, it may be necessary to qualify the corporation to do business in that other state. This involves filing an application for authority in the other state, along with a certified copy of the certificate of incorporation from the state of incorporation.

Activities in a state that constitute no more than interstate commerce do not require a corporation to qualify in that state. For example, selling products through local sales representatives who do not have the authority to enter into contracts does not constitute doing business in another state for purposes of qualification.

—Answer by Thomas M. Pitegoff, attorney,
Pitegoff Law Office, White Plains, New York

- The corporation can own property, sue or be sued, and go on indefinitely, no matter if investors come and go.
- To keep your separate legal status, comply with whatever formalities your state's laws require; when in doubt, be extra cautious and remember that you and the corporation are two entirely different legal entities.
- Chances are, a corporation formed by your lawyers would qualify as a close corporation, which can give you the protections of a corporation without all the formalities.
- Your corporation could also qualify as an S corporation, which could be beneficial for tax purposes.
- Though the minimum requirements for incorporation are more than for other forms of business organization, they may not involve much paperwork. Preprinted forms exist but, like off-the-rack clothes, they might not be a good fit for you.

CHAPTER 14

Limited Trouble—
and Paperwork

*Finding Out Why Limited Liability Companies
Are Sweeping the Country*

*Of course you like the idea of being shielded from corporate lia-
bility, but are corporations worth the trouble? They can come
with lots of strings attached, such as mandated meetings and a
cumbersome three-part management structure. Sometimes corporations are taxed as entities and the shareholders are then
taxed as individuals—a double whammy. A relatively new kind
of legal entity, the limited liability company, has spread like wild-
fire because it combines almost all the benefits of corporations
with fewer hassles, at least in some states. Read on to find out if
it's for you.*

A limited liability company (LLC) combines the best attributes of a corporation and a sole proprietorship or partnership. Since an LLC is not a corporation, it provides the flexibility
of organization of a proprietorship or general partnership—you
don't have to have shareholders, directors, and officers, to say
nothing of the mandatory meetings. And it has the same pass-
through taxation that sole proprietorships and partnerships enjoy.

But because an LLC protects against individual liability, it can
give you the same protections as shareholders of a corporation. As
an owner of an LLC, you won't be at risk for more than the money
you invested—creditors won't be able to come after your personal
assets. However, professionals in one-person LLCs are still responsible for their own acts and omissions so the LLC provides
limited, if any, protection in these circumstances. An LLC is very
attractive to investors because of the combination of flexibility
and limited liability and the avoidance of the two-tiered tax on C
corporations.

ONE-PERSON LLCs ON THE HORIZON?

The major drawback for LLCs is the inconsistency among the states for certain requirements. For example, state laws initially required LLCs to have two or more owners. But new IRS regulations have spurred new laws in most states permitting one-person LLCs.

Three other features of LLCs make them attractive. First, the owners (called **members**) can have full or limited management rights, as desired. The limited partners in a limited partnership can't take part in the management of the business. And the three-tiered management structure of shareholders, directors, and officers of a corporation is often awkward. The members of an LLC can take an active part simply and directly.

Second, as a member you have some protection against unacceptable new members becoming involved in managing the business. Under many state LLC laws, members can freely transfer their *financial* rights in an LLC, but their right to participate in the governance may not be transferred without the consent of the remaining members. (Of course, the flip side is that the restriction may make it harder to dispose of your ownership interest in an LLC than your shares of stock in a corporation.)

Third, you and the other members can be creative in how you agree to divide profits and losses. There's no requirement that these be divided according to the percentage of ownership, but there is such a rule for corporations.

Want some more advantages? There are no restrictions on the number or types of persons who can be members of an LLC, or the types of ownership interests. That means LLCs can be used in far more situations than S corporations, which can have no more than 100 shareholders, all of whom, with the exception of certain types of trusts and estates, must be United States citizens or resident aliens. Your LLC, for example, can have a nonresident alien, a corporation, a partnership, or another limited liability company as a member.

HOW THEY GREW

The first LLC statute in this country was enacted in 1977 by Wyoming. Florida adopted a similar act in 1982. Very few LLCs were formed, however, until after 1988, when the Internal Revenue Service ruled that they would be taxed as partnerships rather than as C corporations as long as they met certain requirements. The two principal requirements were:

1. that the membership interests not be freely transferable; and

2. that the limited liability company not have the same type of continuity of existence as a corporation.

These requirements were relatively easy to meet under the existing LLC statutes. These days, any unincorporated business organization is *automatically* taxed as a partnership if it has two or more owners and as a sole proprietorship if it has only one owner, unless it elects to be taxed as a corporation. This means that LLCs are a very popular form of business for small businesses.

NEWNESS BRINGS UNCERTAINTY

Corporate law has had centuries to develop in the United States, resulting in a fairly stable set of laws dealing with most issues that may arise in operating a corporation. LLCs have existed only since 1977. As a result, state LLC laws differ greatly, and these differences can create uncertainty. Moreover, *state* taxation of LLCs also varies. Most states tax them as partnerships, but some states may still tax them as corporations. Others may impose a high annual license or franchise fee on LLCs.

In addition, because LLCs are "sort of" corporations and "sort of" partnerships, there is still some uncertainty in the law as to whether corporate law should apply to certain issues, or whether partnership law should apply. These and other uncertainties are caused primarily by the relative newness of this type of business organization.

THE WAVE OF THE FUTURE?

LLCs are on the way to superseding partnerships and S corporations as a preferred form of business organization for closely held business entities.

LLCs IN ACTION

LLCs can be used for virtually any type of business. LLCs are often used for businesses where pass-through taxation brings nice tax breaks. LLCs are widely used for:
- real estate ventures;
- extraction of oil, gas, and minerals;
- high-tech ventures—for example, a company formed to exploit a patent;
- corporate joint ventures;
- acquisitions;
- agriculture; and
- venture capital companies.

Because of their corporate-style limited liability, LLCs are also becoming more widely used by such professionals as doctors, lawyers, and accountants (see sidebar). Some states, however, do not yet allow certain professionals to practice as an LLC.

 PROTECTION AGAINST MALPRACTICE, TOO

Several states have laws that protect general partners against malpractice liability. Some even provide more complete protection than professional corporation statutes.

Partnerships choosing this status are called **limited liability partnerships**. They're discussed more fully in chapter 12.

ORGANIZING AN LLC

A limited liability company must have one type of document, and should have a second. The first is generally referred to as the **articles of organization**. This is the birth certificate for the LLC, just as the articles of incorporation is the birth certificate for the corporation. It must be filed in the office of the secretary of state in the state where the LLC is being formed. The legal requirements vary, but generally the articles of organization must contain the same type of information as required in a certificate of limited partnership. One difference is that most of the limited liability company statutes require the articles of organization to specify whether the LLC will be **member-managed** or **manager-managed** (a situation similar to having managing partners in a partnership) and to give the names and addresses of the members or managers.

The second, highly recommended, document is generally referred to as an **operating agreement**. Like the bylaws of a corporation, the operating agreement serves as the constitution for the limited liability company. It is also sometimes called the **member control agreement** or **regulations**. This agreement is similar in format and content to a partnership agreement and must be drafted with great care. It is also, in fact, somewhat like the shareholders' agreements prepared for some (but not all) corporations, but it may be more complicated and costly to prepare and may have to be done sooner than the shareholders' agreements, which can often be delayed. Such agreements do not have to be filed in any public office.

In addition, in some states, such as New York, the law requires LLCs to advertise their formation, and the advertising can cost more than the organization of a corporation.

Like a sole proprietorship and any form of partnership, an LLC must obtain various business licenses, permits, and tax identification numbers before starting to engage in business.

YOU MUST REMEMBER THIS

• Limited liability companies have many of the benefits of corporations but, depending on state law, may require fewer legal
formalities. However, be sure to check out the official filing costs.

• LLCs provide both protection against personal liability and
favorable tax status.

• LLCs are relatively new—expect some changes as this area
of law becomes clarified.

CHAPTER 15

So What's the Best Business Form for You?

We Lay Out Your Options—the Choice Is Yours

Willie and Lillie plan to start a business offering 1950s nostalgia items: instant sock hops for parties, gold lamé suits for him and her—the works. They've got some investors and capital and have done a marketing plan, but they don't know how to dot the legal i's and cross the legal t's. They've at least considered various legal forms for their business, but they're confused and uncertain, and what they really want is someone to tell them what they should do.

Sorry, Will and Lill, there is no answer that will work for all businesses—otherwise we'd have only one form of business organization.

Yes, one choice, the sole proprietorship, will work for many start-up businesses. If there's just you, and you're willing to risk some personal liability or have insurance to cover at least some of your liability risks, then this isn't a bad option.

But not all businesses have just one person—there may be two or three or more principals. For a variety of reasons you may want to give other people a piece of the action. And not all are on shoestrings: Some have investors or other sources of capital. Some want to operate in more than one state. Some "new" businesses may be building on the foundation of existing businesses.

Hiring an experienced business lawyer would help Willie and Lillie and other entrepreneurs who aren't in the sole proprietor mold make this critical decision. The lawyer could take some of the burden off of them by examining their particular situation, suggesting a business form, and then helping them take the steps to meet all the legal requirements. Accountants or other professionals who know about their business can also get

MIX AND MATCH

Don't forget that you may be able to adapt whatever form of business you choose by adding or subtracting characteristics. In other words, your choice doesn't always have to be "either/or." With some planning and legal help, it sometimes can be "both."

For example, if you want to restrict transfers of ownership interest—an inherent characteristic of partnerships—but you also want to be a corporation, you can have the best of both worlds through carefully crafted agreements among the shareholders. For example, in most situations business continuation agreements authorize the purchase of a departed owner's investment and allow the business to continue.

---

involved in these and other important issues that must be dealt with in setting up and operating a new business.

But in the final analysis, the decision must be made by the business owner, and often there are no clear answers, even if you do have professional help. You just can't meld all the relevant tax and nontax factors into a neat set of guidelines. You have to look at your situation carefully. What might be the best choice in one case might not be the best choice in a similar but slightly different set of circumstances.

It is important to revisit the issue on a regular basis. As your business grows, other forms of business entities may become more appropriate for you and your business.

The table on pages 173–176 summarizes the characteristics of the various forms. It will help orient you to the major differences between them. Here are some specific considerations you'll have to keep in mind.

KEEPING COSTS DOWN

If you're on a budget (and what start-up isn't?), you'll have to keep an eye on organizational and administrative costs. Sole proprietorships and general partnerships cost the least. They require no written documents or public filings, except possibly to comply with an assumed name statute. (However, you're certainly well advised to have a written agreement or general partnership agreement defining the rights and obligations of the partners.)

Also, sole proprietorships and partnerships generally pay no annual fees (other than business license fees and the like), but you'll have to contend with written documents and various filing and annual fees for all the other business forms. These expenses can mount up. And neither sole proprietorships nor general partnerships offer limited liability.

WHAT DO INVESTORS WANT/EXPECT?

You'll have to take into account the objectives and backgrounds of the other investors. For example,

• If one or more of the investors is transferring property to the business for an equity interest, that fact may have a big impact on the choice-of-business-form decision.

• Do the investors expect to take part in managing the business or be involved in some other way? Their level of participation is always an important factor in choosing the business form, as is the amount of capital each investor is contributing and whether the capital will be in the form of equity or debt.

 LOOK TO THE FUTURE

While you're weighing the tax factors, how's your crystal ball? Changes in tax laws and regulations can radically change the relative advantages of one form over another. These changes have occurred very frequently in the past several decades. If you or your attorney see one coming, one form of business might become a better choice than you first thought.

• How important is limited liability to the investors? The investors may not be familiar or comfortable with one of the newer forms of businesses, such as a limited liability company or limited liability partnership. And it's not just investors—the demands of the business's creditors can also have a bearing on the choice of the business form.

WHAT ARE THE TAX CONSEQUENCES?

Even though profits are but a glimmer in your eye, you'll want to look at both state and federal tax laws in making your decision. The form of business you select can make a big difference in the taxes you'll eventually pay.

A good basic principle is to have your earnings taxed once, not twice. And that generally means staying away from C corporations. As we previously explained, C corporation income is hit by a double tax. First, a C corporation must pay taxes on its taxable income at the rates specified. Then, in addition, the shareholders must pay taxes at the individual rates applicable to them for any income they receive from the corporation in the form of salaries or dividends.

The double whammy of both taxes is often higher than the taxes would be if the business was operated as an S corporation, partnership, or limited liability company. In all three, the taxable income of the business is taxed only one time to the owners.

The difference can be huge. A business taxed as a corporation that, for example, generates a significant amount of net capital gains income will have that income taxed at the corporate rate and then taxed a second time, in most cases, as ordinary income when distributed to the shareholders as dividends. If the business is eligible for pass-through tax treatment, on the other hand, the net long-term capital gains are passed through to the owners of the business, who pay taxes at the new favorable capital gains tax rates available to individuals. Although the tax laws change frequently, through the 2009 tax year, certain dividends

COMPARISONS OF 2008 INDIVIDUAL JOINT TAX RATES WITH C CORPORATION TAX RATES

Taxable Income	Joint Tax Rate	Taxable Income	C Corporation Rate
Up to $16,050	10%	Up to $50,000	15%
$16,051 to $65,100	$1,605 + 15% of amount over $16,050	$50,001 to $75,000	$7,500 + 25% of amount over $50,000
$65,101 to $131,450	$8,962.50 + 25% of amount over $65,100	$75,001 to $100,000	$13,750 + 34% of amount over $75,000
$131,451 to $200,300	$25,550 + 28% of amount over $131,450	$100,001 to $335,000	$22,250 + 39% of amount over $100,000
$200,301 to $357,700	$44,828 + 33% of amount over $200,300	$335,001 to $10,000,000	$113,900 + 34% of amount over $335,000
Over $357,700	$96,770 + 35% of amount over $357,700	$10,000,001 to $15,000,000	$3,400,000 + 35% of amount over $10,000,000
		$15,000,001 to $18,333,333	$5,150,000 + 38% of amount over $15,000,000
		Over $18,333,333	35%

Note 1: Qualified professional service corporations (i.e., where substantially all of the corporation's activities involve the performance of services in the fields of health, law, engineering, architecture, accounting, actuarial science, performing arts, or consulting) are taxed at a flat rate of 35% of taxable income.

Note 2: These are federal tax rates; the states may apply additional taxes.

and capital gains can qualify for tax rates that range from 0 percent to 15 percent. It is important to note that for short-term capital gains (for investments held less than one year) the tax rate can be as high as 35 percent.

Even if the total taxes paid by the C corporation and its shareholders on taxable income generated by the corporation are less than if the business were operated in another form, the difference in most cases will not be that substantial and will not justify operating a small business as a C corporation. Moreover, there are other tax disadvantages of operating a C corporation, including the tax liabilities incurred in liquidating a C corporation or converting it to another business form, which more than offset the possibility of lower annual taxes based entirely on a tax rate structure that can be changed at any time. Historically, C corporation tax rates have been *higher* than that of other business forms for most levels of taxable income.

A second general guideline is that if flow-through taxation is important, partnerships and limited liability companies usually provide more flexibility than S corporations. This is because of their ability under subchapter K of the Internal Revenue Code, which governs partnerships and limited liability companies, to authorize special allocations of income and losses and to make distributions of capital without triggering adverse tax consequences.

In this connection, "check-the-box" federal tax regulations remove much of the tax uncertainty and complexity of the taxes owed by partnerships and limited liability companies. In effect, partnerships and LLCs have the option of choosing whether to be taxed under subchapter K or as a corporation. This option is available only to unincorporated business organizations and therefore is not available to corporations.

It is possible for some corporations to choose whether to be taxed as C corporations or S corporations for federal tax purposes, but as we pointed out earlier, because of the strict eligibility requirements, not all C corporations can qualify to be S corporations.

LAW CAN PROVIDE FLEXIBILITY

When considering which form of business organization is right for you, remember that the law in your state may give you some particularly good choices. For example, if you want to avoid the sometimes awkward tripartite management structure of corporations, you'll find that some states require fewer formalities for close corporations but still give you the benefits of incorporation.

WHAT DOES YOUR STATE ALLOW?

Another factor to consider is the peculiarities of your state's laws. State laws differ, particularly regarding the newer forms of business entities such as limited liability partnerships and limited liability companies. That means the best choice for a particular type of business in one state may very well not be the best for the same business in another state.

For example, in most states only professional businesses can form a limited liability partnership. And even if the business qualifies, it might not be a good idea to form the business as an LLP because the liability protection of an LLP in that state is not as broad as it would be in, for example, a corporation.

DOING BUSINESS IN MORE
THAN ONE STATE

Do you intend to do business in at least one more state? If so, you'd better look into the laws of the various states where you expect to operate just so you're not blindsided by special problems. For example, you might not want to form a limited liability partnership if you expect a significant income from sales in a state that does not have a limited liability partnership act. That's because the courts of the other state might treat the partnership as

GETTING HELP FROM THE STATES

Many states provide help in selecting a form of business. Look for state information over the Internet by accessing www.state.[two-letter abbreviation of your state].us. Texas, for example, is www.state.tx.us. Once you have accessed the state's official Web page, look for a link for start-up businesses and selecting a business form, or locate a search box and enter a search term such as "business form."

a general partnership, thereby exposing the individual assets of the partners to creditors' claims arising in that state.

ELIMINATE THE IMPOSSIBLE

Finally, a suggestion no one could quarrel with: Eliminate the business forms that are clearly unsuitable or not available. For example, if there is only going to be one equity owner, then forming the business as a partnership is not possible because, by definition, a partnership must have two or more co-owners.

LIMITED LIABILITY BETTER

All things being equal, the less personal liability you have the better. But corporations may be cumbersome to organize and operate, as well as expensive to set up in your state. Maybe your new business should be formed as an unincorporated business entity having limited liability, rather than as a corporation.

Assuming there will be more than one owner, this means that the choice will be between a limited liability partnership, a limited partnership, and a limited liability company (which can have only one owner in just about all states). Which of these three will be the best depends in large part on the state statutes.

Limited liability partnership. If the statutes of the state where the business is to be formed provide some limited liability to general partners, and the business will not be conducting significant business in states that do not have similar LLP statutes, then forming the business as a limited liability partnership may well be the best choice. This is because lawyers and courts are fairly familiar with partnership law, whereas limited liability companies are a relatively new form of business and there are very few court decisions interpreting LLC statutes.

Under the same circumstances, a limited liability partnership will also probably be preferable to a limited partnership. This is because you must have at least one general partner in a limited partnership, and the general partner's personal assets will be exposed to the liabilities of the limited partnership, unless the general partner itself is a corporation, a limited liability partnership, or a limited liability company. In that event, however, there will be two separate entities, the general partner's entity and the limited partnership. This in turn will mean that two sets of business records will have to be maintained, two sets of documents will have to be completed, and two tax returns will have to be filed annually. The extra cost and administrative headaches involved in keeping up with two entities is hard to justify, when it is clear that all your objectives can be met by using one business entity.

Limited liability company. If a limited liability partnership is not available or does not offer the full extent of liability protection you want, then, between a limited liability company and a limited partnership, the best choice in many cases will be a limited liability company. Even though there are some legal uncertainties with regard to LLCs because of their relative newness, you will be able with one legal entity to achieve what it takes two entities to achieve if the business were operated as a limited partnership.

Limited partnership. Nevertheless, there will always be circumstances where a limited partnership will be the best choice, even though two business entities will have to be formed in order to obtain the desired limited liability protection.

IF YOU DECIDE ON A CORPORATION . . .

Another general principle or guideline is, if you decide to set up a corporation, you should form the business as an S corporation rather than as a C corporation. As we explained, this is because of potential tax savings. S corporation income, for the most part, is taxed only once, at the shareholder level, but C corporation income is taxed twice—at the corporate level and also at the shareholder level.

It is important to note that some corporations are not able to qualify as an S corporation. Or perhaps for other reasons—for example, the greater acceptability of C corporations in the securities markets—a C corporation will simply be the better choice.

IT'S UP TO YOU

These are merely a sample of the kinds of questions you might have to consider. Remember that it is you, the business owner, who must make the final decision on the legal form and on any other legal issue that must be resolved. What you are paying your lawyer for is to assemble all the necessary background information and to provide you with his or her best judgment and recommendations so that you can make an informed decision.

CHANGING YOUR MIND

What if you choose one form of business but find that it's just not working for you? Or what if you acquire a business and have to decide whether to keep the business organization it has or change to a different form? Alas, all this can be even more complex than the first decision you made about how to organize your business.

This additional complexity is largely due to tax laws that treat certain types of changes in form as **taxable liquidations** rather than as **nontaxable conversions**. In plain English, that means that some changes trigger certain taxes, while others are just treated as a change in business form that has no tax consequences.

Good conversions. It's generally possible to convert one type of unincorporated business form (sole proprietorship or partnership, for example) into another unincorporated form or into a corporate form without adverse tax consequences. Thus, if you are operating a sole proprietorship, you can convert it into a partnership, a limited liability company, or a corporation on a tax-free basis, assuming all other legal requirements can be met (e.g., to qualify as a partnership, there must be at least two co-owners). Likewise, if you and the other owners of a partnership wish to become a different type of partnership, a limited liability company, or a corporation, these conversions can also be accomplished on a tax-free basis. The same is true if you acquire an unincorporated business—generally you can convert it to another form without big tax headaches.

Bad conversions. On the other hand, if you go the other way—from corporation to an unincorporated form—in the eyes of the tax folks you're liquidating the business, with whatever tax consequences that brings. So if the business you own or acquire is a corporation and you want to convert it into a partnership or limited liability company, under existing federal tax law and the tax laws of most states, the tax would be based on the difference between the tax basis of the business assets and their fair market value at the time of the conversion. In many cases, the combined federal and state taxes will be so high that it may not be practical to make the conversion. This is why so many medical practices that are incorporated as professional corporations retain their corporate status even though the doctors in the firm would prefer to practice as a limited liability partnership or limited liability company.

That's not to say you can never convert from a corporation to another form without getting hit by taxes. In cases where there is very little difference between the market value and the tax basis of the assets, the amount of the total taxes incurred in a taxable conversion may not be too high. Moreover, in some cases

S TO C, BUT NOT C TO S

You can generally convert an S corporation to a C corporation without serious tax consequences, but converting an existing C corporation to an S corporation will trigger tax headaches. So if you've decided that a corporation is the best form of business for you and you meet the requirements of subchapter S, you'd better choose S status at the time you incorporate the business.

it may be possible to avoid the liquidation tax by diverting all new business to a newly formed unincorporated business form that has the legal characteristics you want. The old business entity would then continue in business at least until such time as all of its expenses and liabilities have been paid and all of the income from business transactions that took place before the new business entity was formed has been collected. For obvious reasons, expert tax assistance is necessary to achieve this result.

YOU MUST REMEMBER THIS

• If only one person is involved and the liability issues can be handled, then a sole proprietorship might well do the trick.

• Limited liability companies and limited liability partnerships can give you many of the benefits of corporations without as much hassle and possibly with tax advantages.

• If you do form a corporation, it's probably worth your while to try to qualify as an S corporation for tax reasons.

Characteristics	Proprietorship	General Partnership	Limited Liability Partnership	Limited Partnership	Regular (C) Corporation	S Corporation	Close Corporation	Professional Corporation	Limited Liability Company
Limited Liability	No	No	Yes	No, general partners; yes, limited partners	Yes	Yes	Yes	Yes, other than shareholders' own malpractice	Yes
Management rights of owners	All rights belong to sole proprietor	Yes, partners have equal say in management unless agreed otherwise	Same as general partnership	Yes, general partners; no, limited partners, who, however, have voting and other rights so long as they do not manage day-to-day operations	Shareholders elect directors, who in turn select officers and other agents	Same as regular corporation	Same as regular corporation, but a right to vary by agreement	Same as regular corporation, but a right to vary by agreement	Yes, same as general partnership, but most statutes specify that the members vote in accordance with percent ownership of capital

Characteristics	Proprietorship	General Partnership	Limited Liability Partnership	Limited Partnership	Regular (C) Corporation	S Corporation	Close Corporation	Professional Corporation	Limited Liability Company
Transferability of ownership interests	Freely transferable, but very limited market	Financial rights are transferable but transferee does not become a partner without the consent of all remaining partners	Same as general partnership	Same as general partnership unless agreement provides otherwise	Shares freely transferable and no distinction between financial and management rights as in partnerships and limited liability companies	Shares freely transferable but as a general rule transfers are restricted by share transfer restrictions agreements to protect the remaining shareholders against unacceptable transferees	Same as S corporation	Same as S corporation, but only licensed professionals of the same profession can be transferees	Same as general partnership
Business continuity on dissociation of owner	No	Can be limited; withdrawal of partner can result in a dissolution and liquidation unless all the remaining	Same as general partnership	Can be limited; withdrawal of a general partner results in dissolution unless business continued by agree-	Perpetual existence	Perpetual existence	Perpetual existence	Perpetual existence	Essentially the same as a limited partnership

			partners agree that the business should continue	ment of the remaining general partners; withdrawal of a limited partner generally has no effect on continuity					Can be same as partnership or sole proprietorship, but may elect to be taxed like a regular corporation
								Same as close corporation	
							Will be taxed as either a regular corporation or an S corporation		
						Except in limited circumstances, single tax at the shareholder level, basically similar to partnership			
					Double tax: income initially taxed at corporate level; shareholders pay additional tax on dividends and other distributions from the corporation				
				Same as general partnership					
			Same as general partnership						
		Single tax, partners include their pro rata share of income and deductions on their individual tax returns							
	Single tax, owner taxed directly								
Taxation									

Characteristics	Proprietorship	General Partnership	Limited Liability Partnership	Limited Partnership	Regular (C) Corporation	S Corporation	Close Corporation	Professional Corporation	Limited Liability Company
Distinctive features	There is no legal distinction between the sole proprietor as an individual and a business	(1) Unlimited liability of the partners; (2) lack of continuity because of danger of liquidation when a partner leaves	Available only to professionals in most states. All partners have limited liability to some degree: Partners are protected against vicarious liability for malpractice or torts of other partners	(1) Unlimited liability of the general partners but limited liability of the limited partners; (2) the inability of the limited partners to take part in the day-to-day management of the business	(1) Limited liability of the shareholders; (2) the three-tiered management scheme of shareholders, directors, and officers	(1) Limited liability of shareholders; (2) lack of flexibility because of restrictions on number and types of shareholders (individuals and some trusts)	(1) Limited liability; (2) ability to modify the management and free transferability characteristics of a regular corporation	(1) Exclusion of shareholders' own malpractice from limited liability; (2) only useful for those professionals who cannot have corporate limited liability because of ethical or statutory restrictions	Combination of the same limited liability as a corporation and the tax and nontax flexibility of a partnership

PART IV

A Section About People

Dealing with Employees and Customers

You never want to forget that business is ultimately about people. Whether they're working for you or buying from you, they are the lifeblood of your business.

They have a legal role, too. Depending on their role, they have a relationship with the business that's affected by the law.

Depending on the category those people who work for you fall into—regular staff, independent contractors, temps, etc.—very different laws can impact them. We discuss the legal pros and cons of each.

We look at ways of hiring (and, alas, firing) that will minimize potential legal hassles, and we discuss the many laws that affect how you treat employees on the job. We also look at injuries to workers and regulations governing a safe workplace.

Unfortunately, workers aren't the only ones who might get injured on your property or by one of your vehicles. We look at ways of limiting your potential liability to customers, suppliers, delivery people, and others in contact with the business.

Finally, your business's customers have legal rights that you should know about. We discuss the legal aspects of dealing with customers, including extending credit to them and trying to collect the inevitable slow (or no) payment.

Read on to find out how you can achieve the most from these close encounters of the business kind and minimize the legal risks.

CHAPTER 16

Hiring Employees

Hiring Without Hassles

Doug's business is thriving—the phone is ringing, orders are being faxed in, and he's working twelve hours a day with no end in sight. He'll do even better—and have more time for his family—if he has good help. He's not sure how to find the right people, though, and all the stories about lawsuits in the workplace have got him spooked. Can he add people without adding headaches?

Hiring your first employee is a big step for an emerging business: It's a rite of passage on your way to being truly established. For a growing business on the other side of that rite, adding people is a mark of continued progress. While there's no magic bullet that will absolutely guarantee trouble-free hiring, taking steps to avoid legal hassles dovetails very well with sound business practices.

WHO IS AN EMPLOYEE?

From a legal standpoint, the first question may seem an odd one: What, exactly, is an employee? Plenty of laws regulate the employment relationship, but they apply only if the individual is considered an **employee**. An **independent contractor** is *not* covered by the restrictions and obligations imposed on businesses, which apply only to employees. For example, you're required to pay for workers' compensation insurance for employees but not for independent contractors.

An **employee** is hired by a business to perform work under the control, direction, and supervision of the employer. He or she is paid an hourly wage or a salary. Usually the employer furnishes the equipment the employee uses to perform the job.

The fact that an individual is employed **part-time** does not affect her status as an employee. If she works under your control, for a wage or salary, using your equipment, she's an employee even at ten hours per week. (However, you might get a break in that some laws specifically state that they do not apply to part-time workers who work less than a certain amount of hours.)

An **independent contractor**, in contrast to an employee, is responsible for the costs of her own operation, including equipment and supplies. You generally pay a contractor on a per project basis. You hire her to perform a specific task or project but leave it to her to decide how to achieve the objectives.

Here's an example of an independent contractor relationship. You want a fence built around your business. Jones offers to build the fence for $1,000 and you agree. You do not supervise Jones's work or provide the tools used to build the fence. When the fence is completed, you pay Jones the $1,000, and your relationship ends.

Temporary workers also may limit your exposure to laws regulating the employer-employee relationship. If hired through an employment agency, they're probably not considered *your* employees. If you make an arrangement with an employment agency to send you a typist on a temporary basis and you pay the agency a fee for the typist's services, you will probably not normally be considered the typist's employer. Her employer is the

 A CONTRACT IS KEY

Though using temps and independent contractors might be simpler in terms of employment laws, you aren't completely free of legal concerns. You'll probably have to deal with contracts with the temp agency and maybe with your independent contractors, too. Make sure you know what you're agreeing to, and remember, you can try to negotiate to make the terms more acceptable.

personnel agency. The agency is responsible for making payroll deductions, hiring, firing, and paying the worker.

One way of accomplishing certain tasks is to use independent contractors and temporary workers. This can be simpler and less risky legally. It can reduce the cost of providing insurance to all employees and make it less costly for a business to have a general fringe benefit plan for the principal executives. It also may give you a chance to try out some people, see how they work, *then* decide whether to hire them. (You'll probably have to pay a fee to the temp agency to hire one of its employees.)

The downside is that you may want to have more continuity in your operation, and not want to be training people all the time. And certain jobs aren't suitable for independent contractors.

There are also potential tax risks. Either the business or a worker can file an IRS Form SS-8 to determine the worker's status for employment tax and income tax withholding purposes. (Workers who believe they have been misclassified as independent contractors instead of employees often file this form with the IRS.) The IRS uses a very complex multipart test that considers forty-five factors related to behavioral and financial control, the relationship between the worker and the firm, and interactions between the worker and the firm's customers to determine whether the worker in question should be classified as an employee rather than an independent contractor. If workers are reclassified as employees, withholding taxes and the like are

HEDGING YOUR BETS

Hiring a worker part-time is a good way to try the person out without making a big commitment. You can make a trial period part of full-time jobs, too. It's perfectly legal not to start any benefits until after a probationary period—ninety days is common—has been successfully completed.

assessed against your business. IRS Publication 15-A, *Employer's Supplemental Tax Guide*, provides information on classifying workers as employees or independent contractors.

HIRING? KEEP YOUR FOCUS

When you hire workers, you're obviously looking for people who are able and willing to do the job in question. One easy way to avoid most legal liability related to the hiring process is to focus on job skills, qualifications, and expectations. This places the emphasis where it should be—on filling the job. To the extent that your hiring decisions are based on job-related criteria, you will avoid most legal pitfalls. Decide what qualifications are required to do the job, put those qualifications in a written job description, and focus your hiring efforts on them as objectively as possible.

Most of the laws that impact the hiring process are aimed at status, rather than on a person's qualifications. The table on page 184 lists the major federal laws on employment that can be of concern to small-business operators.

Several federal laws deal with discrimination in hiring because the applicant is a member of a protected class. (A protected class is a group of individuals who are given special status under the law based on a group characteristic such as race, religion, color, national origin, gender, age, disability, or union activity.) **Title VII** prohibits employers from hiring or refusing to hire applicants because of race, gender, religion, national origin, or color. Title II of the **Genetic Information Nondiscrimination Act of 2008** (GINA) prohibits employers from using genetic information in deciding whether or not to hire someone. The **Age Discrimination in Employment Act (ADEA)** prohibits hiring decisions based on age (40 years or older). The **Americans with Disabilities Act (ADA)** prohibits an employer from refusing to hire qualified individuals with disabilities who, with or without reasonable accommodation, can perform the essential functions of the job. The **Uniformed Services Employ-**

ment and Reemployment Rights Act of 1994 (USERRA) prohibits employers from refusing to hire applicants because of their past, current, or future military obligations. The **National Labor Relations Act (NLRA)** prohibits employers from refusing to hire applicants because they are members of a union or because they favor union representation.

As you can see from the table on the following page, many of these federal laws do not apply to smaller businesses. However, almost every state has passed state statutes that overlap with the antidiscrimination prohibition of federal laws, and in some cases may go beyond. These state laws apply to most businesses operating within the state, and usually exempt only extremely small employers, such as businesses with fewer than five or fewer than three employees.

EXAMPLES OF ILLEGAL EMPLOYMENT DISCRIMINATION

- Refusing to hire an applicant because she is pregnant.

- Refusing to provide an accommodation to an applicant with a disability that would enable her to perform the job. For example, a typist who is blind applies for a clerical job. She is capable of doing the work if the computer had a Braille keyboard. You refuse to hire her because you don't want to buy such a keyboard. This refusal would be illegal unless you could prove that the cost of a Braille keyboard would impose an undue hardship on your business.

- Refusing to hire a Latino worker because he speaks with an accent.

- Forcing an employee to retire when he reaches the age of sixty-five.

- Refusing to hire an applicant because she is a member of the Teamsters Union.

- Refusing to hire an applicant because a genetic test reveals he has the potential to develop cancer.

Antidiscrimination Laws

Title	Coverage	Effect
Title VII of the Civil Rights Act of 1964 (Title VII)	Employers with fifteen or more employees	Prohibits employment discrimination based on race, color, religion, gender, or national origin
Title II of the Genetic Information Nondiscrimination Act of 2008 (GINA)	Employers with fifteen or more employees	Prohibits employment discrimination based on genetic information.
Age Discrimination in Employment Act (ADEA)	Employers with twenty or more employees	Prohibits employment discrimination because an employee is forty years or older
Title I of the Americans with Disabilities Act (ADA)	Employers with fifteen or more employees	Prohibits employment discrimination against qualified individuals with disabilities who, with or without reasonable accommodation, can perform the essential functions of the job
Uniformed Services Employment and Reemployment Rights Act of 1994 (USERRA)	All employers	Prohibits employment discrimination against veterans and requires employers to grant time off to employees to perform their military duty
National Labor Relations Act (NLRA)	Employers based on annual dollar volume of business that varies by type of business	Prohibits employment discrimination because employees have engaged in union activity or protected concerted activity

Moreover, many state antidiscrimination laws prohibit discrimination against an even broader range of persons than those protected by federal law. Some states have passed laws protecting applicants from discrimination because of:

- sexual orientation,
- marital status,
- arrest or conviction records,
- off-duty use of tobacco products,
- political party affiliation, and
- personal appearance.

You need to be aware of the employment laws of your state, since they vary from state to state.

SOME HIRING TIPS

Make the whole hiring process as objective as possible. Don't stereotype applicants in any way, but rather focus on what the job requires and how each particular applicant matches up.

Be careful with advertisements. Don't say or imply that a job is for one gender or the other (no "Gal Friday wanted"); don't engage in age stereotyping by saying you're looking for a "recent college grad." Make sure your ads get to a wide segment of the population. It never hurts to put in the ad "Equal Opportunity Employer."

Use checklists. Go into interviews with a series of questions that focus on the specific requirements of the job. Try to ask all applicants the same questions. Take notes.

Avoid questions that show stereotyping. You may want some assurance that an employee will be with you for at least a few years. Don't ask a female applicant, "Do you plan to get married?" "Do you plan to have children?" or "Is there a chance your husband will be transferred?" Keep the focus on the job. Ask, "Is there any reason you might not stay with us for the next few years?" or "Where do you see yourself in five years?" If you want to know if an applicant can work late from time to time, don't ask, "Do you have to be home to make the kids dinner?" Instead,

BENEFITS OPTIONAL

Contrary to popular belief, you're not required to offer employees any vacation time. And the law does not require you to offer health and pension benefits either. In a tight market for good people, you might want to offer benefits, but you don't have to.

---

simply ask, "Is there any reason you wouldn't be available to work late at certain times?" And, of course, ask the same questions of all applicants.

Ask only what you need to know. If filling the job doesn't require you to ask certain questions, then don't ask them. Do you have to know the applicant's marital status? Number of children? Religion? Age? Financial status? National origin? Then don't ask the question. (You may have to ask about some of these matters *after* a person is hired. For example, you might need this information for the purpose of a pension, health insurance, a contact in an emergency, or certification that the person is entitled to work in the United States. However, saving these questions for later ensures that they didn't influence the hiring process.)

USING REFERENCES AND BACKGROUND CHECKS

The law does not regulate requests for references. However, if you unnecessarily pry into private personal information or use unreasonable methods to gather data, you may open yourself to **tort liability for invasion of privacy**—in other words, you might face a personal injury lawsuit from a disgruntled applicant. You will generally be safe if you limit any background or reference check to issues relating to the performance of the job in question.

If you decide to run a credit check on prospective employees, you should be aware that this practice raises questions under both Title VII and the **Fair Credit Reporting Act**. Requiring good credit as a condition for employment has been held to adversely disadvantage minority candidates and thus raises issues of discrimination under Title VII. If you decide not to hire an applicant based on information obtained from a consumer credit reporting agency, the Fair Credit Reporting Act requires you to advise the applicant of that fact and provide him or her with the name and address of the agency that provided the report.

 ## SOME TIPS FOR WRITING JOB DESCRIPTIONS

These suggestions will help you focus on the qualities the person needs to do the job—and should help you avoid problems with laws against job discrimination.

- List the essential functions of the job: What are the core duties to be performed by the person holding the job? What percent of an employee's time is spent on each duty? What is the primary purpose for this job?

- List the requirements needed to perform the essential functions of the job: What skills are necessary to perform the job? What level of formal education or training is necessary to perform the job successfully? What, if any, work experience is necessary? What personal characteristics are linked to performing the job successfully?

- State where the job fits into the business structure: To whom does the person holding this job report? Is the person in this job responsible for supervising others?

- Set a salary level for the job.

USING PREEMPLOYMENT TESTS

The law limits the types of tests you can use to screen out unqualified applicants. To be on the safe side, any test should measure an applicant's ability to perform the job in question. Tests that are not job-related and that screen out disproportionate numbers of minorities or women have been held to violate antidiscrimination laws.

The ADA forbids requiring medical tests of applicants unless you've offered to hire the person and all employees who hold the job in question are required to take such a test. Any information obtained as a result of the test must be kept confidential, in a file separate from the applicant's personnel file, and cannot be used to discriminate against the applicant because of the result or any disability disclosed.

The **Employee Polygraph Protection Act** prohibits you from requesting or suggesting that applicants undergo a lie detector test. You can test for drugs, but several states regulate how you can conduct such a test. Talk to a lawyer experienced in labor and employment law in your state to ensure you don't run afoul of the law.

OTHER LEGAL REQUIREMENTS

Other laws directly affect the hiring process. Federal immigration law requires that all employers complete an eligibility form (**Form I-9**) for *every* employee hired. You can download a copy at www.uscis.gov/i-9 or you can contact the nearest office of the U.S. Citizenship and Immigration Services. The purpose of this form is to ensure that you have verified the legal eligibility of the applicant to be employed in this country.

The federal **Fair Labor Standards Act** (FLSA) regulates the conditions under which businesses can hire children. As a general rule, companies cannot employ anyone under the age of fourteen.

LIMITING THE HOURS OF WORK FOR MINORS

The FLSA and most state laws limit the number of hours that minors can work. As a general rule, children ages fourteen to fifteen cannot work during school hours. Under the FLSA, children are limited to a maximum of three hours of work on a school day and eight hours of work on nonschool days. In any event, they are prohibited from working before 7:00 A.M. or after 7:00 P.M. (9:00 P.M. in the summer). Some state laws have even stricter limitations.

Children who are fourteen to seventeen years old cannot be employed in industries that are defined by the statute as hazardous.

Even if your business does not generate a sufficient volume of business to be subject to the FLSA, every state also has laws on the employment of minors. As a rule, these state laws apply to all businesses that operate within the state, regardless of size.

Under state laws, special licenses are required for certain categories of jobs. In most states, if you want to hire a barber, cosmetologist, or nurse, you must require the applicant to have a specialized state license. Depending on the state, there may be other occupations that require a license as a condition for employment.

YOU MUST REMEMBER THIS

• You can dip your toe in the hiring water—and limit some potential legal hassles—by using temps and independent contractors.

• Lawful hiring means focusing on what the job requires, which also happens to be a very good way of finding the right people.

• Even though federal laws may not cover very small employers, state laws probably cover them. Make sure you know the laws of your state.

CHAPTER 17

Laws Affecting Employees

A Short Course on Law in the Workplace—and How Knowing What's Up Can Benefit You

> Doug has decided to take the plunge and hire his first employees. But he's worried about all the legal requirements of paying them, to say nothing of withholding the right amounts, paying the right taxes, etc. And how can he minimize other legal problems once his employees are on the job? Here's a quick look at the law's requirements and some steps that can lead to peace of mind.

The table on the following pages gives you a quick look at some of the major federal laws that regulate the workplace. Your state may have additional, overlapping, or supplemental laws.

Don't forget that, in addition to these laws, the antidiscrimination laws also apply to how employees are treated on the job (for example Title VII, GINA, ADEA, and ADA). We discussed these laws in the previous chapter on fairness in the hiring process, but they protect current workers, too. That means that you can't discriminate on the basis of race, religion, gender, color, national origin, age, or disability in:

- pay,
- promotions,
- vacations,
- hours of work,
- training programs,
- leave time,
- working environment,
- discipline, and
- discharge.

Employers subject to Title VII and the ADA (as well as similar state laws) are also required to make reasonable accommodations for employees with disabilities and for employees' religious beliefs. Employers are not required to make accommodations if they would cause an undue burden. Unfortunately, there are no hard and fast rules for what is a reasonable accommodation or what would constitute an undue burden—each situation must be decided on a case-by-case basis. A few examples can provide some guidance: An employer is expected to make some adjustments to work schedules, such as break times and working start and end times, as long as the adjustments are not overly disruptive to workflow and are generally fair to all employees; an employer is expected to provide a special chair to accommodate someone's disability, but not to install an elevator; and employers are expected to permit certain religious attire unless there is a significant business reason to prohibit the attire.

This chapter looks at some legal issues that affect all employers. For more information, have a look at another book in this series, *The American Bar Association Guide to Workplace Law.*

PAYING WAGES

The FLSA requires employers to pay a **minimum wage** of $7.25 per hour as of July 24, 2009. Businesses not covered by the FLSA are almost certainly covered by state minimum wage law. Most states' minimum wage is different from the FLSA level, either higher (approximately twenty-seven states) or lower (approximately six states); some have the same level (approximately twelve states), while five states (Alabama, Louisiana, Mississippi, South Carolina, and Tennessee) don't have a state minimum wage at all. In states that have set their minimum rate higher than the federal law, all employers doing business in that state must pay the higher rate, even if that business is covered by the FLSA. You will need to contact your state's department of labor to determine your applicable minimum wage.

The FLSA also exempts a variety of employees from the minimum wage, such as full-time students in retail and service establishments, employees at certain seasonal amusement or

Laws Governing Conditions of Work

Title	Coverage	Effect
Fair Labor Standards Act (FLSA)	Covers employers whose gross annual volume of business equals $500,000 or more	Requires employers to pay minimum wages and overtime compensation; regulates the employment of minors
Occupational Safety and Health Act (OSH Act)	Covers all employers engaged in a business affecting commerce	Requires employers to provide safe workplaces and to comply with safety and health regulations
Equal Pay Act (EPA)	Covers employers whose gross annual volume of business equals $500,000 or more	Requires employers to pay the same wages to male and female employees when they are performing substantially the same type of work
National Labor Relations Act (NLRA)	Covers retail employers whose gross volume of business equals $500,000 or more; covers manufacturing employers that ship or receive at least $50,000 worth of goods across state lines	Regulates the labor-management relationship and prohibits discrimination based on union activity
Family and Medical Leave Act (FMLA)	Covers employers with fifty or more employees (i.e., larger small businesses)	Requires employers to give employees up to twelve weeks of unpaid leave because of a serious medical condition or to care for ill family members, newborn babies, and newly adopted children; requires employers to reinstate workers to

		the same or substantially equivalent job after the leave is over. A recent amendment now provides up to 26 weeks of unpaid leave for a spouse, son, daughter, parent, or next of kin to care for a member of the Armed Forces, including a member of the National Guard or Reserves, who is undergoing medical treatment, recuperation, or therapy, is otherwise in outpatient status, or is otherwise on the temporary disability retired list, for a serious injury or illness.
Consolidated Omnibus Budget Reconciliation Act (COBRA)	Covers employers with 20 or more employees that provide group health insurance.	Allows ex-employees (except those terminated for gross misconduct) to personally pay group-rate premiums to maintain employer-sponsored health insurance for up to 18 months.

TAKING CREDIT FOR EMPLOYEE TIPS

Under the FLSA, if you have employees in jobs that customarily receive more than $30 a month in tips (for example, waiters and hairstylists), you are allowed to credit tips against the minimum wage. But regardless of how much an employee actually earns in tips, you're always required to pay at least $2.13 an hour. Of course, you are allowed to credit only the amount the employee actually receives in tips. The employee must always receive *at least* the minimum wage when wages and tips are combined.

recreational establishments, farm workers on small farms, newspaper delivery employees, and casual babysitters.

Employers must pay the minimum rate for every hour worked. **Hours worked** generally include all time spent by employees performing their job duties during the workday. If the employee's job requires travel during the workday, such as a service technician who repairs furnaces at customers' homes, the time spent traveling is considered hours worked. Hours worked also include preparatory time spent before the start of the workday when the preparation is necessary to perform the job. For example, workers who have to sharpen their knives at a meat processing plant, or workers required to wear special protective clothing at a chemical plant, must be compensated for this preparatory time.

Overtime

The FLSA and comparable state laws also regulate wage rates for **overtime** work. You must pay employees who work more than forty hours *during any workweek* 1.5 times their regular rate of pay for every hour worked over forty. In computing overtime pay, you must use the employee's regular rate of pay, not the minimum wage rate. Although many provisions of the FLSA apply

MYTH EXPLODED

Contrary to popular belief, you are not required to pay overtime because an employee is scheduled to work on weekends or holidays or just because an employee works more than eight hours in a workday. The key is whether the employee worked more than forty hours that week.

only to businesses with annual dollar volumes of $500,000 or more, the overtime regulations apply to all businesses.

You don't have to pay overtime to some categories of workers. The law cuts you a break on (meaning that the law exempts them):

- retail commission salespeople,
- outside salespeople,
- computer professionals,
- executive employees (as long as they earn more than $455 per week, manage the business, and supervise other employees),
- individuals who own at least 20 percent of the business,
- professional employees (including teachers and academic administrators in elementary and secondary schools), and
- administrative employees.

The law specifies certain conditions that must be met for an employee to be classified in one of these exempt categories. Merely giving an employee one of the above titles will not automatically make the employee exempt. Contact your local FLSA field office for a complete list of the factors that are considered in determining exempt status.

A SHORT GUIDE TO PAYROLL WITHHOLDING

You're required to withhold, deposit, report, and pay three separate types of federal employment taxes:

- income tax;
- Social Security and Medicare tax (required by the Federal Insurance Contributions Act [FICA]); and
- unemployment tax (required by the Federal Unemployment Tax Act [FUTA]).

You withhold the income and FICA taxes from employee wages and pay them to the government. You're also required to pay an amount equal to the employee's FICA withholding (in essence, a tax on you). As an employer, you're exclusively liable for FUTA taxes; employees don't pay any portion of them.

You must deposit income and FICA taxes in a financial institution qualified as a depository for federal taxes either monthly or semiweekly. Each quarter most employers are also required to file Form 941 detailing income and FICA tax payments.

Although these requirements may seem pretty daunting, the IRS does offer a guide to federal employment taxes: Publication 15, Circular E, *Employer's Tax Guide*. It's available from your local IRS office or can be accessed at the IRS Web site (go to www.irs.gov and search "Publication 15").

 THE STATES GET INTO THE ACT

Most employers are also required to withhold, deposit, report, and pay at least two separate types of *state* employment taxes: income tax and unemployment tax. The method for paying these taxes and the forms that must be filed vary by state. Contact your specific state department of revenue for information concerning state employment taxes. To find business tax information for individual states, visit www.business.gov, select "Finance & Taxes" from the menu, then select the "Taxes" submenu to reveal a "State Taxes" link.

PREVENTING SEXUAL HARASSMENT

Sexual harassment in the workplace gets plenty of attention in the media. But what is it, exactly—and more important, how can you avoid it in your business?

Two Types of Harassment

The law categorizes sexual harassment into two types of illegal actions. One type of sexual harassment, known as **hostile environment harassment**, consists of unwelcome physical conduct or verbal comments of a sexual nature that create a hostile working environment for the victim. The second type of sexual harassment, known as **quid pro quo harassment**, consists of subjecting the victim to unwelcome sexual advances, the submission to which becomes the basis for an employment decision.

The law gives you more defenses against the first type of harassment (see the following steps). To protect yourself against the second type, you have to be very vigilant that no employment decisions of any kind—from hiring and firing to promotions and demotions—are in any way influenced by supervisors' threatening reprisals for sexual rebuffs or granting preferences to reward employees who comply.

There are some important steps you can take to minimize your exposure to liability for sexual harassment, especially for hostile environment harassment:

1. The first step is to create a policy that clearly and absolutely prohibits sexual harassment ("zero-tolerance") and disseminate it to all your employees. This policy should define what type of conduct is prohibited and should also contain a mechanism by which an employee can bring a harassment complaint to the attention of management.

2. Make sure that all employees understand the policy. You should establish mechanisms to communicate the policy clearly and repeatedly to employees (at the minimum by posting it

WHAT ABOUT FALSE CHARGES?

What if you investigate a sexual harassment charge diligently but find there's nothing there? Are you justified in disciplining the employee who made the charge? The short answer is maybe, depending on the specifics of the situation. It may be that the employee making the charge acted in good faith but was overly sensitive, in which case disciplining the complaining employee could be viewed as illegal retaliation. However, if you feel that the employee is seriously off base or is using the complaint process maliciously against a fellow employee or against the company, you'd be justified in imposing discipline or even termination. If you have any doubt as to the actions you can take in response, consult with your attorney.

prominently on bulletin boards, but also by stressing it in regular employee meetings and training programs).

3. Make sure that the mechanism for making complaints is effective, and give employees an alternative route to complain if they allege that the harassment is by their supervisor.

4. Stress that there will be no reprisals for employees making such complaints.

5. If you do receive any complaints of harassment, actively and promptly investigate the complaints (using outside investigators if necessary) and, if complaints are well-founded, take immediate and effective action to stop the offending conduct and prevent it from recurring.

OTHER WORKPLACE ISSUES

Disciplining Employees

You generally have pretty wide latitude in deciding what rules to set and how to enforce any workplace conduct rules—unless you discriminate on the basis of race, gender, age, religion, disability, and so forth. You can provide employees with a list of punishable offenses, but you don't have to: You can decide on a case-by-case basis. Nor do you have to issue a warning before imposing discipline. (You probably would face certain limitations if your employees were unionized.)

But make sure that you don't violate the antidiscrimination laws. You should treat similarly situated persons the same. If you discipline a woman for missing work but don't discipline a man, you might face problems under Title VII, unless the circumstances were different for each employee—for example, he had a doctor's note justifying being absent and she had no legitimate excuse.

Smoking at Work

You're generally free to restrict smoking at work—to ban it altogether or limit it to certain areas. California bans smoking specifically in the workplace and many states and municipalities ban smoking in publicly accessible buildings, which include most workplaces. However, you may not be able to do anything about off-duty, off-premises smoking by employees. Approximately twenty states forbid you to discriminate against employees for their use of tobacco products away from the workplace.

Dress Codes

Dress codes are generally legal, but you shouldn't have a dress code for one gender and not the other. Dress codes are allowed to reflect social norms and professional dress, if required. Any dress code needs to be related to a legitimate business purpose. For example, a business is allowed to ban excessive body piercings for employees who have customer contact, and for all employees who prepare food. However, employers do need to be sensitive to certain religious requirements. For example, some women may be required to cover their heads with a scarf; some men may be required to grow certain facial hair.

English-only Rules

Requiring English on the job is fine as long as it's job-related and consistent with business necessity. But if the rule requires English during breaks and lunch time, it could run afoul of Title VII, since it could discriminate against persons of certain ethnic and national origins.

Health Insurance

You don't have to provide health insurance, but if you do, you have to make it available to all employees and administer it without discrimination. If you provide health insurance, Title VII requires that it cover pregnancy and pregnancy-related conditions. (Abortions don't have to be covered except where the life of the mother is endangered.)

If your policy covers spouses, it must cover male and female spouses, equally, including pregnancy and pregnancy-related conditions. Dependents' pregnancies don't need to be covered.

 OFF-DUTY CONDUCT

As a practical matter, many employers don't concern themselves with what their employees do in their off time. However, there aren't too many laws that require you to keep hands off of off-duty behavior. Some states, New York for example, forbid interference with employees' political activities. Twenty states prohibit employer discrimination based on marital status, and fourteen on sexual orientation. As noted earlier, approximately twenty states forbid you to discriminate based on employees' use of tobacco off premises. Mostly, though, this isn't a legal matter. One more caution: Prying into employee off-duty conduct may also subject you to tort liability for invasion of privacy, unless you can establish a legitimate business reason for the prying.

Family Medical Leave

The **Family Medical Leave Act** (FMLA) requires employers with fifty or more employees to provide up to twelve weeks of unpaid leave during any twelve-month period for employees for the birth and care of a newborn child, adoption of or foster care for a child, care for an immediate family member (spouse, child, or parent) with a serious health condition, as well as medical leave when the employee is unable to work because of a serious health condition. A recent amendment to the FMLA now provides up to twenty-six weeks of unpaid leave during any twelve-month period for a spouse, son, daughter, parent, or next of kin to care for a member of the Armed Forces, including a member of the National Guard or Reserves, who is undergoing medical treatment, recuperation, or therapy, is otherwise in outpatient status, or is otherwise on the temporary disability retired list, for a serious injury or illness. The FMLA applies to employees who have worked for the employer for at least twelve months. The employer must reinstate the employee to the same or a substantially equivalent position upon his or her return.

Employees' Financial Woes

Your employees' personal finances might affect you. If a creditor of an employee gets a court order of **garnishment**, you are required to withhold a certain amount from the worker's paycheck and pay it to the creditor. If the employee declares bankruptcy, federal law prohibits you from discriminating against him or her on that basis.

YOU MUST REMEMBER THIS

• The laws that prevent discrimination in hiring also forbid discrimination on the job. Make sure you treat similarly situated people equally.

• As an employer, you're a part-time (and unpaid) tax collector. The IRS expects you to withhold a portion of employees' wages. You'll also have to contribute toward employees' Social Security and Medicare and pay an unemployment tax.

• Federal (and sometimes state) laws govern such issues as minimum wage and overtime.

• You can minimize the risk of sexual harassment—but it takes vigilance and commitment.

CHAPTER 18

Terminating Employees

We Cover Everything from Tips on How to Let Someone Go to Noncompete Agreements

Barbara's got a big problem. Her first two hires went great. Her third was a disaster. Greg won't work, can't learn, and has a lousy attitude to boot. How can she get rid of him with a minimum of fuss and the least likelihood of legal trouble?

No matter how much time and effort you spend in trying to hire good workers, you can't be 100 percent successful. At some point you'll have to face the unpleasant task of firing someone. Here are some legal and practical ideas for terminating employees without adding problems.

From a legal perspective, you need to be most concerned about the *reason* for the discharge. Most workers are **employees at-will**. This means that you can fire someone with no notice and for any reason, *so long as the reason is not illegal*.

There are two general categories of illegal reasons: reasons that are specifically prohibited by federal or state antidiscrimination or antiretaliation laws, and reasons that are against state common law public policy.

 PROTECTION IN BIG SKY COUNTRY

Only one state, Montana, has placed a general restriction on an employer's ability to fire workers. The **Montana Wrongful Discharge from Employment Act** prohibits firing employees except for **good cause**. *Good cause* is defined as "reasonable job-related grounds for dismissal" for legitimate business reasons.

ANTIDISCRIMINATION LAWS

Title VII, the ADEA, the ADA, USERRA, and the NLRA all prohibit employers from firing workers if the reason for the decision is membership in one of the protected classes listed in the laws or union activity. (See chapter 17 for the scope and coverage of these laws.)

Most states have passed laws that parallel the antidiscrimination prohibitions of the federal laws but also apply to smaller employers doing business within the state. Thus, even if your business is not covered by federal antidiscrimination laws, your state probably has a law prohibiting the same things.

Moreover, as mentioned in chapter 17, many state antidiscrimination laws contain a broader range of protected classes or activities than the federal laws. A few states, such as New York and Colorado, prevent you from firing workers for *any* lawful off-duty conduct, as long as it has no bearing on the business.

Finally, a federal law, the **Jury System Improvements Act**, prohibits employers from firing workers because they have been called to serve on a federal jury. About three-quarters of the states have similar laws prohibiting firings because employees have been called for jury service in the state court system.

The **Uniformed Services Employment and Reemployment Rights Act of 1994** (USERRA), which applies to all employers regardless of size, provides a special protection against firing. The broad prohibition against firing workers who are or have been members of the uniformed services is supplemented by a special provision dealing with employees reinstated to their jobs after a leave of absence for military duty. USERRA provides that a person who is reemployed cannot be fired *except for cause* within one year after reemployment, as long as the employee's period of military service was more than 180 days. If the employee's period of military service was more than 30 days but less than 181 days, you cannot fire the worker *except for cause* within 180 days after reemployment.

CHECKLIST FOR HOW TO FIRE AN EMPLOYEE

Obviously, few of us look forward to letting an employee go. The experience will never be pleasant, but taking a few precautions can prevent it from being the overture to a lawsuit.

- Identify potential problems early. Don't ignore employee performance or workplace problems.

- Make your expectations clear. Talk with an employee who is having problems and clearly explain how the employee does not meet expectations and what he or she must do to fix it.

- Document the case against the worker. Keep a detailed record of incidents, disciplinary action, and conversations regarding performance.

- Dismiss the worker in a face-to-face meeting, preferably with a witness present.

- Hold the termination meeting in a private place at the end of the workday.

- Have the final paycheck ready to give to the dismissed worker.

ANTIRETALIATION LAWS

Antiretaliation laws prohibit you from firing workers because they have attempted to enforce their rights under various federal and state employment laws. For example, if you fire a worker because he filed a complaint with the Department of Labor contending that he had not been paid overtime, the discharge would be illegal.

A subcategory of antiretaliation laws covers discharging employees who report suspected violations of state or federal laws, rules, or regulations. This type of statute is generally known as

whistle-blower laws. Whereas the antiretaliation laws are limited to the enforcement of the specific rights contained in *employment-related* statutes, the whistle-blower laws are meant to protect workers who report a suspected violation of *any* statute.

The scope of whistle-blower laws varies considerably by state. Federal law protects some whistle-blowers from termination. Some states have no such laws; others protect only government workers. However, a significant number of state whistle-blower laws also protect additional workers. These laws sometimes protect employees only if they have reported the violations to a particular person, such as an appropriate government agency or to an agent of the employer.

PUBLIC POLICY EXCEPTION

In almost every state, the courts have also stepped in to limit, in some circumstances, an employer's otherwise unrestricted right to fire workers. In these states, courts have adopted a **public policy exception** to the employment at-will doctrine. This exception makes an employer subject to **tort** (personal injury) lawsuits for damages an employee suffers when the reason for the firing violates a principle of state public policy. **Public policy** is the lawmakers' view of what is in the best interests of the public. The public policy of the state can generally be found in the state constitution, laws, and regulations, and sometimes in state court decisions.

Courts generally recognize four kinds of reasons for discharge that raise public policy concerns:
- firing an employee who refuses to perform an illegal act;
- firing an employee who reports a violation of state law;
- firing an employee for engaging in acts that state public policy encourages; or
- firing an employee for exercising rights granted to that employee by a specific law.

States vary in the exceptions they recognize. A few recognize all four exceptions, but most recognize only one or two.

EMPLOYEES WHO HAVE CONTRACTS

There is another category of workers who may have protections against being fired for any reason or no reason. Workers with **employment contracts** are not governed by the at-will doctrine. Rather, the specific terms of their contracts govern the circumstances under which they may be fired. Some workers, usually highly skilled professionals or executive employees, have written contracts setting forth the length of employment and detailing the circumstances under which they can be fired. Such contracts are individually negotiated between the worker and the business owner at the time the employee is hired. Employment contracts are rare in the world of small business.

Collective bargaining agreements are another kind of employment contract, and they cover many more workers. They're negotiated between employers and unions and contain the terms of employment for a particular group of workers. These contracts usually provide that employees can be discharged only for just cause.

Lastly, the law sometimes recognizes **implied contracts** between the company and its workers. An employer can inadvertently create such a contract by written manuals or verbal statements that suggest he or she will discharge employees only under certain conditions. An example would be some sort of overly enthusiastic oral welcome or chipper language in an employee manual, something like, "as long as you do your job, your job is secure here at Barbara's Bakeries." The implication is that they can't be let go unless they don't do their job, and that can be hard to prove. And what if you need to let some good people go because business is bad?

You can avoid creating such a binding contract by clearly and unambiguously informing employees in writing that policies contained in any handbook or manual are not meant to create a contract. Also, many employers include a written statement on their application forms stating that if an employee is hired, he or she is employed at-will and can be discharged at any time for any reason, and that no individual within the company is authorized to make any promises to the contrary.

EMPLOYEE CLAIMS FOR UNEMPLOYMENT COMPENSATION

Most employees, when they are terminated, file for state unemployment compensation (UC). In most states, workers are entitled to receive UC if they are unemployed because of plant closure, layoff, or other acts or circumstances that are not their fault. However, workers are disqualified from receiving UC if they voluntarily quit without good cause, if they are fired for misconduct, or if they have not worked the minimum amount of time specified by state law.

When one of your ex-workers files for UC, the state notifies you. You can contest the payment by filing a written statement detailing why the worker is ineligible to collect UC.

Appeals of the initial eligibility determination are heard before an administrative hearing officer in a relatively informal type of hearing. Often, neither you nor the claimant will be represented by an attorney at this hearing.

A hearing officer's decision can be appealed to the state's administrative board, whose decision can be appealed to the state court.

CONTINUING EMPLOYEE HEALTH INSURANCE

The **Consolidated Omnibus Budget Reconciliation Act** (COBRA) is a federal law that gives terminated employees the opportunity to continue their ex-employer's group health insurance coverage. COBRA applies to businesses with twenty or more employees that offer group health insurance coverage for their employees. COBRA is available to terminated employees who had participated in the group health insurance coverage (though it does not apply to employees who were terminated for gross misconduct). The employer is required to notify the health insurance plan administrator within thirty days of the termination, to allow the administrator to send the proper forms to the ex-employee so that the ex-employee has the opportunity to continue the health insurance coverage for up to 180 days (the ex-employee is responsible for paying the premium). The same procedures apply for a surviving spouse and dependents, but note also that longer coverage may be available to spouses and dependents if a qualifying event such as divorce or death occurs.

REFERENCES

From time to time, you'll probably be asked to provide references for ex-employees. This may be because of a request from the worker or a prospective employer.

Generally, you are not legally required to provide a reference. Eleven states, however, have passed laws requiring an employer, sometimes in limited circumstances, to provide, upon the request of the employee, a letter stating the nature of the employee's job, the length of employment, and the reason for separation.

If you do decide to provide a reference, you must be aware of certain legal implications. Most states have **blacklisting** statutes. Blacklisting consists of intentionally trying to prevent someone from getting a job. However, *truthful* statements about someone's ability to perform the job in question are not considered blacklisting.

The content of a reference may also give rise to liability under state tort law for:
- defamation;
- intentional interference with prospective employment contracts;

- negligent misrepresentation; or
- intentional infliction of emotional distress.

Defamation occurs when one person's false statement injures the reputation of another person. Providing false information to a prospective employer with the intent to cause an applicant to lose the job constitutes **intentional interference with a prospective employment contract**. False statements that cause a loss of money (such as a wage-paying job) can be grounds for **negligent misrepresentation**. The premise behind all of these tort actions is that the employer's statement is false. Making truthful statements concerning a former employee usually does not subject you to liability for defamation, interference with contract, or misrepresentation.

Moreover, most states recognize a **qualified privilege** defense to charges of defamation. This defense applies when a former employer provides information to a prospective new employer about the employee's ability, job performance, or other work-related information. The former employer will be protected even if the information turns out to be false, as long as the

CHECKLIST FOR GIVING REFERENCES SAFELY

Because of the potential pitfalls involved, many employers refuse to provide references. Others provide only basic information, such as verifying the former employee's dates of employment and job duties performed. Employers who do provide references can limit their exposure to liability by:

- limiting the number of individuals authorized to provide references;

- avoiding statements based on hearsay or gossip; and

- discussing only issues that have a direct bearing on an individual's work.

information in the reference was provided in good faith. However, you can lose the qualified privilege if:

- you were motivated primarily by ill will in making the statement;
- you provided the information to individuals who did not have a legitimate reason to receive it; or
- you did not have grounds for believing the statement was true.

Disclosing even true information, moreover, can result in tort liability for **intentional infliction of emotional distress.** You can be liable for disclosing even true information if the information is private and personal, the employee has a reasonable expectation that it will be kept private, and the information is unrelated to work.

COVENANTS NOT TO COMPETE

Sometimes employees acquire specialized and valuable knowledge as a result of working for you and your business. You may be concerned that once they leave you they'll use this information to compete against you.

You can protect yourself with **covenants not to compete.** These are written contracts that restrict workers' ability to compete against you after leaving your employment for a certain period of time and in a certain geographic area. For example, a contract might provide that a financial adviser will not provide financial services to customers within a twenty-five-mile radius of the employer's place of business for twelve months after leaving the company.

Because covenants not to compete limit an individual's ability to earn a livelihood, they are valid and enforceable only under very limited circumstances. The purpose behind the covenant is to protect you from *unfair* competition caused by the fact that, while working for you, someone gained:

- specialized knowledge unique to your business (for example, trade secrets);

- access to customer lists that are not otherwise easily accessible; or
- specialized skills.

Thus, a covenant protects a substantial right unique to a particular employer or business. This involves a judgment call, and it's not easy to lay down hard and fast rules. However, a covenant between a securities firm and one of its salespersons may be enforced, because the sales representatives had access to a highly valued list of particular investors. A covenant between a retail store and an in-store salesperson based on that employee's access to customers would not be enforced, since there is probably nothing particularly valuable in the access to an array of people who walk in the door.

Even if your covenant seeks to protect unique and substantial business interests, you have to be careful that the scope of the contract is reasonable in terms of time limits and geographic

NEGOTIATING COVENANTS NOT TO COMPETE

If your business interests require protection through a covenant not to compete, it's generally best to negotiate an agreement when the employee is initially hired. Some states will enforce such covenants only if they were signed at the time the employee was hired. Most states, however, will enforce covenants not to compete that are signed as a condition of continued employment as long as the employee actually worked for a reasonable period of time after signing the covenant. In addition, some states require that independent consideration (such as increased salary or change in status) must be given to a current employee in exchange for the employee's signing a covenant not to compete.

Courts will enforce a valid covenant not to compete either by issuing an order preventing the former employee from working in violation of the terms of the covenant, or by awarding money to the former employer for losses resulting from unfair competition.

area. Reasonableness depends on the specific facts of each case. Generally, time limits of one year are reasonable but over three years are not. Geographic limitations should be restricted to the area in which the employee had worked.

California courts will generally not enforce a covenant not to compete between an employer and an employee; however, they sometimes enforce covenants not to compete arising from the sale of a business or the dissolution of a partnership.

YOU MUST REMEMBER THIS

- Be professional in how you treat employees. Sticking to job performance and avoiding extraneous stuff will help both in terminating people and in giving references.
- Make a record when you fire someone—just in case. Be able to document problems, warnings, etc., that led to the firing, and have someone you trust witness it so there's no question of what was said.
- Be careful what you say when you hire someone—don't imply job security that you don't want to back up.

CHAPTER 19

Maintaining a Safe Place of Business

For Your Employees, Customers, Business Contacts, and Other Folks on Your Premises

As if you didn't have enough to worry about . . . there's a pothole big enough to sink a midsized dog in your company's parking lot, the stairs are worn and slippery, and the carpeting near the door is loose. You're an accident waiting to happen! Of course, you should fix these and other hazards—but what are your legal responsibilities, and how can you minimize your exposure to risk?

U nder the law, maintaining a safe business and working environment is your responsibility as a business owner. As with so many aspects of the law, you're well advised to stop trouble before it starts. Take steps to make sure the premises are safe and stay that way.

No amount of precaution, however, can guarantee that injuries won't take place. When they do, your legal liability may hinge on who is injured. Your liability varies, depending on whether the injured party is a customer or employee. In general:

• injuries to customers are governed by state **tort** law;

• injuries to workers are governed by state **workers' compensation** law;

• the federal **Occupational Safety and Health Act** (OSH Act) imposes an obligation on you to maintain a safe and healthful work environment so as to prevent injuries to your workers.

PREMISES LIABILITY

State tort law is designed to compensate people for harm resulting from someone else's action or failure to act. Tort law—also called

personal injury law—encompasses many different types of things. Automobile collisions, injuries due to slipping and falling, defamation, assault, and intentional infliction of emotional distress are just a few examples. The part of tort law that deals with a business owner's liability (legal responsibility) for personal injuries sustained by people who are present on the property is known as **premises liability**. In general, you can be found liable if the injuries were due to your negligence or fault. You can also be found liable if your employees were negligent or at fault.

The principles of premises liability are based on each state's common law of torts. The specifics vary from state to state. We can't provide an exact answer to your particular situation. We will, however, outline the general rules that can help you assess the possibility of liability when accidents causing injuries do occur.

Premises liability is centered on these basic principles:

• you owe a *duty* to a person on your property to prevent foreseeable harm; and

• your *breach* of this duty is the proximate cause of injury to the person.

The degree of duty you owe to third parties varies depending on which state's law is being applied. In some states, the degree of duty owed is based on the status of the third party. In these jurisdictions, a person present on your premises can be categorized as either an **invitee**, a **licensee**, or a **trespasser**.

Invitees

If the person is an invitee (the most common and most important category of visitor), the law imposes several duties on you. There is a duty to exercise reasonable care to avoid injury to the invitee, as well as a duty to act prudently to discover unreasonably dangerous conditions and either make them safe or warn the invitee of the danger. If you warn, the warning must be specific enough to inform the visitor of the risk. Thus, a sign proclaiming "DANGER" will not suffice, whereas "CAUTION, WET FLOOR" is adequate.

WHO IS AN INVITEE?

Invitee is the legal word that covers most of the visitors to your premises. An invitee can be either public or business in nature.

- A **public invitee** is a person who is invited to enter or remain on the property as a member of the public for a purpose for which the property is held open to the public. Examples are children accompanying their parents to a store, people attending public meetings held on the premises, or social guests of hotel patrons.

- A **business invitee** is a person who is invited to enter or remain on the property for a purpose directly or indirectly connected to your business. Examples are customers in stores, patrons in bars and restaurants, delivery personnel making pickups and deliveries at the business, and independent contractors performing work on the premises.

Licensees

If the person is a licensee, you have a duty to exercise reasonable care not to injure the licensee and to warn a licensee of any unreasonably dangerous conditions that are known to you but that would not be obvious to the licensee. You are under no obligation, however, to inspect the premise for unknown dangers (as is the case for invitees) or to warn against unsafe conditions that would be known to the licensee.

The basic point for both invitees and licensees is that you must conduct your activities on the premises to reasonably avoid injury to these parties. You can also be held responsible for unsafe conditions caused by your employees. You will generally be held liable for injuries caused by employees when they are acting within the scope of their employment.

WHO IS A LICENSEE?

A licensee is a person who is privileged to enter or remain on land only by virtue of your consent as owner. Your consent may be either express or implied. Examples are someone who enters the premises to meet an employee for lunch, people who come onto the premises to get out of the weather, or members of the general public who use your parking lot under circumstances indicating you don't object.

Trespassers

What if the third party is a trespasser? A trespasser is a person who enters or remains on your property without your consent. Examples are burglars or people who cross the property to take a shortcut. With these interlopers you have only the duty of refraining from conduct that constitutes willful or reckless disregard for the trespasser's safety. However, business owners owe a higher duty to trespassing children when they may be attracted to the property by an artificial condition, such as a swimming

 ## NOT IN EVERY STATE

Some states do not use this type of classification scheme based on the status of persons on the property. In these states, you have the duty to exercise ordinary reasonable care **under the circumstance** to prevent reasonably foreseeable risks of harm to third parties. In deciding what is reasonable care under the circumstances, however, the courts in these states often take into account whether the third party is an invitee, licensee, or trespasser.

pool or an excavation site. Owners must take steps (such as fences) to protect children from these "attractive nuisances."

WHAT WILL YOU OWE IF FOUND LIABLE?

If someone successfully proves that his or her injuries were caused through your fault as the business owner, you can be liable for the payment of both **compensatory** and **punitive** damages.

Compensatory damages include medical expenses related to treating the injury, past and future earnings lost as a result of being unable to work or being limited in one's ability to work, and monetary compensation for pain and suffering endured by the injured party.

Punitive damages are recoverable only if the plaintiff can prove that you acted maliciously or with gross negligence. The jury determines the amount of punitive damages based on its reasonable judgment as to the amount necessary to punish the wrongdoer and to deter similar misconduct in the future. Punitive damages are rather rare.

LIABILITY FOR INJURIES TO WORKERS

The system for handling injuries to workers is very different from the way other injuries in the business place are handled. In a

 INSURANCE IS A MUST

Besides making your place of business as safe as possible, you'll want to protect yourself from liability awards by carrying enough insurance. Protection against the risk of being found liable for damages is part of standard business insurance policies, just as it's part of homeowner's insurance. See chapter 10.

nutshell, workers may find it easier to collect damages (they don't have to prove fault), but the benefits are limited (no pain and suffering, for example).

Workers' compensation is a state-based system for compensating employees who are injured in work-related accidents. In establishing workers' compensation systems, the states virtually did away with tort-based liability for employee workplace injuries. Workers' compensation is now the only way an employee can seek money for the vast majority of work-related injuries.

Whereas the plaintiff in a tort suit must prove that you breached a duty owed to him or her, under workers' compensation the employee need not prove that your fault or negligence in any way caused the accident. It is, in essence, a no-fault scheme. The trade-off for the employer, who is being held strictly liable for workplace accidents, is that the amount of recovery is less than what is normally available in a personal injury lawsuit.

 ## THE FEW EXCEPTIONS

As a general rule, an employee cannot bring a tort-based personal injury lawsuit against you or against co-employees when the injury results from a work-related accident. Instead, employees can seek redress through workers' compensation systems. There are, however, a few exceptions to this rule. The most common exceptions are:

- the conduct in question constitutes a nonphysical tort (for example, defamation, intentional infliction of emotional distress, or false imprisonment); or

- the employer acts with willful and wanton negligence (for example, the employer fraudulently conceals from its workers that they have contracted asbestosis as a result of workplace conditions and continues to expose them to the hazard).

What Workers Get

Three types of benefits are payable under workers' compensation:

• medical benefits that cover the cost of treatment and rehabilitation;

• disability benefits that cover the loss of earnings due to the injury; and

• **burial** and **survivor** benefits.

Disability benefits are paid when an injury causes either a temporary or a permanent disability. The level of benefits paid is based on state law and thus varies from state to state. When workers are temporarily unable to work because of injury, they receive a fixed weekly benefit based on a percent of their regular salary (usually 50 percent to 66 percent). A worker who is permanently disabled, either partially or totally, receives a payment designed to compensate for the decrease in earnings due to the permanent nature of the disability. The amount paid may be determined either by a **schedule,** a state-devised list that specifies wage loss for specific disabilities or by a percentage of weekly earnings. (For example, a person who loses an arm may be entitled to the equivalent of 312 weeks' compensation.) However, it appears the trend is moving toward calculating by weeks' compensation as opposed to a set amount.

Survivor benefits are paid to a spouse and children when a workplace injury causes the employee's death. The spouse receives a percentage of the employee's weekly wage until remarriage; the children also receive a percentage of the weekly wage until they reach the **age of majority** (i.e., the age they're considered to be adults).

Who Is Covered?

Almost all states require every employer, regardless of size, to provide workers' compensation coverage for all its employees. A few states, however, exclude extremely small employers (for example, an employer with fewer than three employees). Also, some state laws exclude certain categories of workers, and you're not required to provide coverage for them. Examples are casual employees, agricultural employees, and domestic workers. Of course, since independent contractors are not employees, they too are excluded from workers' compensation coverage.

Who Pays?

Workers' Compensation benefits are funded by insurance paid for exclusively by the employer. You *cannot* ask or require employees to pay any portion of the premiums. You get insurance coverage in one of three ways:
- payroll tax paid into the state workers' compensation fund;
- insurance premiums paid to private carriers; or
- self-insurance.

Although a few states require you, as the employer, to purchase insurance through a state fund, most states require that you purchase insurance through a private insurance carrier. And the larger your enterprise is, the more likely you will be allowed to self-insure, as long as you can present evidence of general financial responsibility or post a security or surety bond.

Whether you should choose coverage through a state fund or private insurance depends on the premiums charged. As with most insurance, the premiums reflect, in part, the claims experience of the particular employer. Ultimately, you will have to check with your state's workers' compensation agency to learn what your state laws require, or which options are allowed.

What's a Work Injury?

The kinds of injuries that will be paid under workers' compensation include injuries caused by defective machinery, fires or explosions at work, repeated lifting of heavy equipment, or slipping on an oily floor. The basic standard is that an employee whose injury or illness "arises out of and in the course of employment" is entitled to compensation. An injury "arises out of" employment if there is a causal connection between the injury and the employment. Thus, an injury suffered at work by a female employee who is hurt by her husband because of a domestic dispute does not arise out of the employment; rather, it is a personal risk. On the other hand, many states would find that an injury suffered by a night clerk at a convenience store who is shot by a thief does arise out of employment.

In determining whether an injury occurs "in the course of" employment, state laws consider the time, place, and circumstances in which the injury occurs. Thus a worker injured in an automobile accident on his commute to work is not covered, whereas a repairperson injured in an automobile accident while driving to a customer's home is covered.

Most states' workers' compensation laws also cover illness or occupational disease caused by working conditions. Generally, in order for an illness or disease to be compensable, the job must present a greater risk of contracting the illness than the normal risk of everyday life. Thus, a clerk who catches a cold from a coworker will not be compensated, whereas a textile worker who contracts brown lung disease would receive compensation.

 ## DETERMINING IF AN INJURY IS WORK-RELATED

Standards to determine if the injury is covered under workers' compensation vary state by state, but there are some common factors that the courts look to in determining that an injury is work-related:

- the activity that caused the injury was for the benefit of the employer;
- the employee was paid for the activity;
- the activity occurred on the employer's premises; and
- the activity was supervised by, or approved by, the employer.

The Claims Process

Most states require employees to notify you as soon as possible after they have sustained a work-related injury. The employee then must file a written claim with either you or your insurance carrier. If you do not contest the claim, benefit payments begin. If you contest, the employee must then file the claim with the state workers' compensation board. The board will hold a hearing to determine whether the employee is entitled to benefits and, if so, the amount due. The board's decision can be appealed to state court.

PREVENTING INJURIES AT THE WORKPLACE

The **Occupational Safety and Health Act (OSH Act)** is a federal law aimed at preventing workplace injuries. Unlike personal injury and workers' compensation discussed in the two previous sections of this chapter, the OSH Act does not provide compensation to people who are injured. Rather, its regulatory provisions are aimed solely at you, the employer. The law imposes on you specific duties and obligations designed to ensure safe and healthy working conditions.

Also, unlike personal injury and workers' compensation, the OSH Act is a federal statute. The requirements imposed by this law are the same regardless of what state your business is located in. The OSH Act applies to all private-sector employers who are engaged in business affecting interstate commerce, regardless of the number of employees or the size of the business. Even if you think your business is strictly local, you're probably affecting interstate commerce. All it takes for your business to affect interstate commerce, for example, is to buy goods produced out of state, supply goods or services to other businesses that are either located out of state or that are engaged in interstate commerce, or use the mail or Internet to conduct business.

The OSH Act imposes three obligations on you:

- First, you are required to furnish a workplace "free from recognized hazards that are causing or likely to cause death or serious physical harm" to employees. This requirement means that you must eliminate recognized hazards that are preventable.

- Second, you are required to comply with the specific safety and health standards of the **Occupational Safety and Health Administration** (OSHA), the federal agency responsible for enforcing the law. There are some generally applicable standards, such as those requiring that places of employment be kept clean and orderly and that exits be clearly visible, accessible, and unlocked. Other standards are tailored to the workplace conditions of specific industries, such as health care or construction.

- The third requirement is that if you have eleven or more employees, you must maintain a log and summary of all occupational injuries and illnesses, along with supplemental records detailing each illness and injury.

 EXAMPLES OF OSHA STANDARDS

- Floor surfaces must be kept as clean and dry as possible.

- Personal protective equipment must be provided if there are hazards capable of causing injury through absorption, inhalation, or physical contact.

- If a place of business is not within close proximity to a hospital or clinic, there must be a person on the premises adequately trained to perform first aid.

- Other standards set maximum levels for noise exposure or specify maintenance requirements for equipment.

You Might Be Inspected

OSHA inspects worksites to make sure they're complying with the law. An inspection is initiated by one of three means:

1. OSHA itself can initiate an inspection;

2. an employee can request OSHA to conduct an inspection; or

3. a workplace fatality or accident can trigger an inspection.

An inspection begins when the compliance officer presents herself at the workplace and requests entry. An employer may refuse entry if the officer does not have a warrant, in which case the officer will obtain a warrant from the court, authorizing the inspection.

During the inspection, the officer is authorized to inspect any condition at the workplace as well as machines, materials, and any records the OSH Act requires. The officer may also question you and your employees. You (or your representative) can accompany the officer during the inspection. Upon completion, the officer will hold a closing conference with you and advise you of any violations discovered during the inspection.

Penalties

If the inspector finds violations, OSHA will issue a citation to you describing the nature of the violations and establishing a reasonable period of time within which you must correct the problem. The citation will also state the penalty imposed for the violation. Penalties are monetary fines, up to a maximum of $70,000 for each violation, the amount of which is determined by the nature and severity of the violation. In extreme and very unusual cases, an employer can be subject to criminal liability and imprisonment for a willful violation that results in an employee's death.

You can contest the citation and/or the penalty by filing a notice with OSHA within fifteen days. A hearing will be held before an administrative law judge, who will issue a decision. The decision can be appealed to the Occupational Safety and Health Review Commission; the decision of the commission can be appealed to the federal Court of Appeals.

The States Get into the Act

States may also regulate workplace health and safety in two ways. First, they may issue regulations covering workplace conditions that are not dealt with by OSHA standards. Second, they may adopt a state safety and health plan that, at a minimum, duplicates the requirements of the OSH Act (it may also provide for higher standards). If OSHA approves the state plan, the state will then be responsible for enforcing safety and health regulations within its borders. OSHA has approved twenty-one state health and safety plans that apply to private businesses.

YOU MUST REMEMBER THIS

• It pays to take precautions. Make your place of business as safe as possible, provide clear warnings of any known hazards, and be sure to carry enough insurance.

• Your legal obligations are highest to the people you invite on your property—your customers and suppliers. They're also the people who may be most important to your business. For both practical and legal reasons, keep them as free from harm as possible.

• Legally, you're responsible for the negligence of your employees. Make sure they're well trained and capable of doing the job.

CHAPTER 20

The Legal Side of Dealing with Customers

All You Need to Know About Consumer Protection Laws

Even though Doug tries to deal honestly and fairly with customers, every so often there are misunderstandings and occasional complaints. These small issues aren't a big deal for Doug; they are something he can live with. But being dragged into court on a consumer fraud charge is something else. How can Doug's business avoid problems in a lawsuit-happy society?

In recent years, states and localities have stepped up efforts to protect consumers. Inevitably, that's placed more restrictions on businesses. As an owner, you're faced with more pitfalls, so it pays to understand the legal environment and the steps to take to protect yourself.

ADVERTISEMENTS

One worry you might have is inadvertently making a contract through an ad. If the product doesn't deliver, might you have a breach of contract suit on your hands? This can go to the back shelf of your worry closet. An advertisement is not often the basis of a contract (though statements in advertising can—and often do—create express warranties that become part of a contract formed by a later offer and acceptance).

A contract can be formed only when there is offer, acceptance, and consideration (see chapter 23). Store advertisements are not usually offers. The law, perhaps somewhat artificially, classifies them as "invitations to bargain." But there are exceptions to this.

Suppose your store advertises that it will give a free gift or a special discount to "the first one hundred customers" or to a person who has made some other special effort. If so, the store has made an offer. A customer can accept it by making the special effort successfully, which constitutes consideration. This could be the making of a contract. In fact, a major department store got into hot water many years ago by carelessly advertising, "Be among the first thousand shoppers at our store tomorrow to win a $1,000 shopping spree." The wording suggested to some people that all one thousand would win—a million-dollar proposition for the store.

False Advertising

False or deceptive advertising has legal implications beyond contract law and is forbidden under federal law and in most states, notably under the consumer fraud laws (see sidebar on page 230).

In false or deceptive advertising, your intent isn't important. The overall impression conveyed is what counts. False or deceptive advertising may mislead a consumer about a product's place of origin, nature or quality, or maker. The product can be property, services, or even credit. Federal and some state laws also regulate credit ads so customers can shop for credit.

An example of creating a misleading impression about a product's place of origin is putting French labels on sweaters made in Arkansas. Similarly, promising first-quality socks and delivering irregulars or seconds is creating a misleading impression about an item's nature or quality. Claiming a cheap counterfeit watch as a Rolex is creating a misleading impression as to its maker. That particular kind of palming off is also a violation of federal trademark law, which is a special type of unfair competition law (see sidebar, page 231). As for services, false advertising might lead consumers into thinking that someone has qualifications (such as being a master carpenter) that he or she actually does not have.

To avoid state and federal strictures against false or deceptive advertising, your advertisements should be accurate about material aspects of the product or service that is offered. *Material* means that a representation, statement, or depiction in the ad would likely affect a consumer's purchase or use of the advertised product or service. In other words, the representation, statement, or depiction would be important to the decision to purchase. If an advertisement led a consumer to expect green spark plugs and you sold him gray ones, the ad probably did not materially mislead him. The standard is what would be material to a reasonable consumer. Most of us would say the color of spark plugs doesn't really matter, no matter how serious an interior designer a car buff is.

It's okay for an advertiser to claim that it makes the best tasting fried chicken on the market. This kind of claim is **puffing**— that is, exaggerated sales talk without the walk. However, it might be deceptive advertising to portray an item in a way that suggests performance far beyond reality. And if the spark plug ad said the plugs would last 50,000 miles and they failed early on, the advertisement was probably misleading.

Complaints about deceptive ads could land you in hot water with state or local consumer protection offices, the state attorney general's office, or the National Advertising Division of the Council of Better Business Bureaus. Another advertising watchdog out there is the Federal Trade Commission, though it typically gets involved only in national or at least multistate ad campaigns.

Here's a checklist to help you avoid problems:

• Be careful of factual claims. It's one thing to puff your product—no one can really prove it isn't the "best." It's another thing to make a claim that can be disproved.

• Be doubly careful of claims you're making about the competition's product. You can try to disparage it, but be sure you have your facts in line before you do—your competitor has every incentive to dispute you, perhaps in court.

• Be clear about whatever offers you're making—don't mislead about price, special offers, "free" gifts, or other special promotions.

• Don't be caught in the bait-and-switch trap—make sure you have enough of the sale item you're offering and that your salespeople know to offer rain checks if you run out.

CONSUMER FRAUD ACTS

If victimized by false or deceptive adverting, a consumer may do more than complain to the authorities. Under the consumer fraud laws, he or she may be entitled to extra damages.

Laws prohibiting unfair and deceptive trade practices in consumer transactions have been enacted in every state. These laws are sometimes known as the "Little FTC Acts," because they establish state law prohibitions and penalties for a wide range of unfair and deceptive trade practices similar to those monitored by the Federal Trade Commission.

The consumer fraud acts apply to almost all consumer sales transactions, and they encompass deceptions involving pricing, defective products, bait-and-switch, and many other practices besides false advertising. They are both extremely flexible and very potent—often providing for treble (triple) damages where a violation is found. They are often the basis for injunctions against a company (a court order forbidding certain actions, such as particular ads or practices). Often they permit a consumer who wins to collect his attorneys' fees from the business he's sued. Sometimes they even provide for punitive damages.

Generally requiring lower legal hurdles than traditional fraud remedies—for example, intent to deceive is usually not a requirement—these laws usually provide for both action by state agencies and recovery by private lawsuits. They can even lead to criminal prosecution.

Bait-and-Switch

Regrettably, a misleading practice known as bait-and-switch has become prevalent enough in some industries that it's specifically prohibited in most jurisdictions. The **bait** is an advertisement luring a consumer with the promise of an unbeatable deal, say on an appliance or a car. The **switch** happens at the dealership, when the salesperson tells the consumer that the advertised model isn't available or is "not for you." Invariably, it's a more expensive model that *is* for the consumer. The salesperson has "switched" the consumer from the one he or she originally wanted to buy.

Bait-and-switch is illegal in most states and under federal law if the advertised model was never available in reasonable quantities, though stores are not necessarily bound by *honest* mistakes in newspaper ads, such as misprints. Bait-and-switch laws probably also apply if disparagement of the advertised product is used to discourage a consumer in favor of another model. A consumer likely has the right under state law to see the model that appeared

TRADEMARKS, TRADE NAMES, AND UNFAIR COMPETITION

Unfair competition law is meant to prevent merchants from engaging in practices that deceive the public about the origin or quality of goods. One way this is done is by the enforcement of trademark rights. As chapter 27 describes, a **trademark** is an authenticating symbol or mark that assures the consumer that a commodity or good comes from a certain source—i.e., a brand. The best-known trademarks are worth millions of dollars. For example, if just anyone could put "Coca-Cola" on a soft drink (and in years past many tried), people would never know what they were buying. But, because of that company's vigorous enforcement of its trademark rights, when you buy a Coke, you know you're getting a Coke. That benefits Coca-Cola, and it benefits consumers. Similarly, a **service mark** is a symbol meant to convey the source of services, as opposed to goods, and is protected by the trademark laws as well. A **trade name** is the name under which a merchant does business.

Illegal use of a trademark is called **infringement**. Willful infringers are subject to serious court action, and possibly criminal penalties, for violation of protected trademarks. Because trademark infringement is a fraud on the public, and because companies have a strong incentive to protect the value of their trademarks, it is one of the most often litigated areas of unfair trade practices.

in the newspaper ad. If the store is "fresh out of them" and refuses to offer a rain check (meaning that the consumer can come back at the later date and receive the same deal), the store also may be guilty of false advertising. Violations can be reported to state or local consumer affairs authorities or the state attorney general.

Price Tags and Window Signs

What about other forms of misleading information, some of which may be honest mistakes that benefit the consumer? Let's say a consumer in your store finds an incredible bargain—a dress she knows is worth at least $100, marked for $10. She takes it to the register, where the salesperson does a double take—there's been a mistake, he or she says apologetically.

Your policy might be to sell her the dress for $10 anyway, on the reasoning that "the customer is always right" and you want to earn a reputation for integrity. However, the general rule under state law is that she is not entitled to get the dress for $10 where there's every indication that the store made an honest mistake.

On the other hand, what if the same dress were displayed in the store window with a prominent sign reading "FINAL CLEARANCE—$10!!"? Here state law might well give the consumer the right to insist on the advertised price (watching out again for the

 ### "GOING OUT OF BUSINESS—FOR OUR THIRTIETH CONSECUTIVE YEAR"

Many cities and states have laws regulating "Going out of Business" sales. Merchants who want to run one of these may need a license or permit, since in past years there was a rash of decade-long "Going out of Business" sales that deceived consumers into thinking they were getting unique opportunities. Now you can't run such a sale in these jurisdictions unless you're really going out of business.

bait-and-switch). While the FTC might consider both displays and price tags *ads*, state regulators may consider a store-window display more like a public advertisement than a price tag is, since the display's intent is to induce a consumer to do something she might not have done otherwise—go into the store.

SELLING BY MAIL, PHONE, FAX, AND COMPUTER

Many companies offer shopping options through catalogs, mail order, and online. If this is part of your business, you should know that most of the rules for ordering by mail apply when ordering by phone for mail delivery or delivery by another common carrier, such as UPS or FedEx.

For example, the FTC's Mail or Telephone Order Rule covers goods that consumers order by mail, telephone, computer, or fax machine. Under this rule, goods that are bought through these means must be shipped within the time you have advertised (e.g., six weeks). If no time period is specified, you must ship the goods within thirty days of the order. If they aren't, you must at least send out a notice (by letter, postcard, phone, e-mail, or fax) informing customers of the delay and of the projected delivery date. You also have to offer to cancel the order and send customers a refund within one week if they don't want to wait any longer. Many states have laws that protect consumers even further than this federal rule.

What about substitute goods? Unless as a seller you have the customer's consent to a substitute, he or she doesn't have to accept one. The customer can send it back and ask for a refund. If the customer keeps it, though, he or she will have to pay the usual price, unless you offer it for less.

Sales Taxes

Fax, computer, telephone, and mail-order sales may also have big tax implications. Traditionally, state laws permitted you not to collect tax for many out-of-state sales, but that's changing as revenue-hungry states are becoming aware of how much business is done in cyberspace. Check with local tax authorities or your lawyer to find the current situation in your state, but here are a few general considerations.

You have to collect sales tax for sales made in person if customers take the merchandise with them or have it sent to an address within the state. You also have to collect it for mail orders to "in-state residents"—people who live in the same state as your company.

In many states, however, you may still not have to collect the sales tax on items sold by mail to out-of-staters if your company doesn't have an establishment (retail store, warehouse, and so forth) in that state. (You may also not have to collect sales tax if customers buy merchandise in person and have it delivered to their home in another state.) However, states may have **use taxes** meant to capture the lost tax on these transactions. The use tax is frequently identical to the sales tax. Likewise, some neighboring states, such as New York and New Jersey, have mutual sales tax–collection pacts (meaning that a New Jersey business that ships to New York will still have to charge and collect the New York sales tax, and vice-versa).

SELLING OUTSIDE A REGULAR PLACE OF BUSINESS

Does your business involve sales door-to-door, or at trade shows, or somewhere else besides your premises? Then certain federal (and probably state) laws apply to you.

Over the years the federal government and many states have passed laws regulating door-to-door sales. These laws usually require your salesperson to provide customers with the following details on their receipt:

- the sellers' name and place of business;
- a description of the goods and services sold;

- the amount of money paid and/or the value of any goods delivered; and
  - the customer's cooling-off-period rights (see below).

Also, if the salesperson makes the sale in Spanish or another language, customers may have the right to all of the above details in that language.

The Cooling-off Period

Federal law requires a three-day "cooling-off period" for door-to-door sales. During that time, customers can cancel purchases made from someone who both solicits and closes the sale at a home, or even elsewhere—such as a hotel—that is not an established place of business.

The customer doesn't have to give any reason for changing his or her mind during the cooling-off period, and the three-day period doesn't start until he or she receives formal notice of the right to cancel. Federal law forbids a company from charging any cancellation fee. The federal law will apply to most such cases. Many states also have similar laws that fill in the gaps and may provide additional rights.

If customers decide to cancel during the cooling-off period, state laws usually require a refund of money, a return of any trade-in, and cancellation and return of the contract. The salesperson

 LEARNING THE LINGO

What's the difference between a **warranty** and a **guaranty**? Both words have the same root, which means "to guard." And for consumers the two terms mean essentially the same thing: The difference for you as a businessperson is that a guaranty usually describes a bundle of obligations you take on as part of the purchase contract, while a warranty can describe the obligations the law imposes on you.

has ten business days to do this under federal law. The customer must make the goods available to be picked up during that period. Under federal law, if you don't pick them up within twenty calendar days, the customer may be allowed to keep the goods for free.

WARRANTIES

Express and Implied Warranties

The law divides warranties into **express** and **implied** warranties. Express warranties are promises to back up the product or service, either written or oral, to support the product or service. Suppose your car dealership sells a used car, and you say, "I guarantee you'll get another ten thousand miles out of this transmission." That's an express warranty. It isn't an opinion or puffing about quality or value, such as "This is the best used car for sale in town." "Best" could mean anything to the speaker—best color, best looking, best status symbol. But an express warranty is a specific statement of fact or a promise. Statements like "excellent condition" and "A-1" have been held by some—but not all—courts to create express warranties. The seller sometimes creates an express warranty without intending to, without ever using the words *warranty* or *guaranty*. The new businessperson should be careful and resist the temptation to oversell.

Implied warranties, on the other hand, are not stated at all, but are automatic, or implied by law, in certain kinds of transactions.

Kinds of Implied Warranties

There are two main types of implied warranties: the implied warranty of merchantability and the implied warranty of fitness for a particular purpose. (There is also an implied warranty of title in a sale, meaning that the property is yours to sell, and an implied warranty against interference in a lease, meaning that a tenant will have use of leased property.)

The implied warranty of merchantability. If you're in the business of selling or leasing a specific kind of product, the law requires that the item be adequate for the purpose for which it is purchased or leased. This is a general rule of fairness—that what looks like a carton of milk in the supermarket dairy case really is drinkable milk, not sour or unusable.

The implied warranty of fitness for a particular purpose. This type of implied warranty is a little different. It means that you're presumed to guarantee that an item will be fit for the particular purpose for which it is being sold, as long as the buyer makes that purpose known and you know that the buyer is relying on you to provide a suitable item. So let's say a buyer comes to your dealership looking for a used car to race and tells you that is his purpose. When you sell him a car, you make this warranty because you know he wants to race it, as opposed to using it for basic transportation. Or suppose the buyer told you he needs a car that can tow a trailer full of granite up steep mountains in the snow. When, with this knowledge, you sell him a car, you make an implied warranty that it can do that. When the car fails in that purpose, there would be a breach of that warranty.

 ## HOW LONG DO WARRANTIES LAST?

Durations of warranties may vary considerably, depending on the type of transaction, the warranty involved, and the applicable law. In most states, customers have up to four years after the start of the transaction to enforce an *implied* warranty. But in cases involving *written* warranties, the period may be much shorter. And unless prohibited by state law, the duration of the implied warranty can be shortened to the duration of the written warranty. A written warranty will disclose how long it lasts. It may be as short as ninety days for a portable radio. A warranty on a new car, on the other hand, may last several years or many thousands of miles.

Express warranties are more or less in your power—after all, they depend on the statements you make to customers. Implied warranties are more troublesome because you have less control and because the implied warranty can last as long as four years.

The Magnuson-Moss Act

A federal law, the **Magnuson-Moss Act**, covers written warranties for consumer goods (purchased for personal, household use) costing more than $10. The act does not require that merchants make written warranties, but if they do make such a warranty, they must meet certain standards. The warranty has to be available for consumers to read before they buy. It must be written in plain language and must include the following:

- the name and address of the company making the warranty;
- the product or parts covered;
- whether the warranty promises replacement, repair, or refund, and if there are any expenses (such as shipping or labor) that consumers would have to pay;
- how long the warranty lasts;
- if the warranty does not cover certain legal damages—usually consequential or "out-of-pocket" damages, beyond the cost of the product—then a statement as to that fact;
- the action consumers should take if something goes wrong;
- if the company providing the warranty requires consumers to waive certain rights in a dispute or submit to arbitration, then a statement of that fact; and
- a brief description of consumers' legal rights.

Some states also have laws that provide consumers with greater protection than the Magnuson-Moss Act. For example, a state may require certain types of warranties to be backed by repair facilities within a certain distance of where the product is sold, or specify that repairs must be completed within a certain time period. Another typical example is state lemon laws, which mandate car manufacturers to refund consumers' money when a new car is so defective that it meets the statutory definition of a "lemon." Some states even have lemon laws for used cars.

Full and Limited Warranties

The difference between a full warranty and a limited warranty can be the difference between night and day. Magnuson-Moss requires all written warranties for consumer products costing more than a few dollars to be designated as either a full or limited warranty.

Full Warranties

A **full warranty** is a promise that the product will be repaired or replaced for free during the warranty period. State and federal laws require that if the warrantor will repair the item, it must be fixed within a reasonable time without charge, and it must be reasonably convenient to get the item to and from the repair site. If the company can't fix the problem in a reasonable number of attempts, it must give the consumer a refund or replacement. In effect, this is a type of lemon law. Many stores will offer a short full warranty of their own (thirty to ninety days), above what the manufacturer offers.

Limited Warranties

A **limited warranty** is much more common. Not surprisingly, it covers less: usually only parts and almost never the cost of labor beyond the first month or so. For more expensive appliances such as cars or computers, however, reputable manufacturers may offer limited warranties that are for a longer period of time and provide greater coverage.

Warranties and the Retailer

Most warranties are offered by the manufacturer, and if you're a retailer you are not usually offering the first-line warranty service yourself (though some stores that offer their own service plans do take over even the early warranty service).

If you are a retailer, your own return policy is important. Do you want to give customers five days? Ten? Thirty? Do you want them to be able to return a product for any reason? Do you want to stand behind all products you sell, even beyond the technical cutoff date for returns?

And, since customer relations are important, you'll want to work with manufacturers to ensure smooth procedures for returns of defective merchandise, refunds, and so forth. Sometimes you might help customers who have warranty problems with the manufacturer. Let's say a customer experiences problems with warranty service, and after several unhappy attempts to fix things has had it with the product and wants a refund. He or she might not get one from the manufacturer, who has little to gain—it has lost the customer either way. But as a retailer you may offer a way around the warranty process, especially if it's fairly soon (say, a few months) after purchase. Stores often are able to return defective products that the manufacturer wouldn't have accepted from the customer directly.

Some Tips on Warranty Disclaimers

Merchants and manufacturers may disclaim warranties with statements that meet certain requirements. A disclaimer means

---

 ### WHO'S LEGALLY LIABLE?

When a product goes bad and the customer is mad enough to seek legal action, who's liable—the manufacturer or the store that sold the product? It depends. Each is liable if it gave an express warranty. Both may be liable for breaches of the implied warranty of general fitness (merchantability). The retailer is liable for a breach of the implied warranty of fitness for a particular purpose, since (presumably) only he dealt with the customer and knew the purposes for which the customer needed the product. Further, there may also be tort liability for any injuries to third parties.

that the warranty has been removed from the transaction. But they are available only if the warrantor follows certain requirements. All disclaimers must be clear, unambiguous, and, if written, conspicuous: **BUYER UNDERSTANDS THERE ARE NO WARRANTIES, EXPRESS OR IMPLIED, INCLUDING THE IMPLIED WARRANTY OF MERCHANTABILITY.** Express warranties and implied warranties of merchantability can be disclaimed orally, but a disclaimer for the implied warranty of fitness for a particular purpose must be in writing. Stating that a product is sold "as is" or "with all faults" will disclaim *both* the implied warranties of merchantability and fitness for a particular purpose in most cases. (Alternatively, disclaimer of the implied warranty of merchantability must use the word "merchantability"). It is important to note that you may not disclaim a warranty *after* the customer has made the purchase.

As explained earlier, warranties may be limited. Thus, with consumer products, a warranty will be stated in the purchase contract the customer signs, which will also state a specific remedy if the product fails. This avoids having to give no warranty while still protecting the seller to some extent. For example, the contract may provide that the seller will repair or replace the merchandise, if necessary, but that the customer has no right to get back any money. This protects the seller against the worst-case scenario (having to give the customer money back) while giving the customer some protection. This is called a **warranty limitation** (also called a remedy limitation).

Warranty limitations may also exclude some or all forms of consequential damages. As explained earlier, these are losses caused by the product's defect, including the consumer's lost time and expenses that result from the defect and repair costs. If, for example, a new computer crashes and destroys weeks of work, the customer may get a new computer. But if the warranty that came with the computer (and the disks) excludes liability for consequential damages, the warrantor will almost certainly not be required to reimburse the customer for the lost time, work, or software—much less a lost job or client.

An important exception to this is that customers may recover

A SAMPLE CONSUMER PRODUCT WARRANTY

Here is a generic example of an express warranty for a product used in the home. You may, of course, adjust your warranty—if you want to provide one at all—based on the degree of service you wish to provide (for instance, this example provides a one-year warranty; you might want to provide a shorter or longer warranty period). Some states, especially California, have additional consumer protections, so you must make sure you consult with your attorney to ensure your warranty complies with all applicable laws. You would also need to provide specific instructions on how a customer would return the product to you for warranty servicing.

LIMITED ONE-YEAR WARRANTY

Manufacturer warrants that your Product will be free of defects in materials or workmanship under normal home use for one year from the date of purchase. Manufacturer will, at its option, repair or replace the Product without charge upon its receipt of proof of the date of purchase. If a replacement Product is necessary to service this warranty, the replacement Product may be new or reconditioned. If a replacement Product is sent, a new limited one-year warranty will be applied to the replacement Product.

This warranty applies only to Products operated in the United States. This warranty gives you specific legal rights, and you may also have other rights that vary from state to state.

THIS WARRANTY DOES NOT COVER CONSEQUENTIAL OR INCIDENTAL DAMAGES SUCH AS PROPERTY DAMAGE AND DOES NOT COVER INCIDENTAL COSTS AND EXPENSES RESULTING FROM ANY BREACH OF THIS WARRANTY, EVEN IF FORESEEABLE. Some states do not allow the exclusion or limitations of incidental or consequential damages, so the above limitation or exclusion may not apply to you depending on the state of your purchase.

Nor does this warranty cover damages caused by services performed by anyone other than Manufacturer or its authorized service providers, use of parts other than genuine Manufacturer parts, or external causes such as abuse, misuse, inappropriate power supply, or acts of God.

THIS WARRANTY IS EXCLUSIVE AND IS IN LIEU OF ANY OTHER EX-PRESS WARRANTY, WHETHER WRITTEN OR ORAL. IN ADDITION, MANUFACTURER HEREBY SPECIFICALLY DISCLAIMS ALL OTHER WARRANTIES WITH RESPECT TO THE PRODUCT, INCLUDING ANY IMPLIED WARRANTY OF MERCHANTABILITY OR FITNESS FOR ANY PARTICULAR PURPOSE. Some states do not allow disclaimers of such implied warranties or limitations on how long an implied warranty lasts, so the above limitation may not apply to you depending on the state of purchase.

---

damages in cases of personal (physical) injury that result from a product's defect. This responsibility may *not* be disclaimed.

YOU MUST REMEMBER THIS

• Consumer protection laws are widespread and often have teeth.

• Knowing what the law requires, and taking care, can help you avoid the vast majority of potential legal problems.

• In warranties, as in advertising, it's important to be clear about what you're offering and what you'll do—you can limit warranties through your contract with the customer.

CHAPTER 21

Extending Credit

Bottom-Line Tips on Accepting Checks and Credit Cards and Offering Your Own Credit

As a consumer, Jane loves credit cards. But now that she and her husband, Paul, have opened a shop, she's not quite so sure. Is this form of credit in the best interests of their business? What about accepting checks? What about cutting out the middleman and granting credit directly? This chapter should help her decide.

F ew businesses today can survive by accepting only cash payments up front for their products or services. Consumers today demand the flexibility of being able to pay with some form of credit.

This chapter begins by looking at some of the general considerations of granting credit and examines the following:

- **indirect credit**—accepting credit cards and checks;
- **direct credit**—credit extended directly from the business to the customer; and
- **other credit issues**, including commercial credit (i.e., credit you extend to other businesses), contracts, and promissory notes.

WHAT DOES CREDIT ENTAIL?

Any payment option other than cash up front constitutes **credit**. Credit includes payment by check, credit card, debit card, or any other form of payment after services are provided or the product has left the store.

The obvious benefit of extending credit to your customers is increased sales. Accepting credit cards or offering your own credit terms to customers makes impulse purchasing easy and painless for consumers. Your business will likely attract more customers with the recognition that they can choose whether to pay up front, pay in increments, or delay the payment until sometime in the future.

Whatever credit option you may decide to extend, they come with a cost. Credit card companies charge you to accept their cards. Accepting checks costs you in terms of increased handling and processing of payment. Any form of credit costs you the time value of money, as you wait to receive a payment. And, with these credit options, you're opening your business up to the world of bounced checks, invalid accounts, stolen cards, counterfeiting, and the wonderful world of debt collection. You must decide if these are risks you want to take, and if so, to what extent.

Prepare your business for these inevitable costs and associated problems by entering into the process of credit extension with your eyes wide open. Developing company policies for handling these issues is the best way to ward off the future headaches that credit extensions can bring.

 TIME VALUE OF MONEY

The time value of money is premised on the notion that a dollar in hand today is worth more than a dollar received at a later date. When you have money in hand, you can put it to work—reinvesting it into your business and earning a return on that money. Obviously, if you do not have that money in hand, you cannot put it to work for you. Normally, you would expect to be paid interest for the time you did not have access to your money to make up for the lost opportunity to make use of the money. However, with checks and credit card accounts, you will not receive any interest during the time between the sale and the money being credited to your account. You should therefore consider that time gap as a cost of doing business.

Preliminary Questions

Start by thinking about what policies you want to institute for your business. For example, what forms of credit will you extend to your customers? Each form of credit brings with it special questions to consider.

When billing a customer, is the payment due upon receipt of the invoice, or due after a certain period of time, like thirty days? Will you ask the customer to complete a questionnaire or application form before extending credit? Will you require the customer to sign some form of contract or promise to pay before he or she leaves the store? Will you offer any incentive discounts to encourage consumers to pay you quickly? Will you impose interest or other penalties to late payers?

If you provide a service, will you require a certain percentage of the estimated cost to be prepaid? Or will payment not be expected until the service is completed? Will you require the customer to sign in advance a contract accepting your offer to provide this service?

Will you accept personal or business checks? Will you require certain forms of identification to be provided with those checks? Will you accept third-party checks, starter checks (those without a name or address preprinted on them), or low-numbered checks? Will you use some form of verification to be sure the account hasn't been closed or has insufficient funds?

 DIFFERENT STROKES

Each business is different and therefore has different needs when it comes to credit. You may be in an industry with certain payment and credit traditions that customers have come to expect. The nature of your business may also require the extension of credit depending on your average transaction size and whether you attract repeat or primarily one-time customers.

Spell Out Your Credit Policy

When developing your own policies, consider what types of credit other local businesses, and especially your competition, accept and what conditions they place on credit extension. You may decide to take a greater risk in extending credit if you feel it will help you break into the market and attract more customers. Or, you may offer more generous credit terms as part of a promotion during the dry spells.

Consider also whether you want to offer different credit terms to different customers. A more flexible policy may be appropriate for those repeat customers who have proven track records when it comes to payment. This may be effective in encouraging customers to make timely payments, so that they too can qualify for this "valued" or "preferred" status. Whatever you decide, your credit policies should be carefully defined and spelled out to your customers, so that you don't feel pressured to bend the rules for each new customer who comes in the door. And you must be careful that your credit policies don't discriminate on any of the bases specified in the Equal Credit Opportunity Act (see page 255).

INDIRECT CREDIT

Accepting Checks

Many businesses accept personal and business checks. Train your employees according to your company policy so they know what to do when accepting a check for payment. If you have established a policy of charging a fee for checks that are returned for insufficient funds, by all means post the policy conspicuously. It may deter bad checks, at least to some degree.

When a check is presented, review it to be sure it is filled out properly (made out to your company, with an accurate date, signature, and the correct dollar amount). If you decide not to accept starter checks, then the employee accepting the check should verify that the check has been preprinted with the name and address. It is always a good idea to ask for one or two telephone numbers, if they are not preprinted on the check.

If it's a personal check, ask for the customer's driver's license number (if that information is not preprinted on the check). Always ask for identification with the check. Train your employees to verify that the names, addresses, identification numbers, and photographs are the same. If the addresses are different on the check and on the I.D., the employee should write down on the check the address that is on the I.D.

If it's a business check, it is probably not appropriate to ask for personal information about the individual presenting the check. Instead, you can contact the bank that the check is drawn on, provide the account number, and ask for the account rating. The bank can tell you, for example, if the account has an average balance in the hundreds or thousands of dollars. The bank can also tell you if the particular amount of the check presented to you would clear if presented at the moment to the bank.

There are also many merchant associations and services that will verify, based on the name and/or account number of the check, whether there have been problems with that customer before. Look into joining one of these organizations so that you have this information, which has been compiled from large numbers of merchants, at your fingertips. These services charge a fee, of course, which generally runs about 1.5 percent of the transaction value. These services usually only provide information to help you decide whether to accept a check—they don't necessarily guarantee payment (though some services will do so for additional fees).

Although you may not see this very often, you should always check the reverse side of the check to be sure nothing is written in the endorsement section. Phrases like "Endorsement of this check constitutes agreement that amounts due and owing are fully paid," or even just "Paid in Full," may be legally binding.

Any time you accept checks for payment, you should deposit those checks with your bank immediately. Don't wait a week to do so, because the chance of the funds being in the account decreases with each day you wait.

CHECK IT OUT WITH THE STATE

With any corporate customer, you can always contact the secretary of state's office for your state to inquire about the date of incorporation, names of corporate officers, and names and addresses for registered agents. This information may help you decide whether the corporate check is likely to be good and certainly can be helpful if you ever need to collect on a bad check.

You should consult with a business lawyer for more information on your particular state laws that apply to accepting and rejecting checks.

Bad Checks

Probably no company can claim never to have received a bad check. So don't be surprised when you get the notification that you were presented with a nonsufficient funds (NSF) check. Develop a company policy for dealing with NSF checks.

When the check comes back to you, there are several steps you can take. Some businesses may take all of them, some may not. You can contact the customer's bank to see if there are now sufficient funds to process the check. If there are, cash the check immediately. If not, you can wait a few days or a week and call the bank again. Many times, the customer will have had an opportunity to deposit more funds at this point, and you may resubmit the check at that time. Even if you don't call the bank, it may be a good idea to redeposit the bad check at least once. Perhaps the customer was temporarily low on funds, and the check will clear the next time around.

If you find that the check cannot clear the bank, contact the customer immediately. Let him or her know that a check with insufficient funds was provided to your company for payment. Explain that you expect another form of payment immediately. Let

AN OUNCE OF PREVENTION . . .

Because of the added difficulty of collecting on out-of-state checks, you may decide not to accept them from customers. You're probably better off also not accepting third-party checks because they too bring with them collection problems.

---

the customer know what other payment options your company accepts. If you have a policy of imposing a fine on any checks returned with insufficient funds, then inform the customer of your fine, as well. Put that customer's name on your list of customers not to extend credit to, at least until the customer can prove his or her credit problems have been corrected.

Accepting Credit Cards

Paying with plastic is a dream for consumers for a variety of reasons: It's fast and convenient, they get extra time before having to pay for the purchases, and they may get cash-back bonuses or free frequent-flier miles.

Any business considering accepting credit cards should research the fees and policies associated with credit card payments and should shop around for the best deal. To accept payment by credit card, your company will be required to pay a regular monthly charge or account maintenance fee.

The credit card service also automatically deducts a certain percentage of each transaction (called the **discount**) as part of its charges. The discount percentage varies from 2 percent to 6 percent of the amount purchased, depending on the volume of sales and the nature of the business. In exchange for paying this discount fee, you get nearly immediate payment from the merchant bank that signed the agreement with your firm. The bank then takes the burden of collecting later from the customer. The bank usually deposits payment for credit card sales directly to your bank account within forty-eight hours, minus the discount.

To get started accepting credit cards, go to your bank or contact some of the different credit service companies. An Internet search for "credit card merchant account" will reveal dozens of companies. Banks usually charge higher transaction and account maintenance fees, but they generally provide better service and make funds available faster. If you contact other credit service companies you will find that many fees are negotiable, and most companies will match or beat their competitors' prices. If you're a small business, a provider that specializes in small businesses may offer you a better deal. You will probably need to either purchase or lease an electronic machine that calls and verifies credit with the swipe of the credit card. These enable you to run a quick electronic check of each credit card by swiping the card through a machine. These checks run the credit card number against a regularly updated database of card numbers to be sure it has not been reported lost or stolen and to verify that the customer is not exceeding his or her credit limit.

If you prefer, there are some services that allow you to forgo the machine and enter the credit card number on your computer or dial with a touch-tone phone into an automated line.

There are other supplies you may need to purchase, including credit card slips that the customer will sign to authorize the purchase.

When you set up your business to accept credit cards, you will also be given a maximum store authorization line. This is the maximum amount your business can allow a customer to put on a credit card, without obtaining specific authorization for the transaction, either through the computer or by a phone call. Be sure your employees are aware of this maximum authorization line.

Be sure to familiarize yourself with the bank's or credit service company's policies on handling customer disputes. Generally, when customers dispute a charge on their credit card, the bank, or credit service company may charge the transaction back to you. To avoid this, and avoid the possibility of accepting lost, stolen, or counterfeited cards, you should set up some preventative company policies.

When a credit card is presented for payment, have your employees check the expiration date of the card and the person's name. Compare the customer's signature on the card with that on the credit authorization slip. If there is any question whatsoever about the validity of the card, ask for photo identification to confirm the information.

CONSIDERATIONS IN OFFERING DIRECT CREDIT

Accepting checks and credit cards are forms of indirect credit that you can offer your customers. Many businesses also find it advantageous to offer direct credit—credit extended directly to the customer from your business. If your business wants to provide products or perform a service for customers prior to receiving full and complete payment, then you are offering a form of direct credit.

Some businesses that regularly extend credit to customers find that not only does it increase sales, but the finance charges paid by customers are an additional healthy source of business income. Be aware, though, that there may be laws in your state capping the rate of interest you can charge.

Think about the financial implication to your business if you decide to extend direct credit. You're running the risk of bad debt, and you have to weigh the cost of carrying receivables and the lag in the inflow of funds against increased sales and other benefits to be gained by extending credit. Since goods and services sold on credit can take days or even years to be repaid by the customer, you will need to have greater funds available, whether through owner's equity, borrowing, or some other source. One rule of thumb is that you need three to five times the amount of such funds to run your business if you extend credit to customers than if you were operating a cash-only business. Consider your company's cash flow requirements in determining whether to extend direct credit to customers.

Other important considerations include the customer application process and the laws regulating credit grantors. These are each discussed below.

Customer Credit Applications

One approach to protect yourself is to request a report on each applicant from one of the credit reporting agencies. Contact the credit reporting agencies in your area to find out the information needed, the costs involved, and the process entailed in requesting a credit report. Generally, you will pay an annual fee based on the size of your business plus a nominal charge for each inquiry to gain access to the credit bureau information.

Or you can choose to gather information from the applicant directly and then do at least some of the verification process yourself. The idea is to assess customers' ability and likelihood of paying by asking them to complete a credit application or information form. You can give this form any name you choose to make it more palatable to your customers, such as "New Customer Questionnaire." One purpose of this form is to help you assess whether customers meet your minimum requirements for extending credit. Another purpose is to gather information about customers prior to extending credit, which will be useful later in collecting the debt, if necessary.

You don't have to request the customer's consent to check his or her credit, but it may be a good practice to do so. Simply add a signature line for customers to consent to having their credit checked on your New Customer Questionnaire.

Your credit information form should ask for the customer's name, address, and telephone number; if the customer has lived there for less than two years, ask for a previous address. It should also ask for the customer's employer, work address, and work he or she has done there. Also ask for his or her Social Security number. Ask the customer to provide his or her bank

DON'T FORGET TO VERIFY

After the customer completes the credit application form, but before you extend credit, be sure to verify at least some of the information provided on the form. You can get a credit report on the customer, which will give you a full picture. Or it's simple enough to take the form to a back office out of earshot of the customer and contact the banks listed to verify that the accounts noted are in existence. You can also contact the customer's employer to verify employment and salary information, if provided. These quick checks are useful in determining whether to extend credit to the customer.

---

name, type of account, and account number. You may also ask customers to supply information about any credit card accounts, including account number and expiration date.

While you don't want your credit information form to be so exhaustive as to ward off potential customers, you should ask enough questions to determine that the customer is a good credit risk. If your determination turns out to be inaccurate, at least you have sufficient information to begin the debt collection process. Remember also that once customers walk out the door with your product or once your services are provided, they have no incentive to comply with your requests to complete this questionnaire, so you must ensure it is completed in advance.

The Legal Side of Granting Credit

Many states regulate the amount of interest, or the **rate**, that you can charge. Others, particularly if the credit is extended to a business, leave it entirely or practically up to the market.

You'll have to check with your lawyer to determine the restrictions in your state. If you are granting credit to consumers, you can also check with your state's department of consumer credit, which can provide you with guidelines for rates and other consumer protection regulations. In addition, a federal law applies to grantors of consumer credit everywhere. In an attempt to make it easier for consumers to shop for the best rate and credit terms, Congress enacted the **Truth in Lending Act (TILA)**. TILA requires that all creditors provide information that will help consumers decide whether to buy on credit or borrow and, if so, which credit offer is best for them.

Under TILA, before consumers sign a contract for credit (such as the installment purchase of an automobile or appliances), creditors must disclose to them in writing, among other information, the following:

- the amount being financed;
- the number of monthly payments; and
- the annual percentage rate (APR).

The APR is an annual rate that relates the total finances charge to (1) the amount of credit that consumers receive and (2) the length of time they have to repay it.

TILA also regulates credit advertising, which makes it easy for consumers to credit-shop but governs what you can say in ads. For example, if your ad emphasizes a low monthly payment (giving a dollar figure), it also must contain other pertinent information, like the APR.

The Law and Credit Applications

When a consumer applies for credit, there are legal rules to make sure that you handle the application fairly and confidentially. In connection with the application, or in setting the terms of credit actually granted, the federal **Equal Credit Opportunity Act (ECOA)** prohibits credit grantors from considering the applicant's

- race,
- color,
- national origin,
- sex,
- marital status,
- age,

- receipt of public aid, or
- exercise of his or her legal rights as a credit-seeker.

As to age, once the applicant has reached the **age of majority** (typically eighteen, though a few states may set it at nineteen or twenty), credit grantors generally may not use an applicant's age against him or her—whether young or old—in determining creditworthiness. (But you can give favorable treatment to the elderly, as defined in ECOA.) You may consider the future of the applicant's income stream if he or she is at or nearing retirement; however, you may not require the applicant to buy life insurance to qualify for credit, nor may you cancel credit simply because the person has retired.

The law permits you to use any of the following factors to decide whether to extend credit and under what terms:

- **Ability to repay.** This depends on the stability of the applicant's current job or income source, how much the applicant earns, and the length of time he or she has worked or will receive income. You may also consider applicants' basic expenses, such as payments on rent, mortgages, or other debts; utilities; college expenses; and taxes. This analysis is typically done by mortgage lenders, rather than companies that grant consumer installment credit.

- **Credit history.** This shows how much money the applicant owes and whether he or she has large, unused lines of open-ended credit. Other important considerations are whether the applicant has paid bills on time and if he or she has filed for bankruptcy within the past ten years or had repossessions or judgments issued against him or her.

- **Stability.** The applicant's stability is indicated by how long he or she has lived at the current or former address, and how long he or she has been with current or former employers. Owning a home is normally a big plus.

- **Assets.** Assets such as a car may be useful as collateral for a loan. You may look at what else you may use for collateral, such as saving accounts or securities, though this kind of analysis is found more often in business loans than in typical applications

A LAW WITH TEETH

The Equal Credit Opportunity Act is a law you should take seriously. It allows for punitive damages of up to $10,000 in addition to any losses that applicants can prove they suffered as a result of such activity.

for consumer credit. Also, the FTC Credit Practices Rule (and the laws of several states) limits these types of cross-collateral clauses.

The Equal Credit Opportunity Act requires that you notify applicants of your acceptance or rejection of their applications within thirty days of receiving them. If you deny the application for credit, the denial must be in writing and must give the reason or allow the applicant to request the reasons. And under the Fair Credit Reporting Act, in the event of a credit denial (or withdrawal or reduction), you must tell the applicant if you based the denial on a credit report and, if so, the name, address, and phone number of the reporting agency that prepared the report.

Involve Your Attorney

Since these documents are subject to federal and state fair credit laws, be sure your attorney reviews any questionnaires or forms that you use to gather information prior to extending credit to customers. As noted above, these laws restrict the questions you can ask in your credit investigation, the criteria you can use to accept or reject credit, and the information you may rely upon to determine a customer's creditworthiness.

Also keep in mind that if you intend to levy any finance or interest charges for unpaid balances, state laws may come into play to dictate the amount you may charge, the manner in which you may calculate those charges, and the disclosure of information regarding these charges that must be provided to the applicant.

Other Ways to Protect Yourself

You can also protect yourself by creating a business policy that requires a portion of the final payment to be paid in advance of shipping the product or providing the service. If the customer is willing to put a substantial amount down, perhaps 50 percent of the estimated total cost, that is a good indication the customer is serious and creditworthy.

If you are shipping a product to a customer, you always run the risk that the customer will claim that the product was never delivered, it arrived damaged, or you shipped the wrong product. One way to avoid this, for larger orders at least, is to make it a practice for you or someone from your company to call the customer a day or two after the product should have been delivered. Record the name of the person you talk to, the date, and the person's responses to your inquiries about whether the product arrived undamaged and whether the customer is satisfied.

SPECIAL CONCERNS FOR COMMERCIAL CREDIT

When another business applies for credit, it can be difficult to determine the financial stability of the business and its likelihood of making good on the credit extended. You'll want to develop a credit application form for businesses that is tailored to businesses rather than individuals (tax I.D. number rather than Social Security number; formal business name; form of business organization, such as corporation, general partnership, and so forth). You can verify bank accounts and other accounts, and you can also run a credit check on the business through a commercial credit bureau.

Relevant information such as the expenses and income of the business may be hard to confirm. For this reason, you may decide to request that all applicants for commercial credit provide a financial statement for their business.

You can also ask commercial credit applicants to provide references of other businesses that you can contact to learn about the business's reputation in the community and with other creditors. You can ask for information regarding officers, directors, and principal place of business, and then verify that information with the secretary of state's office.

It's also important that the commercial credit application provides a place for the applicant company to list the names and job titles of those individuals from the company who are authorized to make purchases for the company.

Written Contracts

Prior to extending credit to another business, you may require a formal written contract to be signed by the other company. This contract should describe what services or products are being provided, in exchange for what dollar amount. It should also clearly indicate the due date for the payment and what additional fines or interest may be imposed if the payment is not received in full when due. If a partial payment is being made in advance, that fact should be reflected in the contract. It should also clearly state the name and address of the customer and the location where the products are to be delivered or where the services are to be performed. You should have your basic contract reviewed by your attorney prior to putting it to use with your business customer.

Promissory Notes

Depending on the type of business you're in, you may want to offer a regular payment plan for your business customers, with a built-in finance charge or interest rate. This agreement should be documented in a promissory note signed by the customer. The promissory note should spell out the total amount owed, the specific due dates for payments, penalties for any late payments, finance charges, and the grand total financed. Be sure to have an attorney review your promissory note, as each state has different laws mandating the information that must be disclosed to customers.

Any written contract or promissory note that you use with customers should contain a clause allowing you to be reimbursed for any collection costs and related attorneys' fees you may incur if the customer breaches the agreement.

YOU MUST REMEMBER THIS

• Extending credit—whether through credit cards or on your own—costs money but may be worth it in increased sales.

• If you do extend consumer credit directly, be sure you know and adhere to the state and federal laws that provide protection to consumers.

• Granting credit to businesses, as opposed to individuals, raises some different issues. Your lawyer can help you come up with policies for granting business credit.

CHAPTER 22

The Check Isn't in the Mail!

Collection Dos and Don'ts
for Small-Business Owners

Penny's new business is going well, except for one thing: She's waiting, and waiting, and waiting for payment for stuff she sold months ago. A big stack of moldy accounts receivable isn't helping her cash flow or her bottom line, yet she hates the thought of harassing people. Read on to find how she could collect the money she is owed more quickly and more effectively.

YOUR ROLE AS A CREDIT GRANTOR

Unless you accept only cash at the time your customers buy your products or services—and not many businesses do that in this age of instant credit—you are not only a small-business owner, but also a credit grantor. That means, simply, that you extend credit or offer installment payment plans to your customers—both other businesses and the individuals who buy your goods and services.

For business owners, there's a close association between credit granting and collections. The better the job you do in making decisions to extend credit, the easier your debt collection will be. But even then, it's nearly impossible to make sure that everyone you extend credit to actually pays the bills on time and in full. While most of the individuals and businesses with which you trade will do so, some obviously will not.

A customer's failure to pay can stem from a variety of factors, ranging from mere inadvertence to a change in financial situation or actual intent. When customers become delinquent in paying their bills, you as the creditor—or the collection agency or attorney you choose to hire—will need to try to collect the money you are owed.

BAD DEBT

Collection industry statistics put the amount of consumer debt that goes bad at 3 percent to 5 percent; while between 2 percent and 4 percent of commercial debts (those resulting from business-to-business transactions) are said to go bad.

Contacting a Customer Who Has Fallen Behind on Payment

To some extent, your collection strategy should be related to the size of the debt. Obviously, the larger the debt, the more time and energy you'll be willing to expend.

Your first contact with an individual or business that owes you money probably should be by letter. You are, however, free to make a telephone call or even make an in-person visit if that better suits your needs. The initial contact about a missed payment should be friendly and sincere, while firm enough to clearly inform the customer that the account is past due, and prompt payment is expected. Also, provide the customer with the amount of the debt, when it was due, the date and reason (the goods or services) the debt was incurred, along with the invoice number for the transaction.

It is important to give the customer a definite date by which you expect to receive payment and emphasize to the customer that he or she will incur late penalties or interest if payment isn't received by that date. In closing, be sure to thank the customer if he or she has already sent payment. That lets the customer know you appreciate the business and look forward to a continuing relationship.

If a customer fails to respond to an initial reminder to pay, a second reminder letter with a stronger tone, along with a request for immediate payment should follow. In this contact, you should

WRITING OFF A DEBT

When small-business owners are unsuccessful at collecting their own past-due accounts, many don't know what to do next. Often, they'll just write off the bad debts as a cost of doing business. The American Collectors Association (ACA), one of the leading trade associations for collectors, estimates that in 2007, business debt write-offs totaled 0.6 percent of total business revenues.

specifically tell the customer that the letter is the second reminder about a past-due account. Let the customer know when the first letter was sent, provide the invoice number again, and give the date on which the late payment was expected.

You should also point out whether part or no payment was received and the amount that is still outstanding. Let the customer know of any late penalty payments or interest that you have added to the outstanding balance. Finally, tell the customer to call to arrange a payment schedule if he or she is unable to make immediate payment.

Be sure to keep copies of all correspondence with the customer, as well as a record of any follow-up telephone conversations. They are important not only for your record keeping, but also if you eventually have to go to court to pursue the debt.

Turning Over a Past-Due Account to Collections

The Association of Credit and Collection Professionals says most consumer accounts are referred to outside collections when they have gone unpaid for an average of eight months and the creditor has received no communication from the delinquent debtor.

The Minneapolis-based trade group suggests that you

TALKING TO A LAWYER: PREVENTING BAD DEBT

Q. How can I reduce my collections problems by reducing the amount of bad debt I have in the first place? Any tips?

A. Many small-business owners fail to realize how important cash flow is to the success of their business. It not only gives you the ability to pay your bills and your employees but also provides the money you might need for expansion or investment—critical steps to helping your business thrive.

There are several quick and relatively easy ways to improve cash flow and reduce the amount of bad debt you have:

Step One. A simple way to increase your cash flow is to shorten the time period you give your customers to pay their bills. While many businesses traditionally have offered thirty-day credit terms, a number of experts today are advising a shortened credit term of fifteen days. All you have to do is to make sure that your customer knows and agrees to that credit term at the time of sale. Let your customer also know if there will be interest or other penalties beyond that time.

Step Two. Whatever the credit terms you and your customer ultimately agree upon, *begin the collection process the day after that payment is due.* Surveys of successful credit operations confirm that the quicker you respond to past-due accounts, the better—that is, the more likely you are to receive payment. Yet for some reason, many businesses today are taking the opposite track and actually are stretching out the time they let accounts receivable age. Statistics suggest that some businesses wait as long as sixty to ninety days before beginning any kind of formal collection effort.

In fact, the probability of collecting from other businesses that owe you money (called commercial collection) drops dramatically—to 72.3 percent—after only three months' delinquency. After six months, almost 44 percent of delinquent accounts will never be collected. And, after one year, the probability of ever collecting on a delinquent account drops to 28.4 percent!

—Answer by Martha Middleton,
attorney and writer, Oak Park, Illinois

should look toward hiring an outside collection agency when any of the following signs are present:

- the customer does not respond to letters or calls;
- the debtor has failed to meet the payment terms for no valid reason;
- the debtor makes repeated, unfounded complaints;
- the debtor denies responsibility;
- delinquency coexists with serious marital difficulties;
- there is repeated delinquency along with frequent changes of address and/or places of employment, if known;
- there is obvious financial irresponsibility; and
- the debtor is a *skip*—a delinquent customer who can't be found at the address or telephone number a credit grantor has on file.

 ## WHAT DOES IT COST?

While agencies' fees on collected accounts used to range from 30 percent to 50 percent of the recovery, increased competition and consolidation in the industry generally have brought fees down—and you may have some room for negotiation, too! Today the high-end fee for *consumer* collections tends to be 33.5 percent, and fees can go down to around 25 percent, particularly when the agency is working a high volume of claims for a client. While the experts say they've heard fees as low as 12 percent being quoted, they caution small-business owners that service may not be as complete with such a low fee.

Fees for *commercial* collections generally run about 25 percent. Smaller accounts handed over to collections can go as high as 33 percent but rarely over that amount, experts say.

Collection agencies are generally able to collect on only 36 percent of the small business accounts referred to them. Of those accounts that they are able to recover from, the agencies generally recover less than 30 percent of total past-due *amounts* referred by small businesses.

FEDERAL AND STATE COLLECTION LAW

Perhaps the most important collection law you must be familiar with as a small-business owner/creditor is the **Fair Debt Collection Practices Act** (FDCPA), a federal law that governs debt collection activities by third-party agencies and attorneys. The FDCPA was enacted in the 1970s to offset growing reports of abusive, deceptive, and otherwise improper collection practices.

The FDCPA, primarily enforced through private lawsuits filed by victims of improper debt collection practices as well as by the Federal Trade Commission, covers collection activities that arise specifically out of **consumer debts,** or debts individuals incur primarily for personal, family, or household purposes. The law currently *does not* apply to collectors trying to collect business or commercial debts.

The good news for creditors, including small-business owners trying to collect delinquent amounts, is that creditors themselves *are not* subject to the FDCPA. Rather, the law applies to collection agencies and other third parties that may attempt to collect debts on behalf of creditors. Nonetheless, many of the

HOW THE FDCPA IS ENFORCED

Suits brought under the FDCPA are filed in federal court. Under the law, individuals can bring suit within a year of the offense and may recover actual damages plus statutory damages up to $1,000. Individuals also can receive **injunctive relief** in the form of court orders forbidding a third-party debt collector from continuing any improper practice. **Class actions**, which involve a group of people suing a third-party debt collector, also are possible under the FDCPA. The class can recover damages up to $500,000, or 1 percent of the collector's net worth, whichever is less. If it's determined that an individual has filed suit in bad faith, he or she must pay the other side's attorneys' fees and court costs.

federal law's provisions are relevant to fair and effective debt collection, and prudent creditors engaged in their own debt collections should follow them.

Creditors aren't totally off the hook legally when doing their own collections, though. While they are not subject to the FDCPA, nearly half of the states have their own laws regulating debt collection activities against consumers that *do* apply to creditors!

Here's the Law

The main provisions of the Fair Debt Collection Practices Act are:

- A debt collector may contact an individual only by mail, in person, or by telephone during convenient hours. Unless an individual agrees in writing (or with court permission), a collector may not contact the individual at inconvenient times or places, such as before 8 A.M. or after 9 P.M.

- A debt collector is not permitted to contact an individual at work if the collector knows or has reason to know that the debtor's employer forbids employees from being contacted by collectors at work. Individuals can tell the debt collector what times and places are inconvenient to receive the calls.

- A debt collector is not allowed to contact a debtor if the collector knows a lawyer is handling the matter for the debtor.

- A debt collector must leave an individual alone if he or she instructs the collector, in writing, to do so. Once that is done, the collector may confirm only that there will be no further contact and that some specific legal action may be or will be taken (and only if the collector means it).

- A debt collector must leave an individual alone if he or she notifies the collector in writing during the first thirty days after being contacted that all or part of the debt is being disputed, unless the collector provides proof of the debt.

- A debt collector must send a written notice, within five days of the first contact with an individual, stating the name of the credit grantor to whom the money is owed; the amount owed;

that the debt collector will assume the debt is genuine unless the individual challenges all or any part of it within thirty days; what action to take if the individual believes he or she does not owe the money; and that, if requested, the debt collector will provide the individual the name and address of the original creditor, if different from the current creditor.

- A debt collector may contact anyone needed to locate an individual but may not speak to anyone more than once nor mention the debt. (That includes mailing an otherwise innocuous letter in an envelope indicating it comes from a bill collector.)

- A debt collector may not harass, oppress, or abuse anyone. Specifically, a debt collector may not threaten violence to an individual, his or her property, or reputation. A collector may not use obscene or profane language; annoy an individual with repeated phone calls; make him or her accept collect phone calls; or publish an individual's name on a public roster of "deadbeats." Nor may a collector misrepresent the amount of the debt; attempt to collect amounts beyond what the contract calls for; falsely imply that the collector is a lawyer; or threaten legal or other action that the collector does not intend to take or that is not available.

FTC Action Against Creditors

Although the federal Fair Debt Collection law doesn't apply directly to you as a creditor, the Federal Trade Commission has been keeping a closer eye on the collection practices of creditors. The agency receives numerous complaints about creditors' in-house collectors, including stories that some of them use extreme collection tactics in their dealings with consumers. While the Commission cannot pursue such creditors under the FDCPA, it can and has done so under the Federal Trade Commission Act.

A federal court in 2007, for example, upheld claims against Discover Financial Services in a case involving in-house Discover Card debt collection practices that led to a debtor committing suicide after the company improperly threatened criminal action against the debtor. In 2008, the FTC received 26,000 complaints regarding in-house debt collection practices, compared to 78,000 FDCPA-related complaints. Both in-house and FDCPA-related debt collection complaints represented approximately 25 percent of the total consumer complaints the FTC received in 2008.

Even though the FTC is far more apt to pursue cases such as these, which cover major retailers and thousands of consumers, than cases involving a small business, you should be aware that state and local authorities *are* likely to pursue smaller cases.

And it's possible that the FDCPA might apply to a small business. Even though the FDCPA does not apply directly to creditors collecting their own debt, creditors have been brought under the law in specific circumstances. Under the act, a debt collector is defined to include a creditor that, in the process of collecting its own debts, uses any name other than its own to indicate that a third person is collecting or attempting to collect the debt.

In 2008, the FTC settled an action filed in June 2007 against Tono Records and related companies and individuals (the defendants) whose representatives allegedly victimized Spanish-speaking consumers nationwide by posing as debt collectors seeking payments for purported debts that consumers did not owe. Because the defendants presented themselves as if they were third-party debt collectors, they were subject to the FDCPA as well as the Federal Trade Commission Act (the FTC Act, which prohibits deceptive trade practices). The settlement included a $1.9 million fine against the defendants and a permanent injunction to prevent them in the future from trying to collect amounts that were not yet due and otherwise harassing victims. Also, in late 2009, the FTC and the State of Nevada entered a $1 million settlement with a number of related Internet payday lenders and their principals for violating the FTC Act and other statutes by, among other things, using abusive and deceptive debt collection tactics.

The message for small-business owners is to take debt collection seriously. You don't want to be on the other side of a lawsuit that alleges you have mistreated or harassed a delinquent debtor.

WHAT TO DO WHEN THE
CHECK IS NO GOOD

You can try several routes when a customer's check bounces. First, contact the customer, who truly may have thought his or her checking account had enough money to cover the check. If that's the case and the check can now be covered, tell the customer you'll redeposit it.

If the check does bounce and you can't get satisfaction from the customer, plenty of third-party agencies specialize in the check collection business. District attorneys (DAs) or their counterparts also collect on nonsufficient funds (NSF) accounts. A 2006 amendment to the FDCPA allows local prosecutors to hire collection agencies to collect NSF checks, and county prosecutors in approximately half the states now do so. It is up to you to decide whether to use a private collection agency or a DA's program. You don't pay anything to turn over your bad check to either the DA's programs or private collectors, which make money by tacking on service charges that the check writer is required to pay. For private collectors, that fee is regulated by law in most states and must stay between $15 and $30.

Luckily, numerous high-tech point-of-sale verification and authorization systems are also available so that small-business owners can find out whether they should take a customer's check right at the time of purchase.

BOUNCED CHECKS, A
BILLION-DOLLAR PROBLEM

Historically, only about 1 percent of checks written are NSF, but they represent $20 billion per year. However, as debit cards become more popular (over 75 percent of Americans now have one), and since they are verified for sufficient funds at the point of sale, it can be expected that NSF checks will decrease over time.

SEE YOU IN COURT!

While most creditors don't like to end up in court with their bad-debt cases, sometimes that route becomes inevitable. The good news for the creditor: More than 90 percent of all collections cases filed, once the summons has been appropriately served, result in the entry of a **default judgment** (a judgment entered against the defendant because he or she didn't show up in court). A creditor who has secured a default judgment is entitled to collect interest on unpaid balances until they are paid. Default judgments, in turn, can give rise to **garnishments** (wage attachments or bank attachments) and other judgment remedies.

Title III of the Consumer Credit Protection Act (the Federal Garnishment Law) permits garnishments only up to 25 percent of a person's disposable earnings in any pay period or amounts over thirty times the current minimum wage during the pay period, whichever is less. If a state wage garnishment law differs from the Federal Garnishment Law, the employer must observe the law resulting in the smaller garnishment. Laws on wage garnishments vary from state to state. Texas, for example, prohibits all wage garnishment, while New York limits garnishment to 10 percent of gross income or the federal maximum amount, whichever is less. The rules for garnishing property and money also vary from state to state. A number of items may be exempt from collection in your state, so check carefully before proceeding. It is not necessarily the laws of the state where you are located that will apply—the laws of the state where the debtor or the property is located will control.

As long as the amount is low enough, suing in your state's small claims courts might be relatively easy and cost-effective for you. Be aware, though, that in some states businesses are not permitted to sue as plaintiffs in small claims courts. Also, in some states, a party may sue as plaintiff only a limited number of times.

For a variety of reasons, you may decide to—or have to—sue your delinquent account holders in a higher court. That route can get expensive and takes more time, too. Collection professionals have several rules of thumb for when a delinquent account should end up in court. Accounts that merit litigation are those that are likely never to be paid voluntarily, something you've probably uncovered during the course of your earlier collection activity. If the balance of the debt were large enough, this claim would be a natural for suit.

Don't just consider the balance of a debt, though. Another thing to think about is its freshness—the newer it is, the more likely you are to recover on it. You'll also want to find out whether the defendant is employed and how stable that employment is. With stable employment, there's a greater likelihood of being able to successfully garnish a debtor's wages. Credit experts say you should also try to find out a debtor's other attachable assets, such as bank accounts.

If your small business involves sales of goods such as cars, trucks, large appliances, or other durable goods, those purchased with credit may be subject to **repossession** (you can take the items back) for nonpayment. To repossess an item, you have to have a **security interest** in it (that is, your contract with the purchaser must have specified that you had the right to take the property back in the event of nonpayment). Some states require advance notice before you can repossess. You also must be careful to avoid a **breach of the peace** in repossessing an item. *Breach of the peace* is a legal term describing the act of creating disorder or a public disturbance.

There are times when you should avoid litigation. There may be merit in pulling debtors' credit reports to see how they stand with other creditors and if they are already facing legal actions. Is the debtor a skip? If so, litigation is not the answer, because if you can't find the debtor, you're not going to get paid. Does the debtor have other judgments against him or her? If so, watch out for a possible bankruptcy in the near future; a bankruptcy could wipe out your claim. And uncollected judgments of other creditors should be a sign that litigation may not be cost-effective for that account. The bottom line? Never file suit against an uncollectible debtor.

TALKING TO A LAWYER: SMALL CLAIMS COURT

Q. *Some people in my field collect (or try to) by suing debtors in small claims court, but I've never tried that and have no idea of how to begin. Any ideas for me?*

A. For debts ranging up to a maximum of $10,000 (amounts vary depending on the state), you may find that small claims court is the best avenue for you to recover debts your customer owes you. In small claims court, procedures are simple, and there's often not much of a backlog of cases. To prevail, you need to prove the debt exists, its amount, when payment was due, and that the person you are suing hasn't paid it or has only partially paid it.

You normally don't need a lawyer to file and/or handle a claim in small claims court. If you can't appear in court, however, someone will have to appear in court on your behalf.

—Answer by Martha Middleton,
attorney and writer, Oak Park, Illinois

ALTERNATIVE DISPUTE RESOLUTION

Increasingly, **mediation** and **arbitration** are being used as alternatives to litigation, especially in commercial situations that several years ago almost certainly would have ended up in court. In mediation, a neutral third party meets with both sides to help them reach a mutually acceptable resolution. Arbitration occurs when a dispute is submitted to a neutral third party, who hears the matter and makes a decision.

Both mediation and arbitration come into play at the time a claim normally would be turned over for legal action. A number of companies, in fact, have put arbitration and mediation clauses into their credit applications, contracts, and other agreements. Some courts have begun to order companies with disputes into mediation or arbitration. The reasoning behind such a development is that accounts become delinquent for a reason, but the traditional adversarial processes do not uncover that reason. Such information can be especially critical in a commercial or retail setting because the goal is a continuing relationship between the parties.

YOU MUST REMEMBER THIS

- Nip problems in the bud—don't give debtors too long to pay, or put off trying to collect debt.
- Try to resolve problems informally, through negotiation or alternative dispute resolution, rather than rushing to court.
- Collection agencies might be an attractive alternative for really troublesome debt—at least you might get something.
- If you personally try to collect debts owed to you, be aware of laws governing collections in your state.
- Small claims court might be a relatively attractive, simple alternative; save higher courts for a very small number of cases in which the delay and expense of a lawsuit might be worth it.

PART V

Running the Business

The day-to-day operations of almost any business are loaded with legal issues. Whenever you buy from a supplier or lease property or sign up to run a package of ads, you're entering into a contract. You might not call it a contract, and it doesn't always have to be written, but *it is a contract* if it involves promises exchanged between you and the other person in exchange for money or any other thing of value.

We give you the basics on contracts in this section, including a rundown of some important clauses to watch for and some tips on how to get the benefit of the bargain in particular kinds of contracts. And since this is an imperfect world where things can go wrong, we talk about how to handle disputes as easily and inexpensively as possible.

This part of the book also looks at ways you can protect your business. We issue warnings on some common scams against small businesses and tell you the steps you can take to shield yourself against predators. We also discuss how you can protect a special kind of property—intellectual property. This includes any patents, trademarks, trade secrets, or other property that has value and might be appropriated—unless you know how to use the law's protections.

CHAPTER 23

Contracts

*Understanding Legally Enforceable
Agreements in Your Business's Transactions*

*As a savvy businessperson, you probably already know better
than to sign any business contract before your lawyer reviews
it. But every contract need not be in writing to be enforceable.
And, more important, unless you know what constitutes a contract, you may inadvertently sign a document that is, indeed,
a legal, enforceable contract. This chapter will help you understand the fundamentals of contract law so that you can answer many of your own questions about everyday business
transactions, as well as enhance your ability to use other parts
of this book.*

WHAT IS A CONTRACT?

Basically, a **contract** is a voluntary promise or group of
promises that the law will enforce. These promises must
be made between competent parties to do—or refrain from
doing—something. These binding promises may be oral or written. In most cases, a contract obligates you to perform your side
of the agreement even if you want to call the deal off before receiving anything from the other side. The details of the
contract—who, how, what, how much, how many, when, and so
forth—are called its **provisions** or **terms.**

You don't need a lawyer to form a contract. If you satisfy the
maturity and mental capacity requirements, discussed on page
279, you don't need anyone else (besides the other party). But
most businesspeople turn to competent lawyers to review complex contracts, such as business deals involving large amounts of
money. After all, the devil is in the details, and unless you have a
thorough understanding of commercial laws, you probably won't

understand all the details of a complex contract. But even simple contracts can be troublesome, as so many businesspeople discover when they're dragged into court. Knowing the basics could help you avoid a big mistake.

To qualify as a contract, a promise must be supported by the exchange of something of value between the participants or parties. This is called **consideration**. Consideration is most often money in exchange for property or services, but it can be some other bargained-for benefit or detriment (as explained more fully later in this chapter). The subject of the promise (including the consideration) may not be illegal.

Let's consider the example of an exhibitor getting ready for a big trade show. He e-mails an order to a supplier to buy 1,000 miniature flashlights engraved with his company's logo. The order says that he will pay $4 per flashlight, but the supplier must deliver them one week before the trade show. The supplier signs the order and faxes it back to the exhibitor. That's a contract, right? Right.

Now, suppose the exhibitor and supplier merely agree to this arrangement over the phone: There's nothing in writing. Is that a contract? Yes, although either one of the parties might find it difficult to defend in court. In both cases, consideration has been offered and accepted, and both parties have agreed to terms. Even if the exhibitor finds out the next day that he can

---

 ## THE LAW COVERS IT

Just about all the examples we use in this chapter (and many more) are covered by the **Uniform Commercial Code (UCC).** The code is the work of legal scholars under the aegis of the Commission on Uniform State Laws, an organization that drafts model laws and urges that they be adopted by the states. Thanks to the UCC, the laws governing contracts involving goods are essentially identical in every state. Laws governing contracts involving services, however, can vary from state to state.

CONTRACT LANGUAGE

A valid written contract does not have to be a printed, legal-looking document. Nor does it have to be called a contract. A typed or even handwritten "agreement," "letter of agreement," or "letter of understanding" signed by the parties will be valid if it meets the legal requirements of a contract. Don't sign something assuming that it is not a contract and, therefore, not important.

It is also common for the word *contract* to be used as a verb meaning "to enter into a contract." And we speak of **contractual relationships** to refer to the series of sometimes complex relationships or transactions that may constitute one or many contracts.

---

buy the flashlights for $3.75 each from another supplier, he is bound to the terms of his oral or written contract to buy them from the original supplier.

Now, in all likelihood, the exhibitor would call his supplier and say, "Hey, I can get these flashlights for $3.75 each from So-and-So Co. What gives?" And, in all likelihood, the supplier would agree to match the price—especially if he wants to continue doing business with the exhibitor. The point, however, is that many business transactions constitute a contract, whether they're in writing or not.

CAPACITY

Not just anyone can enter into a contract. People have to be able to understand what they are doing to create an enforceable contract. That requires both **maturity** and **mental capacity**. Without both of these, one party could be at a disadvantage in the bargaining process, which could invalidate the contract.

For businesses, capacity generally comes into play in sales to minors. In this sense, maturity is defined as a certain age a person reaches, regardless of whether he or she is in fact "mature." State laws permit persons to make contracts if they have reached the **age of majority** (no longer considered a minor), which is usually age eighteen. That doesn't mean a minor cannot make contracts, by the way. But courts may choose not to enforce some of them, raising concerns for you as a businessperson if you have a contract with a minor.

The law presumes that minors need to be protected from their lack of maturity and won't allow, for example, a salesperson to exploit a minor's naïveté by enforcing a signed sales contract whose implications a young person is unlikely to have comprehended.

In practical terms, sometimes this results in a minor receiving benefits (such as goods or services) and not having to pay for them, though they would have to return any goods still in their possession. This may apply even to minors who are **emancipated**—living entirely on their own—who get involved in contractual relationships, as well as to minors who live at home but are unsupervised long enough to get into a contractual fix.

A court may require a minor or the minor's parents to pay the fair market value (not necessarily the contract price) for what courts call **necessaries** (what you and I would likely call "necessities"). The definition of a *necessary* depends entirely on the person and the situation. It probably will always include food and probably will never include CDs, MP3 players, or Porsches. Minors who reach the age of majority and do not disavow their contracts may then have to comply with all their terms, and in some states, courts may require a minor to pay the fair market value of goods or services purchased and received under a contract that a minor has disavowed.

There are other people besides minors who may not be able to form enforceable contracts. While the age test for legal maturity is easy to determine, the standards for determining mental capacity are remarkably complex and differ widely from one state to another. One common test is whether someone has the capacity to understand what he or she was doing and to appreci-

WHO ARE YOU DEALING WITH?

We've discussed the fundamental requirements for competence to make a contract—maturity and mental capacity. Of course, it should go without saying that there's an even more fundamental requirement:that both parties be people. In the case of a corporation or other legal entity that the law considers a person, this could be an issue. A problem in the formation or status of the business entity could cause it to cease to exist, legally thus making it impossible to enter into a contract. In that case, however, the individuals who signed the contract on behalf of the legally nonexistent entity could be personally liable for fulfilling the contract.

ate its effects when the deal was made. Another approach is evaluating whether someone has self-control of his or her understanding.

That brings up the question of whether an intoxicated person can be held to a contract. Very often someone who is under the influence can get out of a contract. The courts don't like to let a voluntarily intoxicated person revoke a contract with innocent parties this way, but if the evidence shows that someone acted drunk when making a contract, a court may well assume that the other party probably was trying to take advantage of the situation. That means if you cut a deal with your supplier's sales representative over a three-martini lunch, that deal could be jeopardized. On the other hand, if someone doesn't appear to be intoxicated, he or she probably will have to follow the terms of the contract unless he or she can prove a lack of capacity. (The key to this may be a person's medical history: A person who can show a history of alcohol abuse, blackouts, and the like may be able to void the contract, regardless of his or her appearance when the contract was made. This is true especially if the other party involved knew about the prior medical history.)

VOID VERSUS VOIDABLE CONTRACTS

A *void* contract is so improper or illegal that a court will not recognize or enforce it. For example, an agreement between two individuals to rob a store and split the take is a void contract. No court will uphold this contract if one of the robbers takes all the money. A *voidable* contract is also an improper contract, but the victim has the choice of whether to avoid (cancel) the contract. For example, if the seller of a car significantly misrepresents the quality of the car, the buyer may choose to avoid the contract and get his money back, or go ahead and enforce the contract because he wants the car anyway.

WRITTEN AND ORAL CONTRACTS

As with a written contract, the existence of an oral contract must be proved before the courts will enforce it. But as you can imagine, an oral contract can be very hard to prove: You seldom have it on tape. If our exhibitor had an oral agreement for his flashlights, and the supplier failed to deliver them on time, would the exhibitor be justified in refusing payment? A plaintiff usually can prove an oral contract by showing that outside circumstances would lead a reasonable observer to conclude that a contract most likely existed. The exhibitor might say, "Sure, we had a contract, but he failed to deliver them for the show." The supplier might say, "He failed to specify a due date." Sounds like a split decision. Taking a few more minutes to put a contract in writing can avoid this situation.

But ignore oral contracts at your peril. Although oral contracts can be difficult to enforce, courts will look at whatever evidence is available to establish whether a contract exists and what its terms are. In particular, the courts will look at the conduct of the parties; is there correspondence between the parties, did the buyer review samples, did the seller send an invoice? In our example, the flashlights with the exhibitor's name printed on them would be considered specially manufactured goods—and the court will enforce an oral contract for them because the supplier would not be able to sell them to anyone else (and why else would the supplier have printed the exhibitor's name on the flashlights but for their agreement?). Without a written contract, the real problem will be proving the exact terms of the agreement, such as the price and when the flashlights would be delivered.

Although most states recognize and enforce oral contracts, the safest practice is to put any substantial agreement in writing. It cannot be said enough: Get any promise from a salesperson or an agent in writing, especially if there already is a written document that might arguably be a contract covering any part of the same deal. If it ends up in court or mediation, the written document—a handwritten "letter of agreement" or "understanding" or even an order form—may be assumed to contain all its terms and be a complete statement of all understandings between the parties. The court or mediator would be very hesitant to add words or terms to the document.

The reluctance to add words or terms to a written contract comes from what is known as the **parol evidence rule**. Under this rule, courts typically look only to **unrefuted** (uncontested) testimony to help them fill in the blanks of a contract. Anything excluded from that written contract would be deemed not part of the deal. Writing down terms of a good-faith agreement is the best way to ensure that all parties are aware of their rights and duties, even if no party intends to lie about the provisions of the agreement.

While oral contracts may be legally enforceable, there are some contracts that are completely unenforceable if they are not in writing. This requirement for written contracts, which exists in varying forms in nearly all the states, had its origins in the famous **statute of frauds**, an English law dating from 1677. It refers to frauds because it attempts to prevent fraudulent testimony in support of nonexistent agreements. In most states, courts will enforce certain contracts only if they are in writing and are signed by the parties who are going to be obligated to fulfill them. These contracts often include:

• any promise to be responsible for someone else's debts in the event that person fails to pay—often called a **guaranty**, such as an agreement to pay off the debts of a business you purchased;

• any promise that the parties cannot possibly fulfill within one year after they made the promise;

• any promise involving the change of ownership of land or interests in land such as leases;

• any promise to pay a broker a commission for the sale of real estate;

• any promise for the sale of goods worth $500 or more (this is the amount in the Uniform Commercial Code);

• any promise to **bequeath** property (give it after death);

• any promise to sell stocks and bonds (this provision is not present in some states).

Some states have additional requirements for written contracts. These statutes are designed to prevent fraudulent claims in areas where it is uniquely difficult to prove that oral contracts have been made or where important policies are at stake, such as the dependability of real estate ownership rights. Promises to extend credit are often in this category.

Such state requirements are also typical in the automobile repairs industry; many states require that estimates for repair work be given in writing. If they are not and the repairs are done anyway, the contract may not be enforceable, and the repair shop may not be able to get its money if the customer disputes authorizing the repairs.

Where a written contract is required, a signature by the **party to be charged**—the person by whom the contract will be held—is also necessary. In other words, you cannot sue a party who has not signed the contract. A signature can be handwritten, but a stamped, photocopied, or engraved signature is often valid as well, as are signatures written by electronic pens. Even a simple mark or other indication of a name may be enough. What matters is whether the signature is authorized and intended to

ONLINE SIGNATURES

State courts are beginning to rule that e-mail messages are signed writings for purposes of the statute of frauds when the sender types his or her name at the end of the message, signifying an intent to authenticate the contents of the message. Courts are also enforcing online agreements in cases where the Web site user selected an "I agree" button (as long as there was an opportunity for the user to first review the terms and conditions of the transaction).

authenticate a writing—that is, indicates the signer's **execution** (completion and acceptance) of it. This means that you can authorize someone else to sign for you as well. But the least risky and most persuasive evidence of assent is your own handwritten signature.

Incidentally, hardly any contracts require notarization today. Notary publics or notaries, once important officials who were specially authorized to draw up contracts and transcribe official proceedings, act now primarily to administer oaths and to authenticate documents by attesting or certifying that a signature is genuine. Many commercial contracts, such as promissory notes or loan contracts, are routinely notarized with the notary's signature and seal to ensure that they are authentic, even when

 HOW TO FIND A NOTARY PUBLIC

Most banks and credit unions provide complimentary notary public services for their customers. One can also usually find a notary public in city hall, the county clerk's office, and law offices. Just make sure you do not sign the document before you are in front of the notary public, and make sure you have photo I.D. to prove you are who you say you are.

this is not strictly required. Many technical documents required by law, such as certificates of incorporation and real property deeds, must be notarized if they are going to be recorded in a local or state filing office.

OFFER AND ACCEPTANCE

Offer and acceptance are the fundamental parts of a contract once capacity is established.

Offer

An **offer** is a communication by an **offeror** (the person making the offer) of a present intent to enter a contract. The offeror initiates the offer. The exhibitor's offer was to buy one thousand flashlights at $4 each to be delivered by a certain date. He did not invite the supplier to bargain or negotiate. For the communication to be effective, the **offeree** (the one who is receiving the offer) must receive it. In a contract to buy and sell, all of the following must be clear in order for the offer to be valid:

- Who is making the offer?
- What is the subject matter of the offer?
- In a goods contract, what is the quantity of goods to be sold?
- How much is offered (price to be paid)?

Our exhibitor made the offer, the supplier received it, and the flashlights are the subject matter. Describing the flashlights, such as referring to an order number, ensures that the supplier is reasonably aware that both of you are talking about the same flashlights. Finally, the price is $4,000. It's a perfectly good offer.

Advertisements are not offers, as much as they seem like they are. Instead, courts usually consider advertisements an "expression of intent to see" or an invitation to bargain. See chapter 20 for a more detailed discussion of the legal consequences of advertising.

An offer doesn't stay open indefinitely, unless the offeree has an irrevocable option (options are discussed in detail below).

The offeror is generally in control of his or her offer. Unless there's an option, an offer ends (expires) when:

- the time to accept is up—either a "reasonable" amount of time or the deadline stated in the offer;
- the offeror cancels (revokes) the offer;
- the offeree rejects the offer;
- the offeree makes a counteroffer; or
- the offeror dies or is incapacitated.

An offer is also closed, even if the offeree has an option, if a change in the law makes the contract illegal or something destroys the subject matter of the contract. For example, if Sam has made an offer that is good for one week to buy Mark's cottage, and two days later the cottage burns down, the offer is considered closed.

The general rule for offers is that the offeror can revoke (cancel) his or her offer anytime before it is accepted by the offeree. But there are two exceptions to this rule. As noted above, there are special kinds of contracts called options. An **option** is an agreement, made for consideration, to keep an offer open for a certain period of time.

For example, let's consider the example of a florist who wants to buy a greenhouse. She is very interested in buying one

 WHAT IS A REASONABLE AMOUNT OF TIME?

It depends on the circumstances. An offer to enter into a complex contract or one involving a substantial amount of goods or services to be provided over a long period of time may require a good deal of thought on the part of the offeree. On the other hand, an offer to purchase an item the offeree/seller has in stock shouldn't take more than a day or two to accept or reject. In any event, an offer will expire on its own once the point is reached in which the offeree cannot perform within the time specified in the offer.

a few blocks from her shop, but she and the owner have been wrangling over the price. Now she discovers that a greenhouse a few miles away is on the market. While she would prefer the nearby greenhouse, she doesn't want the other one to slip away. (There's a hot market for greenhouses!) So she offers the owner of the second greenhouse $500 for the right to match any other offers the owner receives in the next three months. (This also is called a **right of first refusal**.) That way, the florist can continue to negotiate for the closer greenhouse, but if someone else makes an offer on the second greenhouse, she won't be out of luck. The $500 is not a down payment or deposit; it's the price of the option in case another buyer comes along. The consideration given in exchange for the option usually is not refundable. In this case, the seller might agree to allow the option payment to be applied against the actual closing price.

The second exception involves offers by merchants. A merchant is someone who regularly deals in goods that are the subject of the offer. (For example, in our flashlight transaction, the exhibitor would not be considered a merchant since he does not regularly buy flashlights—they are just for this one exhibit—but the supplier is a merchant of flashlights since it regularly sells them.) If a merchant makes a written offer to buy or sell goods he or she regularly deals in, and states in the offer that it will remain open for a set period of time (up to three months), then the merchant/offeror cannot revoke (cancel) the offer during that

 GIVE AND TAKE

A contract can come about only through a bargaining process, which may take many forms. This chapter discusses the definitions of consideration, offer, and acceptance. Even though they may not be labeled with the terms we have used, all the principles discussed here will have to be present, in some form, in any contract.

stated time. In other words, the offer is irrevocable for that stated period of time. And the offeree does not have to pay any consideration to keep the offer open.

Acceptance

A contract is not complete unless the offer is accepted. But what exactly constitutes the acceptance of an offer? **Acceptance** is the offeree's voluntary, communicated agreement or assent to the terms and conditions of the offer. **Assent** is some act or promise of agreement. Generally, a valid acceptance requires that every material term agreed upon be the same as in the offer.

Does it matter how an offer is accepted? Unless the offer specifically limits the mode of acceptance, you just have to communicate your acceptance by some reasonable means (not by carrier pigeon, smoke signals, or channeling, but by telephone, mail, e-mail, or fax). If the offer requires acceptance by mail, you must accept by mail for the offer to be effective. Be aware that under the **mailbox rule**, an offer accepted by mail is usually effective when you put the letter in the mailbox, not when it is received, unless the terms of the offer state otherwise. While the mailbox rule got its name when the mail was the primary form of long-distance communication, the same rule is applied generally to fax, telephone, or e-mail communication, as well. In other words, at the time when the fax is sent or the message is left on the answering machine, the acceptance becomes effective. And, when using e-mail, as long as you can show you sent your acceptance to the appropriate e-mail address, an acceptance is effective when you send the e-mail message (even if it winds up in the recipient's junk e-mail folder).

In the example of our exhibitor, the supplier's faxed agreement of the order would constitute acceptance. On the other hand, an assent that is not quite so specific but is crystal-clear in its meaning would also suffice, such as the supplier's calling and saying "It's a deal. I'll deliver the flashlights on May 3." The standard is whether a reasonable observer would think there was an assent.

THE REASONABLE PERSON

Throughout this and any other law book, the word *reasonable* will appear many times. Very often you'll see references to the **reasonable man** or the **reasonable person**. Why is the law so preoccupied with this mythical being?

The answer is that no contract can possibly predict the infinite number of disputes that might arise under it. Similarly, no set of laws regulating liability for personal or property injury can possibly foresee the countless ways human beings and their property can harm other people or property. Because the law cannot provide for every possibility, it has developed the standard of the "reasonable person" to furnish some uniform standards and to guide the courts.

Through the fiction of the "reasonable person," the law creates a standard that the judge or jury may apply to each set of circumstances. This standard reflects commonsense community values, rather than the judgment of people involved in the actual case. Thus, a court might decide whether an oral contract was formed by asking whether a "reasonable person" would conclude from the parties' actions that one did exist. Or the court might decide an automobile accident case by asking what a "reasonable person" might have done in a particular traffic or hazardous situation. In the case of a business, be aware that the reasonable standard will apply to you in terms of the conventions and customers of your industry or market.

In most cases, silence does not constitute acceptance of an offer. It isn't fair to allow someone to impose a contract on you unless you go out of your way to stop it. Hence, the exhibitor cannot force a contract for the flashlights simply because the supplier failed to reject his offer. Nonetheless, there are circumstances where failure to respond may have a contractual effect.

Suppose an insurance company, with which you have had a

policy in the past, sends you a renewal policy for casualty insurance (which is, in effect, a new contract for insurance) and bills you for the premium. If you didn't cancel the policy but later refused to pay the premium, you would be liable for the premium. This works to everyone's benefit: If your warehouse burned down after the original insurance policy had expired but before you had paid the renewal premium, you obviously would want the policy still to be effective. And the insurer is protected from your decision to pay the premium only when you know you have sustained a casualty loss.

Speechless *acts* can also constitute an acceptance. Any conduct that would lead a reasonable observer to believe that the offeree had accepted the offer qualifies as an acceptance. Suppose you say to one of your office workers, "Sally, I'll pay you time-and-a-half to come in Saturday morning and get these files in order." If Sally shows up at 8 A.M. and begins filing, she adequately shows acceptance (assuming you're in the office or you otherwise would know she showed up).

To take another example, you don't normally have to pay for goods shipped to you that you didn't order. You would only have to allow them to be taken back at no cost to you. However, let's assume that the laws on unordered merchandise in your state are limited to consumers and don't apply to business recipients of such merchandise. If you own a shop, receive unordered items, put them on display in your store, and sell them, you might have accepted the offer to buy them from the wholesaler and you thus are obligated to pay the invoice price. Sometimes this is called an **implied** (as opposed to an **express**) contract. Either one is a genuine contract.

A contract usually is in effect as soon as the offeree transmits or communicates the acceptance—unless the offer has expired or the offeror has specified that the acceptance must be *received* before it is effective or before an option expires (as discussed previously). In these situations, there's no contract until the offeror receives the acceptance, and in the way specified, if any.

WHEN AN AGREEMENT ISN'T A CONTRACT

An **agreement to agree** (sometimes referred to as a letter of intent) is seldom a contract because it suggests that important terms are still missing. Rarely will a court supply those terms itself. An agreement to agree is another way of saying that there has not yet been a meeting of the minds, although the parties would like there to be.

Another common question people have, as funny as it sounds, is whether a joke can be an offer. That depends on whether a reasonable observer would know it's a joke and on whether the acceptance was adequate. In our exhibitor's example, you probably couldn't get out of the contract by saying, "How could you think I'd sell these for $4,000? I meant it as a joke!" On the other hand, if someone sued you because you "backed out" on your "promise" to sell him your multimillion-dollar business for $15, the joke would be on him. No one could have reasonably thought you were serious.

Rejection and Counteroffer

Once an offer has been made, the offeree has the power to accept it, reject it, or make a counteroffer. We discussed acceptance above. A **rejection** is simply a "no" by the offeree. Rejections are usually considered effective when received by the offeror (yes, an offeree could mail a rejection to the offeror and then change his mind and call the offeror to accept the offer—the acceptance would create a contract as long as it was made before the earlier rejection was received by the offeror). And rejections are final; once received, the offeree cannot later accept the offer.

A **counteroffer** is a "no, but" response by the offeree. A counteroffer is technically considered a rejection of the original offer while, at the same time, a new offer by the original offeree (and now the roles are reversed—the original offeror is now the counteroffer's offeree). Care must be taken to distinguish between a counteroffer and merely an inquiry. In our exhibit flashlight example, if the supplier responded to the exhibitor's offer by stating, "No, I cannot sell you the flashlights for $4.00 each, but I will sell them to you for $4.25," that is a counteroffer. However, in the bargaining process, the supplier might be interested in doing the deal but is hoping the exhibitor might be flexible on price; so the supplier may say, "$4.00 each is pretty tough for me to do, can you be flexible on price?" This would be neither a rejection nor a counteroffer.

CONDITIONS

Most contracts have conditions. People often use the word *condition* to mean one of the terms of a contract. But a more precise definition is that a **condition** is an event that has to occur before one or both parties may be required to perform. A condition can be a promise. For example, when the exhibitor requires the flashlights to be delivered by a specific date, and the supplier accepts that condition, the delivery date is made a condition of the contract.

On the other hand, many conditions involve uncertain events not under the direct control of the parties to the contract. Thus, neither of them can promise anything about the conditions, but the conditions still must be fulfilled for the contract to go forward.

Let's look at an example of our florist. She is bidding for a contract to provide flowers for a wedding. The florist, the bride, and the groom have discussed the number of arrangements and general price range. Now the couple expects a contract. But in the floral industry, the price of flowers fluctuates daily based on availability. Let's say the florist writes the contract to provide the floral arrangements for a specified price, but the contract does not specify which flowers will be used in the arrangements. If the couple agrees, they sign the contract. The florist can choose any type of flowers to create the arrangement, but both she and the couple are locked into the price.

Let's say this particular bride and groom are very picky. They want some exotic flowers, which the florist's suppliers do not regularly carry. The florist believes she can obtain the flowers, but she cannot guarantee it. So the florist writes the offer to specify that she will provide the desired flowers to the customer at cost plus a modest markup, contingent on availability. In short, this condition lets the florist off the hook if it is impossible to obtain the desired flowers. Given that this is a wedding— and the couple expects to have flowers—most likely she also would ask the couple to provide a second choice of flowers in case she could not get their first choice.

CONSIDERATION

In order for a contract to exist, both sides must give some consideration. **Consideration** is any promise, act, or transfer of value that induces a party to enter a contract. Consideration is a bargained-for benefit or advantage, or a bargained-for detriment or disadvantage. In our flashlight example, the consideration exchanged is $4,000 for 1,000 flashlights. The supplier receives $4,000 (a benefit) in exchange for no longer having 1,000 flashlights (a detriment); the exhibitor gives up $4,000 (a detriment) in exchange for having 1,000 flashlights with his name embossed on them (a benefit).

Consideration can be a bit more complex. For example, the supplier could agree to sell the exhibitor the flashlights for $3,500 in exchange for the exhibitor's promise to also buy something else, such as key chains, from the supplier. The exhibitor is giving up what is presumably his right to buy the key chains elsewhere in exchange for a better price, while the supplier receives a lower price in exchange for the promise of more business later.

Another type of consideration includes a promise to compromise on an existing dispute. For example, if a buyer believes she did not receive the value of what she paid, the seller may be willing to accept a lower amount to avoid a prolonged dispute.

Consideration is key to a crucial principle in contract law called **mutuality of obligation**. It means that both sides have to be committed to giving something or doing something. If either party reserves an unqualified right to bail out, that person's promise is illusory: no promise at all.

There is no minimum amount of consideration required to effect a contract. A price is only how people agree to value something, so there is no absolute standard of whether a price is fair or reasonable. The courts presume that people will only make deals that they consider worthwhile. So if you enter a contract to sell 1,000 flashlights for $4,000, a court will probably enforce it. (But watch out if you sell them for $5,000 and just report a $4,000 sale to the state to avoid paying the full sales tax. It's unethical, illegal, and dangerous: Many states have systems in place to check for just such abuses.)

The exception is something that would "shock the conscience of the court," which might help a consumer get out of a particularly onerous contract. However, this doctrine, which was created by courts to provide protection to consumers who have been grossly taken advantage of, is not much use for businesses claiming that they agreed to pay too much for a product or service.

Consideration has to be a *new* obligation, because someone who promises to do what he or she is already obligated to do hasn't suffered any detriment or bestowed anything to which the other party wasn't already entitled.

For example, suppose the florist contracts to have her office space painted for $1,000. The contract covers the cost of labor ($700) and paint ($300). Before the job is done, the price of paint goes up, and painters demand another $100 to finish the job. The florist is under no obligation to pay the extra $100, because she is getting no consideration she wasn't already entitled to—having her office painted. The painters must fully perform their part of the bargain for $1,000. However, in contracts involving the sale of goods (i.e., tangible, movable items), no new consideration is required for contract modifications made in good faith. For example, if our florist agreed to provide flowers (which are considered "goods" in the business world) for a dinner banquet for $1,000 and because of a freeze, her cost for the flowers will now be $1,100, she could ask for the price to be modified. If the client agrees to a higher price, the client must now pay the higher price, even though the client is really getting no additional benefit for the extra cost.

No one can force another party to renegotiate. While it's true you can go to the other party and ask for more money, keep in mind that whenever you get involved in a deal, you are taking a risk that it might be less beneficial for you than you planned when you agreed to the contract terms. The other party doesn't have to ensure your profit, unless the two of you include that in your bargain. That's why many business contracts include a cost-plus provision to cover uncertainty, as in our earlier example of the florist.

RELIANCE

We said earlier that consideration is a two-way street. That means both parties must get some consideration for a contract to be formed. There is an exception to that rule. Sometimes a contract will be formed by the reliance of one party on another person's promise, even if the one making the promise hasn't gained anything. The concept of **reliance** is that a contract may be formed if one party reasonably relies on the other's promise. That means that he or she does more than expected to receive what was promised. He or she has to do something that wouldn't have been done, or fail to do something that would have been done, but for that promise. If that reliance causes some loss, he or she may have an enforceable contract.

Suppose our florist has a good friend, Kathy, who is also a customer. Kathy orders many floral displays from the florist for her company's events, as well as her own parties. Now Kathy is planning her own wedding, and she has promised our florist that she wants her to do the arrangements for her wedding. Our florist knows that the wedding is set for June 3. Another customer asks the florist to handle her wedding on June 3, but the florist declines, saying she is already booked for that day. As the date draws near, the florist calls Kathy to discuss the flowers for the wedding. It turns out that Kathy has hired another florist, a friend of the groom's mother. It's now too late for our florist to get another booking for that date. Kathy claims you can't enforce a promise. But our florist relied reasonably on Kathy's promise in declining the other wedding, which she would otherwise not have done. The florist probably could prove that Kathy induced her to decline the other wedding. Of course, the florist certainly couldn't expect to get future business from Kathy, so she probably wouldn't pursue her claim. The most important point of this example is to remember that even when you're dealing with friends, get it in writing.

AGENTS

You can have someone enter into a contract on your behalf, but only with your permission. The law refers to such an arrangement as **agency**. We couldn't do business without it. For example, when a shop owner buys supplies, he usually bargains and finally cuts a deal with the sales representative, not the owner. The sales rep is an **agent**, someone with the authority to bind someone else—in this case, the owner of the supply business. The law refers to that someone else as the **principal.** Most of the salespeople you deal with are agents.

As long as agents do not exceed the authority granted them by their principals, contracts they make bind their principals as if the principals had made the contracts themselves. If something goes wrong with the contract, you sue the principal—not the agent—if you cannot resolve the dispute in a friendly manner. An agent normally does not have any personal obligation.

While acting on behalf of principals, agents are required to put the principal's interests ahead of their own. Therefore, an agent may not personally profit beyond what the principal and agent have agreed to in their agency contract. That means an agent cannot take advantage of any opportunity that, under the terms of the agency, should be exploited for the principal.

When an agent exceeds her authority, a number of factors

**AGENTS WHO EXCEED
THEIR AUTHORITY**

On occasion, while making a contract, an agent might exceed the authority granted by the principal. An example would be an automobile salesperson who signs a contract on behalf of a car dealer, which, without the dealer's authority, gives the customer a warranty for 40,000 extra miles. In that case, the dealer might very well be bound by the contract, under the principle of apparent authority.

determine whether the contract can be enforced against the principal. Under the doctrine of **apparent authority,** if the person the agent is dealing with doesn't reasonably understand that the agent is exceeding her authority, the principal may be bound by the contract negotiated by the agent. So if an insurance agent wrote you an insurance policy from her company that exceeded the policy amount she was authorized to write, but the insurer never told you this, you may be acting reasonably to assume she was authorized, and you probably would be entitled to collect on a claim up to the higher limit.

If the other person was *not* being reasonable in believing that the agent was acting within her authority, the contract will be enforceable against the principal only if the principal has knowingly permitted the agent to do this sort of thing in the past, or in some other way led the other person to believe that the agent was authorized. For example, a buyer would not reasonably expect a kickback from a salesperson. However, if the principal knows about the kickbacks and never objects, it could be assumed the salesperson is authorized to make them.

DELEGATIONS AND ASSIGNMENTS

You can transfer your duties under a contract to someone else, unless the contract specifically prohibits such a transfer. The law refers to a transfer of duties or responsibilities as a **delegation**. If, however, someone contracts with you because of a special skill or talent only you have, you may not be able to transfer your duty. Such cases are quite rare. There are arguably no car mechanics who are so good at tuning an engine that they may not delegate the chore to someone else—unless they specifically promise to do it themselves. On the other hand, let's go back to our florist, whom the bride and groom have hired for her particular creative talents. If the florist becomes ill the week of the wedding, she probably could turn the job over to another talented florist without breaching her contract. If, however, she simply hired a group of teenagers to make the floral arrangements, and the bride and groom were unhappy with the result, they probably would have good cause to refuse to pay the bill. And, in some cases, you cannot substitute without permission. For example, if you hire specific entertainers to entertain at a company party, they may not send other entertainers (no matter how talented) as substitutes without your permission.

On the other hand, a transfer of rights, called an **assignment**, is more flexible than a transfer of duties. For example, you may wish to transfer the right to receive money from a buyer for something you have sold. Generally, a contract right is yours to do as you wish with it, as long as you didn't agree in the contract not to assign the right. You can sell it or give it away, though most states require you to put an assignment in writing, especially if it is a gift. Our florist could assign to her bank her right to receive payment for flowers she supplied for a wedding.

There are exceptions to the rule that assignments may be made freely. If an assignment would substantially increase the risk, or materially change the duty of the other party to the contract, the contract may not be assignable, even if its terms contain no explicit agreement to the contrary. Such an assignment would be regarded as unfairly upsetting the expectations the other party had when he or she entered into the contract, so that party would no longer be obligated by the terms of the contract. Generally, having someone send a required payment to a different party is not considered a substantial change.

Suppose, however, that the florist's supplier had granted her a special at-cost pricing arrangement as part of a favored-client bonus program. If she assigned the contract to a known competitor of the supplier, a court could find the assignment invalid.

SPECIAL BUSINESS CONTRACTS

Many standard forms are available for typical business correspondence and contracts. In fact, you can download many standard forms from the Internet, such as a free promissory note from www.legaldocs.com. The Web site also sells sample contracts such as guaranties, noncompete agreements, and settlement and release agreements. In most cases, however, you'll want your attorney to review complex contracts, such as those used in mergers and acquisitions, marketing and licensing agreements, and partnerships. In this section, we give you some basic knowledge about some of these contracts so that you can understand what your attorney is talking about and ask the right questions.

Marketing and Licensing Agreements

If you're negotiating a marketing or licensing agreement, make sure your attorney reviews it carefully. A **marketing agreement**, also called a **reseller agreement**, allows someone to sell a product or service for a fee. The seller usually benefits in broader distribution of his product, and presumably more profit, than he could obtain with his own sales force. Marketing agreements are especially useful in foreign markets. For example, the manufacturer of a small machine part might find it a lot easier to sell his product in South America by working with a large distributor of machine parts in that part of the world.

One of the most important issues to negotiate when creating a marketing agreement with someone in another state or a foreign country is where any disputes will be resolved. In most cases, you want any dispute to be resolved in a court in your home state. Other items to consider in a marketing agreement are whether the business obtaining the marketing agreement will be allowed to sell competing products and/or be allowed to compete against your sales force.

 ## WHAT TO WATCH FOR IN LICENSING AGREEMENTS

If you're considering an agreement in which you're the **licensee** (that is, paying for the right to use a product or service), here are some important points to consider:

- Is the license exclusive? In other words, what are your rights and your markets? Does it cover specific geographic markets?

- Is the cost of the license to be paid up-front or in periodic payments? If periodic, do they terminate at some point in time or are they perpetual? Are they related to revenue payments or sales, or are they a straight payment?

- What rights do you acquire with the license?

- Are there any restrictions on your ability to expand your business?

- What warranties is the licensor making to you, and will the licensor defend its product in court?

If you're a **licensor** (that is, the seller of the license), your checklist includes:

- Is the term of the license limited or finite? What assurances are in place if the licensee fails to perform?

- How will you deal with product improvements over time?

- What rights do you retain to change pricing?

- What liability do you assume if the licensee is sued?

- What restrictions will you impose on the licensee with respect to uniformity of product quality, standards, and services?

In contrast, a **licensing agreement** allows someone to use—not sell—a product or service. The most common example today of a licensing agreement is a computer software license. Microsoft owns its software. If it's on your computer legally, you have licensed it from Microsoft: You don't own it, and you don't have the right to make a copy of it for someone else. Like marketing agreements, licensing agreements are used frequently in foreign markets, particularly in those where laws and regulations

---

 ### TALKING TO A LAWYER: BUSINESS CONTRACTS

Q. *What is the primary value of contracts in the business setting?*

A. The fundamental essence of contract law is to establish clear terms of rights and responsibilities. The reason business transactions have contracts is to foresee and avoid conflicts by giving everyone involved a clear understanding of what they must do or avoid doing.

In many ways, contracts are a good example of the concept of **preventive law** (like preventive medicine, the process of preventing problems from developing or nipping them in the bud before they become major). With the help of a lawyer familiar with the issues, a contract can define the rights and responsibilities of the parties, whether at the formation of the business itself or at the beginning of the business transaction. A good example is defining the terms of a partnership dissolution as part of the partnership agreement at the beginning of the partnership, when no one anticipates that the business will fail. With any luck, these provisions will never come into play. But if the partnership does run into trouble, having them in place can prevent countless hours of turmoil and many dollars.

—Answer by Will Hornsby, staff counsel, Division for Legal Services, American Bar Association, Chicago, Illinois

require that the work be performed in their country or where the necessary permits are difficult to obtain.

Acquisitions, Mergers, and Partnerships

Contracts involving a change in control of a business—whether they be acquisitions, mergers, or partnerships—are so complex that almost anyone would be considered foolish to forgo the services of a professional during the negotiations. If someone approaches you about selling all or part of your business, get a professional on board from the get-go. Otherwise, you run the risk of saying or doing something that could jeopardize your ownership. Many small-business owners happily brag about their sales and profits without realizing they may be inviting a hostile takeover by a competitor. Even if you want to sell or merge your business, you want to do it on your terms—not someone else's—and any information you provide can tip the balance in favor of the buyer.

YOU MUST REMEMBER THIS

• A contract is a legally enforceable, oral or written, promise or group of promises made between competent parties to do—or not to do—something. The contract must be supported by the exchange of something of value between the participants (the parties), called consideration. Consideration is any promise, act, or transfer of value that induces a party to enter a contract. The subject of the promise (including the consideration) may not be illegal.

• Putting the terms of a good-faith agreement in writing is the best way to ensure that all parties are aware of their rights and duties, even if no party intends to lie about the provisions of the agreement.

• Most contracts have conditions, which are events that must occur before one or both parties must perform their duties under the contract.

- When someone enters into a contract on your behalf with your permission, the arrangement is considered an agency. As long as agents do not exceed the authority granted them by their principals, contracts that agents make bind their principals as if the principals had made the contracts themselves.

- Many standard forms are available for typical business correspondence and contracts. In most cases, however, make sure your attorney reviews complex contracts, such as those used in mergers and acquisitions, marketing and licensing agreements, and partnerships.

CHAPTER 24

Special Contract Terms

Some Tips on What Those Strange Clauses Will Mean to You

Business owner Amy has started a successful local coffee shop. It is expanding and growing every day. Each week, Amy has more customers, more suppliers, and is signing more and more contracts with suppliers and vendors: the phone provider, her technology company, the shipping company, her coffee suppliers. She is busy and really doesn't have a lot of time to read each contract line by line. And Amy figures most of it is legal mumble-jumble that is used in contracts—does she really need to read it? Isn't all that stock language the same?

You've now learned the basics of contract law. With this foundation, you should be able to appreciate this chapter's discussion of the types of contract terms that are an important part of commercial contracts.

Many form contracts contain standardized language that can look strange to a nonlawyer. Sometimes it's so odd that it seems to be another language—legalese. However, these standardized terms have usually evolved over the years to have precise meaning in the law. These terms may thus help you form contracts with customers, suppliers, and so forth, since their meanings and legal implications may be well settled in the courts and in a given industry.

This chapter focuses on a number of the most important terms, especially the various types of **waivers**. You have given a waiver when you have knowingly surrendered (waived) one of your rights. After reading this chapter, you should have a good idea of what these types of clauses are about when you see them.

WAIVERS IN GENERAL

A **waiver,** as we said above, is the voluntary relinquishment of a known right. By "voluntary," the law does not mean you necessarily *wanted* to give the right up, but rather that you were *willing* to give it up in order to make the deal happen. In that sense, a waiver of a right is merely a type of consideration, little different from money. You don't, in an absolute sense, really *want* to give up your warehouse, but for $150,000, you're *willing* to do it.

Waivers may be express or implied. An **express waiver** is a written or oral statement that the party is willing to forgo a right he or she has. Some contracts provide, however, that no waiver of any of the contract terms will be effective unless done in writing. This means that any oral promises concerning one party's right to enforce a specific contract provision are unenforceable.

Even then, however, there are courts that will, given the totality of the circumstances, decide that the "no oral waiver" clause *itself* was waived! The most common example of this is when a homeowner tells a contractor to do additional work not covered in the contract. The contractor goes ahead with the work, but the homeowner refuses to pay, pointing to the "changes in writing only" clause. Most courts will say that, by authorizing the work and watching as it is done, the homeowner has waived the right to rely on that clause.

In the last example, watching the work as it is done without protest is called an **implied waiver**. That means that one party's behavior is as good as an explicit statement that he or she does not intend to enforce a certain condition or requirement of the contract. For example, let's say you rent a shop under a lease that requires payment of rent by the first of each month. One month, you forget to pay on time but send the check a week later in the hope that the landlord will accept it, which happens. In doing so, the landlord might have implicitly waived the right to evict you for failing to live up to the contract. If so, the landlord could not after accepting the check, have you evicted for violating the lease. This is also an implied waiver. (Most leases and state laws are not this simple; for more, see chapter 9.) Alternatively, if you wrote and asked the landlord to take the check, and the landlord wrote back saying that he or she was willing to give you a break this time only, it would be an express waiver limited to the one late payment.

Many contract forms have another kind of non-waiver clause that says that, even if the landlord accepts late payment once, the landlord has not waived the timely payment requirement for all time. That means the landlord could insist on strict adherence to the contract terms next month, even after letting you slide this month. This is a fundamentally fair clause and may actually result in a looser, more forgiving relationship between the parties. They don't need to fear that giving the other guy a break from time to time will alter their long-term expectations under the contract. But it does mean that you should not get into the habit of paying late because anytime—be it the second or the fourteenth time—you miss the contract deadline, the landlord could claim you are in breach of the lease. (However, that pattern could lead a court to say you were entitled to notice of a return to strict enforcement before breach is claimed. As soon as the landlord claims a breach, you should consult a lawyer.)

What type of waivers do form contracts frequently contain? Here are a few common ones:

• **Consequential damages.** Consequential damages are compensation for the harm that a person suffers as a consequence of the actual wrongdoing. The best example is losing your business files because your computer crashes. The computer's warranty will invariably state that the manufacturer does not cover consequential damages. The manufacturer may repair your computer or even give you a new one, but under the contract, it will not pay you for your files or compensate you for the time you'll have to spend re-creating them. Most states will uphold limitations such as these, although compensation for other consequences—such as personal injury as a result of a malfunction—may still be available under contract or tort law as a matter of a public policy, notwithstanding the purported limitation. The idea behind these clauses is that the seller cannot know what use you intend to make of its product, nor the extent to which you take your own precautions. After all, considering all the things that can go wrong with a computer, if you don't back up your data on a regular basis you have only yourself to blame.

• **Punitive damages.** A waiver of the right to claim **punitive damages**—a damage award that punishes the breaching party over and above damages that may be awarded to remedy the breach itself—is a variation on the waiver of consequential damages. Some states will not enforce these waivers, regardless of the circumstances of the contract. The reasoning is that punitive damages cannot be waived as a matter of public policy.

• **Defenses.** The law recognizes a number of possible defenses that a party can raise when accused of breaching a contract. These range from **duress** and **undue influence** in the making of the contract to **fraud** and **impossibility of performing** its terms. It is common, except in consumer credit contracts, for certain legal defenses to be waived by the consumer. The enforceability of these clauses frequently depends on the state the business or consumer resides in and the overall situation of the contract.

• **Jury trial.** This is one of the most common waivers found in contracts used by large businesses. They know that juries often start out more sympathetic to the "little guy." Jury trials are also more expensive, complicated, and time-consuming than trials where a judge makes both the legal and factual decisions. For that reason, if you decided to sue, you might not want a jury anyway. On the other hand, if there is a lot at stake, you may not want to give up this constitutional right. (Cases where little money is at stake are often heard in small claims court, where jury trials are not available.)

As we said before, there are as many possible things to waive as there are rights of parties in a contract. Certainly, there is no reason for you to agree to pay, for instance, attorneys' fees in a contract to supply flowers for a wedding. But in some cases, you may have no negotiating power. Then you have to choose how valuable the right that the contract wants you to waive is to you, compared with what you stand to gain by losing it (or the cost of losing the entire contract). In other words, waivers are just like any other contract provision; it is up to you to decide what to negotiate for. Below, we look at some other specific types of contract clauses.

ATTORNEYS' FEES AND LEGAL COSTS

Many contracts specify that in the event of a dispute, the prevailing party can recover from the other party its attorneys' fees and other legal costs associated with the dispute (e.g., filing fees and other costs of litigation). This type of clause is especially common in mortgages and other extensions of credit, requiring the borrower to pay any attorneys' fees and other legal costs incurred by the creditor in its efforts to collect money owed on the contract, as long as the creditor is successful. This is usually an enforceable clause and in itself can amount to a substantial penalty on a party that breaches a contract. In addition, some states, such as California, provide that any party prevailing in a contract dispute is entitled to receive attorneys' fees and legal costs.

ARBITRATION CLAUSES

If your contract contains an **arbitration clause**, you are likely surrendering any legal right to sue in court the company with which you are contracting. Instead, you could be agreeing to submit your dispute on matters related to the contract to **binding** (final) **arbitration**, the most common form of **alternative dispute resolution** (ADR).

Arbitration is less formal than a full-fledged court proceeding, and its procedures are usually simpler. Because of this, it is often much faster and less expensive than a court suit. However, arbitration might not be best for disputes in which the facts are not clear. Discovery, the process of trading documents and information before a court trial, is more limited in arbitration, so you might not be able to get additional information that might help you press your claims. For example, if you have an arbitration clause in an exclusive contract with a subcontractor, and you suspect that the subcontractor is working for a competitor, you would likely have no chance to interview the subcontractor's employees or obtain his financial records in discovery. And there is usually no appeal from binding arbitration, except in very limited circumstances.

 FORM CONTRACTS

We're all familiar with form contracts. Every time you rent a car, for example, you sign a contract that you probably don't bother to read. As a businessperson, you might be asked to sign a standard contract by a supplier.

Rule number one for anyone presented with a so-called standard or form contract is to read it, ask for clarification on any points that aren't clear, and ask for changes if the terms aren't satisfactory. Later on, if there's a dispute, it does you no good to base your defense on not having read and understood the contract. At the outset, you have to act as if you're going to be held to every word in every contract you sign because you might be—particularly if you get involved in a dispute.

There is one slim chance of getting off the hook: The law recognizes that certain take-it-or-leave-it contracts, full of hidden terms and legalese, in a high-pressure situation—in legal terms, **contracts of adhesion**—may be so one-sided as to be unfair. You may be excused from performing them or adhering to their terms if those terms in question are ambiguous or unconscionable. That, however, is a fallback position, and not one that you should rely on. One aspect of adhesion contracts that courts are more unwilling to enforce, particularly when the complaining party is a consumer (as opposed to a businessperson), is the arbitration clause. Courts are very concerned about individuals waiving their right to a trial through a contract in which they did not have a real chance to negotiate the terms.

REQUIREMENT FOR ARBITRATION CLAUSES

The **Federal Arbitration Act** establishes a policy of enforcing arbitration agreements and somewhat limits the ability of states to regulate how such clauses are to be enforced in their courts. You should investigate your state's laws or consult your lawyer to make sure that an arbitration clause would be enforced in your state.

In most cases, for an arbitration clause to hold up in court, it should state all of the following:

- Arbitration is final and binding.

- The parties are waiving the right to seek remedies in court.

- Pre-arbitration discovery (trading of documents and information) is different and more limited than that available in court proceedings.

- Arbitrators are not required to spell out the legal and factual bases for their decisions, which virtually cannot be appealed.

Arbitration clauses vary in their restrictiveness because they may also include other elements, such as a wavier of any right to punitive damages, as discussed above. Others give customers a forty-five-day "window," or forty-five days after a dispute arises, to go to court before losing that right. Compared with the four years you may normally be allowed by state law to bring a lawsuit for a breach of contract, forty-five days is not much time.

In contracts between businesses, courts generally uphold an arbitration clause, citing a general policy in favor of avoiding litigation by use of arbitration.

FORUM-SELECTION CLAUSES

The place to go for legal relief—a court, for example—is a *forum*. A forum-selection clause tells the parties where to go for the adjudication of claims or disagreements about a contract.

Generally speaking, **forum-selection clauses** limit the parties (or sometimes just one party) to a certain state, or federal district, where lawsuits may be initiated. The right to choose the forum in which to sue can be very important. Where there is no forum-selection clause, courts, with some limitations, give the plaintiff the right to choose in which forum to sue.

For example, returning to our example from the previous chapter, let's say our exhibitor's business is located in Michigan, and his contract for 1,000 miniature flashlights etched with his company logo is with a supplier in Wisconsin. He gets into a dispute with the company when he opens the flashlights and discovers that the supplier has misspelled his company's name. He's already paid for the flashlights, and the supplier refuses to refund his money or replace the flashlights. He decides to sue. Legally, he could choose to sue the supplier in Michigan or Wisconsin. The courts traditionally defer to the forum chosen by the person who starts the lawsuit, if the chosen forum is technically correct.

So where would the exhibitor choose? Chances are, even if he felt completely comfortable with the Wisconsin court system, the exhibitor wouldn't want to take the time and expense to find a lawyer in Wisconsin or trot over there to plead and pursue the case.

But the exhibitor needs to take a good look at this agreement with the supplier. Is there a forum-selection clause? If there is, it might require the exhibitor to bring a lawsuit only in Deere County, Wisconsin. For the exhibitor, the inconvenience of a Wisconsin forum may be as good as taking away the right to sue. It's now utterly impractical to sue.

Forum-selection clauses aren't always so strict, but they can be. In business-to-business disputes, the courts routinely enforce them, though there's a smidgen more scrutiny applied to forum-selection clauses than to arbitration clauses.

There is an important difference, though, between forum-selection clauses and arbitration clauses: There is more variation in forum-selection clauses among types of contracts. If you're in a position where bargaining is not practical, you may very well be able to get what you want from another service or goods provider who will enter into a contract without a forum-selection clause or without a clause that is as limiting. And, of course, remember that if the forum-selection clause requires you to use the courts of your own state, you're probably not giving up much agreeing to it.

CHOICE-OF-LAW CLAUSES

Another common clause in contracts is one that designates which state's legal doctrines and substantive laws will govern interpretation of the agreement or any dispute over its meaning. This is called a **choice-of-law clause**. Because it is so frequently found in form contracts used by big companies, it is also hard to negotiate away. You should, therefore, understand what these clauses do.

Every state, as well as the District of Columbia, each territory, and every other jurisdiction in the United States, has its own laws. Making those laws is what each state's legislature, courts, and administrative bodies do. Part of the federal system is that the democratically elected lawmakers of each state make laws that, within the bounds of the U.S. Constitution, reflect the policy preferences of the people of that state.

In many states, the substantive law reflects a traditional approach, which, short of a voter uprising, remains central to its legal tradition. States also have to consider what their legal regime offers to businesses that have the right to set up shop wherever the legal climate is most favorable to them. Therefore, different states have different approaches to contract interpretation, consumers' rights, and the like. Some are very pro-consumer; others are very pro-business.

For a company doing business all over the country, having to contend with the laws of many states is fraught with difficulty. Designating a choice of law provides a measure of predictability when you know that you have to consider the legal doctrines of only one jurisdiction, instead of two or more, whose laws might otherwise be applied without a choice-of-law clause. For companies with many thousands of similar contractual relations, that can mean a considerable cost savings, as well.

The traditional rule regarding contracts is that, regardless of where a lawsuit involving a contract is initiated, the law that will be applied in the suit is related to either the place where the contract is made or the place where the parties intended the agreement to be performed. The latter is often more persuasive if the contract is executed in a geographically convenient neutral ground or a place that has little to do with the contractual relationship.

The choice of which law applies in interpreting and enforcing a contract is called the choice of **substantive** law. The applicable **procedural** law is always the law of the forum. Thus, you could have a Pennsylvania court applying California law to a contract, but the procedural law—the technical rules and procedures by which a court proceeding is governed—will remain Pennsylvanian. (Understanding this, incidentally, can give you some insight into one reason why a party might prefer a given forum, as discussed previously: Choice of forum equals choice of procedural rules.)

As a businessperson, you probably would prefer to make your legal claim in a pro-business state. You can't simply pick a pro-business state out of the air. There has to be some connection between your business and the state whose law is chosen. But if you do business in several states, the **choice-of-law clause** can give your business its preference. Typically, the clause will simply say: *"All disputes arising out of this contract shall be determined in accordance with the law of the State of New York."*

The choice in the last example was no accident, by the way. Most lawyers agree that New York's law is very favorable to business, especially in areas such as insurance and employment, particularly compared to California, which has a number of pro-consumer laws. That does not mean, however, that its *juries* are favorable to business. So a business can have its cake and eat it too by not designating the New York courts as a forum—or by designating another forum—but nonetheless requiring the application of New York's law to interpretation of the contract.

Some courts have balked at applying choice-of-law clauses in consumer contracts (i.e., where the buyer is purchasing the goods or services for personal, household use). They reason that a company should not be able to escape the consumer-protection laws of its customer's home state with such a clause. If that were allowed, eventually those laws would be rendered less meaningful. Thus, some courts hold that, as a matter of policy, such clauses will not be enforced where they deprive consumers of the protection of their state's consumer-protection scheme. Some state laws dictate this result. However, in states that do not require this result by statute, courts have taken a more traditional approach. If there is no evidence of fraud or abuse of bargaining power, they will enforce the clause. As you can see, you'll want your attorney to review any choice-of-law clause that you want to include in your contract or that is presented to you to consider its ramifications.

SECURITY INTERESTS

Jerome thought he was only having his dental office redone. The price seemed right, and the contractor was prepared to finance the work, too, so he could avoid dealing with bankers. When the drywall started peeling off the walls and the electrical wiring kept shorting, however, he was disappointed. When the contractor refused to return his calls, he was angry. When Jerome stopped making payments, he was smugly satisfied. When he got a notice of foreclosure, he was more than a little shocked.

Jerome didn't appreciate the fact that his financing agreement for the office remodeling included a mortgage. Perhaps he should have because both federal and some state laws require disclosure of this, but many people ignore this information. Under that document, he made his office building **collateral** for payment of the contract. Breach of a contract that includes a mortgage or a **security interest** allows the creditor to turn to the

PAYING THE PRICE

Contracts between businesses often include a clause called a **liqui-dated damages** clause. This odd term simply means that the parties have attempted to specify, at the time the contract was made, what the loss will be in the event that the contract is breached. In other words, they've looked ahead and put a dollar figure on the damages that will ensue. Obviously, the benefit of such a clause is that the parties avoid having to go to court.

If the other party insists on a clause specifying liquidated damages, you should insist on a clause that requires the other party to fulfill any of its obligations that could threaten your ability to carry out your own. Sup-pose the exhibitor from our example contracts with the supplier to pro-vide items for three trade shows in the following year—miniature flashlights, key chains, and tote bags. All are to be embossed with the exhibitor's logo. But the exhibitor doesn't state the amounts he will be ordering for each show. Then he includes a clause that says, "Failure to deliver the items at least three days before the date of each show will nullify the order and result in liquidated damages in the amount of $3,000." A smart supplier would insist on an additional clause that re-quired the exhibitor to notify him in writing at least two months (or what-ever time he needs) before each trade show of the number of items required for each order.

---

collateral to make sure the money is paid. *Turn to* means "take it and sell it." Even without foreclosing, as long as someone holds a security interest, or **lien**, on the property, you will be unable to pass on clear title—that is, you will have a hard time selling it.

Is it worth risking your office building for a remodeled of-fice? Maybe. Analyzing that risk is up to you, but it may be a bet-ter deal for you to get a line of credit from a bank to pay for the remodeling, rather than financing through the contractor.

COSTS AND FEES

The most fundamental contract terms, of course, are the price terms—how many products are being ordered and what they're going to cost. Beware of terms that subtly change the economic formula behind your back and give away what you worked so hard to negotiate. Even if the deal is one that required little negotiation, such as an agreement to open a credit line or some other kind of "take it or leave it" transaction, you must find, read, and understand any such clauses to determine whether you can afford the transaction at all.

Typically, fees of this type include:

• high deductibles in service contracts, such as those offered by manufacturers of copiers and other office equipment, which often negate their practical value;

• service charges on checking accounts, including fees for returned checks of $10 or more (try to negotiate with your bank for a waiver of fees for your business accounts); and

• credit insurance, which is very costly term life insurance to cover the amount of credit you're getting.

The possibilities are endless. But the idea, again, is that it does pay to read the whole contract and see what a transaction will really cost before you sign it.

YOU MUST REMEMBER THIS

• Often you will be asked to sign contracts that require you to waive (surrender) certain rights. Make sure that you understand what you're being asked to give up; if it's too much, address the issue in negotiations or seek another source of the products or services being offered.

• Arbitration clauses often offer certain advantages to businesses; consider adding them to your standard contracts. By the same token, be aware of what you're giving up if you agree to someone else's contract that includes such a clause.

TALKING TO A LAWYER: SPECIAL CONTRACTS

Q. *I'm considering becoming a distributor for one of my suppliers. It's for a technical product line that's new to my business; the supplier has always sold directly and never used distributors, so neither of us has much history with this kind of arrangement. We need a written agreement to specify the terms, but where can we find a model? What parts of such an agreement are most important?*

A. The legal issues raised by distributorship agreements are simply too complicated to be handled without lawyers. Many lawsuits are brought by former distributors who claim they were wrongfully terminated. Others are brought by wholesale purchasers who claim they actually were distributors.

They do this because there are special legal protections available for distributors in some states. Distributorship arrangements may also involve antitrust laws. Therefore, you and your supplier must discuss these issues with separate lawyers. This is an investment that will pay off well, because a clear, straightforward distribution relationship can last for decades. Both sides profit from a healthy distribution relationship. Often the main point is that each side understands its rights and obligations.

To some degree, the fact that your supplier has never used distributors before makes it even more important that these contracts be worked out very carefully. Neither you nor your supplier has a track record of experience. Critically, neither of you has any expectations or ways of doing business relevant to the new relationship besides what will be in that written contract. So the words you choose in this new agreement will be construed very strictly.

Going into your lawyer's office, which issues should you clarify? Here are some important ones:

- What is the territory (geographically) that the distributorship covers?
- What is the term (in years) of the distributorship?
- Does this term automatically renew?

- If it does renew automatically, whose responsibility is it to prevent renewal if that is desired? Can either side do so, and if so, how much notice of nonrenewal is necessary?

- Are there grounds for termination of the distributorship by the supplier before the term? These must be spelled out clearly.

- Do you have permission to use the trademarks and other intellectual property of the supplier? Are you obligated to do so?

- In what state's courts, or through what alternative dispute resolution mechanisms, will any dispute be settled?

- If there is a dispute, which state's law will apply?

- Many suppliers put a clause into distributorship agreements requiring the distributor to pay the suppliers' attorneys' fees in the event of a dispute. Try to avoid this at almost any cost.

- Other dispute resolution clauses include the waiver of certain rights in litigation that small businesses find very valuable, such as the right to a jury trial. This may be worth waiving as part of the bargain, but think hard about it.

- Can you sell the distributorship rights? What rights does the supplier have to veto the buyer, if any?

As you can see, there can be much more on the table than meets the eye in these types of relationships. This is one of those times when experienced legal advice is absolutely essential to your future business's success.

—**Answer by Ron Coleman, attorney, Clifton, New Jersey**

- Be particularly aware of clauses requiring you to give up certain legal defenses or the right to a jury trial. Equally troublesome are clauses that require you to pay the other side's attorneys' fees and costs. Penalty clauses can also cause headaches.

CHAPTER 25

What If There's a Dispute?

Keeping the Lid on Time, Hassles, and Costs

Amy's coffee shop is still a success—more customers order lattes and scones every day. And she has started to take more time to read over the contracts she signs and make sure that she understands everything. However, she just realized that the cups she ordered three weeks ago never arrived. Amy has paid 40 percent up front for the cups and really needs them—what will she sell the coffee in? What can she do? Is she out of luck? Does she have to go to court?

FAILURE TO PERFORM A CONTRACT

A lot of the disputes you'll have involve a contract of one kind or another between your business and another business. A **breach of contract**—also called a **default**—is one party's failure, without a good legal excuse, to live up to or perform any of its responsibilities under a contract. A breach can occur by:

• failure to do what was promised under the contract—either a complete failure to perform or performing only part of the bargain;

• one side making it impossible for the other party to perform; or

• one party **repudiating** the contract (announcing an intent not to perform).

Someone who has not performed a material part of the contract by a reasonable (or agreed-upon) deadline has "failed to perform." Suppose a customer agrees to buy a car for $1,000 from your used-car lot. You promise to have it ready "sometime early next week," and the customer leaves you a $100 deposit. It would be a material breach for you never to make the car ready for delivery, or even to string the customer along for weeks and weeks by saying that it will be "ready soon."

"TIME IS OF THE ESSENCE"

What does the phrase "time is of the essence" mean in the law? It's not philosophy. It means that the time for performing, or doing what a contract obligates you to do, is considered a central part of the bargain you made. If time is not made "of the essence" in the contract, you may be required to perform only within a "reasonable" amount of time.

A breach doesn't have to be so straightforward. Sometimes a party breaches by making performance impossible. Suppose you hire a cleaning service to clean your showroom on Sunday. But you are closed on Sunday and forget to send someone to let the cleaners in. You've breached the contract by making performance impossible. The law would require you to pay the service the money, since the cleaning service was ready and able to do the job and presumably turned down requests to clean from other clients.

Also, a breach can be **partial**. That happens when the contract has several parts (for example, when the performance has several installments), each of which can be treated as a separate contract. If a supplier breaches some of those parts, you could sue for damages to make up for those parts of the contract that were not performed. The bargain as a whole, however, may remain intact. You would have to pay for those parts that were performed according to the agreement.

Another kind of breach is a **repudiation**. Repudiation is a clear statement made by one party before performance is due that states through words, circumstances, or conduct that the party cannot or will not perform a material part of that party's contractual obligations. Suppose that on the day before your customer was to pick up the car you promised to sell her, you sent her a message that you decided to sell the car to someone else, or you sold it already. That message or act would be a repudiation. In contrast, it's not repudiation if one party will not perform because of an honest disagreement over the contract's terms (but it may still be a material breach!).

REMEDIES FOR BREACH OF CONTRACT

When someone materially breaches a contract with you (i.e., they completely or substantially fail to perform), you are no longer obligated to keep your end of the bargain. However, you might want to consult with your lawyer for guidance at this stage, since any action you take could have repercussions if the dispute escalates, and especially if it winds up in court. All things being equal, you may proceed in several ways:

- urge the breaching party to reconsider the breach;
- handle the matter unilaterally, usually by denying payment to the other side (but beware that this could put you in breach of contract yourself, if a court or other forum decided that the alleged breaching party had a good reason to stop his/her performance);
- seek to resolve the matter through alternative dispute resolution;
- sue for damages or other remedies.

Suing is listed last here because it's probably your last recourse. Lawsuits can be expensive and time-consuming. That's why more than 90 percent of all civil cases are settled before trial. Even after suits have been filed, the courts actively work to encourage settlements before trial and will often require the parties to engage in pretrial settlement conferences to see if some mutually satisfactory compromise might permit them to avoid the need for a full-blown trial.

Let's Talk About This

A simple first step is to ask the other party to reconsider. This has the virtue of being cheap. Often the only cost is the price of a telephone call and a little pride. The party may have breached the contract because of a misunderstanding. Perhaps the breaching party just needs a little more time. Or maybe you could renegotiate. You may very well be able to come up with a solution that will leave both of you better off than if you went to court. If you do hire a lawyer, the first thing your lawyer is likely to do is try to persuade the breaching party to perform.

Starting with that offer to settle the matter, keep good records of all your communications with the other side. If you see you're in for a struggle, make a file. Keep copies of any letters you send and receive, and move all receipts, bills of lading, and the like to this file.

If you get nowhere with personal communications, the next step before getting courts and lawyers involved may be to go over the other side's head, so to speak. If the dispute is between you and an authorized distributor or exclusive supplier, it is likely that the manufacturer has some interest in the goodwill associated with its product. Therefore, you might want to contact the manufacturer.

 INSUFFICIENT FUNDS

If you believe the other party has breached a contract for which you have already sent a check, don't try to avoid the payment by reducing your bank balance so the check won't clear. The bank can't read your mind, so other checks you've written may not be paid, or the bank might even honor the check you don't want paid in an attempt to accommodate you (although they may charge you an additional fee for the overdraft). More important, you will have gone from exercising a legal right (stopping payment) to committing a legal wrong (passing a bad check). And remember that a business is generally expected to stand behind its checks. The loss of your reputation from a bounced check or wrongfully stopped check could be permanent.

Self-Help

If you don't want to negotiate with the other side or your attempts have been fruitless, you might be able to help yourself by denying payment to the other party.

Stopping payment. If you're involved in a transaction where you paid by check, and the other person refuses to refund your money, you may call your bank and **stop payment** on that check. That prevents the bank from paying the check, assuming the check has not yet cleared your account. Remember, you're still liable for that amount until a court decides otherwise. The seller may sue you for the amount in dispute, and unless you have a legal excuse not to pay, you'll end up writing another check. Also be aware that when you stop payment, you raise the stakes. You also diminish the chance of a settlement, and make a future business relationship with the other party much less likely—and potentially become the subject of a debt collection action.

Credit card purchases. These days, of course, many purchases are made with credit cards. Some sole proprietors routinely use their personal credit cards to purchase items for the business. If you do, then perhaps you can take advantage of certain legal rights not to pay for items in dispute. (Be aware that, by the same token, your customers who pay by credit might use these same protections against you.)

The Fair Credit Billing Act may affect a business's ability to be paid for a credit card purchase. The act regards charges for products that a consumer refuses to accept on delivery or that aren't delivered according to an agreement as billing errors, which the card issuer must investigate. During the investigation the consumer doesn't have to pay, meaning the credit card issuer will not credit the business. The card issuer may resolve the matter by granting the buyer a permanent credit, and the business will not be able to recover. Consumers are also protected from having to pay for shoddy or damaged goods or poor service, if they could refuse payment under state law and the merchant refuses to make an adjustment.

Have Someone Else Help Resolve the Dispute

Another option is to resolve your dispute through arbitration or some other form of **alternative dispute resolution** outside the formal court system.

Alternative dispute resolution is a popular, inexpensive, relatively stress-free, and fast way to resolve disputes. Nearly all states have established dispute resolution centers. These centers may be known as neighborhood justice centers, dispute resolution centers, or citizens' dispute settlement programs. For example, there are centers that specialize in resolving disputes commonly encountered by consumers, employers and employees, landlords and tenants, neighbors, and family members.

Probably the two most common forms of dispute resolution are mediation and arbitration. In **mediation**, a trained mediator will help you and your opponent resolve your disagreement by identifying, defining, and discussing the things about which you disagree. The mediator won't function as a judge deciding the case but will help you and the other party work out your differences. This is an informal, cooperative, problem-solving process and does not require you to know the law or to hire a lawyer. It's very often used in divorces, neighbor-versus-neighbor disputes, and other situations where the parties may have a continuing relationship. As a businessperson, you might find it at least worth a try in disputes with customers.

Arbitration, on the other hand, is a more formal proceeding in which you and your opponent will be asked to present evidence and witnesses to the presiding arbitrator, who usually will issue a written decision to resolve the dispute. In most cases, the decision of the arbitrator is binding on the parties and final.

Arbitration is not necessarily a bad thing. Indeed, it can sometimes be to your advantage. It gets rid of a lot of the formalities and technicalities of court proceedings, and it is often much faster and cheaper. It is also possible to select an arbitrator who has experience in your particular business or industry. There are

GETTING OUT OF A CONTRACT

Sometimes you'll find yourself in a position where you have to breach a contract. Breaching a contract isn't always a bad thing to do, as long as you're ready to take your lumps. Sometimes the price you pay through a remedy for breach is less damaging than performing a contract that has just become a big mistake.

some areas, however, where seemingly simple issues are really much more complex than they appear. Then arbitration might cause problems—for example, there may be limited opportunities to discover evidence. And there is usually no appeal from binding arbitration except perhaps for limited reasons, such as fraud. The contract can specify nonbinding arbitration—i.e., neither party has to comply with the arbitrator's decision. However, this approach will not directly settle the dispute, though it can help both parties better appreciate their respective positions and can lead to a voluntary settlement of the dispute.

Binding arbitration also may not be possible unless both parties agree in advance to accept the arbitrator's decision as final. Be aware that written agreements between businesses often specify arbitration or another type of dispute resolution and courts almost always enforce these provisions. If either you or your opponent does not want to forgo the right to appeal an adverse decision, arbitration will not be helpful.

SUING FOR A BREACH OF CONTRACT

There are times when all these forms of self-help and alternative dispute resolution will take you only so far, after which point you will have to consider other legal options.

Can They Pay?

In deciding whether to sue, you have to consider the other party's ability to pay. There's little point in proceeding if your opponent is **judgment-proof**—that is, unable to pay a judgment the court might eventually hand down.

If the company you sue has gone through the bankruptcy process, your contract could be legally disavowed. If the company has ceased doing business or is under the protection of the bankruptcy laws, your chances of recovering anything of value are small. You will then have to contact the bankruptcy court, and you may need a lawyer's help to put in your claim. If your claim isn't substantial, though, it isn't usually worth the trouble.

If you have a contract that still is in force with a troubled company, you may have to get the rest of your contract needs filled by another company if the one with which you have a contract can't come through. Then you may have a damages claim against the first company, but you have to decide whether it's worth pursuing the matter, given its shaky status.

And if you sue an individual consumer, you could get a judgment but end up paying more in attorneys' fees than the consumer's entire worth.

What Does Your Contract Say?

The second point to consider is how the contract itself may limit your opportunity to sue. Before entering into a contract, and before suing, you must consider all the contract terms that affect your right to sue. These clauses, which are almost always enforced by the courts, include attorneys' fees, choice of law, choice of forum, and alternative dispute resolution, mediation, or arbitration provisions. For more information on these clauses, see the discussion on contract clauses in chapter 24.

These clauses are potentially critical. Some of them make your suit subject to dismissal, in which case you will have invested your time (and money—filing fees can range from $20 or so for small claims court to hundreds of dollars to sue for larger amounts) with no return.

What Will You Ask For?

Assuming you have the right to sue, and the terms in the contract don't make a lawsuit a practical impossibility, the next question is what you hope to get by a lawsuit. The most common legal remedy for breach of contract is a **suit** for damages, usually **compensatory damages**. This is the amount of money it would take to put you in as good a position as if there had not been a breach of contract. The idea is to give you the benefit of the bargain.

What's an example of compensatory damages? Imagine that you hired a contractor to paint your warehouse for $5,000. This job could cost as much as $6,000, but you've negotiated a great deal. Now the contractor regrets agreeing to the $5,000 price and breaches. If you can prove all the facts just stated, you may recover $1,000, or whatever the difference is between $5,000 and what it ultimately costs you to have your warehouse painted (by someone else).

There are other kinds of contract damages. The most common ones are:

• **Consequential damages,** which compensate a party for all the harm the broken contract caused. These may be available in a contract suit; it depends on the language of the contract. Some contracts, however, and especially warranties, are explicit in actually excluding these kinds of damages.

• **Punitive damages,** which are available if the breaching party's behavior shocked the conscience of the court, or if the behavior was willful or reckless. Punitive damages are virtually never awarded in a suit for breach of contract, but it may be possible to get punitive damages or some form of **statutory damages** (legal penalties) under a suit for fraud or other kind of business tort (see sidebar).

• **Liquidated damages,** which are an amount built into the contract in the event of a breach. Even if both parties effectively have breached the contract, this amount may still be awarded as

BUSINESS TORTS

Not all legal disputes between businesses are a matter of contract law. More and more commonly, businesses are also resorting to noncontract, or **tort**, claims. These claims allege that even though there is no contractual relationship between two businesses, one business did something unfair that resulted in a commercial loss to the other one. These claims include unfair competition, intentional interference with contractual relations, and other types of claims.

Lawyers and judges have crafted creative tort theories to describe types of unfair business behavior that the law will prohibit. Sometimes lawyers will add tort claims to existing contract claims, though most judges are skeptical of such a strategy. One of the big dangers of a tort claim is the availability of punitive damages if the plaintiff is successful.

---

damages, as long as it fairly estimates the cost of the breach. The courts will not enforce a **penalty clause**, which is an amount of liquidated damages that is way out of line with the actual loss. Some contracts try to get around this and state that you agree that the liquidated damages are set at a legitimate amount, but courts will not necessarily respect such clauses.

Other Remedies

There are other, equitable, remedies in a contract suit besides damages, which are a legal remedy. Equitable remedies are discretionary remedies awarded by the court where legal remedies are inadequate. The main one is **specific performance**, a court order requiring the breaching party to perform as promised in the contract. Courts used to avoid this because it is hard to enforce, but more and more courts will impose specific performance. It's used if there is no other remedy available because of the contract's subject matter, such as real estate. It might be used in a contract for the sale of goods, if the seller fails to deliver a very unique good—for example a painting by a specific artist. It will almost never be applied to personal services contracts, however—that is, to force a person to render the promised service.

A court may also **rescind** (cancel) a contract that one party has breached. The court may then order the breaching party to pay the other side any expenses incurred. It could also order the return of goods sold. Or, the court could **reform** the contract. That involves modifying the contract according to what the court concludes, based on evidence at trial, the parties actually intended. Although these remedies are not commonly requested, they are being requested increasingly under the provisions of many states' consumer fraud laws.

Going to Court

If you end up having to sue another person or business, you should seek the advice of a lawyer. Real court is not for amateurs. The procedural rules, knowledge of the law, and courtroom methods are much more complex than they seem on television. In the courtroom, the judges have busy dockets and no time to assist sincere but overwhelmed parties acting *pro se* (meaning representing themselves). However, the legal training necessary to make the case is well within the competence of an experienced attorney, whom you can find through references from friends, family, or your local bar association.

There's another reason you need a lawyer to go to court: Corporations, most types of partnerships, and in fact nearly any business entity that is not a sole proprietorship (see chapters 11 through 15) are required by law to be represented by an attorney. (A rare exception in some states is that property managers are allowed to represent landlords in housing court.) Without a lawyer your claims could be bounced out of court before the other side even has to respond to your claim.

Reasons Not to Sue

Another reason not to sue, besides the obvious ones discussed above, is even more obvious—you could lose. The contract defenses discussed previously are a two-way street. Any one of them may be asserted as a defense against your suit for breach, including the defense that there was never a contract at all.

It is also possible that the defendant could make a claim against you in turn, called a **countersuit**. That means the person or company you're suing could sue you back, perhaps making a claim for back payments that it otherwise may have let go. You might emerge from the courthouse not only without satisfaction, but also with a judgment to pay.

All in all, undertaking a lawsuit can be a very annoying, time-consuming, expensive, and disappointing process. Think hard about whether suing is worth it, in terms of both economic and spiritual cost. Then think again.

YOU MUST REMEMBER THIS

• You have a number of options when you think someone has breached a contract against you.

CONSUMER FRAUD ACTS COULD BITE YOU

We discussed consumer fraud acts in chapter 20, but these potent weapons for consumers ought also to be part of your calculations in deciding whether to pursue certain legal actions. They don't apply to other businesses, but they do apply to protect consumers (people who buy goods or services for personal, household use). Not only do they make fraud more unwise than ever, but they also could end up as part of a countersuit brought by a consumer whom you originally sued to make good on an invoice or to pay the amount promised in a contract. Since they often provide for treble (triple) damages, or recovery of the consumers' attorney's fees, they could be costly to you if the court decides against you.

- It usually pays, at least initially, to talk with the other party, to try to come to an agreement, or to take other steps short of a lawsuit.
- Your right to file suit, and the terms under which you do so, may be limited by the contract.
- Remember, disputes are rarely cut-and-dried, and the other side has the right to its day in court also.

CHAPTER 26

Too Good
to Be True

Watch Out for These Scams
Against Your Business

*John got a phone call from a man who said he was from an of-
fice supply firm John's company has used before. He wants to
let John in on a deal: The man's firm just had twenty cases of
copy paper returned from another customer who made a mistake on the order. He needs to reduce the inventory. If John
will take this paper off his hands today, he can let it go for 30
percent off the normal price. John thinks this sounds pretty
good; he can always use copy paper. So he agrees to the deal.
Later, when the paper is delivered, John notices it's not as
good as he is used to. But in the press of daily business, he
doesn't do anything about it. Five weeks later his accounts-
payable clerk receives an invoice from the supplier. It appears
legitimate, so the clerk pays it without question. No one notices that the price paid for this shoddy paper is five times
higher than John normally pays.*

Small businesses are frequent targets for con artists looking to profit from people's inattention to detail. Usually,
small businesses have no centralized accounting department or
security department. It's up to you, the owner, to take care of a
myriad of details, and examining every invoice may be far down
the list of priorities. Too often the same company gets fleeced
more than once by the same scam, as the supplier puts the
company on an automatic shipment program in hopes of the
invoice being paid by the accounting department as a routine
matter.

The first step to protecting your business from con artists is
knowing how these people operate. Here's a look at some of the
most common scams.

RED FLAGS

The unscrupulous can always find new ways to swindle your business. Here are some warning signs to watch out for:

- Deals that sound too good to be true, such as rock-bottom prices or big prizes to thank you for ordering;

- Aggressive or intimidating sales pitches;

- Offers that must be accepted immediately;

- Evasive answers to reasonable questions;

- Unwillingness to provide references from satisfied customers (especially other businesses you've heard of); and

- Name dropping—if the promoter mentions one of your customers or suppliers, it might be an attempt to appear legitimate.

The Office Supply Scam

This common scam is often called "Toner Phoner" because early versions involved shipments of photocopy toner. It typically begins with a caller who says he's a repairman updating his records and asks for the make and model of the office copier, fax machine, or printers. (If one employee won't provide this vital information, he'll try another one until he finds someone who'll cooperate.) A few days later a salesman calls (or stops by the office), saying he's overstocked on the paper or cartridges or toner you use in your equipment. The salesman offers what he says is a sizable discount if you'll order it today. What you don't know is that the base price is up to ten times higher than market price for the same supplies. If you bite, someone claiming to be a supervisor or credit manager will call back the next day to confirm the order and price and make sure the person who placed the order has the authority to do so.

When the shipment arrives, it's normally of mediocre to low quality. The invoice doesn't come for another five or six weeks—

typically long enough for someone to have opened the boxes and started using the supplies—and it usually goes to someone other than the person who ordered the product and noticed the poor quality. The accounts-payable department may not notice that not only is the base price grossly inflated, but there's a shipping and handling charge that adds another 10 percent to 17 percent to the "discounted" price. After the company pays the bill, the supplier may put your company on an automatic reorder program, sending even larger shipments from time to time until someone catches on. To add insult to injury, if you figure out what's going on and return a shipment, the supplier may charge for shipping costs, plus a sizable "restocking fee."

This scam can be particularly damaging because the shoddy office supplies—such as remanufactured toner cartridges—can void the warranty on your equipment. That can blot out any savings you'd have had if the discount were on the level.

The best way to avoid this scam is to educate employees about it. Centralize purchasing and tell the person who orders supplies to shop around. Then refuse to pay any invoice that doesn't come with a valid purchase order.

PHONY INVOICING

Some con artists don't even bother to send merchandise. Instead, they send an invoice (or what looks like an invoice) demanding payment for certain goods or services that were neither ordered nor delivered. One of the most popular versions is invoicing a company for advertising that supposedly ran in a magazine. The invoice often contains the name of a company executive who supposedly ordered the advertising—lifted from a business directory or Web site. Some scammers lend credibility to their invoice by enclosing one of the company's real advertisements, scanned onto a page that looks as if it came from the magazine where the ad supposedly appeared. Some send the same phony invoice to the company twice, in hopes it will be paid twice by inattentive accountants.

TO FIND OUT MORE

To find out more about a business proposition or to report a suspected con artist, call your local Better Business Bureau. You can also contact:

Council of Better Business Bureau
4200 Wilson Blvd.
Arlington, VA 22203
www.bbb.org

Federal Trade Commission
800-554-5706
www.ftc.gov

National Fraud Information Center
800-876-7060
www.fraud.org

More resources can be found in the World at Your Fingertips section starting on page 463.

Of course, sending a phony invoice is illegal. Some scam artists skirt the law by sending what looks like an invoice but putting a disclaimer in fine print: "This is a solicitation. You are under no obligation to pay unless you accept this offer." It's against the law to send a solicitation styled as an invoice without the disclaimer being in conspicuous, large print, but these con artists flout the regulations.

THE BUSINESS DIRECTORY SCAM

Businesses routinely pay invoices for business directory and Yellow Pages advertising. What many people don't recognize, though, is that neither the term *Yellow Pages* nor the walking fingers logo is copyrighted anymore. Anyone can offer to advertise your business in a Yellow Pages directory—but that doesn't mean it will be distributed to the public. Scammers can send deceptive solicitations claiming to publish a Yellow Pages directory—which a business can advertise in for a hefty fee. These publishers actually do publish directories, but they are often purse-sized volumes, often disturbed to a limited number of people. It's a profitable scam. Scammers also send fake invoices for listings in business directories that you never requested. Make sure you examine any advertising solicitations and bills carefully to make sure you're getting what you think you are paying for.

ADVERTISING SPECIALTIES

Here's a scheme that could embarrass your business for years. Again, the high-pressure pitch typically comes over the phone: You can order key chains, ice scrapers, mugs, pens, or other merchandise emblazoned with your company's name, to use for promotion. And to thank you for ordering the merchandise, we'll send you a DVD player! A cell phone! A cruise package!

When the stuff arrives, chances are it's of such poor quality that you wouldn't want to use it to represent your company. It'll sit in your storeroom for years, an embarrassing reminder of the time you thought you could get something too good to be true. The prize, though, is usually even worse. One business owner thought he had a deal when he ordered promotional mugs that came with a motorboat as a prize. The mugs turned out to be ugly tan plastic, not ceramic, and the company logo was just painted on. The motorboat turned out to be inflatable, with a tiny angler's motor.

Some con artists avoid prosecution because the recipient is too embarrassed to complain. In some cases, if the employee who ordered the products does complain about the quality, the promoter threatens to inform the boss about the prize, which looks like a bribe.

WHO'S WHO?

Proud of your booming business? There's a scam artist out there hoping to make a quick buck by playing on your vanity. An official-looking letter informs you that you've been selected because of your success for a listing in a forthcoming edition of a book, titled something like *Who's Who in the Business World*. Just complete and return the enclosed biographical form. Or it might say you've been nominated for an award or special membership. Don't expect instant fame, though, because chances are no one will read the book or use it for reference. What you can expect is to be charged a hefty price for a copy of the book. You might also have to pay a subscription or listing fee. A better title might be *Who's Who Among Suckers*.

ADVANCE FEE LOAN BROKERS

Need money to stay afloat or to expand your business? If you've had trouble finding financing, you might be tempted by the pitch of a loan broker. Some are legitimate, but most are not. The "broker" advertises the availability of money to lend. You answer and meet with the "broker," often in a coffee shop or hotel, fill out an application, and sign a contract for the "broker," to prepare a plan and present it to prospective investors. You pay a $1,000 advance fee for finding the loan or risk capital—and that's the last you hear from the loan broker.

ROGUE REPAIRMEN

An unfamiliar technician appears at the loading dock or some other work area, away from whoever normally orders service, and offers a free inspection of your office equipment or a "two-for-one" deal on service. At best, you'll get a shoddy repair job. At worst, you find out later that the technician swapped your good

DOS AND DON'TS TO AVOID GETTING FLEECED

- Don't make commitments to people you don't know, especially over the phone.

- Do insist that all sales pitches, charitable appeals, and advertising propositions be sent in writing.

- Don't agree to advertise in a publication without verification of circulation figures, sample copies, publication dates, and the name of the publisher.

- Do keep an approved list of publications where your advertisements appear, so employees won't fall for the claim that your company has advertised there before.

- Don't pay invoices that can't be matched with a purchase order.

- Do centralize authority for supply and repair orders.

- Don't contribute to charities without the full name, address, and purpose of the charity, along with the latest financial statements, indicating that most of the money collected actually goes to the work of the charity.

- Do issue charitable contribution checks to the charity itself, rather than an individual solicitor.

- Don't order supplies from an unknown supplier without first comparing prices and quality with known suppliers.

---

equipment for something inferior. Or, mentioning that this model is being recalled, he may take it out the door and never come back.

"IT'S FOR CHARITY"

How often is your business asked to buy a block of circus tickets for underprivileged kids or donate to a local police fund or contribute to some other charity? Be aware that not all charity solicitors are on the level. In some cases, less than 2 percent of the money raised goes to the charity, with most of it going into the solicitor's pocket. Be sure you ask for information about the charity, including a financial statement.

 ## START-UP SCAMS

Sadly, scamming business start-ups is a growth industry. With more and more people looking to begin a small business, often at home, there's no shortage of potential victims who lack savvy in the wiles of the world. Some common business opportunity scams targeting the self-employed include:

- Work-at-home opportunities, in which you make crafts, stuff envelopes, or do something else that promises you a big return without even leaving home. Pitfalls include having to buy a big inventory to get started and no guaranteed markets or volume of business.

- Pyramid schemes, in which the core of the business is the new distributors whom you bring in. If the business itself is not profitable, selling new people on investing is a risky way to make a living. The history of pyramids is that the first few people do well, but everyone else loses when the pyramid collapses.

As always, your best defense is to resist high-pressure tactics and go slow. Ask for documentation. What percentage of people do well at this business? Who are they? Can you contact them (and not just the ones the promoter steers you toward)? Ask for a written statement verifying the earnings claim. Check the company out with the Better Business Bureau and your state and local departments of consumer affairs. Get all promises in writing and in the contract you sign. Make sure you have advice from people on *your* side—a lawyer, accountant, or experienced businessperson.

PHONE AND E-MAIL FRAUD

A caller claims he's with your bank, credit card company, Internet service, or cell phone provider—anything to try to trick you or your employees into providing various forms of account information. Shortly thereafter, bogus charges begin to appear on the account. The information sought changes with the technology, but the technique remains the same. Don't provide any account information to anyone who calls your business unless you are absolutely certain you are talking with an authorized representative. And don't just take his or her word for it; hang up and call the company's regular customer service number to verify whether there truly is a question with your account.

You can also assume that any of these scams that are or were tried over the phone will now come in through e-mail. The most infamous scam now has its own name, the "Nigerian Scam," because many of the original perpetrators were located in Nigeria. The sender usually claims that substantial sums of money are being held by a bank or government entity, and if you will help free these sums, you will receive a percentage. To proceed, however, you will be asked to provide a bank account number, which, if you do, will be shortly emptied. There are many variations on this scam, but they all have one thing in common—someone you do not know wants your bank account number.

Corporations in a number of states have received solicitations that appear to come from a government agency, but actually do not. These solicitations usually offer to assist the corporation in performing a nonexistent or not legally required service, such as registering with a fictional corporate registry or filing corporate minutes (which is not required in any state).

You and your employees need to be vigilant in order to avoid becoming victims of "phishing" e-mails (the word *phishing* comes from the cyberspace underworld) in which the senders are fishing for account information. They appear to come from valid, and important, sources, such as your bank or even the IRS. They will state they need to verify information such as passwords, account numbers, and Social Security numbers. But don't be fooled, this is exactly the information scammers need to steal your identity. Some of these phishing e-mails look very realistic. However, banks, other financial institutions, and government agencies will never send you an e-mail requesting sensitive information (unless you are already working with a representative on a matter and have agreed in advance to communicate via e-mail).

You should also be wary of online offers, whether through Web sites or e-mail messages, that offer you free software. Many of the programs actually infect your computers with programs (commonly referred to as a virus) that can track your keystrokes, sending back the information—which can include passwords and account information you entered at legitimate Web sites—to crooks. Other forms of this nefarious software can take control of your computers, causing them to start sending out spam e-mail messages over your Internet connection. It is imperative that you invest in quality antivirus software that can detect and remove these rogue programs. You can also invest in anti-spam software, which can detect and reject many phishing e-mails, along with the plain old junk e-mails that clutter all our in-boxes.

CASHIER'S CHECK SCAMS

You've decided to sell some excess inventory through an online auction or classified ad site. You receive an e-mail from an interested buyer who has a cashier's check that is a few hundred (or a few thousand) dollars more than your asking price. You are asked to accept the cashier's check and send the buyer the difference—maybe even told to keep a little extra for the inconvenience. Where's the risk in that; after all, a cashier's check is as good as cash, right? Wrong, at least in this case. The cashier's check is fake. The problem is, your bank will initially accept the cashier's check and you'll send the extra money and the inventory. A few weeks later, your bank will notify you the cashier's

DID YOU KNOW?

If your company falls for a scam once, chances are you'll be hit again and again. Con artists buy and sell mailing lists of easy targets.

check is fake and now you are out your inventory and that "extra difference" you sent to the scammer.

PLAIN OLD THEFT

Keep your eye out for strangers in the workplace. Thieves will dress in business attire, or sometimes like a maintenance person, and wander through office buildings. Busy people just assume the person belongs there because he or she looks like they do. When the opportunities present themselves the thieves pick up laptops, cell phones, purses, and briefcases and disappear down the closest stairwell. Requiring employees to wear picture I.D. badges can help alleviate this problem.

YOU MUST REMEMBER THIS

- Be skeptical of pitches, get everything in writing, and watch for red flags. It's not hard to avoid these scams if you're vigilant.
- Check out any suspicious company with the Better Business Bureau, the authorities in your state, or those in the state the company is headquartered in.
- If you've been victimized, complain to the Federal Trade Commission, attorney general's office in your community, or the consumer-protection bureau. If the mail has been used in the scam, contact the U.S. Postal Service.

CHAPTER 27

Protecting Your Intellectual Property Rights

The Lowdown on Patents, Copyrights, Trademarks, Service Marks, and More

Bill and Diane have a nice little business that involves, in part, designing greeting cards. And, because they're designers, they have a really good logo for this business. They have been told that they ought to protect their intellectual property. What is intellectual property? Bill has enough trouble keeping track of the car keys, and now he has to figure out how to protect an abstraction? Help!

It is easy to understand property you can see—a building, a fleet of vehicles, the products you make, the office equipment you use—and to take steps to protect it from being stolen and used by someone else. But what about property that comes from your imagination, not from an assembly line? A surprising number of small businesses have a stake in what is called **intellectual property**. Perhaps it is their logo or slogan. Maybe it is an audiovisual work, an original writing, a Web site design, or some other creation for which a copyright is possible. Maybe it is a trade secret, such as a secret formula, or even a design that can be patented.

Intellectual property is subject to special legal and tax rules, which we describe briefly. This chapter will provide an overview of intellectual property law. However, because of the highly technical nature of intellectual property rights, you should consult a good attorney who specializes in intellectual property or small businesses as soon as it becomes evident that intellectual property rights exist or may exist in your business. That is the best way to ensure that you are most effectively protecting your intellectual property rights.

TRADEMARKS AND TRADE NAMES

A trademark is any
- word or words,
- name,
- symbol or picture, or
- device

that a company or business uses to distinguish its goods from someone else's. A trademark can be any combination of the above and can even be a saying or slogan, such as Coca-Cola's "It's the Real Thing." The Nike "swoosh" is a trademark, as is the Gap logo and thousands of other familiar marks. Trademarks that have been registered with the U.S. Patent and Trademark Office can be easily identified by the ® after the mark on the product or its packaging. Trademarks that have not been registered with the U.S. Patent and Trademark Office may be entitled to certain protections, which will be discussed later. Such unregistered trademarks may be identified by the familiar ™ after the mark.

A related property right is a **service mark**. A service mark is essentially the same as a trademark except that it identifies services rather than goods. A service mark is usually indicated by ˢᴹ after the mark. For example, "Nike" is a trademark because it identifies a product, while "Macy's" is a service mark because it identifies a retail service.

Certification marks, such as seals of approval, and **collective membership marks**, used to indicate membership in an organization, are also related concepts. They are rarer, but they too have a value that would be lost if they could be used by just anyone, especially people not authorized to use them. An example of a certification mark is the Lawn Institute Seal of Approval. An example of a collective membership mark is the American Bar Association. These two types of marks are probably not relevant to most small businesses, but keep them in mind in case your business expands or its focus changes.

WEB SITES

If your business has a Web site, your business is automatically national or even international, in which case trademark protection could be imperative.

Protecting Your Mark

If you are just starting your business, or if your business is local and will likely remain local, you may find that common law protection of your trademark or service mark provides sufficient protection. Common law protection of a trademark occurs automatically as soon as you begin to use your mark—such as on signs, your letterhead, your product, or your ads. Common law protection of a mark simply means that the first entity using a particular name or slogan has a certain right to the use of that name. If your business and its mark are limited geographically and not all that valuable (yet), this simple form of protection might well be enough.

But, like most things that are free, such protection might not be best. If there is a chance your product or business will become active in more parts of the state and maybe even in different states, you should consider obtaining official registration from the state in which your business is located and from the U.S. Patent and Trademark Office.

State trademark registration is a relatively simple and inexpensive option that a small business may wish to consider. State-level registration provides trademark protection beyond common law protection but only in the state in which the trademark is registered. For a company with only a local focus, this may be the optimum level of protection. State trademark registration is generally quicker and less expensive than federal trademark registration, but it prohibits others in that state only from using the mark and can be superseded by a federal trademark.

MORE ON TRADEMARKS

You can access the basic trademark forms, as well as information about applying for a federal trademark, through the U.S. Patent and Trademark Office Web site—www.uspto.gov—or you can call 800-786-9199 for a hard copy of the *Basic Facts* brochure or for answers to specific questions. The U.S. Patent and Trademark Office has a system that allows a registrant to apply for a trademark electronically, and information regarding this system is available on the Web site as well.

Advantages of Federal Trademark Registration

- Protection of the mark in more than one state;
- Better protection in case of a court fight over the mark—federal registration provides evidence of ownership of the mark and allows for invocation of the jurisdiction of the federal courts;
- "Instant protection"—if you file an "intent to use" application with the U.S. Patent and Trademark Office, your right to obtain a particular mark will be protected from the date the application is filed, even before the trademark is officially approved and even before the trademark is used; and
- Indefinite protection—unlike copyrights and patents, which are good for only a certain number of years, trademarks can last forever, provided the registrant properly maintains the registration, as discussed later in this chapter.

Disadvantages of Federal Trademark Registration

- The process is lengthy—from nine months to a year;
- It will also cost you money—application fees of $375 and legal fees (you can file on your own, but this is one of those cases in which hiring an attorney specializing in the area will probably be worth it);

- Though your mark can last indefinitely, you have to take several steps to maintain proper registration: Namely, you must continue to use the mark; between the fifth and sixth years from the date of the initial registration you must file an affidavit setting forth certain information; you must renew the mark every ten years.

You may not register a trademark if it is confusingly similar to another registered mark. Also, you cannot register a mark as a trademark if it is merely descriptive of the goods or services identified by the mark. For example, the words *soft drink* likely cannot be trademarked because they merely describe the product they name. Federal law also prohibits the registration of marks that are immoral, scandalous, or disparaging.

 SEARCHES FOR TRADEMARKS

One part of the process of trademark registration is to search to make sure that no existing mark is similar enough to yours to cause problems, such as confusion among consumers about the origins of goods or services. The examiner at the U.S. Patent and Trademark Office will do this in deciding whether to register a mark. However, it is a good idea to conduct your own search first to avoid unnecessary expenses in applying for a trademark for a name or design that has already been trademarked by someone else.

Your attorney will help you search to discover whether there is an existing trademark that may conflict with yours. The Web site of the U.S. Patent and Trademark Office—www.uspto.gov—has a free database of registered and pending trademarks. It permits you to search in a variety of ways and can help you determine whether a particular mark has already been taken.

Trade Names

A **trade name** is another form of intellectual property that you should protect. A trade name is generally defined as the name a business uses for advertising and sales purposes that is different from the name in its articles of incorporation (or other officially filed documents) or its official name. An example of a trade name is the use of the name "Tom's Burger Shack" by a company whose official registered name is Smith's Restaurant Service, LLP. Most states authorize the protection of a trade name by filing certain documents with the county clerk of court or other appropriate officials in the state. This process is discussed in chapter 2.

Many companies choose to file for trade name protection before or at the opening of the business. However, you can file to protect a business's trade name even after it has begun. It's a good idea to do so, since failing to register a trade name properly can result in liability to the individuals actually involved in the business venture. For example, let's say Smith's Restaurant Service, LLP, failed to register its trade name with the appropriate county or state officials but conducted business as Tom's Burger Shack. Then the individuals signing documents and incurring debt on behalf of Tom's Burger Shack may be held personally responsible for the company's debts and other obligations.

 MORE ON TRADE NAMES

For more information on registering a trade name, contact your local clerk of court, secretary of state, or your attorney.

Taxation of Trademarks and Trade Names

The cost of developing and registering a trademark or trade name must be capitalized (i.e., you depreciate the cost over time rather than deduct it as a straight expense). The advertising and promotional expenses incurred in marketing goods and services subject to a trademark or trade name, are, however, deductible as selling expenses. The sale of a trademark or trade name can result in capital gains treatment. Instead of an outright sale, a trademark or trade name is frequently **licensed** to one or more third parties, often as part of a franchise agreement. The income received from this licensing arrangement is treated as ordinary income rather than capital gains.

DOMAIN NAMES

Increasingly, small businesses are finding it advantageous to create Web pages for communication and advertising purposes and even direct commerce. Many such businesses have established their own Web domain names, which are alpha-numeric Internet addresses. Given the worldwide scope of the Internet, domain names are issued without regard to whether trademark or trade name protection might exist under the laws of the United States.

Where does that leave you if you own a trade name or trademark and find someone using it as a domain name? The International Corporation for Assigned Names and Numbers (ICANN) was formed in 1998 to develop policy on the Internet's unique identifiers (i.e., domain names). It has adopted a Uniform Domain-Name Dispute-Resolution policy, which most courts and Internet service providers comply with. Whenever there is a dispute as to who is entitled to a particular domain name (or one that is possibly confusingly similar to an existing name), a panel of experts reviews the domain name(s) in question, examining existing trademark and trade name registrations, the length of time the name(s) has/have been in use, and the good faith use of the name(s). Internet service providers will generally follow the decision reached in this dispute-resolution process by allowing the registration of a particular domain name or removing it from the Internet. This dispute-resolution process was initiated particularly to fight *cybersquatters*—companies or individuals who register confusingly similar domain names only for the purpose of later selling them to the legitimate business that needs those names. As explained below, you may still have additional recourse against an entity improperly using or even registering the trademark as a domain name.

The best approach is to get there first. Small businesses interested in Internet exposure should act quickly to ensure that they are able to register the domain name desired.

The registration of domain names in the United States was originally limited to only a few broad categories: ".net" for network service provides, ".org" for nonprofit organizations, ".com" for commercial institutions or service providers, ".edu" for educational institutions, ".mil" for military organizations, and ".gov" for government institutions or agencies. Domain names outside the United States end in two-letter country codes, for example, ".ca" for Canadian sites. New domain extensions have been added, such as ".biz" for businesses, ".info" for sites just providing information, and ".tv" for media sites. However, ".com" still remains the most popular domain name extension.

Federal trademark protection will become increasingly important as the new domain name system moves closer to becoming a reality. For example, if a company is called Rainbow Women's Stores, it might have a domain name such as www.rainbow.com. The addition of new categories to the domain system will allow another entity to register the domain name www.rainbow.biz, which may be confusing.

The proposed new system of domain name registration seeks to minimize this problem by giving some effect to the federal registration of trademarks, regardless of which country issued the trademark. The new system will allow the holder of a trademark to bring a complaint and possibly cancel another entity's improper registration of that trademark as a domain name.

One foreseeable problem with this system is that trademarks can be obtained very easily and inexpensively in countries outside the United States. Therefore, many companies may rush to obtain foreign trademarks, hoping to avoid the delay and hassle of a United States trademark application.

TRADE SECRETS

A trade secret is something referred to as "know-how." It is data or information, not generally known in a particular industry, that gives a business an advantage over its competitors. Common examples of know-how are:

- formulas (and not just chemical ones—trade secrets include recipes and directions for making everything from lipstick to soft drinks to succotash);
- manufacturing techniques and processes (how to do something better, faster, cheaper);
- customer lists (you have them—and the competition would kill to get them); and
- computer software (not the stuff users can see on their screen, but the source code that makes it all work).

Other possible trade secrets are designs, patterns, programs, systems, forecasts, specifications, and other technical data. Even magic tricks could qualify as trade secrets. A trade secret is not patentable, nor can it be registered as a trademark. However, trade secrets *are* recognized legally as a form of property, and you can turn to the courts to protect against their unauthorized use.

Protecting Trade Secrets

How do you get the most protection possible for your secret? The key is to take steps to protect it from disclosure and maintain its confidentiality. Of course, you want to keep it hidden from as many people as possible. Reveal nothing to outsiders, and as little as possible to a trusted few of your consultants, em-

YOUR LEGAL OPTIONS

Your legal options in the event of a breach of confidentiality or noncompete agreement depend on the laws of your state, as well as the particular contract you have with employees. You might be entitled to **injunctive relief**—a court order stopping the thieves from using your secrets. You might also be entitled to money damages. And the **Economic Espionage Act of 1996** makes stealing trade secrets a federal criminal offense. You might also be able to get federal injunctive relief under this act.

---

ployees, and others. Require employees and selected outsiders who have access to trade secrets to sign confidentiality agreements, by which they acknowledge that the information is a secret and agree not to reveal it.

Obtain further protection by requiring employees, particularly those with positions of power and access to trade secrets, to execute covenants not to compete (see chapter 18). A covenant not to compete protects a business from the dangers associated with key employees leaving the business and going out into business on their own—or joining a competitor—and taking the secrets with them.

Your attorney can draft strong noncompete/nondisclosure agreements for you. Make sure you use them.

Notes About Trade Secrets

- Unlike patents and copyrights, you can protect trade secrets forever.
- Trade secrets are immediately protected—no waiting for registration, such as for trademarks and patents.
- There are no filing fees or expensive procedures; all you need is a security system and agreements not to disclose or compete. However, if someone improperly discloses your trade

secret, although you can sue them for damages, the trade secret protection is lost forever.

• They can be more confidential than a patent (to get patent protection you have to disclose at least portions of your secrets).

• You could lose the secret if someone can legitimately figure it out (e.g., by analyzing that formula).

• Precisely because they are secret, it is harder to prove in court that you developed them, making legal enforcement more of a problem.

TAXATION OF TRADE SECRETS

Trade secrets are not specifically covered by the Internal Revenue Code. Nevertheless, the tax treatment of trade secrets and know-how is fairly well established by the courts. You can either amortize or deduct the expense you incur in developing a trade secret—it is a legitimate business expense. And there are no other tax consequences associated with trade secrets unless they are transferred, for example, as part of the sale of all the assets of a business. Then they are considered assets and are subject to tax on their sale. However, in some situations, the amount allocated to the trade secrets upon transfer may qualify for capital gains treatment, and that could save you money.

PATENTS

The founders of our country thought that protecting patents and copyrights was so important that they included it in the Constitution. Among the powers the Constitution gives Congress is the power "to promote the Progress of Science and useful Arts, by securing for limited Times to Authors and Inventors the exclusive Right to their respective Writings and Discoveries." Since its very first session, Congress has enacted laws designed to stimulate creativity by giving "authors and inventors" the exclusive rights to their intellectual property for a period of years.

Kinds of Inventions That Are Patentable

A **patent** gives you an exclusive right, within the United States, to make, use, and sell your invention for a period of years. Not every invention is patentable. By statute, the invention must fall into at least one of four classes:
- process (for example, the manufacturing of chemicals or treating of metals),
- machine,
- article of manufacture, or
- composition of matter (for example, mixtures of chemicals).

In addition, based on existing technology (known technically as **prior art**), the invention "would not have been obvious at the time the invention was made to a person having ordinary skill in the art to which said subject matter pertains." This is usually referred to as the **unobviousness** (or **nonobviousness**) **test**. Not only must the invention meet these criteria, but it must also have some utility, not be frivolous or immoral, and not be naturally occurring (sorry, you can't patent gravity).

The invention must be more than just an idea or scientific principle—there must be proof that it can be made operative (no perpetual motion machines unless they really work). Moreover, a patent will not be issued if the invention has been described in any printed publication anywhere in the world or was in public use or offered for sale anywhere in the United States for more than one year prior to the time an application for a United States patent is filed. If all these conditions are met, is your patent application out of the woods? Not necessarily. The patent may still not be issued because of existing valid conflicting patents.

Obtaining a Patent and the Advantages of Having a Patent

You apply for a patent by filing an application with the U.S. Patent and Trademark Office. This is a highly technical and lengthy process that may take several years to complete. Patent registration can cost several thousand dollars in filing fees, legal fees, costs of drawings, and costs of patent searches.

Though there is no legal requirement that you have an attorney, most people seek to protect their rights to the maximum extent by working with an attorney who specializes in patent law or who is a **patent agent**. (The distinction is that a patent agent might be better for more routine work, while a patent attorney might be better for more complex work, particularly if you anticipate a legal challenge to your patent.)

If your invention is for the ornamental design of a manufactured item (a **design patent**), your protection lasts for fourteen years after approval of your patent application. If it's for the functional features of the invention (a **utility patent**), the period of a new patent is twenty years from the date you filed the application.

You should know that if your application is successful, you become the **grantee** of the patent. That gives you the nonrenewable exclusive monopoly in the United States to use or assign rights to use a utility patent for twenty years from the date the patent application is filed. Maintenance fees are required after the first three and a half years of the patent and then every four years over the next eight years to keep a patent in force. These fees can be as high as $4,000.

All this effort is worthwhile because you can then prevent anyone from selling or using your invention without your permission. However, there are no patent police to do this for you— you must file (and finance) a lawsuit against the infringers, and that might take years of litigation.

A patent issued in the United States does not provide any protection in another country. For foreign country protection, you have to obtain additional patents. To have maximum protection in all other countries that are signatories to various treaties and conventions establishing reciprocal priority rights, you have to file foreign patent applications in the United States. Since patents in many other countries are subject to onerous taxes and in some cases compulsory licensing within the country, it is often advisable not to seek foreign patents directly, or to seek them only in countries where it will be economically worthwhile to do so.

The time involved in pursuing all the procedural steps in obtaining a final decision on a patent may take several years. Since an infringement claim can cover the period between the filing of the application and the issuance of the patent, your rights are not prejudiced by the delay, assuming you ultimately get a valid patent.

You can maintain total control of a patent and, as its sole owner, manufacture and market goods with a patent. Or you can sell or license the patent to others on an exclusive or nonexclusive basis in return for a payment called a **royalty**. Another option if you are the inventor is to sell or assign the invention to a new or existing business in which you are an investor, with the expectation that the business will develop and market the patented product.

Even if you cannot obtain a patent, it may be possible to get basic protection for your invention through the trade secret doctrine, or in the case of a design invention, by means of a trademark or copyright. You can explore these and other possibilities, such as an unfair competition claim against unauthorized users of the invention, with a good patent law firm.

Tax Consequences of Patents

The various methods of marketing a patent have different tax consequences.

For tax purposes, marketing an invention involves two stages. The first is the research and development stage, when the invention is refined and reduced to practice. The expenses incurred in this stage are generally deductible.

The second stage involves the tax consequences of sale or license of the patent once it is issued. Exploiting a patented invention in your own sole proprietorship has no particular tax consequences. Selling or licensing rights of an invention, however, can produce either ordinary income or capital gains.

Capital gains are taxable at a lower rate than ordinary income under current law. However, the Internal Revenue Code has very stringent requirements for obtaining capital gains treatment, and

BE CAREFUL

Phony patent development and marketing firms are a persistent scam, probably because there is an unending supply of people out there with a "great idea" that they could make a bundle from if only they knew the steps to take. There are legitimate firms, too, and the best way to find them is through personal recommendations from people you trust. Check any company out with the Better Business Bureau, your bureau of consumer affairs, the district attorney in your area, or the attorney general in your state or in the state in which the company is located.

it is very important to seek the early assistance of an attorney who is familiar with the tax consequences of patents. This is particularly true if there is any possibility the patent will be transferred to a business with the expectation that the owners of the business will receive capital gains treatment on the royalties generated by the patent. For this plan to work, the invention must be transferred to the business prior to the time the invention has been tested and successfully operated or has been commercially exploited, whichever is earlier. It is often difficult to determine when an invention has been reduced to practice.

If you are the inventor of the patented creation and you are going to transfer a patent to a business in which you have an ownership interest, it is generally easier to achieve favorable capital gains tax treatment if the business is a partnership or limited liability company than if it is a corporation.

COPYRIGHTS

A **copyright** is literally a right to copy. If you have copyrighted your creations, you can prevent anyone else from appropriating them—that is, copying or manufacturing them—without your permission.

Copyrights basically protect artistic endeavors. Under the law, seven types of works can be copyrighted:

- literary works;
- musical works;
- dramatic works;
- pantomimes and choreographic works;
- pictorial, graphic, and sculptural works, including fabric designs;
- motion pictures and other audiovisual works; and
- sound recordings.

These categories are broad enough to cover all sorts of media, old (books, plays, records) and new (CDs, DVDs, MP3s, video games, software, and so forth). But your "work" cannot just be an idea (the notion of pizza-eating Ninja Turtles, for example) to qualify for copyright protection. It must be realized in a "fixed form"—a book, a computer disk, a Web site, an actual television series about pizza-eating Ninja Turtles. And, it has to have originated with you and be the result of at least some creativity.

Getting Copyright Protection

In some ways, getting copyright protection is easier than getting a patent or trademark. You have basic, common law copyright protection automatically whenever you put your idea into a fixed form (write an article, record a song, make a videotape, store your software on disk).

You can get better copyright protection—i.e., protection that's more apt to stand up in a legal fight—by placing the symbol ©, the year of first publication, and the name of the copyright holder prominently on every publication of the material. It also helps to file a copyright application for the artistic work with the Federal Copyright Office (www.copyright.gov). There is a small fee (less than $100 in most cases) to file and it requires only filling out a simple form and sending in two samples of the work.

You can even file for copyright registration years after your artistic creation is published, but if you file within three months of publication, you will have certain important advantages in

GET HELP BY WEB

The Copyright Office's Web site, www.copyright.gov, has application forms you can download, a database of registered copyrights and other records, and electronic versions of many of its publications, such as *Copyright Basics*.

litigation with any infringers. If you win, you will be eligible for statutory damages of up to $150,000 and attorneys' fees, in addition to any actual damages you can show, in the event of infringement.

Copyright lasts the lifetime of the creator plus 70 years if the

 ## TALKING TO A LAWYER: COPYRIGHT

Q. *I have a script for a play, and I'd like to put together a group of friends to do a production of it. Do I need something in writing so I protect my own script? Since it's my script, wouldn't I continue to own the play no matter who produced it? What happens if it's a big success and a big producer wants the rights to it?*

A. You can protect your script by placing the symbol ©, your name, and the date of the first publication prominently on every copy of the script that you distribute. You might also consider contacting the Federal Copyright Office or an attorney regarding federal copyright registration. In the event a producer would like to use your script to produce a play or movie, it is possible for you to license the right to use the script in a very limited purpose, such as to produce a movie, while retaining the copyright to the work.

—Answer by Scott Withrow, attorney,
Withrow, McQuade & Olsen, LLP, Atlanta, Georgia

creator is an individual, and between 95 and 120 years if the copyright is held by a business. Copyright gives you the right to sell the whole bundle of rights, or to unbundle the rights and sell or license them in a variety of ways. For example, in book publishing you could license the right to reproduce the work to publishers abroad and to a paperback publisher in this country, as well as the right to prepare derivative works (a movie, play, TV show, and so forth) based on the original work.

Taxation of Copyright Royalties or Sales Proceeds

An individual who creates an artistic work, unlike the inventor of a patentable product, cannot obtain capital gains treatment upon the sale or transfer of the rights to the work. However, capital gains tax treatment is available when the copyright is held by a corporation or business entity taxed as a partnership. Thus, sales of films produced by a corporation, partnership, or limited liability company can, under some circumstances, qualify for favorable capital gains tax treatment.

TALKING TO A LAWYER: WEB PROTECTION

Q. As a businessperson whose business is her art, how do I best protect my intellectual property after posting it on the Internet?

A. When posting art or any other creative work on the Internet, you can protect such work by placing the symbol ©, your name, and the date of first publication of the work on every copy posted on the Internet. You might also contact an attorney regarding registering the work with the Federal Copyright Office. Even if you have already posted some of your work on the Internet or otherwise published it, you can still obtain federal copyright registration.

—Answer by Scott Withrow, attorney, Withrow, McQuade & Olsen, LLP, Atlanta, Georgia

Q. I know that a lot of small businesses are doing well after setting up a Web site, but I'm concerned about the legal side of choosing an Internet name or slogan. What's the general situation, and what special steps can I take?

A. You can use almost anything as an Internet name. Your name on the Internet will be your domain name—the unique address used by the Internet's infrastructure to allow other computers to find you on the Internet. Your domain name is a word or phrase ending in one of the now ubiquitous top-level domain extensions such as ".com," ".org," or ".net." Your preferred domain name might be the name of your business followed by the popular ".com" extension—"yourbusiness .com"—or you might use a phrase or slogan such as "worldsgreatest widgets.com." The ".com" top-level domain extension was originally intended to refer to a commercial enterprise, while ".org" refers to a not-for-profit enterprise and ".net" signifies that the domain name is held by an Internet-related organization.

Once you have selected a domain name you would like to use, you need to find out whether it is available. Domain names at the same level of the Internet's nomenclature hierarchy must be unique. That means there can be only one ".com" top-level domain, and there can be only one "worldsgreatestwidgets.com." If a company has already registered a domain as its own, then you are too late. But even if a domain name is available, it may not be a wise choice. Other businesses may be using the same word or phrase or an almost identical word or phrase as a trademark or trade name.

These businesses may not choose to register their trademarks as domain names, but they might still be very interested in protecting their trademarks. They have the money to try to prevent you from using your chosen domain name on the grounds that it infringes on their trademark. A trademark owner might obtain a court order preventing you from using your chosen domain name if the trademark owner shows that either consumers will be confused about who is behind your domain, or that your business will attract consumers unfairly because its trademark is so well-known and consumers will seek it out on the Internet.

Or, your domain name might be put on hold by Network Solutions,

Inc. (NSI), the private company that, since the early days of the Web, has been primarily in charge of registering the ".com," ".org," and ".net" domain names. Network Solutions will do this if a trademark owner submits proof of a registered trademark that is identical to the domain name and claims prior use of the word or phrase in question. The domain name holder will not be able to access or use the domain name in any way during the period it is on hold, which will last until the parties resolve or settle the dispute. It doesn't matter if your business is not competitive with that of the trademark owner, and if you believe you can show you used the name first, you still cannot prevent Network Solutions from putting it on hold. If you believe you started using the name or phrase first, you will have to litigate to prevent Network Solutions from putting the name on hold and to prevent the trademark owner from taking the domain name away from you.

Once you have decided upon a domain name, the next step is to reserve the domain name through your Internet Service Provider (ISP) and to have your ISP register the domain to you as its exclusive owner. (Of course you also need to have Internet access and a place to house or host your Web site on the Internet. Most ISPs offer Web site hosting along with e-mail service and Internet access.) You can register your domain name yourself, over the Network Solutions Web site, www.networksolutions.com, or through www.register.com, the most recently approved registrar of top-level domains. NSI charges a fee of $70 for two years to register your domain name to you. Or, for $119, NSI will register the name and "reserve" it for you for two years, which means it will host the name on its server and allow you to use it to send and receive e-mail and build a Web site.

The U.S. Department of Commerce has recognized the nonprofit Internet Corporation for Assigned Names and Numbers (ICANN) as the organization chartered to oversee various administrative functions relating to Internet domain names and numbers, including accrediting additional companies to register ".com," ".org," ".net," ".biz," and ".info" top-level domains. Hundreds of organizations worldwide have been approved to register these domain names.

You might also choose to register your domain in more than one top-level domain extension (both ".com" and ".org," for example), or in one of the many other top-level domains that refer to a country. These usually are restricted to businesses or individuals within the particular country; for example, the extensions ".co.uk" and ".org.uk" may be used by commercial and personal sites in the United Kingdom. Increasingly, many of these top-level domain extensions are available to businesses regardless of their actual location. For example, the domain extensions ".ms" (Montserrat) or ".ky" (the Cayman Islands) are available for use by commercial or personal Web sites. The extension ".md" (the Republic of Moldova) is available for use by commercial sites relating to the medical profession. Registration of domains with these extensions is handled through a number of sources, but NSI or register.com will also help you register domains with some of these extensions.

—Answer by Gerald V. Niesar, attorney,
Niesar & Diamond, LLP, San Francisco, California

YOU MUST REMEMBER THIS

• It is important to protect your intellectual property—both to protect your bottom line, and to help prevent possible headaches and consumer confusion.

• The U.S. Patent and Trademark Office can be very helpful if you are trying to decide on a trademark or want to register one.

• If you have any plans to do business internationally or on the Internet, you will want to make sure your intellectual property rights are still accounted for.

PART VI

The Taxman Cometh

We won't repeat the old bromide about death and taxes—you already know that you'll face taxes on your business. What you may not know is that state and federal tax laws are very complex, and this complexity might be a good thing for you.

At just about every level of government, the authorities are of two minds about business taxation: On the one hand, it's a source of revenue, but on the other hand, businesses create jobs, generate wealth, and add to the community. Thus, tax laws are at least in part written with an eye to encouraging (or at least not stifling) business and business expansion.

That means that the laws on business taxation may provide special opportunities for *your* business to lighten its tax load. We point out a number of these opportunities for both federal and state taxes, and conclude by providing guidance on dealing effectively with tax people in the event of a dispute.

CHAPTER 28

Business Taxes 101

Knowing the Basics of Taxation Can Help You Plan—and Save Money

Your new business has not only survived for nearly a year, it's even made some money. But as you ring in the new year, you have more to think about than planning for growth. Spring is rapidly approaching, and with it that dreaded date: April 15th. Now what? Where do you begin the convoluted process of reporting income and paying taxes? How do you even find out what you need to know? What do you do with all those records on your computer (or are they stuffed into a shoebox)?

If you thought your individual taxes were complicated, wait until you try managing taxes for a business. First there's income tax on business earnings, whether they're reported on a corporate tax return or on your personal tax return. When you expect the tax for the year to exceed $1,000, you have to pay quarterly estimated taxes. (The $1,000 figure—like all of the specific dollar amounts and percentages in this chapter—is as of the 2008 tax year.) And you have to withhold income tax and Social Security and Medicare payments for each employee. While you're at it, there's the self-employment tax for you (unless you're an employee of your own corporation) to make your own contributions to the Social Security and Medicare systems. Your business may also be subject to state income taxes, federal or state unemployment taxes, federal excise taxes, business license fees, property taxes, and state and local sales taxes. All of these are subject to a raft of rules and regulations, filing deadlines, and penalties for late filing or failure to withhold.

What's more, the tax law has certain changes built in to existing law (such as dollar amounts triggering certain consequences that may vary year to year depending on a schedule included in the tax code). And Congress and state legislatures are often (if not always) contemplating new tax laws that affect business.

MAJOR FEDERAL TAX FORMS AND SCHEDULES

I

Form 1040	Individual or married couple return
Form 1040-ES	Estimated tax for individuals or married couples
Schedule A	Itemized deductions
Schedule B	Interest and ordinary dividends
Schedule C	Profit or loss from business
Schedule C-EZ	Simplified profit and loss statements
Schedule D	Capital gains and losses
Schedule E	Supplemental income and loss
Schedule F	Profit or loss from farming
Schedule SE	Self-employment tax
Form 8829	Reporting expenses for business use of your home

II

Form 1040-ES	Payment voucher that accompanies estimated payments
Form 2210	Calculates the penalty for underpayment of estimated tax

III

Form 1120	Corporate tax return, long form

IV

Form 1120-S	S corporation tax return

V

Form 1065	Partnership information return
Schedule K-1	Allocation of partnership results

Tax laws are so complicated that it takes an expert just to know and understand all of them. Many business decisions have tax consequences, so it pays to consider the options ahead of time. Would we save money on taxes if we did this rather than that? Are those savings offset by added expenses elsewhere? What if we tried this other plan? An experienced attorney or accountant can help you evaluate the tax implications of plans you're considering, avoiding unhappy surprises later. And he or she should be well versed in the latest changes in the law.

FIRST, THE GOOD NEWS

Despite the complexity, there's good news for you as a business owner. The U.S. government has a penchant for small businesses, the backbone of our economy. One reason the tax code is so complicated is that Congress wants to provide certain benefits to promote small businesses, families, family farms, nonprofit groups, minority-owned businesses, and other institutions our society favors. The government attempts to guide the nation by manipulating tax policy and tinkering with the tax code in hopes of making the system fair to everyone—and keeping special-interest groups happy, but that's another story. Being a small-business owner does have some advantages.

What's the lesson? Keep your eyes open because your business may be eligible for certain business credits to offset all the taxes. At any time, the federal government offers dozens of tax credits for businesses, ranging from efficient energy use, to hiring certain classes of employees, to making your business more accessible to disabled individuals. IRS Form 3800 contains a summary of all available business tax credits. One of the largest sources of business tax credits are investment credits, which currently are focused on energy research and use. IRS Form 3468 contains investment credit opportunities.

In the same way, because you're a small-business owner you may be able to take some unexpected deductions. Basically, most ordinary and necessary business expenses can be deducted from the income that your tax is based on. These include wages and salaries, supplies, office expenses, utilities, pension and profit sharing plans, rent or lease payments, legal and professional services, employee benefits programs, insurance, and interest. You can deduct advertising, bad debts from sales or services, bank service charges, business cards and stationery, car and truck expenses, charitable contributions, commissions, credit card fees and finance charges, education, gifts, Internet and e-mail services, parking, professional memberships and publications, postage, public relations, repairs, telephone service, trade shows

 THE SELF-EMPLOYMENT TAX

The good news is that even if you're self-employed, you're covered under the Social Security system. (That is good news, right?) You pay a self-employment tax instead of FICA (Social Security). The bad news is that, since you have no employer, you have to pay the entire tax. However, you then can deduct 50 percent of the self-employment tax on your federal tax return. Here are the basics:

- The self-employment tax is composed of two elements and is taxed at two different rates. The Social Security portion is currently 12.4 percent of wages, tips, and net earnings, up to $102,000. The Medicare portion is currently 2.9 percent of net earnings, with no limit. The percentage and self-employment income figures tend to increase every year.

- To compute the self-employment tax, use Form 1040, Schedule SE. You must file a Schedule SE if you expect to owe taxes on your final return, including the self-employment tax, of $1,000 or more.

- Include the self-employment tax in your estimated quarterly tax payments.

- Take your deduction for half the self-employment tax on line 27 of Form 1040.

and conventions, and (subject to limitations) business-related travel, meals, and entertainment. State and local taxes can be deducted from the taxable income reported on your federal return. If some of your equipment is stolen or destroyed in a fire or earthquake, you may be able to deduct part of your loss from taxable income.

When you invest in buildings, vehicles, equipment, computers, furniture, or other tangible property, you generally can't deduct the entire cost in one year, but you can write off part of the expense every year for the expected life of the purchase. This is called **depreciation**. You can even get the lion's share of the tax benefit early by claiming **accelerated depreciation**, on the theory that new vehicles and equipment drop significantly in value the first year, just because they're no longer new. IRS Publication 946 provides an overview of depreciation. Finally, a special provision in the tax code allows taxpayers (subject to some limitations) to directly expense as much as $250,000 of the cost of eligible personal property placed in service during a tax year. This is called a "Section 179 Deduction." If you operate at a loss for a year or two, you can deduct the loss from taxable income in more profitable years, up to twenty years later (loss carry forward) and/or up to five years earlier (loss carry back).

NO BROKEN RECORDS

The only way you can save money on all these items, though, is to keep track of what you spend and save receipts to prove it. If there's one general rule for business taxation, it's the same as the general rule for individual taxation: Keep good records. Here are some common ways to keep your records straight:

• Deposit all business receipts in a separate bank account and make all disbursements by check, so you'll have an accurate record of both income and expenses.

• Avoid writing business checks payable to "cash."

• Write checks payable to yourself only if you're withdrawing income from the business for your own use.

HOME OFFICE DEDUCTIONS

Some people might say that claiming a home office deduction is the same thing as stamping "Audit Me" on your return. That's not quite true. You just have to be careful that you meet the criteria. If you do, you may deduct direct expenses (those that apply only to the home office) and indirect expenses, such as a proportional share of rent, heat, electricity, insurance, depreciation, and so forth. (Remember, though, that the home office expenses you deduct can't exceed your business income, though you can carry over the excess to the next year's return.) You can even deduct home office expenses for a sideline business, if you meet both of the criteria for the home office.

Principal place of business. The home office must be your principal place of business. Whether yours meets that standard depends on its relative importance to the business and the amount of time you spend there. You can claim the home office is the principal place of business if you have no other fixed location for administrative/management activities. For example, if you are a traveling anvil salesman and you use your home for your reports and such, even for relatively few hours per week, you may be entitled to take the deduction because you don't have another office.

Regular and exclusive use. The home office must be used regularly and exclusively for your business. This means you can't claim your dining room as an office if the family eats there, too. But you could claim the corner of your dining room where you put your computer, if you didn't use it for anything else (and didn't let the children play games on it). However, if you are a day care provider you may meet this standard even though the children are all over your house, mingling with your family. There's also an exception for storage of inventory and/or product samples.

If you conduct more than one business from a home office, you must meet the test for each business. If one business qualifies and another doesn't, the IRS will not allow you to take deductions for even the one that qualifies.

Use Form 8829, "Expenses for Business Use of Your Home," to calculate the percentage of your home allocated to the home office and figure your deduction.

- Keep a record of any transactions between you and your business.
- Create a permanent record to keep track of deductible expenses and any assets you can depreciate.
- Create an orderly file for canceled checks, paid bills, deposit slips, receipts, and other papers that support the entries in your books.
- Save tax returns indefinitely, and save supporting records for at least three years or until the statute of limitations for that return runs out.
- If you change your accounting method, keep records supporting the change indefinitely.

Good record keeping is no more fun than paying taxes, but it can help things go much more smoothly.

DON'T RELAX, IT'S INCOME TAX

Since the biggest slice of the business tax pie is income tax, let's start there. Where you report your business income, how you pay it, and whether it's taxed once or twice depends on the structure of your business. (And how you structure your business may have a lot to do with how you prefer to be taxed.)

- A **sole proprietor** files taxes as an individual. You (and your spouse, if you're filing jointly) will file one tax return, Form 1040. That's the easy part—it's the same form you've already used to file as an individual. Your business income or loss will be determined on Schedule C and reported on line 12 of your federal income tax return. Your net profit or loss is how much you made, minus how much you spent on the business.

Schedule C is the tool required to figure net profit or loss by entering gross receipts minus returns and allowance, then subtracting deductible expenses and the cost of inventory, supplies, and labor (other than your own). You can file Schedule C-EZ if you have less than $5,000 in business expenses, no net losses, no employees, and no home office deduction—in other words, if you have a very small operation.

• A **partnership** is a reporting entity, which means the partnership must file a tax return, Form 1065, along with a Schedule K-1 for each partner. However, a partnership does not pay taxes. The Schedule K-1 allocates the partnership income to you and your partner(s), and you include it on your Form 1040. As a partner, you pay tax on your share of income and take the losses on your individual returns. You will owe taxes on your share of partnership income even if you don't actually receive it. The partnership return is due on the fifteenth day of the fourth month following the close of the partnership tax year. (Got that?)

Some transactions must be separated rather than reported as part of the partnership's regular taxable income. These include:

    o   capital gains and losses,
    o   farm-related gains and losses,
    o   dividends,
    o   casualty gains and losses,
    o   tax-exempt income and retirement contributions,
    o   charitable contributions, and
    o   most credits.

These items are separately reported on the individual tax returns because they're subject to special calculations or limitations. An individual partner also needs to file quarterly estimated tax payments, including self-employment tax.

• A **corporation** counts as a legal entity, as if it's a separate person, so it not only files a Form 1120 Corporate Income Tax Return but also pays corporate income taxes on its income. The shareholders then pay tax on their dividends, so the income is taxed twice. (A regular corporation is called a C corporation for tax purposes. The letter comes from the subchapter of the Internal Revenue Code that covers tax rules for corporations.) Federal corporate tax brackets are different from those for individuals, ranging from 15 percent to 39 percent. However, unlike individual tax brackets, corporate brackets aren't adjusted each year for inflation.

One good thing about C corporations is that they're best for fringe benefits. The corporation can deduct the cost of health insurance, dependent care assistance, and some term life insurance, and you don't have to pay tax on them.

• If you own a small corporation and you don't like double taxation, you can declare your business an **S corporation**, which makes it a reporting entity with a tax status similar to a partnership. The S corporation reports its income on Form 1120-S but does not pay tax, while you as a shareholder pay taxes on your share of the income. This is a fluid status, which you and any other shareholders may declare on IRS Form 2553 during the prior year or the first two and a half months of the current tax year to obtain the status for the current year. (Again, the name comes from the corresponding subchapter of the Internal Revenue Code, as these are often called "subchapter S corporations.") The taxable income for an S corporation is computed in a similar fashion as for a partnership.

As a shareholder, you report not only your share of the income, but also your share of credits and deductions, capital gains and losses, farm gains and losses, charitable contributions, and tax-exempt interest. As with a partnership, if the S corporation loses money, you can't deduct a loss greater than your investment, that is, your adjusted basis in the corporate stock plus the amount of any loans from the shareholder to the corporation. Any loss above this amount can be carried forward.

As a shareholder who works for the S corporation, you're treated as an employee, so your business pays the employer share of FICA, plus workers' compensation and unemployment insurance. However, you can't get all the fringe benefits available to a C corporation because for those purposes you count as a partner.

• A **limited liability company**, the new form that combines the best of partnerships and corporations (see chapter 14), can choose whether to be taxed as a partnership (or, if your state allows a sole-owner LLC, a sole proprietor) or a C corporation. (Choosing not to be taxed at all is not allowed.) You can imagine how many prefer C corporation status so they can be double taxed. If you choose to be taxed as a corporation, you must file a Form 8832 with the IRS.

BUT WE *REALLY* NEEDED TO HAVE THE MEETING IN TAHITI . . .

Now that you're getting the hang of this business deductions game, how about deducting the box seats in the stadium where you sometimes take a customer? Be careful, because you're not the first one to think about stretching the law a bit here. Excessive travel and entertainment deductions are likely to raise the eyebrows of an IRS auditor. IRS Publication 463 explains travel, entertainment, gift, and car expenses.

Here are the rules of thumb:

- **Local travel.** You can deduct taxi, train, or bus fare related to your business, as long as you have the dates and receipts to back it up. You cannot, however, deduct the costs of commuting between your home and the business.

- **Business travel.** When you travel overnight for a conference, convention, or business trip, you may deduct all trip-related expenses, including transportation, lodging, meals, Internet or phone charges, laundry, and tips. Again, keep a log and save receipts. If your trip combines business and pleasure, you can deduct travel and business expenses only if 50 percent or more of your trip is devoted to business.

- **Entertainment.** You can deduct 50 percent of the expense for entertaining a client, customer, or employee if it's directly related to your business. This includes meals, tickets, parties, and other entertainment expenses. But you'd better keep a log handy to write down all the details: the date, the amount, the place, the business relationship, and the business purpose of the event. Likewise, keep a guest list for that business-related party and identify each guest by business relationship. Keep receipts, filed neatly so you can find them if needed.

I Estimate We'll Make Five Dollars . . .

All these forms won't pay the bills, so when does the government actually get its money? More good news, bad news. . . . If

NAME, RANK, AND EMPLOYER IDENTIFICATION NUMBER

One of your first steps in starting your business is to obtain an Employer Identification Number (EIN) from the IRS. If you're a sole proprietor with no employees, you can use your personal Social Security number, but it's better to get an EIN anyway to keep business finances separate from personal finances. You must have the EIN before paying estimated taxes or filing a return. Some banks require an EIN before you can open a business banking account. You use the EIN on all business tax returns, checks, and other documents sent to the IRS, and possibly on state tax forms*, as well.

To apply, obtain Form SS-4, the Application for Employer Identification Number. This form is basically self-explanatory. Note that "name of applicant" means the official company name, or your full name if you're a sole proprietor. For "closing month of the accounting year" in space 12, talk to your accountant or lawyer about whether it's advantageous for your company to choose a fiscal year different from the calendar year. If you decide to go with a fiscal year, the IRS will want a substantial business reason for doing so.

IRS addresses, phone numbers, the Internet, and fax numbers for your region are listed on Form SS-4. You can apply for and immediately receive an EIN through the IRS Web site, www.irs.gov (look for a "Business" menu selection, then a link for "Employer ID Numbers"). You can also receive an EIN immediately by calling the IRS's toll-free "Business & Specialty Tax Line." You can mail the form to the IRS and wait four weeks for your number, or you can fax the form to the IRS and receive your EIN within four business days.

You need a separate EIN for each business that you operate. If your corporation changes into an S corporation or vice versa, there's no need to change the EIN. However, you need a new number if you:

* incorporate the business;
* convert it into a partnership or limited liability company;

---

* Note that you may also need a state sales tax identification number, along with a state unemployment compensation identification number.

- take over the business from your partners and operate it as a sole proprietorship;

- terminate an older partnership and begin a new one; or

- buy or inherit an existing business that you plan to operate as a sole proprietorship.

---

you're the owner of a sole proprietorship or a partner in a partnership, you naturally will not have tax withheld from your paycheck. (You will have it taken out if you're the employee of your corporation.) That's the good news. The bad news is, you must make estimated tax payments on April 15, June 15, and September 15 of the tax year, and January 15 of the following year. The quarterly payments are based on your estimate of income tax liability for the year. The self-employment tax is included in your estimated tax payments. Some details:

- You do not need to pay quarterly taxes if your estimated annual tax, including tax on self-employment income, can reasonably be expected to be less than $1,000.

- If you are employed in addition to your business, or your spouse is employed, consider increasing withholding on the regular salary to eliminate quarterly payments.

- The required annual estimated payment is either 90 percent of the tax shown on the current year's return or 100 percent of the tax shown on the previous year's return (provided it covers a full twelve months), which becomes 110 percent of last year's tax if your adjusted gross income exceeded $150,000.

You may need help to figure this as closely as possible. You don't want to pay too little because there's a penalty, but there's no reason to pay taxes any earlier than necessary to avoid a penalty. By keeping your money as long as possible, you are borrowing, interest-free, from the government. Therefore, use the method that results in the lowest amount of estimated tax. For example, when your business really takes off, you can base your estimated payments on the previous year's return, without

DON'T FORGET THE W-2s

You must issue a Wage and Tax Statement (W-2) to any employee by January 31, or within thirty days of a written request from an employee if employment was terminated. You must file these with your state and the IRS. The form may be obtained from the IRS.

penalty. Just be sure to plan for the rest of the tax due when you file, or you will face penalties and interest.

No, Really, It's a Business

But what if your business doesn't do very well the first few years and you actually lose money? That's normally bad news, but there's a silver lining to this cloud. If you lose money, the business is not subject to income tax for that year (although property taxes, payroll taxes and sales taxes still apply). If your business is a partnership, S corporation, or LLC, the amount of business loss you can deduct on your personal income tax depends on your tax "basis," which is, broadly speaking, the value of your investment in the business. The deduction is limited to the amount of the basis at the end of the year in which the loss was incurred. If your tax basis is zero (which means that your business has no value for tax purposes), then you can't take a loss and you can't reduce the basis. But unused losses may be carried forward (tax-speak for kept until you need them) and reported in a more prosperous year. If your business is a C corporation, you can not only deduct losses on the corporation's tax return but also carry losses forward up to twenty years against future profits.

In the opinion of the IRS, this sort of thing can get out of hand. The agency is willing to support your struggling efforts to launch a business, but after a while enough is enough. Suppose you have outside income to support you, but your little dog-breeding business keeps losing money year after year. The IRS may declare that it's really a hobby and nix your loss write-offs. In that case, you have to prove that you really intend to make money at it and you're trying to do so. Here's what the IRS considers in determining profit motive:

• Do you carry on the activity in a businesslike fashion, with such indicators as good records, a separate business bank account, and a separate telephone line?

• Do you put in a lot of time and effort? This isn't to rule out part-time businesses, but full-time effort is more convincing.

• Do you depend on the income from this business for your livelihood? Steady losses that conveniently offset regular income from other sources look suspiciously like hobbies.

• Do you seek expert advice on how to turn the business around and make it profitable?

If your business makes a profit three out of five years (or two out of seven years if your business is related to horses), you're presumed to have a profit motive.

But Can I Defer Income?

If (and when) you become wildly successful, you may have the opposite problem: how to keep your business income from bumping you into the next tax bracket. It's possible to defer the income to the next year, when you expect to owe less tax. The legal way to do this is to delay your billing or collection at the end of the year (assuming you are operating on a cash basis). Then the money rolls in come January or February, so you don't have to report it until April of the following year (unless your business is a C or S corporation, in which case you must report it by March 15).

HAVE EMPLOYEES, WILL WITHHOLD

Ah, the joy of hiring your first employee! One day you're harried and overworked, wishing you had someone to help you manage all the paperwork. The next day you have an employee, together with the responsibilities of keeping records of wages and hours, paying unemployment and workers' compensation, and withholding income tax and FICA—and you're wishing you didn't have such a load of paperwork to manage.

If you've only hired one part-time secretary, do you really have to do all that? Unfortunately, most likely you do. The IRS considers you an employer if you pay wages of $1,500 or more in any calendar year, or if you had one or more employees at any time in each of twenty different calendar weeks. (Special rules apply for farm workers and household employees.) According to the IRS, an employer gives the worker the tools and place to work and has the right to fire the worker.

You might be tempted to avoid having to withhold taxes by claiming that the people who work for you are independent contractors, not employees. But true independent contracts operate their own businesses and are responsible for their own taxes. If the IRS questions your classification, its primary question will be the degree of management and control you exercise over the worker. An IRS agent might ask whether the workers hold themselves out to be operating their own businesses, whether they advertise their services, and whether they decide when to be at work, what to do, and how to do it. If not, they probably count as employees.

So let's suppose you do have employees. You need to be withholding **income tax** from your employees' paychecks, based on their filing status (single or married), number of dependents, and amount of wages or salary due. Keep the W-4 forms your employees complete for you, in case the IRS questions the number of deductions an employee claims or his or her claim to be exempt from withholding. You also must withhold the employee's share of the **Social Security tax** and **Medicare tax** (FICA, for Federal Insurance Contributions Act), and pay the employer's share. Then there's **federal unemployment tax** (FUTA), which your business is responsible for paying. Use Form 940 or 940-EZ to calculate and pay FUTA. Note that sole proprietorships and partnerships don't have to pay FUTA on the owner's compensation. You also have to file Form 1099-MISC if you have paid more than $600 to nonemployees.

The frequency with which you must deposit withholding tax depends on the amount of withholding you collect. The IRS will require you to deposit your employees' withholding at least quarterly; most small businesses do so monthly. You must also file Form 941, Employer's Quarterly Federal Tax Return. Be careful here—some businesses have faced fines because they sent the tax directly to the IRS instead of depositing it in an authorized financial institution, usually a bank. The IRS sends you coupons to use when making these deposits. Generally, the deposits must be postmarked on or before the due date. (Check with your bank—you may be able to make the deposit directly to it.)

Two unpleasant words sum up the basic consequences of not paying such taxes on time: *penalties* and *interest*. The amount of the penalty will depend on how late the payment is, but it's often steep enough to drive a company out of business. Depending on your state's laws, you may be committing a crime. So don't give in to the temptation to ease your financial troubles by using the employees' contribution to pay creditors or delay depositing these taxes until a few weeks after the deadline. This money is not yours; it's a trust fund. If the IRS determines that a "responsible person" willfully paid other creditors before paying payroll taxes, that person may be held personally liable for the unpaid tax. And while other creditors' debts can be wiped out if your business goes bankrupt, liability for payroll taxes stays with you.

Note that there's no break for small business. If you're a one-person corporation, you're both your own boss and your own employee. When you pay yourself a salary from corporate funds, you have the same payroll-tax liabilities as a corporation with a hundred employees.

Given the stakes, it may be worthwhile to engage the services of a payroll service to keep track of payroll and employment taxes, issue the checks, and remind you of what's due when. At the end of each quarter, the payroll service will fill out quarterly payroll tax returns for your business and tell you how to file them. It will also prepare W-2 forms for employees at the end of the year. The cost is reasonable. Another option is to look into software designed to help small businesses manage payroll and taxes.

One tip for reducing unemployment taxes: Make sure former employees collecting unemployment benefits are actually eligible. Some employees who are fired or leave on their own accord apply for unemployment benefits. So document the reasons for termination and take it to the unemployment office to prevent a tax charge from being made against your account. Lots of employers fail to do this and end up paying needlessly.

 ### SHE'S MY . . . UM . . . SECRETARY

If your spouse works in your business, it may make sense from a tax perspective to put your spouse on the payroll. Here are some advantages:

- If you take business trips together, you can deduct your spouse's expenses, provided that your spouse is an employee of the business.

- Suppose you have a sole proprietorship. Ordinarily, you can deduct only 60 percent of the cost of your own health insurance premiums. However, if you set up a health insurance plan for all employees and make your spouse your only employee, the business can potentially deduct 100 percent of the cost of premiums for your employee, your employee's spouse (that is, you), and your dependents.

- If your spouse isn't already working outside the home, earning a salary from the business will provide Social Security benefits in later years.

- Suppose you operate a regular C corporation. Paying your spouse a salary allows you to take money out without having it taxed twice. If you take it out as a dividend, that money is taxed once as corporate income and again on your joint income tax return. Money paid out in salaries, though, is deducted by the corporation and taxable only on the wage earner's return.

Be careful, though. Your spouse must perform legitimate work for the business and receive a salary that's not out of line. You also have to pay payroll taxes on that salary, which will offset some of the benefits gained.

YOU MUST REMEMBER THIS

- Pay quarterly taxes, including self-employment taxes, on time to avoid a penalty.
- Pay all your employees' taxes. Don't try to float them—you'll be in over your head before you know it.
- Substantiate all your deductible expenses carefully.
- Don't forget that free help is available from the IRS.

CHAPTER 29

Then There's the State and the City

A Quick Look at How You Can Owe Less

Robert was trudging along on his own running his consulting business. He was taking care of his business and paying his federal taxes. But if that is all he is doing, he could be in some serious hot water.

If federal taxes weren't enough, chances are you'll have to pay state income tax or, if your business is a corporation, a state corporate tax. As with federal taxes, there are strategies to make the tax burden less, well, burdensome. Read on to find out more.

You understand what income tax and corporation tax mean. But do you know what a **franchise tax** is? Sometimes that's what a state's business tax is called, because it's a tax imposed on the privilege of doing business. (The name has nothing to do with whether or not your business is a franchise.) Then there's property tax, license fees, state unemployment tax, and sales tax on your own purchases (in addition to collecting and turning over sales tax on your customers' purchases). In fact, in many states the state tax bill is growing as the federal government cuts back on funding for social programs. Some states are increasing corporate or sales tax rates, while others are subjecting more services to state sales tax. It's become the fastest growing tax burden for U.S. companies.

At the same time, many states are increasing their enforcement efforts, exchanging information with other states, and finding new ways to track down companies they believe aren't paying the right amount of state tax. Some have increased their auditing staff.

Accordingly, make sure you understand the tax laws and regulations in your state and be careful to comply. Find out about licenses required for your kind of business and pay any fees on time. Fortunately, many of these taxes are deductible.

STATE AND LOCAL INCOME TAXES

While states need revenues to maintain their infrastructure, they also need businesses to provide jobs. Accordingly, many states offer incentives, exemptions, and credits to reduce the tax burden on small businesses and compete with other states as a prime location for business. Check with your state's or city's economic development council to see if it offers any of these. For instance, equipment used in research and development may qualify for a tax exemption or credit. Or you might get tax credits for establishing new jobs in an economic target area.

If your business is a corporation and your state has a corporate income tax, consider doing business in more than one state. You may be able to reduce your taxes overall. Why? Because if you're taxable in only one state, you have to report 100 percent of your income in that state. But if your business is taxable in more than one state then you might be able to apportion the income between the states, which might put your company in lower tax brackets. Having inventory or one sales rep in a rented office may be enough to establish a business presence in a neighboring state, but the issue would be whether you could justify spreading the income between the states. Check with an attorney who understands the tax rules in both states to make sure this strategy would meet your goals.

SALES AND USE TAXES

Don't assume that because you have a new business operating at a loss, you don't owe any state or local taxes. While you generally wouldn't have to pay state or local income taxes, you'd still be responsible for sales and use taxes. (A **use tax** is a form of sales tax, imposed by some states on personal property purchased outside the state—and designed to keep residents and resident businesses from buying outside the state to avoid paying the state's sales tax.) Your sales tax liability continues whether or not you collect sales tax from customers and remit it to the state government, so if you shirk in this area, you could be stuck paying 5 percent to 10 percent of your gross receipts.

If your business is the end user of a product, you usually have to pay any applicable sales taxes to the state or municipality. But if your business is selling the product to someone else or using it in manufacturing your own product, you're often exempt from sales tax. A grocery store, for example, doesn't have to pay sales tax to its suppliers. If you're exempt, apply for a **sales tax permit** from your state department of revenue and display it prominently. When you deal with wholesalers, you can give them resellers' certificates with your sales tax number, essentially stating that you don't have to pay sales tax.

To collect sales tax, you need a state sales tax identification number, available from your state department of taxation. It takes about a month to get one. Generally, most services are exempt, while most products other than food and drugs are subject to sales tax. Many states, though, have been adding to the list of services subject to sales tax. Consult your state department of taxation to see whether your product or service is taxable.

Be sure to collect sales and use tax in each state where you do business. If you neglect to collect them and remit them to those other state governments, you could be held personally liable for the tax, plus interest and penalties. States are on the lookout for businesses that fail to collect these taxes.

PROPERTY TAXES

It's a great thing when your business opens its first office or store in its own building—except that your business now becomes subject to property tax. You may have to pay property taxes even if you don't own your own place, because more commercial leases are requiring the lessor rather than the landlord to pay the property tax.

The property tax rate is based on the assessed value of the real estate. In many areas, commercial or industrial property is assessed at a higher rate than residential property. If you believe your assessment is too high, you can file a request for a new one. In most jurisdictions you can appeal the assessment if you feel it is too high.

Ask your state department of taxation whether your business is liable for **personal property taxes** on other property it owns, such as furniture, fixtures, vehicles, equipment, and inventory. As the years go by, make sure the state isn't taxing you for vehicles you've traded in or machines you've hauled to the junkyard.

YOU MUST REMEMBER THIS

• Check with state and local tax authorities to see what taxes/fees you're responsible for. It's better to know in advance what you have to do (and perhaps pay on some regular basis) than to get an unwelcome surprise at the end of the year.

• Often, these fees and taxes can be deducted from your income and thus lower your federal tax burden.

• Be on alert for state and local incentives, exemptions, and credits. Governments often offer such incentives to certain types of businesses, businesses in certain locations, and so forth— make sure you take advantage if you qualify.

CHAPTER 30

Tangling with the Government

You Have Rights—Know How to Use Them

Jeremy filed the taxes for the café he and his wife run. He sent in the forms, paid the necessary fees, and April turned into May. However, come August, Jeremy opened up his mailbox to find a dreaded letter from the Internal Revenue Service, and he could see only one word: AUDIT.

Tax audits rank right up there with root canals as popular activities. Nonetheless, this isn't exactly the Spanish Inquisition. You do have rights. This chapter will give you some dos and don'ts.

Dealing with the government isn't necessarily tangling with the IRS monster. When you're working on your tax return, estimated payments, employment taxes, or other tax paperwork, you may decide to take advantage of the IRS's telephone hotline or take your questions to someone at your local IRS office.

Just remember to take your free advice for what it's worth. While most IRS agents and employees are courteous and well meaning, not all are trained in every detail of tax law. It's common to receive poor oral advice. If you rely on inaccurate advice and the result is that you are assessed with penalties, the agency won't rescind them just because you did what your accountant or lawyer told you to do.

Now, let's consider what to do in case of—better sit down—an audit. The good news is that, statistically speaking, you won't get audited. Fewer than 1 percent of all individual tax returns get audited. However, the IRS and state tax authorities do check up on businesses and individuals with suspicious deductions and other irregularities, such as very high income and income not subject to tax withholding (for instance, self-employed taxpayers and those with high investment income). Some businesses and professions are targeted in a given year for audits. And a few lucky people get chosen each year for extremely thorough random audits. These are designed to determine how well Americans are complying with the tax laws.

However nervous you may be about the possibility of an audit, do not ignore correspondence from the IRS. It may just be a Notice of Proposed Changes, pointing out the ways in which the IRS disagrees with your return and proposes to alter it. You typically have thirty days to respond. Read the notice, compare it with your tax return, and decide whether to go along with the proposal or to send a letter explaining and documenting your position. Of course, you should also ask your tax professional to provide insight and guidance.

If you do get audited, don't panic. The examination can take place by mail, at your office or home, or at an IRS office. The agent will arrange a date depending on your respective schedules. You can authorize an attorney, CPA, or other individual authorized to practice before the IRS to represent you. If you have an attorney, as opposed to other representation, anything you tell the attorney will be privileged—that is, he or she cannot be forced to repeat anything you have said. So you can and should be completely open with your lawyer.

Here are some tips on coping with an audit:

• **Be prepared.** Review your entire return, especially the points in question, to make sure it's complete and accurate. Gather records to document the items in question.

• **Be a step ahead.** Anticipate questions the auditor might ask and plan your answers.

• **Watch your attitude.** Be polite, confident, and businesslike. Answer questions accurately, but don't volunteer information that isn't required. Being belligerent can get you in trouble.

• **Don't get ambushed.** If the agent asks for information that wasn't on the audit request, ask for another appointment so you'll have time to gather your records and prepare your responses. The agent may just drop the question.

If you are unhappy with the results of your audit—they generally don't produce refunds—you may request a conference. After the conference, or if you don't request a conference, you will be issued a Notice of Deficiency, commonly called a "ninety-day letter." It's called that because the IRS will assess the tax ninety days from the date of the letter. At that point you can pay, pay and claim a refund, or sue. If you sue, you definitely need an attorney. There is a small-tax procedure for disputes of $50,000 or less.

 THE TAXPAYER BILL OF RIGHTS

Worried about the horror stories you've heard about IRS agents running roughshod over taxpayers? The Taxpayer Bill of Rights of 1996 and the Internal Revenue Service Restructuring and Reform Act of 1998 put high-caliber legal weapons into the hands of taxpayers.

- The laws make it easier to get your money or property back if the IRS wrongfully seized it.

- If you receive a penalty for inadvertently sending payroll tax money to the IRS instead of depositing it in a government depository, the IRS can now waive the penalty.

- If your business has been the victim of outrageous conduct by IRS agents, you can sue and recover up to $1 million in damages—ten times the limit on such suits before.

- If you win a lawsuit against the IRS, it's now easier to obtain reimbursement for reasonable attorneys' fees.

- The laws mitigate the consequences for failing to properly deposit payroll deductions, particularly if the error relates to the business's first deposit.

- By federal law, taxpayers also have a right to privacy and confidentiality, professional and courteous service, professional representation, being required to pay only the correct amount of tax, help from the Problem Resolution Program, appeals, and judicial review.

You may be able to recover legal fees from the IRS if you "substantially prevail" in the key issues in your case or in the amount of tax. To defeat your claim for attorneys' fees, the IRS has to show it was "substantially justified" in its position. The courts have ruled that "substantially justified" means reasonable.

Occasionally you might be able to successfully sue for damages if the IRS takes unauthorized collection action or fails to release a lien.

YOU MUST REMEMBER THIS

- Don't panic if you get audited.
- Have a strategy for the audit session and watch your attitude.
- Remember that you have legal rights, including the right to be represented at the audit.

PART VII

Various Endings
Some Happy,
Some Not

Nothing lasts forever, so you've at least got to consider some of the possibilities at the end of the line.

The sad truth is that many small businesses don't make it—but perhaps more would if their owners were aware of the legal protections that may be open to faltering businesses. Bankruptcy law provides some options for restructuring a business and keeping it going through a tough period. And legal help and some negotiating tips might enable you to get more time from creditors—time that might make all the difference.

Other possible ends include selling the business, and we give you information on business brokers, various ways of structuring deals, and valuing the business, along with other tips that will help you get what your business is worth.

The tax laws give you a number of attractive alternatives for retirement plans for you and your employees, but we remind you that it's up to you to select a plan and get the ball rolling. We give you the pros and cons of each option, and suggest ways of taking the maximum tax benefit.

Finally, there is the issue of how to pass along the business to your family or others. The sad fact is that very few family-owned businesses make a successful transition to the second generation. And even fewer make it to the third generation. You can beat these odds by knowing the attractive options the law gives you for saving taxes and then planning ahead to get the maximum benefit. Once again, we give you the information you need to take care of business—literally.

CHAPTER 31

Sink or Swim—Facing Financial Difficulties

The Law, and Your Lawyer, May Be Able to Help

Your worst fear has come true—your business is in financial trouble. Don't panic. This is not the end of the world. You're not the first to meet this fate, and you won't be the last. The law—and your lawyer—can help, but you must try to keep your nerves from jangling too loudly. You still have options.

As this chapter explains, there are many options when faced with financial difficulties, but we open our discussion with the most draconian of them all: bankruptcy. Why? Because financial difficulties occur—legally at least—in "the shadow of bankruptcy." Since both the businessperson and his or her creditors know that bankruptcy is a legal option, the alternatives tend to be examined by both debtors and creditors with an eye to how the business and creditors would fare if the business chose to declare bankruptcy.

BANKRUPTCY

Bankruptcy is probably the most well-known option. Just seeing the word may put a knot in your stomach, and it should. Bankruptcy can make a person feel embarrassed, guilty, and inept at managing money. Nevertheless, unless you win the lottery (and soon), it could be your best bet at climbing out from under excessive debt.

What It Means to Be Bankrupt

Businesses and individuals typically explore the option of bankruptcy when they are having trouble paying debts when the debts become due. When this happens to a person or business (known as the **debtor**), that person or business may then be entitled to file for bankruptcy under the federal bankruptcy laws, also known as the **Bankruptcy Code**. The parties to whom the debtor owes the money are known as the **creditors**.

One of the immediate benefits of bankruptcy is what is known as the **automatic stay**. This means that when a company or individual files for protection under the Bankruptcy Code, almost all other legal actions against the company or individual are barred. This is important if the business is facing numerous lawsuits that could destroy the company.

The Bankruptcy Code is divided into chapters, such as Chapter 7, Chapter 11, and Chapter 13. As we'll explain later, each of these *may* be available to you if your company is facing financial difficulties.

The Bankruptcy Code grants relief to debtors and creditors when debtors are unwilling or unable to pay their bills. A **voluntary bankruptcy** is one filed by a debtor. In some circumstances, creditors can also file a bankruptcy petition to force a debtor into bankruptcy. This is known as an **involuntary bankruptcy**. Bankruptcy is strictly a federal law; there are no state bankruptcy laws. In addition, bankruptcy proceedings are initiated and conducted in specific federal bankruptcy courts.

In a **bankruptcy liquidation**, the debtor's assets are distributed among the creditors, and most remaining debts are **discharged** (dissolved). The Bankruptcy Code determines which

 LEARNING THE LINGO

Creditor: A person or business that has a monetary claim against the debtor.

Debtor: The person or business who has a financial obligation to repay debts.

DEALING WITH STRESS

Facing financial difficulties can throw you into emotional turmoil. Be prepared to go through the same emotions as you would if dealing with the death of a loved one: denial, depression, panic, remorse, anger, and shock. Don't let it ruin your personal relationships, especially with your spouse. Take comfort in knowing that you have legal options, and focus on the solution.

---

creditors get paid and in what order. Keep in mind that although *your* debt may be discharged in bankruptcy, anyone who co-signed a loan with you will still be held responsible. Debts that will not be discharged include most taxes, alimony, child support, student loans, and some property settlements.

Types of Bankruptcies

There are three main types of bankruptcy that apply to business owners. All are available to individuals (and thus sole proprietors), and the first two are also available to business entities:

• Chapter 7 is available to business entities themselves—that is, to partnerships, corporations, and LLCs. This Chapter is also available to individuals (including a sole proprietorship owned by an individual). Because legally there may be no distinction between the sole proprietor and his or her business, the business assets of a person filing under Chapter 7 would be included in the **bankruptcy estate** (the property controlled by the bankruptcy proceedings). As explained below, Chapter 7 (sometimes called **straight bankruptcy**) enables you to discharge your debts (not pay them), but within limits set by law, and your property could be sold and the proceeds split among your creditors (this is called **liquidation**).

• Chapter 11, by contrast, enables you to keep your business open as you **reorganize** your business debts. It is open to all forms of business entities, including sole proprietorship.

• Chapter 13 also provides for debt reorganization. It is not available to businesses per se, but, because there may be no legal distinction between the sole proprietor and his or her business, a sole proprietor filing under Chapter 13 may include business debts that he or she is personally liable for. Unlike Chapter 11, it has stringent limits on the amount of debt involved in the bankruptcy—no more than $336,900 in unsecured debt or $1,010,650 in secured debt (see the sidebar for an explanation of these types of debt).

Sometimes, a business will file for one form of bankruptcy and later have it converted to another form.

While weighing your options, do not destroy any financial or business records. Doing so could cost you your right to have your debts discharged in bankruptcy.

Each form of bankruptcy will cost you money out of pocket. As a general rule, Chapter 7 is the least expensive, followed by Chapter 13 and Chapter 11. The cost of many individual bankruptcies increased after the Bankruptcy Reform Act of 2005.

 ## LEARNING THE LINGO

Liquidation: When the debtor's assets are sold and the proceeds are distributed to the creditors.

Trustee: The person appointed by the court to be in charge of managing the bankruptcy.

Secured debt: If you don't meet your financial obligations, you will lose a specific piece of property (known as the **collateral**), such as your home or car, pledged to secure the debt.

Unsecured debt: Your financial obligations are not backed by any property (collateral). Credit cards are examples of unsecured debt.

Under the Reform Act, attorneys representing consumer debtors must verify the accuracy of the information contained in filings, meaning more up-front work and higher fees. In addition, individuals must complete credit counseling from an approved credit-counseling agency before filing for Chapter 7 or Chapter 13 bankruptcy. Workouts, discussed later, are less expensive than Chapter 13 and Chapter 11 bankruptcies.

Chapter 7

Simply put, a company in Chapter 7 bankruptcy stops all operations and goes out of business. A trustee is appointed to sell the assets of the business for cash. This is known as **liquidation**. This money is then used to pay administrative and legal expenses and to make partial payments to your creditors. Chapter 7 usually takes only a few months and is fairly straightforward.

Chapter 7 is for companies that are so far in debt that they cannot continue business operations. The court may authorize the trustee to operate the business for a limited time if the court finds it is necessary for an orderly liquidation. Secured creditors are paid first from the collateral used for their loans. If there isn't enough from the collateral to pay secured creditors in full, these creditors are lumped into a group with unsecured creditors for the rest of their claims. There usually isn't anything left over for the business owners. The stock of a Chapter 7 company is almost always worthless.

The goal of Chapter 7 is to give creditors a fair share of the proceeds from the liquidation. In the case of individual Chapter 7 bankruptcies, another goal is to wipe the slate clean and provide for a fresh start. If an individual's debts (including business debts) are discharged in a Chapter 7 bankruptcy, then he or she is no longer liable for them. This is the fresh start. However, the fact of having declared bankruptcy will be part of the person's credit history and could be reported on credit reports for as long as ten years.

Though giving debtors a fresh start by discharging their debts is a goal of *individual* bankruptcies, it doesn't apply to the business as an entity. Typically, a corporation or other business entity will be dissolved when all of its assets are distributed. There is no fresh start for this entity. It has ceased to exist.

However, the clean slate for business bankruptcies may not be quite as clean as it is for individual bankruptcies. Yes, shareholders in a corporation or limited partners in a partnership won't have any liability for the company's debts (unless, for example, they signed loan agreements in their individual capacities), but the situation may be different for other forms of business organization.

For example, if a business partnership files for bankruptcy, its *general* partners are liable to the bankruptcy estate. Even though the company goes through bankruptcy, the partners are not discharged of their personal obligations. The bankruptcy trustee appointed by the court has a claim against the general partners for the debt owed by the business. The filing won't show up on the partners' personal credit history, but they are responsible for the debts of the company as general partners.

Individuals filing for Chapter 7 relief must also pass a "means test," which is designed to determine whether an individual with regular income has the means to repay some of his or her debts over time rather than go through liquidation. Using a fairly complex formula, the court will compare the debtor's household income (with some adjustments) to the median household income in the state where the debtor resides. If the debtor's adjusted income is $6,000 or more than the median income, filing Chapter 7 will be considered a "substantial abuse" of the Bankruptcy Code and the petition will most likely be converted to Chapter 13. The theory is that if the debtor has an "excess" of $6,000 in income per year, he or she can afford to repay creditors by that amount each year for the next five years. From a business perspective, the means test would be applied if a sole proprietor filed for Chapter 7 liquidation, since a sole proprietor would have to file as an individual; it would not apply if any other type of business (i.e., partnership, corporation, or limited liability company) filed for liquidation.

Chapter 11

A Chapter 11 bankruptcy is used to restructure a business. As noted earlier, it may be available to some individuals (sole proprietors). Chapter 11 allows a business to continue operating while it repays creditors through a plan approved by the bankruptcy court. It gives breathing room to businesses that are having financial problems. The goal is to give the business a chance to get back on its financial feet.

Under Chapter 11, management is allowed in most cases to continue to run the day-to-day business. The bankruptcy court, however, must approve significant business decisions.

At least one committee will be appointed to represent the interests of the creditors. The committee will work with the company to develop a plan of reorganization to get the business out of debt. This plan must be accepted by the creditors and approved by the court. If the creditors reject the plan, the court may still approve it if the court finds the plan to be fair.

The irony of Chapter 11 is that it pulls management in different directions. It demands a lot of the debtor's attention just when the debtor needs to spend more time focusing on the business's financial health.

 STEPS IN APPROVING A CHAPTER 11 BANKRUPTCY

- The debtor business develops a plan with the committee of creditors.

- The business prepares the plan and files it with the court.

- Creditors vote on the plan.

- The court approves the plan.

- The business carries out the plan by making the payments called for by the plan.

LEARNING THE LINGO

Cram down: When the court approves a Chapter 11 bankruptcy plan over the objection of creditors.

The assets of the business (debtor) will be used to pay at least some of the costs associated with a Chapter 11 restructuring. For example, the expenses of the committee of creditors may come out of the assets. However, creditors will pay for the services of professionals (lawyers, accountants, and so forth) working for them.

This type of bankruptcy is costly and time-consuming. The courts (and lawyers) are extensively involved. Some Chapter 11 bankruptcies end up being converted to Chapter 7 bankruptcies if the business can't meet its obligations under its plan.

Chapter 13

Chapter 13 bankruptcy is, in general, a repayment plan available only for individuals. (Hang in there—we'll get to an exception to this rule.) You make regular payments to a court-approved trustee. The trustee then makes payments to your creditors. This type of repayment plan usually stretches out over three to five years. Here's the key: You can file for Chapter 13 as an individual and, if you own a business as a sole proprietor, you might be able to include business debts for which you are personally liable. This is worth looking into, although it will not be an option for most people. If you're a stock or commodity broker, don't waste your time. You're not allowed to use Chapter 13 at all.

The benefits are that Chapter 13 costs much less and is much easier than Chapter 11. The fees for filing under Chapter 13 are much less than those for Chapter 11, but the biggest cost difference is in professional fees. A Chapter 11 bankruptcy involves more lawyers and accountants, is more complicated, and takes longer than Chapter 13. The more hours put in by those lawyers and accountants, the bigger the bills.

In a Chapter 13 bankruptcy, you write one check every month to the court, rather than separate checks to your creditors. In a Chapter 11, you write separate checks and pay quarterly administration fees. Chapter 13 does not require those quarterly administration fees.

On the other hand, businesses filing for Chapter 13 must have regular income and meet the law's debt limitations. At present, the business cannot owe more than $336,900 in unsecured credit or more than $1,010,650 in secured credit. Chapter 11 does not have those limitations.

In a Chapter 13 bankruptcy, the business has to file a plan of reorganization within fifteen days of filing for bankruptcy. Most businesses will be hard pressed to have that reorganization ready by that time. In Chapter 11, there is no deadline for filing a reorganization plan, although after four months other creditors can file a plan. If the business has less than $2.19 million in debt and is not primarily engaged in owning or operating real estate, it can file for Chapter 11 as a "small businesses debtor" and may have up to 300 days to file a reorganization plan. With Chapter 13, you don't get a bankruptcy discharge until you are done with the payments—usually three to five years later. You are considered to be in bankruptcy for that entire time. In a Chapter 11, though, once you file your plan you are out of bankruptcy and get your discharge.

Bankruptcy and Your Credit Rating

If you file as an individual and go through the bankruptcy process, the bankruptcy will tarnish your credit rating. There's no way around that. A bankruptcy will stay on your credit report for up to ten years. If you do not declare bankruptcy, but simply fail to pay your bills, this unpaid debt will typically remain on your credit report for seven years. Keep in mind, though, that a debtor with a large amount of unpaid debt is considered as big a risk as one with a bankruptcy. At least with a Chapter 11 or

Chapter 13 bankruptcy, the business works with its creditors, pays part of its debts, and gets back on track.

During this time, beware of advertisements promising to fix your credit instantly. These are scams that will take your money and leave you feeling worse than ever. The good news is that you cannot be discriminated against for declaring bankruptcy. You cannot be denied a job or a driver's license because of it.

Once you've bitten the bankruptcy bullet, it's time to begin rebuilding your financial reputation. Open a savings account. It doesn't have to be big; you just have to contribute to it consistently.

Obtain a secured credit card. Most banks offer these cards now. Make payments on time, every time, for everything. Find consistent employment. With any luck, when the entrepreneurial bug next bites you, your credit history won't trip you up.

ALTERNATIVE TO BANKRUPTCY

Out-of-Court Restructuring or Workout

In an out-of-court restructuring, or **workout**, the financially distressed business and its major creditors, such as lenders or suppliers, agree to adjust the business's obligations. That means that your creditors will cancel some of the debt you owe them. This can be a slow process. Creditors will want to bring in accountants and lawyers to understand and negotiate the restructuring. While you may believe that your initial restructuring plan is the fairest to your creditors, the creditors will most likely consider it your first offer and begin negotiating from that point.

A workout may be draining, but it is usually faster than a Chapter 11 restructuring. In addition, it is almost always a better deal for your business than bankruptcy. An out-of-court restructuring doesn't carry the stigma associated with bankruptcy. Third parties may decide that if the business's creditors are willing to do a workout, the creditors must feel the business can regain sound financial footing. Thus, other parties will have more

HANGING ON TO YOUR PRIVACY

A workout is also the best way to protect yourself from having to disclose information you want to keep confidential. A workout does not require a filing with the bankruptcy court. When a company files for bankruptcy, though, it has to disclose how it operates its business, with whom it does business and on what terms, its financial records (including a summary of assets and liabilities), and other information. This information is filed with the bankruptcy court and becomes public record. That means anyone—including creditors, competitors, neighbors, and your in-laws—can look at it. Oh, and they can look at it without charge.

confidence in doing business with you when you're in a workout than if you're in bankruptcy.

Unlike Chapter 11, a workout allows the business to choose those creditors it believes are necessary to the restructuring. The business gets to decide how to approach those creditors and has more flexibility in negotiating the plan.

Another advantage of workouts is that they are less obtrusive. In a Chapter 11 bankruptcy, the financially strapped company's executives are required to appear at a meeting of the company's creditors. At this meeting, the creditors get to question the executives, who are under oath. The creditors can also get court orders to make the executives available for questioning at other times, and to force the company to hand over copies of documents that deal with the company's business affairs.

A workout, on the other hand, gives the company more control. It allows the company to limit the release of its financial records to those creditors the company considers essential. The company can also require that this information be kept confidential.

The biggest problem is getting the creditors to agree to the plan. Each creditor will have to decide whether a workout is more beneficial than the outcome of a bankruptcy. Creditors may distrust the business's management. They may not have confidence in the restructuring plan. They may believe they would be better off if the company went through a Chapter 11 reorganization or was liquidated. Creditors will have less say, however, if the business goes into bankruptcy court. Thus, the threat of bankruptcy may convince creditors to agree to the plan.

When Chapter 11 Is Better Than a Workout

Nevertheless, Chapter 11 may still be the best option for financially troubled companies. Let's assume that all your creditors agree to your workout plan. You've successfully avoided bankruptcy, at least for the time being. Guess what—Uncle Sam is watching, and he wants a cut for the coffers. In most instances, you will have to report the canceled debt as gross income on your federal income tax return. Chapter 11 bankruptcies do not have this requirement, although state sales and use taxes do still apply.

As noted earlier, all bankruptcies, including Chapter 11, also carry the benefits of the automatic stay, which means that when a company files for protection under the bankruptcy code, all other legal actions against the company are barred. This may help save your business from lawsuits that could destroy the company. It is not possible to get an automatic stay for a workout.

The Option of Doing Nothing

You always have the option of taking no action at all. There is no longer a debtor's prison for people who don't pay their bills, so you can't be thrown into jail. Bear in mind that your vendors and suppliers will stop working with you, but in some situations this could be the route to take.

Specifically, if you have very little income or property, you may be what is known as **judgment-proof**. That means you don't have enough assets to make it worthwhile for creditors to sue you. You simply don't have anything they can take. Instead, creditors will write off your debt and treat it as a deductible business loss for income tax purposes. In seven years, it will come off your credit record.

EXAMINING YOUR OPTIONS

Consulting a Bankruptcy Attorney

First of all, this is one of those times when you shouldn't try to do it yourself. A lot of money may be at stake—to say nothing of the survival of your business—in an area that's saturated in law. When you are facing financial difficulties, it is better to seek legal advice sooner rather than later. Bankruptcy attorneys have many stories about business owners who could have avoided bankruptcy altogether, if only they had sought legal advice as soon as they hit rough waters. Early intervention is the key.

The best way to find a good attorney is to ask your colleagues and associates if they can recommend someone. This does not necessarily have to be a bankruptcy attorney. An attorney experienced in business or corporate law will suffice. If bankruptcy becomes your best option, that attorney can refer you to a skilled bankruptcy attorney. You can also call your state bar association and ask for a listing of the names of the attorneys in the bankruptcy section or committee. This is no guaranty of the attorneys' skills, but these attorneys tend to be more active attorneys in the practice field.

A good attorney will help guide you through your options, but you will have to be honest and forthcoming when consulting a lawyer. It is the only way that an attorney can help you decide on the best course of action. Your lawyer will need some very specific information. Try to bring along as much information as possible to any legal consultation.

At the very least, bring along tax and employer identification numbers, as well as the specific date the business was started. List the names and addresses of any partners or members of a limited liability company, and the percentage of ownership held by each partner or member. Bring your partnership agreement,

WHAT TO BRING?

Here is a quick checklist that can help you make sure you are bringing the necessary documents when you meet with your attorney, saving you both time and money. Try to bring:

- tax and employer identification numbers;
- the names and addresses of any partners or members of your business;
- the percentage of ownership held by each partner or member;
- the partnership agreement/limited liability company agreement/ incorporation documents;
- information about any shareholders, including the number of issued, outstanding, and authorized shares;
- financial records, including inventory counts, loans, property owned, and tax returns;
- a list of your major creditors and the amounts they are owed; and
- any previous court documents regarding your business.

limited liability company agreement, or incorporation documents with you. Specify the name and address of all the officers and directors.

If the business has shareholders, your attorney will need to know the total number of shares. That includes issued, out-

 A FINAL WORD

Whatever you decide, remember that this is not the end of the world. It probably provides little comfort to know that others have been in your shoes, but it's true. They survived, and you will, too.

TALKING TO A LAWYER: CAN A BUSINESS FILE FOR PERSONAL BANKRUPTCY?

Q. *Is there any way my business can file for Chapter 13 bankruptcy? We are a partnership, but there are only three partners.*

A. Although Chapter 13 is reserved for individuals and sole proprietors, there is a way you can file under that chapter. You and your partners can transfer all the assets to one individual as a sole proprietor. Then the sole proprietor can file under Chapter 13. This is knows as "rolling up" the company. Keep in mind that bankruptcy will show up on the new sole proprietor's credit report.

—Answer by Cindy Moy, attorney and author,
Golden Valley, Minnesota

standing, and authorized shares. If you've been a business owner or officer in a business other than the one with financial difficulties, you'll need to bring that information, too.

Your attorney will also want to see all of your financial and business records, including inventory counts, loans, property owned, and tax returns. You should also have a list of your major creditors and the amounts they are owed (including any past-due amounts). If your business is or has been sued, have available the pleadings, court documents, and any judgments rendered. The same goes for lawsuits brought by your company against someone else.

Don't be surprised if your attorney requests other documents, as well. These are complicated matters, and your lawyer needs to be fully aware of your situation.

YOU MUST REMEMBER THIS

• Seek legal help at the first sign of financial difficulties. The earlier the intervention, the better.

TALKING TO A LAWYER: PERSONAL CREDIT

Q. I'm a general partner in a partnership. How will my business bankruptcy affect my personal credit?

A. As a general partner, the business bankruptcy will not appear on your personal credit report. You are, however, still liable for the debts your business owes, which will affect your personal finances. If the business debts are substantial, you could be forced into personal bankruptcy, as well, which will go on your personal credit report and stay there for ten years.

—Answer by Cindy Moy, attorney and author,
Golden Valley, Minnesota

- A workout is quicker and almost always a better deal for a business than a Chapter 11 bankruptcy. There are some instances, though, when a workout will not be feasible.
- Some business owners can file a Chapter 13 bankruptcy, although that is generally an option only for individuals.
- Going through bankruptcy can be emotionally taxing. Do not let the bankruptcy ruin your personal relationships.

CHAPTER 32

Selling a Business

There Are Plenty of Possible Arrangements—but You Want the Best

Janet's business has been very, very good to her—a steady source of income for years. But all good things come to an end. She has started to think about what will come next: retirement? relocating to warmer weather? or maybe trying a new profession? Whatever the reason, she thinks—make that, she knows—that the business has value. But how does she find a buyer? How can she ensure that she gets value for the business? How can Janet safeguard her legal rights? This chapter has answers.

Selling a business and buying one are two sides of the same coin, so you'll want to look at chapter 5 on buying a business for additional insights. As noted there, providing information about the business and the parties is central to the process. As a seller, you'll want to know a good deal about the buyer, particularly if he or she will be making payments over time and you will in effect be financing the purchase. And of course the buyer will be requesting plenty of information about the business. These exchanges of information have legal dimensions, and there may be important legal documents at various stages—and certainly at the end, when the purchase contract is signed.

THE BUSINESS BROKER

One of your first decisions will be whether to use a broker. Generally, your advisers—such as lawyers and accountants—will work for an hourly rate. While each of these advisers may be able to do some of the things a broker will do, brokers do have some definite capabilities that can make them indispensable in certain situations. And brokers usually work on a commission basis, in which the commission is not payable until the sale is closed.

The advantages of using a broker include:

• brokers will generally be more aware of market conditions and understand better how to offer the property;

• they have the ability to keep the business identity secret until they can identify and qualify a buyer; and

• once a buyer who is financially qualified is making serious inquiries, you'll want to meet face-to-face to size each other up, ask specific questions, and begin to establish a working relationship; the broker can help with this process.

Of course, the major disadvantage in using a broker is the cost. However, the broker's commission may be more than paid for by the better sale he or she can arrange. You should never have to pay a broker any money in advance.

YOUR AGREEMENT WITH THE BROKER

If you're using a business broker, you should certainly have a written contract—there's too much at stake, and too many controversies that can come up, to be satisfied with a handshake agreement. The broker will probably ask you to sign a listing agreement. It's not a bad idea for your lawyer to advise you on this legally binding contract, since a lot of money can be on the line and you may be able to negotiate some terms to your advantage.

Though brokers use preprinted forms, these agreements are "standard" only in that many brokers use them. Like all legal contracts, they are subject to negotiation.

Among the negotiable points are:

• type of listing (can you sell it yourself and avoid a commission?);

• when the commission is due (when the sale is actually consummated or when the broker finds a ready, willing, and able buyer?);

• the percentage of the sales price that is due as commission

MAINTAINING CONFIDENTIALITY

Very few sellers want customers, vendors, creditors, and debtors of the business to know that the business is for sale. Besides using a broker, you can keep matters confidential by asking serious candidates to do their investigation under a confidentiality agreement that they will not divulge or use information discovered but not readily available to the general public. This can be included as an addendum to the selling prospectus that they are to sign (see page 414), or you can ask them to sign a letter to that effect, perhaps binding their co-investors and advisers, as well.

(10 percent to 12 percent is a common range, but it can sometimes be negotiated down);

• whether the broker can represent a prospective buyer as well as you, the seller; and

• how long the listing is with the broker (less time will be better in the event you become dissatisfied with the broker).

Other important points often covered in the listing agreement are what happens in the event of a dispute between you and the broker; who holds the earnest money in the event of a sale and, if the broker holds it, what happens in case of a default; legal liability for misrepresentations; legal liability for damage to or loss of property while the property is being shown; and what happens in the event the seller withdraws the authority to sell the business.

SO WHAT'S IT WORTH?

As anyone who has tried to sell anything can tell you, it's impossible to determine exactly what a product is worth. However, you don't have to pick a figure out of the air. Certain tangible assets—vehicles, machinery, inventory, and so forth—may be fairly easy to put a price tag on. More troublesome will be intangible assets, including intellectual property (a patent, trademark, or copyright) and especially goodwill. Sellers probably tend to overvalue goodwill as a component of the sale. Yes, it may exist, but how much of it inheres to the business per se, and how much to the hard work and presence of you, the seller? Or, to put it another way, how much goodwill can the buyer expect once you're out of the picture? Perhaps an agreement that you would stay on for a period of months as a consultant will help maintain the goodwill (and keep up the value of the business). A noncompete agreement might have the same effect.

One way to establish a value for your business is to have it appraised. If you use a business broker, you should have no trouble finding someone to do the appraisal. If you're handling the sale without a broker, you can probably find a good appraiser through recommendations from your lawyer or accountant.

Two factors the appraiser will look at are your earnings and sales history. One or both of these figures can be multiplied by a certain factor—which varies by industry—to come up with a rough estimate of the business's worth as a going concern. Say, for example, your annual profits average $50,000. If the standard multiplier in your industry is five, then that aspect of your business might be worth $250,000. Adding this to the value of the business's assets would give you a ballpark figure of what the business is worth.

THE SELLING PROSPECTUS

You should provide certain preliminary information about the business for the broker to market the property and the prospective buyer to determine whether he or she is interested. A **selling prospectus** allows you to provide this information, anonymously if necessary, and to make certain important features of the business evident. In the selling prospectus, you can also document the story of the business and specify your reasons for selling.

A TIP ON AVOIDING LIABILITY

A word of caution concerning your selling prospectus: The selling prospectus is a **disclosure document** and may be the basis of subsequent legal action by the buyer. This is not the place to fantasize about the business. Be sure to mention all the **material** (important) facts about the business, since failing to state a material fact could be the basis of a lawsuit. Make sure all facts stated in the selling prospectus are true. Avoid misleading statements. Or course, you'll have a tendency to puff the status of the business, but it should not override the need to document all items of fact. Identify clearly what is a statement of opinion and what is a statement of fact.

You should cover the following items in the selling prospectus:

• **The story of the company.** This narrative should cover the history of the business and convey the mission of the business now and into the future.

• **Area of operations.** Indicate the location of the business—including the premises of the business operations as well as the area of customer or client activity.

• **Assets.** There should be a description, not a listing, of the physical assets of the business. This should indicate what items used in the functioning of the business are leased or owned.

• **Operations.** Describe the process of operating the business, with an emphasis on the role of the owner.

• **Employees.** Provide the number of employees, with a breakdown of general numbers devoted to operations and management tasks, along with information about payroll.

• **Profit and loss information.** This should not be in the form of an accounting schedule, but should be a narrative describing the nature of revenue and expense experience. Sales information should be related to customer or client activity or marketing reactions as appropriate.

- **Competition.** You should not denigrate the competition; you should be accurate about the standing of competitors with respect to the business.
- **Owner requirements.** You should state the obligations that the owner will have to assume for the business to be successful. Make sure this section accurately indicates what the owner's involvement should be.
- **Owner's reasons for selling.** You need to state a true and accurate reason for why you're selling the business, but you do not have to give all reasons or give a reason that will render an inaccurate view of the prospects of the business.
- **Financial statements.** Summary statements may be appropriate, but you should not provide detailed financial statements that may be incorrectly interpreted.
- **Price and terms.** You should indicate the range of acceptable terms, from all cash to all seller-financed. State the security necessary for any part of the purchase price financed. Also anticipate asset allocation issues, including values for covenants not to compete, and tax issues.
- **Confidentiality.** You should include a confidentiality statement that is to be signed by the prospective buyer. It should state, in effect, that the prospective buyer is aware that customers or clients, as well as suppliers and others important to the business, are not aware of the possible sale and that all material delivered to a prospective buyer is considered to be confidential information. By signing, the prospective buyer agrees to keep the fact of the sale, discussions, and the information received confidential.

STATEMENT OF INTENT

This is a working document designed to help the parties clarify where they are and where they're going. It's really an agreement to agree. It's *not* a contract, and it's not enforceable. Make sure this fact is prominent in the language of the document and that you and the buyer fully understand the limitations of the document. And don't put agreements that *are* intended to be enforceable in the statement of intent document.

Once you and the prospective buyer understand how to use the statement of intent, it can let the parties see the possible parameters of the deal—its overall structure and price. And it can then set the stage for the final steps in the process—drafting the contract for purchase and sale of the business.

CONTRACT FOR PURCHASE AND SALE

The process of preparing the contract for purchase and sale of a business determines the whole basis upon which the business is sold or purchased. The structure of the contract will depend upon whether the contract will be one to purchase specific assets of the business or to purchase the entity conducting the business.

What are you selling? Are you selling the business per se, or merely some of its assets? A purchase of the assets will involve a purchase of specified assets and liabilities of the business and will not include an assumption of any undisclosed liabilities—such as lawsuits against the business that may not have even been filed yet or regulatory hassles that are on the horizon but are not yet known to you, the seller. For these reasons, buyers often prefer to purchase the assets and use them as the basis of a business with a new legal organization, such as a new corporation or partnership. (This is another reason goodwill may be less of a factor than you think. If the business is going to be reconstituted, then the goodwill of the existing business is an almost negligible factor.) Buying the assets may also provide significant tax benefits for the buyer—for example, the ability to depreciate them even though they've already been depreciated by the selling business. This can enable the buyer to show a "paper" cost, and thus in essence shelter some profits from taxation.

On the other hand, when the business per se is purchased, there is a benefit of continuity of the entity, and sometimes buyers prefer this. Yes, there is the risk of known or unknown liabilities

ASSUMING SOME OF THE RISK

By agreeing to give the buyer your personal warranty against undisclosed obligations and liabilities of the business, you are giving the buyer legal recourse against you if certain kinds of trouble develop, maybe months and even years down the line. You might have to agree to something along this line to make the sale, but obviously you are opening yourself up to risk, and you'll want to consider this carefully and seek good legal advice before you commit.

---

that will accrue to the entity, but buyers can protect themselves to some extent through diligent investigation, insurance, and **personal warranties** from you, the seller (see sidebar).

While it is more obvious in an asset purchase agreement, even in an entity purchase situation there must be a method to define exactly what is being sold. This is frequently accomplished by attaching detailed schedules to the contract that specifically identify the assets and liabilities, or specifically define the balance sheet of the entity, so that the exact nature of what constitutes the business and what is being transferred can be identified, item by item. At closing, you'll provide a bill of sale with general **warranties of title.**

For what price? The sales price is a factor but not the sole element in determining the net proceeds you'll receive. You will often have a price in mind without knowing what the entire transaction will be. Often you can lower the price for a business where a tax advantage to you occurs, giving you the same net cash and making the business more attractive to the buyer. Keep this in mind both in setting your asking price and in negotiations.

How much up front? You will want a significant portion of the purchase price paid at closing, since it's important to have the buyer committed enough to the business that he or she would not walk away from a hardship situation.

What if the business runs into problems after the sale?
Assuming that not all the purchase price will be paid at closing,
you will want to be able to regain ownership and control of the
business if the buyer fails to run it successfully. This is especially
important in an asset purchase situation. Have your lawyer craft
a **security agreement** assuring you of the right to take back the
secured property of the business if the required payments aren't
made. The buyer's obligation to pay the unpaid portion of the
purchase price after closing should be a personal obligation on
the buyer's good credit. This aspect also requires your lawyer's
careful attention and skillful crafting in the debt instruments
used. In many situations, requiring the buyer to assign a life insurance policy to provide security for the purchase price payment will give additional comfort to you as the seller.

Will you stick around? If you are to continue participating
in the business, whether as employee or consultant or in some
other capacity, the exact terms of this participation should be
part of the agreement to purchase the business. In certain cases,
especially for employment or consulting arrangements, it should
be the subject of an additional employment/consulting agreement.

Any additional papers? You should assure the buyer that
you will sign additional documents needed between the parties
to accomplish the intent of the purchase and sale agreement.

Could premises be a special issue? The status of the business premises could be very important to the sale. For example,
if the business currently has a lease, the buyer will want to be
sure that it is acceptable to him or her, and, if it is, it must be **assignable** to the buyer (that is, the buyer must be able, under the
terms of the lease, to step into your role as tenant).

If you own the real estate constituting the premises, it may
be under another entity controlled by you. If so, and the sale of
a real estate parcel is involved in the purchase and sale of a business, the purchase of the real estate will likely involve the other
entity in a separate real estate purchase and sale transaction.
Whether the property is owned by the business directly or by another entity, it's important that the sales document gives clear

title to the property and that all appropriate environmental considerations be addressed.

When does possession shift? Usually, possession of the business is delivered at closing. Frequently, part of the closing and delivery of the business is an agreed-upon procedure for a final inventory. Often this affects the purchase price, if that price is based upon a variable such as an inventory on hand.

What about costs already paid? Maybe you've made certain payments applying to fixed periods of time, in effect paying in advance for taxes, insurance premiums, and certain utility charges. If so, these should be appropriately prorated, so that you receive credit for the amounts that cover the period after the business is in the buyer's hands.

While the agreement should prorate taxes, there should also be a clear statement of who is responsible for the payment of taxes that will become payable after closing. It's a good idea to do a thorough inventory of taxes previously paid to all governmental entities. That will probably prepare you and the buyer to assign responsibility of payment and correctly prorate taxes at closing. Pay special attention to **use taxes** or other taxes that may be caused by the transaction itself.

What are the default provisions? Legally, **default** means failure to live up to the terms of a contract. Your agreement to sell the business should define acts of default broadly to include the deviation from any of the required terms of any agreement between the parties involving the purchase and sale of the business. The default provisions of all standard form documents used—such as notes, security agreements, bills of sale, and leases—should be consistent with the default clause in the purchase and sale agreement.

You might want to give the buyer the right to receive **notice of the default** and a **right to cure** the default (fulfill the duty in the contract). Generally, with repetitive obligations, such as payments, a right to cure is less of a concern. However, where the obligation may be a onetime duty or a similar act that might be overlooked, the right to cure provision makes very good sense—you'd probably rather have the buyer do whatever the contract called for than have the right to pursue the buyer in court for money damages, which could take years and wind up with you getting nothing. Of course, the default provisions will probably run both ways—both parties will have to adhere to them.

Especially where there are notice-to-cure provisions (but also in any case), the notice provision should account for certain hypothetical situations, such as what if the buyer has abandoned the business, or what if the seller has died and the status of the seller's estate is unclear?

Even if the buyer is not in possession, the seller must be able to accomplish the required notice to complete the default process. The buyer must be able to complete the payment process even if it is not clear whom to pay. A well-drafted contract can cover these and many other contingencies.

Any provision for attorneys' fees? You won't have the right to receive attorneys' fees in a legal action (lawsuit), even if you win, *unless* there is a provision in your agreement to that effect or a statutory provision provides authority for such an award. That means that if you want to be able to recover such fees, you'd better make that a provision of the contract. As for collecting payments that you are due, expenses of collection (without

 NONCOMPETE AGREEMENT

The buyer will probably want an assurance that after the sale of the business, you will not compete with or remove personnel from the business. The noncompete agreement could be a part of the purchase and sale document or a separate document. The tax effect for you is that payment for the noncompete agreement is ordinary income. To spread this out (and not take a tax hit in one year), the payments can be extended over a number of years, even though the agreement itself will probably not restrict your ability to compete for more than three years. (Courts tend to frown on longer terms than this as an unreasonable limitation on your ability to earn a living.)

legal action) may be as important as attorneys' fees. Your contract can provide that you have the right to these, as well. As long
as the buyer agrees, it will be part of the agreement.

What is the role of the broker? The agreement should
clearly specify the lack of or fact of broker involvement. If possible, complete broker compensation at closing.

TAX FACTORS

What if your business entity is being purchased by another business entity? (That is, what if you're not just selling assets, but the
business itself?) Will you continue to have an **equity** (ownership) interest in the combined entity after the acquisition? Or
will you instead sell your entire interest in exchange for cash or
financial instruments that do not represent a continuing propri-
etary interest in the successor business entity? How you answer
that question will have big tax implications—implications you
should be aware of early in the negotiations so that you can take
maximum advantage of the tax laws.

If you're a shareholder in your corporation disposing of your
interest in the corporation with a taxable transaction—that is, if
you're selling your shares to the new owners—generally you'll
recognize a gain or loss equal to the difference between the basis
of the stock (its cost to you) and the amount you realize on the
transaction. If you sell at a profit, you'll pay taxes on that profit.

If, on the other hand, the acquirer is a corporation, you can
dispose of your interest in your company with a "tax-free reorganization" and you will not have a recognized gain or loss on the
transaction and you retain your original basis. In this transaction, stock of the acquiring corporation is used to purchase the
stock and/or assets of the target (i.e., your) company. It is not
strictly a tax-free transaction, really a tax-deferred transaction,
as you will most likely pay capital gains tax later when you sell
the acquiring corporation's stock.

There are five types of "tax-free reorganizations." In a **statutory merger**, your company (the target company) is absorbed into

the acquiring corporation. A statutory merger qualifies as tax-free as long as the consideration paid by the acquiring corporation consists of at least 45 percent of its stock. In a **stock-for-stock exchange**, the acquiring corporation exchanges its voting stock for at least 80 percent of the target corporation. This transaction is available only if both businesses are corporations. If only assets are being purchased, an **exchange of stock for assets** transaction can be tax-free if at least 80 percent of the consideration paid for the assets is in the form of the acquiring corporation's stock, which is distributed to the owners of the selling business upon liquidation of the business. A **forward triangular merger** can be tax-free if the target company is merged into a subsidiary of the acquirer and at least 45 percent of the total consideration paid by the acquirer is in the form of the acquirer's stock. Finally, there is the **reverse triangular merger**, in which a subsidiary of the acquirer is merged into the target company. Here, at least 80 percent of the consideration paid to the target company must be in the form of the acquirer's voting stock. In all of these transactions, any nonstock consideration received by the target company and/or its owners is immediately taxable.

A company selling its assets in a taxable transaction will generally recognize a gain or loss on the sale, and the owners or the business (depending on the type of sale) will have to pay taxes on any recognized gain. A target company's owners in a tax-free reorganization, however, will generally not recognize either gain or loss, insofar as they receive stock of the acquiring corporation, so there is no immediate tax liability on any gains received via stock.

Transactions that are treated as tax-free reorganizations obviously have an advantage from a tax standpoint. Generally, they entail a continuing equity interest in the acquiring enterprise by former owners of the acquired company. In other words, instead of selling and receiving money, you're getting shares in the acquiring corporation as consideration, and these shares indicate your ownership interest in it.

A transaction can qualify as a tax-free reorganization only if a substantial portion of the consideration paid is in the form of stock of the acquirer (i.e., the buyer if this were a straight sale).

If you and the other owners of the acquired company want liquidity and diversity of investment (both of which may be inconsistent with retaining an equity interest in the acquiring entity), a reorganization probably isn't for you.

How do you figure in the tax consequences during negotiation? Typically, the parties reach a mutual understanding by agreeing upon a purchase price amount. In many cases, getting to that number has a great deal to do with the structure of the transaction. That determines the economic results and drastically affects the consideration (money, stock, assets, and so forth) received by each party. The tax structure must be a part of the early negotiation and must be a factor in determining the purchase price.

Let's take a look at an example. Assume that your buyer will acquire all the stock of your corporation from you, for the amount of $1,000. Your basis (i.e., your cost from a tax perspective) in the stock is $100. With a taxable acquisition structure, you would recognize capital gain in the amount of $900, and the buyer would acquire the stock of the corporation with a basis of $100.

If structured as a reorganization in which you received $1,000 worth of stock in the acquiring corporation, however, you would recognize no gain (consideration being in the form of qualifying stock), and the buyer would acquire the stock with a basis of $100.

Let's take another example. Let's say you're the CEO of Me, Inc., a corporation in which you are the only shareholder. Its assets have an aggregate basis of $100 attributable to depreciable assets. Me, Inc., has available net operating losses that can shelter up to $800 of gain on the sale of its assets. Another corporation wishes to acquire Me, Inc. It offers to acquire Me, Inc.'s stock from you for an aggregate price of $1,000 (the fair market value of the business). If the sale were to close, you would recognize a gain of $900, and the acquiring corporation would acquire the stock of Me, Inc., with a basis of $1,000 and with its loss carryforward. Instead, the acquiring corporation may offer to acquire the assets for $1,000. Me, Inc., would have a gain of $900, less the operating loss of $800 to recognize $100 gain. For you to receive proceeds, Me, Inc., would have to liquidate.

Those transactions that fall within Section 368 of the Internal Revenue Code as meeting the definition of a reorganization are capable of being tax-free. Other transactions will be taxable, but note that there are several exceptions:

- Use of Section 351 to provide tax-free treatment to certain shareholders in an otherwise taxable transaction;
- use of a newly formed holding company to acquire stock of both parties; or
- the formation of a joint venture subsidiary.

 TALKING TO A LAWYER: SELLING A BUSINESS

Q. *Someone advised me that it's very important that the buyer of the business be satisfied. He said that I should aim for negotiations in which both sides think they've done well (win-win). Why is this so important, and how do you recommend we go about getting this result?*

A. The most important way to make sure the buyer is happy is to make sure he or she encounters no surprises during the negotiations and closing of the transaction. To avoid surprise, the parties should agree to a comprehensive term sheet. The term sheet should include the price, how the price will be paid, and the post-closing role of the seller(s) (that is, a noncompete or consulting agreement). After appropriate nondisclosure protections have been obtained, the term sheet should also list the major assets to be transferred, the customer list, and most recent financial statements. After this type of full disclosure, the parties can proceed to enter into a definitive contract and move to closing without major surprises causing the buyer to be dissatisfied.

—Answer by Michael E. Flowers, partner, Bricker and Eckler, LLP, Columbus, Ohio

CLOSING

The closing process involves the signing of the final purchase papers. At closing, the seller, and often the buyer, will be required to certify that the warranties and representations given in the contract—which will remain the basis for a legal action after the closing—were and are true, accurate, and correct. The buyer will want the lawyer for the seller to provide the buyer with a legal opinion—often called **legal opinion of seller's counsel**—that the seller has taken all legal steps required to close the transaction properly. All the documents of transfer will be executed, and you'll receive payment of the purchase price.

It's often only at closing that the final purchase price will be determined in accordance with procedures set forth in the contract for purchase and sale. For one thing, this may involve calculating the effect of certain allocations of payments or deposits between the parties. These events include inventories of assets, final accounting for payments received for accounts receivable, and identification of certain receipts after an initial period of operation under the new owner.

YOU MUST REMEMBER THIS

- Selling a business involves the same basic process as selling a home, but everything from appraisals to setting the price is more complicated.
- How the deal is structured—with special regard to the tax ramifications—is absolutely crucial.
- Getting good advice from a lawyer and accountant will increase your chances of getting the most for the assets you sell.

CHAPTER 33

Retirement Planning for the Business Owner

The Law Gives You a Lot of Attractive Options

John and Lois would LOVE to retire. They're in their sixties, the kids are grown and scattered across the country, and they want to travel and do some serious work on their golf game. The problem? They have a growing business, but no business-related retirement plan. Unless they can sell the business for enough to live off the proceeds, they're chained to the cash register.

When you started up your business, most likely you envisioned a time when you could walk away with enough money to live as you'd grown accustomed. That's a doable goal, but you have to plan for it—now. Whether you want to stop working at age fifty or to work as long as possible and pass your money on to your children, you can set up a retirement plan to help you achieve your goals.

This chapter gives you a basic approach to follow when deciding whether to establish a retirement plan for your business. The law gives you plenty of options. For example, Congress has opened a door to retirement plans for small employers with the so-called SIMPLE (Savings Incentive Match Plans for Employees) plan. This is attractive at first glance but might not be right for you—it could stick you with a retirement plan that does not measure up to your retirement goals and creates financial demands that cannot be met (as the employer must make minimum contributions to the plan). Traditional retirement plans can often meet retirement goals without the monetary demands of SIMPLE plans. This chapter gives you the pros and cons of a variety of approaches. At least one of them will work for you.

LEARNING THE LINGO

The world of pensions has a language of its own. We'll help you make sense of it. For example, in this chapter we'll focus on **tax-qualified plans**. These give you a tax break, so they're usually most attractive to you. However, you should be aware that **nonqualified plans**, which are not tax-favored, are also available to meet your retirement needs.

DO YOU NEED A PLAN?

If you have no interest in saving for a time when you will no longer be working, stop right here. If you are happy with the limited contributions you have made to your individual retirement account (IRA), you need not read on. However, if you have realized that the funds in your IRA are insufficient to retire on and want to receive additional tax-favored treatment for money you contribute to a business-related retirement plan, take a look at the advantages and disadvantages of tax-qualified plans.

A tax-qualified plan is an agreement between the employer and its employees that complies with the requirements of the Internal Revenue Code. In basic plans, an employer can contribute up to $49,000.

As a business owner, you wear two hats—you are an employer but also an employee. As the employer, you provide the benefits of a tax-qualified plan to you, as the employee. Under a tax-qualified plan, the benefits provided by you as the employer must benefit all employees. You as a business owner also gain tax advantages for your business. Even if you're the sole employee and have self-employed income from moonlighting while you have a job, or if your business is unincorporated, a retirement plan is available. Such plans are commonly referred to as **Keogh plans**. Except for certain prohibited transactions, the same rules apply.

When deciding whether to begin a retirement plan, the first place to look is your pocketbook. If you are a start-up company that does not have a lot of cash flow to invest, now is not the time to set up a retirement plan. For a retirement plan to work, you need money to put into it. While you will not be locked in to making contributions to some plans during bad financial years, you need to feel that you are at a state in your business where you can make a commitment to finance the plan.

PROS AND CONS OF A
TAX-FAVORED PLAN

Advantages

- A retirement plan could give you a competitive advantage over other businesses to attract and keep qualified employees.
- As the employer, you receive a current tax deduction for all contributions to the plan. As an employee, you are not taxed on the contribution when it is made on your behalf, but rather when you actually receive the money on your retirement, death, disability, or termination. Generally, when you receive the proceeds at the later date, you have less income and therefore pay a lesser tax rate on these distributions. Plus you can continue to defer this tax until age $70\frac{1}{2}$ by not taking distributions.
- The funds contributed by you as the business owner to the plan are held in a separate trust account. These assets may not be touched by the business and are exempt from creditors of both your business and your employees. The funds in this tax-sheltered trust are to be invested by you as a trustee of the retirement plan. All of the income generated by the investment of these funds is also tax-deferred. The trust will not pay any tax when the income is earned, and the tax will be deferred until the investment income is actually distributed to you.

Disadvantages

• You have to meet all the requirements of the Internal Revenue Code to receive tax-favored status. That prohibits you from contributing to your own account at a rate that discriminates against employees who are not owners of the company. Additionally, as an owner-employee, you will have to meet special requirements in order to maintain the plan's tax-favored status, and only a certain amount of contributions to the plan will be tax deductible.

• Plans can be expensive to administer, and you will be required to file an annual form with the Internal Revenue Service. However, the expenses of administration and filing annual reports will be paid from the plan assets and not out of your business.

• The Department of Labor requires that it and, in some instances, employees be notified about certain plan provisions.

• To ensure the tax-exempt status of your plan, it must comply with Internal Revenue Service requirements. You can have your plan administered by a provider (such as a bank, insurance company, trade or professional association, or a mutual funds company), in which case it will use what is essentially a pre-approved master or prototype plan. You can design your own plan, which doesn't require pre-approval by the IRS. However, you would be well advised to have the IRS review it and, if it is approved, issue a determination letter (that the plan complies).

WHAT TYPE OF PLAN SHOULD I CHOOSE?

If you decide that you're willing to suffer through the red tape to reap the tax benefits of a retirement plan, you need to decide what type of plan will achieve your retirement goals.

"Plans at a Glance" (see page 440) is a comparison of different types of tax-favored retirement plans. The first two, SIMPLE (Savings Incentive Match Plans for Employees) and SEP (Simplified Employee Pension), are **statutory plans**, which means their requirements are established specifically by the Internal Revenue Code. The next three, profit sharing, 401(k), and money purchase pension, are forms of **defined contribution plans**. The final category is **defined benefit plans.**

"Plans at a Glance" and the brief discussions in the next few pages will give you an idea of the smorgasbord of possibilities. With a little looking, you'll find something that's right for you— but don't make that decision alone. You'd be well advised to consult an attorney with retirement planning experience. This is one of those times when expertise really pays off.

Statutory Plans

The statutory plans have little flexibility, since the law specifies their eligibility and vesting requirements.

• **SEP-IRA.** A SEP allows you to contribute to an IRA for each of your employees. Your contribution is limited to the lesser of 25 percent of the employee's compensation or $49,000 (in 2009). Your employees do not contribute to the plan and all employees who have worked for you for three of the past five years and earned at least $550 in the previous year are eligible. As the business owner, you can contribute to your own SEP-IRA, though you have to separately calculate your maximum deduction. You do not have to make a contribution to the plan every year. However, you must include all eligible employees in your plan.

• **SIMPLE-IRA.** If you go the SIMPLE route, you can adopt the plan as an IRA or as a 401(k) (a type of defined contribution plan that's available as a separate option). Both employees and the employer contribute to the plan. One disadvantage of SIMPLE plans is that you have to contribute to them every year regardless of your financial success for that year. (There are two types of SIMPLE plans, and one lets you reduce your contribution to 1 percent of payroll if you have a bad financial year and have chosen to adopt a SIMPLE-IRA.) If you choose to set up a SIMPLE-IRA, funds are held in an IRA, while funds contributed to a 401(k) are held in a qualified trust.

Employees can allocate some or all of their contributions to a Roth IRA. Among the major differences between a Roth IRA and a traditional IRA are:

• Contributions to a Roth IRA are made after taxes are deducted from the employee's wages.

• Since taxes have already been paid on the funds invested in a Roth IRA, distributions are not taxed.

• Employees may begin withdrawals not only when they turn 59½ but also five years after the first contributions to the Roth IRA were made.

A potential downfall of the SEP-IRA and SIMPLE-IRA is that the employee will have access immediately to any amount contributed. Any contributions made to these types of plans are 100 percent **vested**, meaning that the employee is entitled to receive 100 percent of the funds in his or her account regardless of length of service with your business. Even though the employee will face a penalty for early withdrawal, the temptation may be too great.

Another problem is that many part-time and seasonal workers will be eligible under the statutory plans. With defined contribution or defined benefit plans, you can exclude more employees from coverage.

In addition, with defined contribution and defined benefit plans, you can establish a schedule so that your employees may become gradually vested in their accounts over a period of years. For example, an employee may be entitled to only 20 percent of the amount in his or her account after two years of service. This amount would then increase by 20 percent each year until the account was 100 percent vested. A beneficial side effect of a gradual vesting schedule is that when an employee leaves and his or her account is not 100 percent vested, the remaining amount is forfeited. The forfeited amount is then redistributed to the accounts of the remaining employees. And, of course, gradual vesting rewards employees who've been with the company longer.

IT'S A MATTER OF DEFINITION

Another part of the pension puzzle deals with how benefits are paid out.

- **Defined contribution plans** are where you and your employees put in a certain percentage of income, but benefits depend on how the investments you make with this money perform.

- **Defined benefit plans** pay you a certain amount depending on how many years you've worked. These are the traditional pension plans of big corporations and government. They're not as common in small businesses, but they're an option, too.

- **Keogh plans** are either defined benefit or defined contribution plans established for a self-employed person. The same rules apply, except you may not:

  o lend any part of the plan's income or principal to an owner-employee;

  o pay any compensation to the owner-employee for services rendered to the plan; or

  o acquire any property from or sell any property to an owner-employee.

Defined Contribution Plans

Besides their vesting and eligibility flexibility, defined contribution plans are attractive to small businesses because they are inexpensive and easy to administer. With a defined contribution plan you must keep a separate account within a qualified trust for each individual employee, so that at any time the employee may know the balance in his or her account. Defined contribution plans are easy to "sell" to employees because they can see how much money they have in their individual accounts. However, because of this account segregation, the investment risk falls on the employee.

Profit sharing plans and money purchase pension plans are two types of defined contribution plans.

• **Profit sharing plan.** Although it is called a "profit sharing plan," you do not actually have to make a profit for the year in order to make a contribution (except for yourself if you are self-employed). A profit sharing plan can be set up to allow for discretionary employer contributions, meaning the amount contributed each year to the plan is not fixed. An employer may even make no contribution to the plan for a given year. Employees do not contribute to the plan, which must provide a definite formula for allocating the contribution among the participants and for distributing the accumulated funds to the employees after they reach a certain age, after a fixed number of years, or upon certain other occurrences.

• **Money purchase pension plan.** By contrast, if you elect a money purchase pension plan, you will make a fixed percentage contribution each year. If you choose to make a 3 percent contribution, it will be 3 percent of compensation to all employees.

Defined Benefit Plans

A defined benefit plan is just what it sounds like: In a defined contribution plan, the employer defines the amount of **contribution** it will make each year. The benefits the employees ultimately receive are undetermined (because they are based on how the contributions are invested). But in a defined benefit plan, contributions are based on what is needed to provide definitely determinable **benefits** to plan participants. An actuarial calculation has to be made to determine the amount the employer must contribute today in order for the employee to receive that determined amount on retirement. Because of this setup, the investment risk falls on the employer and not the employees. Because of this calculation, a defined benefit plan is more expensive to administer.

Benefits in a defined benefits plan are guaranteed. The employer pays an insurance premium to the Pension Benefit Guarantee Corporation (PBGC), which insures the funds in the plan

AN ADVANTAGE IF YOU'RE OLDER

Are you a "senior" employee at your business? If so, there's an advantage in a defined benefit plan. If you're older than most employees, you can receive greater benefits under the plan than the younger employees.

at a certain level. If the plan or the employer goes belly up, the employees will be entitled to receive payments from the PBGC, though not their full entitlement.

WHAT PLAN FEATURES SHOULD YOU SELECT?

You can tailor a defined contribution or defined benefit plan to accomplish your retirement goals. Most of these features are not available with a statutory plan. When selecting features and options for your plan, you should ask yourself the following questions:

Which of Your Employees Do You Wish to Cover with Your Plan?

Generally, you will want to benefit employees who stay with you for a period for time before they are allowed to participate in your plan and who are employed by you on more than a part-time basis. You may require an employee to complete up to two years of service before becoming eligible to participate in your plan. In addition to a waiting period, you may require the employee to be at least twenty-one years old. You may also exclude part-time employees from participation in your plan by requiring your employees to complete at least 1,000 hours of service during the year before becoming eligible for your plan or to continue participation in your plan.

Who Do You Want to Receive the Greatest Benefit from Your Plan?

You may decide that your employees should be entitled to 100 percent of the contributions made to the plan on their behalf at the time the contribution is made. However, it is more likely that you will wish to reward employees who stay with your business long-term. Vesting is the legal term that refers to the point after which an employee's accrued benefits cannot be taken away— i.e., the benefits must be paid to the employee upon retirement or switching jobs. If this is the case, you may adopt a **vesting schedule** that rewards long-term employees. There are two types of vesting schedules:

• **Cliff vesting.** The employee is not entitled to any of the benefits contributed on his or her behalf until the employee has completed a certain number of years of service. At that point, the benefits become 100 percent vested. The number of years required prior to 100 percent vesting cannot exceed five.

• **Graded vesting.** The employee's entitlement to benefits gradually increases over a period of time. The gradual increase may not exceed a seven-year period prior to 100 percent vesting. At the least, the employee must be entitled to 20 percent after three years of service, increasing by 20 percent each year until the contributions are 100 percent vested.

Additionally, as a business owner, you will most likely want to design the plan so that you can receive greater benefits than employees who are not as integral to your business as you are. If you receive more compensation from the business than your employees, you can integrate your plan with Social Security. Your contributions are then based on the Social Security taxable wage base. In allocating contributions, you are allowed to take into account the amount of Social Security benefits attributed to each employee. Because the Social Security taxable wage base at present is $106,800 (in 2009), employees receiving compensation above this amount will be entitled to greater benefits because there is no Social Security benefit attributed to amounts in excess of $106,800.

How Should Funds Be Contributed to Your Plan?

We've briefly discussed traditional contributions by you as the employer to your plan. However, there are other means of making contributions to your plan. One such way is by adopting a 401(k) feature. This profit sharing–plan feature allows an employee to contribute $16,500 (in 2009) of current salary, pretax, as an investment in your plan.

When Will the Money Be Available to Employees?

Employees are eligible to receive distributions from your plan on retirement, death, disability, or termination. You have the option of selecting a retirement age for your plan. You may not elect a retirement age in excess of sixty-five years. You may also want to allow an earlier retirement date after the completion of a certain number of years of service by the employee—for example, age sixty, if the employee has completed seven years of service with your company.

You may allow employees to borrow funds from the plan based on the employee's account balance. The amount must bear a reasonable rate of interest and be paid off by periodic payments in a reasonable amount of time. The loan amount cannot exceed $50,000 or half of the employee's vested account. The

 ONLY IF YOU REALLY NEED IT . . .

There's a stiff penalty for taking money out of your 401(k) before you're 59½, but the law does take hardship into account. Amounts contributed by the employee under a 401(k) plan may be distributed, without penalty, to an employee who demonstrates hardship. The law specifies several examples of hardship, such as medical care, the purchase of a principal residence of the employee, and payment of tuition.

loan period may not exceed five years unless the loan is for the employee's residence.

How Should Your Plan Funds Be Invested?

The traditional model for a plan is for you to select yourself as the plan trustee. You will then consult with your investment adviser to decide how the plan funds will be invested. An alternative model is to allow self-direction of investments by your employees.

With self-directed investments, you will select several investments for the employees to choose from. The employee will then allocate his or her funds among these options. The employee must agree in writing that you are relieved from all liability for any loss resulting from investments made pursuant to his or her direction of investments. Many companies have set up toll-free numbers or Web sites for employees to call to check on the status and adjust their investments on a daily basis.

IT MAY NOT BE TOO LATE

What if you've waited a long, long time to plan for retirement like John and Lois? All is not necessarily lost. Fortunately for John and Lois, their daughter Emily has decided to move home to run the business so her parents can retire. While John and Lois did not manage to save a lot for retirement, the business is extremely profitable.

One of the first things Emily decides to do is set up a 401(k) plan. She will keep her parents on as consultants and pay them a salary. She may occasionally hire a part-time worker for vacations and holidays, but Emily, John, and Lois will be the only employees eligible for the 401(k) plan. John and Lois will receive a salary large enough to live on and make the maximum 401(k) contribution, thereby deferring tax until they draw on the funds later. In addition, they will receive matching contributions from the company. Better late than never.

Of course, Emily, at age thirty, will also be well on her way to building a substantial retirement nest egg.

YOU MUST REMEMBER THIS

- Establishing a pension plan can help you get and keep good employees.
- A plan can also benefit you, save you money on taxes, and give your business a tax break.
- You can find (or create!) a plan that's right for you—the law gives you plenty of options.

Plans at a Glance

Provisions	SIMPLE	SEP	Profit Sharing Plan
Employee eligibility	Age 21, earned $5,000 in any two preceding years and is expected to earn $5,000 in current year	Age 21, worked for employer any three of last five years and earns $550	Age 21, and 1,000 hours of service; can wait two years with 100% vesting
Maximum number of eligible employees	100	Unlimited	Unlimited
Maximum employee deferral	$11,500 (higher amount permitted for older employees)	Not an option	Not an option
Employer matching contribution	Dollar-for-dollar match up to 3% of compensation, which may be reduced to 1% of compensation in same year	Not an option	Not an option
Employer Contribution	2% of compensation (up to $4,900) to eligible employees only in lieu of match; in either case, no additional contributions allowed	Not to exceed 25% of compensation or $49,000, whichever is less	Not to exceed 25% of compensation (20% if self-employed), up to $49,000; possible integration with Social Security
Vesting Schedule	100% vested at all times	100% vested at all times	Gradual vesting; forfeitures
Employer control of distributions	None of IRA; 401(k) defined by qualified plan and trust; all distributions need employer approval	None	Defined by qualified plan and trust; all distributions need employer approval
Participant loans	Not available	Not available	Available

401(k)	Money Purchase Pension Plan	Defined Benefit
Age 21, and 1,000 hours of service; can wait two years with 100% vesting	Age 21, and one year of service; can wait two years with 100% vesting	Age 21, and one year of service; can wait two years with 100% vesting
Unlimited	Unlimited	Unlimited
$16,500 (higher amount permitted for older employees)	Not an option	Not an option
Optional	Not an option	Not an option
Combined employer & employee contributions cannot exceed $49,000 (higher amount permitted for older employees)	Mandatory contribution, not to exceed 25% of possible compensation, up to $49,000; integration with Social Security	Mandatory actuarially calculated amount not to exceed 100% of employee's highest three-year average compensation, up to $195,000
Gradual vesting; forfeitures	Gradual vesting; forfeitures	Gradual vesting; forfeitures
Defined by qualified plan and trust; all distributions need employer approval	Defined by qualified plan and trust; all distributions need employer approval	Defined by qualified plan and trust; all distributions need employer approval
Available	Available	Available

CHAPTER 34

'Till Death Do Us Part

What Will Happen to Your Family Business When You Die? Plan Ahead to Avoid Disaster.

It's a month after your sudden death, and the powers on high have allowed you to return to your old company, just to see how things are going. You were the president and sole owner, but two of your three children (a son and a daughter) worked in the business, and you'd assumed (but not really planned in detail) that they'd take over when you died. The first thing you notice as you stand unseen in the corner is that there's an internal crisis going on. Your son and daughter cannot agree on how to run the business, who should be in charge, or even what client to call first. Naturally, the most talented and valuable employees have started to look for other jobs at the time when your company needs them most. What's worse, your estate is facing a whopping tax bill that could drain the business's assets just when your children need them most.

If you're like most people, chances are you've entertained the fantasy of attending your own funeral, like Tom Sawyer and Huckleberry Finn, seeing who shows up, and listening to what all your loved ones have to say about you. But take it a step further and consider what you'd see if you dropped in on your business a week or two after your death. Is everything running smoothly? Unless you've taken time to plan ahead and prepare an estate plan that extends to the business, chances are things will be pretty rugged.

In the scenario above, the internal crisis is just the beginning of the problems your successors may face. Customers, bankers, suppliers, competitors, and predators are all very interested in what will happen with the business now that the owner and the president has died. Will a sale actually take place—and when? Will the new owners want to change any of the key relationships with outside parties?

WHAT IF YOU BECOME DISABLED?

Don't limit your estate planning to preparing for your death. Keep in mind the possibility that you might suffer a significant physical or mental disability that could impair your decision making. Disability may even be worse than death, because you might not recognize the seriousness of your impairment. The law makes it extremely difficult for others to take away your freedom of choice and responsibility for making decisions. Great damage to the business can be done before you return to good health or control is transferred through legal proceedings that result in conservatorship. Ask your attorney what steps you can take now to avoid harm to your business should you become disabled.

Meanwhile, there is a chance that loan documents, franchise agreements, and other legal contracts contain termination or renegotiation clauses in the event of the death of the majority or sole business owner. Can there be any worse time for the business to renegotiate financing or a distributorship relationship? Worse yet, numerous relationships with key customers are dependent upon personal contact with you, the owner. Now that you're dead, will those accounts be up in the air?

Then there's the issue of control. Since there was no plan for succession, no one knows who will take charge, and for how long and under what mandate. Does the successor have the right to make the decision to sell the business—to whom, for how much, for cash or notes? In many cases, the law will naturally favor a request of the surviving spouse to have control of the business interests. Can a surviving spouse with experience in another line of work but none in this business take on responsibility for critical decision making for the business? And things can get really nasty if this is your second spouse and you have children from a prior marriage. Do your family members get along with your other employees? Do you have an employee who was expecting to take over the business one day?

PLAN AHEAD TO MINIMIZE TAXES

The threat of heavy taxes upon the death of the business owner is one of the principal reasons businesses don't make it into the next generation. Using estate planning to minimize taxes is very important, regardless of whether the business is going to be sold or continued. This chapter can't examine this mammoth subject in great detail, but here is a very abbreviated primer that may help you understand some of the issues and help you and your lawyer plan for the maximum advantage.

To decide what the property in your estate is worth, including your business, the IRS does not look at what you paid for it, but generally uses the fair market value of the property at your death—or, if the total value six months from the date of death is lower, your executor may elect to use that alternate valuation.

Significant changes were made to estate taxes through the Economic Growth and Tax Relief Reconciliation Act of 2001. Only estates with a taxable value (as calculated by the IRS) exceeding $3.5 million have to pay a federal estate tax, but estate tax rates can be as high as 45 percent. It is important to remember that in 2011 the federal estate tax exemption will revert to $1 million and the top tax rate will be 55 percent unless something is done with the current federal tax law. (Your state may impose additional taxes, but we concentrate on federal taxes for this discussion. Many of these states have decoupled from the federal estate tax with amounts as low as $1 million or less, so do not assume that estate taxes are not an issue in your case. Check with your lawyer to determine if your state has decoupled from the federal system. This will greatly impact your business succession plan as well as your personal estate plan.) The assets subject to tax at death, besides your business, may include the family home, the family farm, life insurance, household furnishings, money owed to you, benefits under employee benefit plans, as well as other items that produce no lifetime income. If you own property on the date of your death, it will be part of your estate for estate tax purposes. In short, you may be richer than you think. If your estate is likely to exceed the threshold ($3.5 million as of 2009), good estate planning can sharply reduce the amount of money that goes to the government instead of to your beneficiaries.

Warning: Federal and state tax laws change frequently, so be sure to review your estate plan periodically. Under the Economic Growth and Tax Relief Reconciliation Act of 2001, estate taxes are set to be eliminated in 2010; however, Congress and President Obama's administration have indicated that they may maintain estate taxes for estates exceeding the $3.5 million threshold. Again, if there is no action by Congress, we will revert to a $1 million threshold in 2011. It is important for you and your attorney to work as a team to plan for changing circumstances and laws.

SOME TAX-SAVING IDEAS

In addition to your own $3.5 million federal estate credit, you can pass your entire estate without any federal estate taxes to

A TAX BREAK FOR FAMILY BUSINESSES

The United States Congress passed legislation in 1997 that provided special benefits for family-business owners by reducing estate taxes. If the decedent owned an interest in a qualifying family-owned business, a deduction from the gross estate in the amount of up to $1,100,000 may be available. In other words, when determining whether the estate exceeds the $3.5 million threshold, the first $1.1 million within the estate may be excluded from the calculation. As might be expected, there are a number of complex rules and requirements that must be met in order to qualify for these special tax provisions. This should be a part of the estate planning process with advice from a qualified attorney.

your spouse. (This is referred to as the **unlimited marital deduction**.) Don't celebrate too soon, though, since without planning all this would do is defer taxes. If you simply leave your estate to your spouse and don't create an appropriate trust to take advantage of your $3.5 million exemption, your spouse's estate will pay taxes on this sum when he or she dies.

Let's say Susan has an estate worth $4.35 million. She dies and leaves it all to her husband, Bob. When he dies a few years later, there is a hefty federal estate tax that could have been avoided altogether through the simple use of marital deduction planning. If she were the owner of a business, even more might have been saved had Susan taken advantage of the qualified family-owned business interest exclusion.

To take maximum benefit of both her $3.5 million exemption and that of her husband, Susan could establish a **bypass trust** or **credit shelter trust** (also called **exemption trust**). It's called a bypass trust because as much as $3.5 million bypasses the surviving spouse's taxable estate and goes directly into a trust that ultimately benefits the children, grandchildren, or other beneficiaries when the second spouse dies. Remember that this planning is going to be different in states that have decoupled from the federal estate tax. In such states, planning that was good for many years relative to the federal estate tax could trigger hefty state estate taxes at the death of the first spouse to die. The laws of the affected states provide different consequences and options that are important to discuss with your attorney.

Here's how it works. Let's assume Susan dies survived by her husband and several children. The adjusted gross estate (her estate after deducting funeral expenses, expenses of administration, and claims) totals $4.5 million. Her will, or trust, creates a gift of $1 million for her husband. The remaining $3.5 million goes into the bypass trust. The income is payable to her husband for as long as he lives. The trust can be drafted so that he is entitled to the principal of the trust under ascertainable standards commonly known as maintenance, education, support, and health. Finally, he can have power of appointment and act as trustee. On his death, Susan's estate and the trust go to the chil-

GIVING IT AWAY—WHILE YOU'RE STILL ALIVE

Gifts you make during your lifetime are another good way of avoiding or limiting taxes on larger estates. The law allows you to give up to $13,000 worth of assets *per recipient* to as many people as you wish each year (married donors giving a gift as a couple are allowed a $26,000 per recipient per year gift exclusion). The people who get the gifts don't have to be related to you. This is called an **annual exclusion** in IRS-speak. You can also make tax-free, direct payments of tuition and medical expenses beyond the $13,000 limit. There is no gift tax on any gifts made between spouses in any amount, or on gifts to political organizations. And gifts to charitable organizations can be deductible.

Let's say Tom, the owner of a small business, has an estate large enough that his estate will owe money even if he creates a bypass trust and takes advantage of the qualified family-owned business interest exclusion. One way to lessen the eventual tax burden would be to give money away while he's alive. He could give $13,000 a year (and his wife could give an equal amount) to each of his three children and seven grandchildren (possibly in a trust for younger grandkids). That's as much as $260,000 *a year* that could escape taxes. This also removes the growth and appreciation of the $260,000 from the estate. Tom could also transfer some of the value and control of the business during his lifetime (e.g., give shares of stocks). It may be possible to do so at a discounted value for minority interests.

The drawback to lifetime gifts is that you lose control of the money. Even assuming you leave yourself enough to live on comfortably, the beneficiary (usually a child) may not be responsible enough to handle that kind of money wisely. One method of retaining some control over your gift is to give the money via a trust. Trusts can also be used to reduce the cost of gifts and to leverage costs. A number of types of trusts can be used to help clients with these objectives.

dren. Moreover, whatever is in the trust can pass to the children free of the federal estate tax regardless of its worth. This means that years of growth and appreciation in the bypass can pass free from the estate tax.

This arrangement eliminates federal estate taxes. On Susan's death, her estate owes no estate tax. Because unlimited property can be passed to a spouse without being taxed, her gift to her husband is exempt from federal estate taxes when she dies. It is added to her husband's taxable estate, but then *his* $3.5 million credit, or whatever is available during the year of death, kicks in, so no taxes will be owed on his death if the taxable estate is not larger than $3.5 million. The bypass trust utilizes *his wife's* $3.5 million exemption as a credit shelter on her death but is not included in his adjusted gross estate on his death.

FAILURE TO PLAN

The death of a business owner is a particularly difficult event because the personal grief and pain is compounded by the abrupt change in the business. Many business owners hope that one or more children will enter the business and carry on a legacy that will be special to family members in current and future generations. Unfortunately, approximately 70 percent of family-owned businesses fail to make a successful transition into the second generation. Only 15 percent or so are successfully transferred to a third generation of family members. These statistics reveal both the difficulty of transferring from one generation to the next and the lack of planning for successorship.

Many business owners continue to retain ownership and control of the business well beyond normal retirement age. Even when doing estate planning, business owners persist in saying "if I die" rather than facing the certainty of death. This makes the event of death an almost certain crisis, as previously described. How can the business leaders in the next generation emerge and gain actual experience if the older generation fails to pass the torch?

Clearly, to avoid subjecting your family, partners, and employees to the turbulence of coping with business disasters after your death, it's crucial to devote the time and resources needed to develop a plan for succession. This chapter outlines different possibilities for dealing with the transfer of your business interest in the event of your death or disability. In some cases, a sale is inevitable. In other cases, your plan will anticipate a transfer

 IN THE MINORITY

What if you own less than 50 percent of the family business? As a minority business owner, chances are you lack the control and flexibility you'd need to direct the sale or other disposition of your business interests after your death. The minority business interest represents an investment or employment opportunity for you—one that won't necessarily extend beyond your lifetime.

When you die, the challenge to create financial value for your heirs out of a piece of paper representing a small proportion of ownership emerges. It's very difficult to determine the fair market value of a minority business interest. Accordingly, it's extremely important to have a buy-sell agreement (see page 455) that deals with transfer at death or other specified event. Otherwise, your family will find itself in a very precarious position of converting the business into a liquid asset.

Because it's difficult to get regular cash flow out of a minority business interest, don't count on your minority interest in the family business to provide financial security for your surviving spouse. It's better to address that need from other financial resources, such as savings, additional investments, life insurance proceeds, and retirement plan accounts. In many cases, it's more logical to pass the minority business interests on to your children.

However, depending on the nature of the business and your relationship with other business owners, you may be able to work something out with them. It almost never hurts to explore options.

of the business interest by gift or inheritance to family members. There are also important differences between sole- and majority-control business interests and minority business ownership interests (see sidebar on page 449).

IF YOU INTEND TO SELL

Let's begin with a rather simple scenario, where you're the sole or majority owner and you intend for the business to be sold when you die. If the planning process successfully addresses each of the following factors, your partners or heirs should be able to obtain maximum value for the business interests while avoiding disruption of the business and conflict within the family.

Internal Crisis

Consider first the reaction of employees who know that the business is about to be sold, as they fear for their jobs and start looking for ways to jump ship. The crisis may also begin if they see a decline in the health or interest of the major personality and force behind the business. The strategic business plan should include the designation of new leaders in the event of death or disability, with instructions that these people should immediately communicate as much accurate and helpful information to employees as soon as possible after the critical event.

External Crisis

If your business loses key customers or distributorships because of the uncertainty following your death, it will be difficult to sell the business for an optimal price. Some distributorship agreements require pre-approved successors, in effect forcing you to plan for your succession. You should also plan ahead to make sure that customers feel comfortable dealing with at least one other person in the business—especially as you get older and the risk of your death or disability increases. When renewing contracts with franchisers and suppliers, ask for a modification of any clauses stating that the contract be terminated or renegotiated upon the death of the owner. Perhaps you could amend them to specify renegotiation three months after the death of the owner, to give your business a chance to get over the hump. There is no guarantee that franchisers and suppliers will agree to these changes, but you'll never know unless you try, and the time to try is *now*.

Control

Any prospective buyer will want to see a business that's running smoothly. Make sure that the new leaders named in your plan for succession are specifically granted the authority to make decisions concerning the business immediately after your death or disability. The issue of control should be addressed through a

 LIFE INSURANCE: YOUR TICKET TO CASH FLOW

In many cases, the biggest business-related problem for the grieving heirs is cash flow. They may have to pay estate taxes, cope with legal expenses associated with transferring the business to new hands, and possibly buy out heirs who don't want their inheritance tied up in the business. A major infusion of cash can make it all go more smoothly.

Any life insurance policy will be much more helpful if it's coupled with a well-prepared estate plan. Through planning, you can get the value of the insurance out of your estate (and thus not have to pay taxes on it). The key is to not own the policy directly but to set up a life insurance trust that owns the policy on you. That gets it out of your estate and accomplishes significant tax savings. Careful estate planning can dramatically enhance the value of the life insurance for the financial benefit of the business and family members after your death.

will, living trust, or other appropriate legal document. Appoint one or more competent, experienced individuals or entities to make business decisions. Proper planning can allow your potential successors to rehearse their roles while you are alive and healthy. If they do a good job then you can have a sense of security. If they do not do well, then you will know that you need to adjust the plan before you find yourself and the business in the middle of battle conditions.

Value

If you're anticipating the sale of the business after your retirement or death, you may want to maximize business value to attract interest from potential buyers. Let's say you've been operating the business to maximize compensation and minimize taxable income. That's fine, but annual earnings may suffer under such a plan, and you might want to bump them up if you anticipate selling the business.

In many cases, key managers and employees approach the family wanting to purchase the business. These potential buyers may ask the estate and surviving family members to finance the purchase price. A sale to an employee stock ownership plan sounds fine on paper until family members realize that financial security for the surviving spouse and the children depends upon the future success of the business enterprise.

IF YOU INTEND FOR THE BUSINESS TO CONTINUE

Internal Crisis

It's important to convince employees that a sale of the business is not imminent. Especially if you serve as president and chief executive officer, make sure that you've planned in advance for a new leader to emerge quickly. If you know the identity of the new leader, you should share this information with employees and other owners so there are no surprises. Do you want to take steps to ensure that key employees stay with the business? Do they have, or should they have, the ability to acquire some ownership interest in the business? If the business interest is extremely valuable and constitutes the vast majority of the deceased owner's estate, it's natural to expect concern and anxiety on the part of family members whose financial assurances—and financial opportunities—are at risk.

External Crisis

Again, it's extremely important to convince outsiders who have dealings with the business that business operations will continue without significant changes or surprises.

Control

The issue of control is extremely important if the business will be continued rather than sold. Family members who are active in the business will naturally have a different point of view from family members who are not. Insiders want generous compensation and no dividends paid. Outsiders receive no compensation and require dividends to receive any financial benefit from the family-owned business.

The natural love and affection that family members have for one another is typically very strong. Unfortunately, significant financial issues can test these relationships. Sibling rivalries are common. If the surviving spouse has control after the death of the business owner, what assurances are there that he or she will be able to meet these responsibilities? Should control by the surviving spouse continue until his or her death, which may occur when he or she is ninety years of age or older—and it is the children who are thinking about retirement? Have family members made assumptions that have not been communicated? Has the business owner communicated with the family about his or her plans? The lack of communication can create many problems. Think of your plan as a means of articulating your goals, wishes, and directions in an appropriate fashion to ensure the smooth transition of your business and the well-being of your loved ones. Make sure your loved ones know about your plans and what they entail.

Value

If the business will not be sold, there is no interest in maximizing the value of the business. In fact, every effort is usually made to establish an extremely low value in order to minimize estate taxes. Even if no estate taxes are payable at the death of the first spouse (which is usually the case), low values will accommodate interfamily gifts, sales, and other transfers designed to minimize future estate taxes that may be projected at the death of the second spouse. However, be aware that the IRS does have hefty undervaluation penalties that can apply.

Estate Planning

Estate planning is just as important if you want the family business to keep going as it is if you intend for the business to be sold. Your plan should provide a legacy for children and future generations of family members after your death or disability. At the same time, it must adequately address the financial needs of a surviving spouse. It must also provide for the fair distribution of estate assets among children and other family members. Will one or more children receive ownership interests in the business to the exclusion of other children? How do you compare the value of an illiquid business interest with cash or marketable securities? Should one child receive a controlling interest in the business, or should it be shared among several children? If one child receives the business, how will that impact that child's total share of the estate? Is that child's share of the remainder of the estate adjusted? What is the impact of these decisions on family relationships?

Only you and your family can answer these questions. As always, communication is key—be sure you involve your family in these decisions so you know their concerns and they know your evolving thinking. If your beneficiaries (your spouse and/or children) are interested in taking over the business and in your judgment possess the expertise to do so, it's relatively simple to transfer your interest directly to them. If stock is involved, you might want to leave voting stock to the children who will be involved in operating the business and nonvoting stock to the others. Or you can leave the child who will be running the business enough cash (perhaps through life insurance proceeds) to enable him or her to buy out the rest of the estate and thus avoid conflicts.

BUY-SELL AGREEMENTS

Buy-sell agreements are typically made between owners of a business, whether they be shareholders, partners, or members of an LLC. Though, as we'll see later, they come in many varieties, their main purpose is to provide a mechanism for the smooth transfer of the business, whether at the death of one of the principals or before. They're typically used when your beneficiaries will not be actively involved in the business after you're gone.

If two or more people own an interest in your business, you should have a buy-sell agreement or other legal document that imposes restrictions on the sale or transfer of ownership interests. As an example of how one might work, let's say you're in a partnership and you want the other partners to remain in operational control of the company after your death. You and your partners could craft a buy-sell agreement in which all the remaining partners agree to purchase the interest of any partner who dies. This allows the business to continue running smoothly with the same people in charge, minus one.

Buy-sell agreements typically provide that at the owner's death, his or her interest in the business will be acquired by the remaining partners or shareholders, leaving the decedent's family with the proceeds of the sale. Life insurance is often the vehicle used to finance these arrangements, which lets the business itself avoid a drain on its cash. The principals buy life insurance on each other's lives, and the proceeds go to the surviving spouses or children in return for the deceased partner's share of the business.

A lengthy and more comprehensive agreement will probably answer more questions than a relatively short and simple agreement. Don't be satisfied with a cheap Band-Aid document that leaves many questions unanswered. Review old buy-sell agreements and make certain that their terms and provisions continue to provide a reasonable and clear result in each circumstance. As a rule of thumb, you should review your buy-sell agreements at least every other year, or immediately if there are significant changes in the law or in the business itself.

There are many kinds of buy-sell agreements. Consider the following general matters in the context of your specific circumstances and with the advice of a competent attorney.

Force Out Provisions

This variety of buy-sell agreement, unlike the others described in this chapter, operates while all the principals are still alive. It allows individuals, during the administration of the business, to buy out other owners. One helpful provision is to allow any owner to offer to buy out another owner's share. The owner making the offer has to come up with the dollar figure. The owner receiving the offer either accepts the offer or buys out the owner proposing the offer at the price proposed. This provision guarantees that a fair price is offered.

Right-of-First-Refusal Agreement

A buy-sell agreement may simply provide that the company or other business owners have a right-of-first-refusal to purchase an owner's interest in the event of death. Typical provisions include a specified price at which the business interest may be purchased and whether payment must be in cash or paid over a term of years at a specified rate of interest. Collateral and secu-

FOR THE NEXT GENERATION

Are you hoping your family business will continue into the next generation, providing employment and prosperity for your children and grandchildren? Avoid dissension in the family with a carefully drafted buy-sell agreement.

One variation of the standard right-of-first-refusal agreement is to provide an opportunity for the ownership interest to remain in the same branch of the family before it is offered to either the company or other branches of the family. This can be extremely important when the balance of control among different branches of the family is an issue.

Buy-sell agreements for family-owned businesses should address lifetime gifts of stock, sales, and other transfers. Lifetime transfers to family members, as well as bequests at death, are typically permitted under the terms of the buy-sell agreement without invoking a right-of-first-refusal that would otherwise apply. Gifts and other transfers to trusts may also be addressed in the buy-sell agreement. Nevertheless, these specific provisions must be clearly spelled out in the agreement in order to avoid a later controversy.

rity provisions should be included if installment payments are allowed. The price or price formula, of course, is very important to purchasers and sellers of the business interest. In addition to death, buy-sell provisions and a right-of-first-refusal can be granted under other circumstances, such as disability, attempted sale to another party, retirement, bankruptcy, or termination of employment.

Mandatory Purchase

Mandatory purchase provisions in a buy-sell agreement provide that the business interests will be sold by the heirs of a deceased business owner and purchased by the company or other business owners. This element of certainty is very important for all parties. As long as all of the detailed terms and provisions are clearly spelled out in the agreement, action is automatic. There is no room for concern, conflict, anxiety, or further negotiation at a difficult time. Again, mandatory purchase provisions may also be applied under circumstances other than death, as desired by the parties to the agreement.

Price and Value Provisions
in Buy-Sell Agreements

The specified price or value contained in a buy-sell agreement may be dramatically less than the value of the business interest if the entire business were sold under favorable circumstances. Be sure you carefully consider the price and value provisions of your buy-sell agreement, and update the language from time to time to reflect changes in facts and circumstances. Does the agreement distinguish between minority ownership interests and majority ownership interests? If an appraisal is required, is the appraiser given guidelines concerning discounts for minority interest or lack of marketability? Who gets to pick the appraiser? Does the agreement provide that the company picks one appraiser and your family picks a second appraiser?

Funding

When you die, how will the company and remaining business owners finance the purchase of your interest in the business? Life insurance is an obvious option. Another possibility is seller financing through installment payments over a number of years. Payouts over long periods of time tend to create issues that can be avoided through other options. Make sure you carefully explore the potential ramifications of such pay-out agreements. Does the company or the other business owners have the capacity to borrow additional funds to finance the obligatory purchase? Will your family members be protected from financial risk associated with installment payments? Is their risk increased if remaining business owners dramatically increase the indebtedness of the company for expansion and acquisitions?

PLANNING TIPS

Here are some specific planning tips for your review and consideration. You may find one or more of these planning tools helpful to resolve a particular issue.

• **Revocable trusts.** As a family-business owner, you may choose to transfer the business interest and other assets to a revocable trust. A business owner may serve as sole trustee, if desired. The terms of the trust usually provide for the appointment of a new trustee in the event of disability or death. This eliminates a crisis that could otherwise occur in terms of control when the business owner is stricken by disability or dies. In many states, revocable trusts avoid an otherwise costly probate process. In some cases, these trusts are superior to wills because they're more likely to survive if contested. The trust has the big advantage of protecting the privacy of the business after your death. The last thing you want is to have the books and records of your business become matters of public record for all, including your competitors, to see! Also, you can avoid administrative hassles by having your living trust control what happens to your business and other assets in the event of your disability and after your death.

• **Last will and testament.** If you don't establish a revocable trust, it's imperative that you execute a complete, adequate, and comprehensive will providing for distribution of the estate, including applicable business interests.

One of the most significant functions of the will or trust is appointing executors, trustees, and other fiduciaries who control business decision making after your death. In appropriate circumstances, the will or trust should include special provisions that guide executors and trustees in dealing with valuable business interests. And the will, like a trust, can be used to appoint special advisers or committees to assist your executors in making business decisions. Your will may also include a provision on compensation of the executor.

If you have neither a living trust nor a will, the state in which you are domiciled (likely where you live) has laws that will take force that are not interested in protecting your best interest nor concerned about saving you taxes.

- **Business details tape.** It's a good idea to use an audiotape or a written document to convey important facts and details that would be helpful in dealing with your business interests after death.

- **Board of directors.** If a business is incorporated, most states require that a formal board of directors be formed. Unfortunately, many privately held businesses that are not corporations do not utilize a formal board of directors to oversee the president and business operations. Think about appointing a board that includes some outsiders with objective opinions. The void in leadership occasioned by your death can be quickly and competently filled by a veteran board of directors that has been working together for many years.

- **Family business successorship plan.** If you're serious about retaining the family business as a legacy for future generations, actively pursue a plan of successorship. The successorship plan should deal with the present facts and circumstances, as well as anticipate future changes. The plan, for example, should provide for alternative control and leadership in the event that any child successors are not yet ready to assume responsibility. The plan should provide financial security for your surviving spouse that is separate from the business enterprise. Business successorship should be coordinated with the estate plan to be fair to all children and other family members.

- **Stop procrastinating.** Important advice to all business owners: You will die someday! Take the time to put together a thoughtful and effective estate plan. With any luck, you will have many opportunities in future years to fine-tune and update the plan.

TALKING TO AN EXPERT: CONVEYING THE BUSINESS AT DEATH

Q. *I'm nearing retirement age, but I'm not sure I (or my kids) want the business to continue as a family business. What are some of the considerations?*

A. All too often, I find that families haven't discussed succession at all, or if they do it involves Dad meeting with an estate planner. Instead, families should start at the beginning, with the root of the vision—continuing as a family business. Do you want to continue as a family business? If so, why is it important?

The first question addresses individual goals. Maybe all of your children are not interested in the family business, or maybe some are but you wouldn't know because you've never asked.

The advantage of the second question is its focus on the positive, what the family stands to gain. I suggest that families have a brainstorming session and list all the answers on big sheets of paper. Then the typed results serve as a benchmark when conflict erupts. For example, siblings Joe and Mary are arguing about Joe's late expense report. When they notice their list on the wall, including "We get to work with those whom we love the most," they may want to continue the discussion, but it loses its heat in the light of the long-term dream.

—Answer by Dr. Patricia (Pat) Frishkoff, founding director of the Austin Family Business Program at Oregon State University, a resource for business owners and their families, www.familybusinessonline.org.

YOU MUST REMEMBER THIS

• Not only do you have to plan ahead for what will happen at your death, you've got to make plans for the business in case your health deteriorates and you become disabled.

- Regardless of whether the business interest will be sold or continued, the estate planning process is not for your personal benefit. It's for the benefit of family members and employees who are left behind. Good tax planning can benefit them to the tune of hundreds of thousands of dollars.

- With the help of your lawyer, you can create documents—a will, a trust, a business successorship plan—that will ease the transition for your partners and employees, provide for your family, and reduce the chances that people will fight over the assets.

The World At Your Fingertips

Throughout this book, we've given you resources to help you find more information on certain topics. But we aren't done yet! In this section, we compile all those resources—and add many more.

GENERAL RESOURCES

All Business.com: www.allbusiness.com—Provides a vast array of information for business owners, including forums, legal forms, and numerous experts' articles and blogs.

Small Business Administration: www.sba.gov—The Web site of the federal agency charged with helping small businesses includes resources, articles, forms, and information about services.

Association of Small Business Development Center Network: www.asbdc-us.org—Seeks to help new entrepreneurs establish new businesses and provide support for current business owners.

Findlaw Small Business Center: www.smallbusiness.findlaw .com—Provides resources on the legal side of small-business creation and ownership.

Nolo.com's Small Business Section: www.nolo.com (click on "Business, LLCs, and Corporations")—Provides legal information and forms for small-business owners.

Service Corps of Retired Executives: www.score.org—This Web site enables you to obtain free, confidential e-mail advice from former executives in your field.

Small Business for Dummies, 3rd edition, Eric Tyson and Jim Schell, Wiley (March 2008).

The Big Book for Small Businesses: You Don't Have to Run Your Business by the Seat of Your Pants, Tom Gegax and Phil Bolsta, HarperBusiness (February 2007).

LEGAL SERVICES AND INFORMATION

American Bar Association: www.abanet.org—Provides information on legal topics generally, on finding a lawyer in your area, and on where to find additional information and resources. You can also find your local bar association by visiting www.abanet.org/barserv/stlobar.html.

Martindale-Hubbell: www.lawyers.com—A leading resource for information on lawyers practicing in the United States and abroad. Offers a free Web site with profiles of over 440,000 lawyers and law firms, as well as tips on selecting a lawyer.

Finances

Bankrate.com: www.bankrate.com—Offers up-to-date information on interest rates.

Quicken's Small Business: www.quicken.com—Provides accounting products and support for home businesses.

How to Collect Debts and Still Keep Your Customers, David Sher and Martin Sher, AMACOM (May 1999).

Franchising

The Federal Trade Commission (FTC): www.ftc.gov—The FTC offers information about the FTC Franchise and Business Opportunity Rule. The Web site has many resources relating to franchising, including commentary about the federal rule, state rules, and FAQs.

Franchise Handbook Online: www.franchise1.com.

International Franchise Association: www.franchise.org.

American Franchisee Association: www.franchisee.org.

Working with Employees and Customers

Equal Employment Opportunity Commission (EEOC): www
.eeoc.gov—Provides information on the law regarding workplace
discrimination and the employer's obligation to offer equal opportunity in hiring and in all aspects of employment.

Department of Labor: www.dol.gov—Here you can find general
information on the Fair Labor Standards Act, as well as the related regulations.

United States Department of Justice: www.usdoj.gov—Look
here for information on federal laws on hiring practices. You can
also access the Office of Special Counsel for Immigration-
Related Unfair Employment Practices.

National Labor Relations Board (NLRB): www.nlrb.gov—This
agency is charged with enforcing the National Labor Relations
Act, which governs relationships between agencies and employers.

Business Scams

National Fraud Information Center: www.fraud.org—Provides
information on small-business scams.

Federal Trade Commission: www.ftc.gov.

Better Business Bureau: www.bbb.org—Can be a helpful re-
sourse for ensuring that your business isn't victimized by another
business with a questionable reputation.

INDEX

ABOUT THE AUTHOR

Robert Sprague (JD, MBA) is an assistant professor in the University of Wyoming College of Business Department of Management & Marketing, teaching Law for Managers, Business Law for Entrepreneurs, and Commercial Law courses. Professor Sprague previously practiced law, primarily counseling small businesses, and has started and managed small businesses. Professor Sprague has published several articles addressing business-related legal issues.

Also Available:

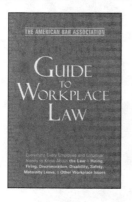

THE AMERICAN BAR ASSOCIATION
Guide to Workplace Law, Second Edition

978-0-375-72140-3
$16.95/ $22.95 Can.

This guide provides essential insight for employers including advice on hiring, firing, retirement, sexual harassment, maternity leave, workplace safety, and more—all explained in clear, non-technical language

THE AMERICAN BAR ASSOCIATION
Guide to Credit and Bankruptcy,
Second Edition

978-0-375-72300-1
$16.99/ $21.99 Can.

This new edition is updated with recent changes in bankruptcy laws. It also includes information on how to apply for, build, and protect your credit; handle credit card rates and home equity loans; and make the right choices about debt management and bankruptcy.

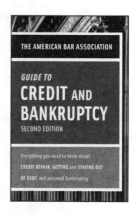

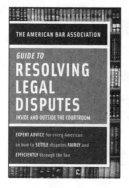

THE AMERICAN BAR ASSOCIATION
Guide to Resolving Legal Disputes

978-0-375-72141-0
$16.95/ $21.95 Can.

This comprehensive guide contains dozens of situational examples and important information about mediation, arbitration, small claims court, and civil court procedures. It also features tips on how to save time and money when working with a lawyer.